Death

THE OPEN YALE COURSES SERIES is designed to bring the depth and breadth of a Yale education to a wide variety of readers. Based on Yale's Open Yale Courses program (http://oyc.yale.edu), these books bring outstanding lectures by Yale faculty to the curious reader, whether student or adult. Covering a wide variety of topics across disciplines in the social sciences, physical sciences, and humanities, Open Yale Courses books offer accessible introductions at affordable prices.

The production of Open Yale Courses for the Internet was made possible by a grant from the William and Flora Hewlett Foundation.

RECENT TITLES
Paul H. Fry, *Theory of Literature*
Shelly Kagan, *Death*
Dale B. Martin, *New Testament History and Literature*

FORTHCOMING TITLES
Christine Hayes, *Introduction to the Old Testament*
Ian Shapiro, *The Moral Foundations of Politics*
Steven B. Smith, *Introduction to Political Philosophy*

Death

SHELLY KAGAN

Yale

UNIVERSITY PRESS

New Haven and London

Yale University Press books may be purchased in quantity for educational, business, or promotional use. For information, please e-mail sales .press@yale.edu (U.S. office) or sales@yaleup.co.uk (U.K. office).

"Separation" by Friedrich Klopstock, translated by Walter Kaufmann, "To the Parcae" by Friedrich Holderlin, translated by Walter Kaufmann, from *Existentialism, Religion and Death* by Walter Kaufmann, copyright © 1976 by Walter Kaufmann. Used by permission of Dutton Signet, a division of Penguin Group (USA) Inc.

Set in Minion type by Westchester Book Group
Printed in the United States of America

Library of Congress Cataloging-in-Publication Data

Kagan, Shelly.
Death / Shelly Kagan.
p. cm. — (The open Yale courses series)
Includes bibliographical references and index.
ISBN 978-0-300-18084-8 (pbk. : alk. paper)   1. Death.   I. Title.
BD444.K26 2012
128'.5—dc23
2011045265

A catalogue record for this book is available from the British Library.

This paper meets the requirements of ANSI/NISO Z39.48-1992 (Permanence of Paper).

10   9   8   7   6

*This book is dedicated
to the memory of my parents
Rosh and Abe Kagan*

Contents

Contents

Acknowledgments

This book is based on a course on death that I have taught for a number of years at Yale University (and before that, at the University of Illinois at Chicago). In the spring semester of 2007, my lectures for that class were videotaped as part of the Open Yale Courses project. (The lectures can be found online at oyc.yale.edu/philosophy/death.) The written transcripts of those lectures formed the first draft of the book that you have in your hands.

In revising those transcripts for publication, I have eliminated certain repetitions, corrected errors, and altered the presentations of ideas or arguments whenever I felt my original attempts were inadequate. I have eliminated some of the asides (and significantly shortened the discussion of Plato). I have altered the setting and some of the examples. But I have kept the informal tone and language of my original lectures. Death is a serious topic—but we don't have to discuss it or write about it in ponderous academic prose.

I am grateful to my students for their many comments and questions over the years. I am grateful as well to those who have watched the online lectures and emailed me with some of their thoughts and reactions. I am confident that I would never have written this book were it not for the encouraging feedback from people who watched (or listened to, or read) the lectures online and helped me see that the ideas that I discuss here may be of interest to people outside the academy. I am particularly indebted to Yale for inviting me to participate in the Open Yale Courses project. The experience was (and continues to be) an extraordinary one.

In my lectures and this book I constantly draw on ideas that have been developed and debated by a large number of contemporary philosophers. I have only marked a few of these philosophical debts with explicit citations (in keeping with the book's introductory nature); but little that I say here is particularly original to me.

CHAPTER 1

Thinking about Death

This is a book about death. But it is a work of philosophy, and what that means is that the topics that we're going to discuss are not identical to the topics that other books on death might try to cover. So the first thing I want to do is to say something about some of the subjects that we *won't* be discussing, things that you might reasonably expect or hope that a book on death would talk about, so that if this is not the book you were looking for, you'll realize that right away.

What I primarily have in mind are psychological and sociological questions about the nature of death, or the phenomenon of death. For example, a book on death might well have a detailed discussion of the process of dying or coming to reconcile yourself with the fact that you're going to die. We're not going to talk about that. Similarly, we're not going to talk at all about the process of grieving or bereavement. And we're not going to discuss the funeral industry in America, or the troubling attitudes that we take toward the dying, or how we tend to try to keep the dying hidden from the rest of us. These are all perfectly important topics, but they're not, as I say, topics that we're going to be talking about in this book.

So what will we talk about? We will be discussing philosophical questions that arise as we begin to think about the nature of death. Questions like, what happens when we die? Actually, though, to get at that question, the first thing we're going to have to do is think about this question: what *are* we? What kind of an entity is a person? In particular, do we have *souls*?

I might as well explain—right here at the start—that in this book I am going to be using the term "soul" as a bit of philosophical jargon. By "soul" I'm going to mean something immaterial, something distinct from our bodies. So one thing that we will be asking is, do we have immaterial souls, something that might survive the death of the body? And if not, what does that imply about the nature of death? What happens when we die?

Here's another question we'll be asking: what would it take for me to *survive* my death? Indeed, we need to ask more generally, what is it for me to survive at all? For example, what does it mean for me to survive, say, *tonight*? Here, roughly, is what I mean by that question. At some point tomorrow afternoon somebody is going to be sitting here at my computer, working on this book. I certainly presume (and hope!) that it will be me. But what exactly *is* it for that person, who will be sitting here typing tomorrow, to be the very *same* person as the person who is sitting here typing today? That's a question about the nature of personal identity across time. Pretty clearly, if we are going to think properly about death and survival, and the possibility of my continued existence after my death, we first have to get clear about the very nature of personal identity.

These sorts of questions—questions about the existence of souls and the nature of death and the possibility of surviving death—will occupy us for roughly the first half of the book. And then we'll turn to value questions. If death is really the end, can death be *bad*? Of course, most of us are immediately and strongly inclined to think that death *is* bad. But there are philosophical puzzles about how death *could* be bad.

Let me try to give you a quick feel for one of these puzzles. Suppose that after my death I won't exist. If you stop to think about it, then, it becomes hard to see how death *can* be bad for me. After all, it seems that death can't be bad for me when I am dead: how can *anything* be bad for something that doesn't even exist? But if death can't be bad for me when I am dead, how can it be bad for me at all? After all, it certainly doesn't seem that it can be bad for me *now*, while I'm still alive!

Don't worry. I am not going to try to convince you that death *isn't* bad. But as we'll see, it actually takes a bit of work to pin down precisely what it *is* about death that's bad, so as to see how death *can* be bad. (It's also worth asking whether there is more than *one* thing about death that makes it bad.) Now if death is indeed bad, then one might wonder, would immortality be a good thing? That's another question that we'll think about. And more generally, we need to ask: how should the fact that I'm going to die affect the way that I *live*? What should my attitude be toward my mortality? Should I, for example, be *afraid* of death? Should I despair at the fact that I'm going to die?

Finally, we'll turn to questions about suicide. Many of us think that given the valuable and precious thing that life is, suicide never makes sense. After all, you're throwing away the only life you're ever going to have. So we'll end the book by examining the rationality and morality (or, perhaps, the irrationality and immorality) of suicide.

That's where we're going. For those of you familiar with the relevant philosophical jargon, we can say that, roughly speaking, the first half of the book will be metaphysics, and the last half of the book will be value theory.

Now there are, I think, two different ways to write a philosophy book, especially an introductory book like this. In the first approach, you simply lay out the various alternative positions, pro and con, and you try to remain neutral. You don't openly take a stand; you avoid letting on which particular positions are the ones you actually accept. That's approach number one. But there is a rather different approach you can take instead, and I should warn you that in this book it is this second approach I will be taking. In the second approach, you *do* tell the reader which views you accept, and you *argue* for them—you do your best to defend them. That's closer to what I will be doing here. There is a particular line of thought that I am going to be developing and defending. That is to say, there's a set of views I hold about the issues that we'll be discussing, and what I'm going to try to do in this book is to convince you that those views are correct.

To help give you a quick sense of what those views are, let me start by describing a *different* set of views—one that many other people accept. As you'll see in a moment, this common point of view involves a number of logically distinct claims. Logically speaking, then, you could believe some of these things and not all of them. But lots of people do believe all of them, and I imagine that it's pretty likely that you too believe at least some of these things.

So here's the set of common views. First of all, we have a soul. That is to say, we are not just bodies. We're not just lumps of flesh and bone. Instead, there's a part of us, perhaps the essential part of us, that is something more than physical—it's the spiritual, immaterial part of us. As I say, in this book we'll call that a soul. Most of us believe in souls. Maybe you do too. Certainly most people in America believe in some sort of immaterial soul. And given the existence of this immaterial soul—the common view continues—it's a possibility, indeed a fair likelihood, that we will survive our deaths. Death will be the destruction of my *body*, but my soul is immaterial, and so my soul can continue to exist after my death. Of course, there is much that we can't know about death; death is the ultimate mystery. But whether or not you do believe in a soul, you probably at least *hope* that there's a soul, because then there would be a serious possibility of surviving your death. After all, death is not only bad, it is *so* horrible that what we would like is to live forever. Immortality would be wonderful. And armed with a soul, as it were, there's at least the possibility of immortality. At any rate, that's certainly what we *hope* is the case—that we are immortal souls—whether or not we *know* that it's the case. And if there is no soul, if death really is the end, then this is such an overwhelmingly bad thing that the obvious reaction, the appropriate reaction, the universal reaction, is to face the prospect of death with fear and despair. Finally, given how horrible death is, and given how wonderful life is, it could never make sense to throw your life away. Thus, on the one hand, suicide is always irrational; and on the other hand, it is always immoral as well.

That, as I say, is what I take to be a common set of views about the nature of death. And what I'm going to be doing, what I'm going to be arguing in this book, is that that set of views is pretty much mistaken from beginning to end. I'm going to try to convince you that there is no soul. I'm going to try to convince you that immortality would not be a good thing. That fear of death isn't actually an appropriate response to death. That death isn't especially mysterious. That suicide, under certain circumstances, might be both rationally and morally justified. As I say, I think that the common picture is pretty much mistaken from start to end, and I am going to try to convince you of that. That, at least, is my goal. That's my aim.

Unsurprisingly, then, I hope that by the end of the book you will agree with me about these things. After all, I think the views I will be defending are true, and I very much hope you will end up believing the truth.

But I should also say that the *crucial* point isn't really for you to end up agreeing with me. The crucial point is for you to think for yourself. Ultimately, the most important thing that I am doing is inviting you to take a good, hard look at death, to face it and think about it in a way that most of us never do. If you, at the end of the book, haven't agreed with me about this particular claim or that particular claim, so be it. I'll be content. Okay, I won't be *completely* content, but at least I will be largely content—as long as you've really thought through the arguments on each side of these various issues.

Before getting started, I need to make one or two more remarks. First, as I have already explained, this is a work of philosophy. What that means, basically, is that we'll just be thinking very carefully about what we can know or make sense of with regard to death using our reasoning capacity. We'll be trying to think about death from a rational standpoint.

So I need to make it clear that one kind of evidence or one kind of argument that we *won't* be making use of here is an appeal to religious authority. You may, of course, already believe in the existence of an afterlife. You may believe you're going to survive your death. You may believe in immortality. And you may believe in all of these things, of course, because that's what your church teaches you. That's fine. It's not my purpose or intention here to try to argue you out of your religious beliefs or to argue against your religious beliefs. But I do want it to be clear that I will not appeal to such religious arguments—whether revelation, or the authority of the Bible, or what have you—in the course of this book.

If you want to, you can think of this book as one big hypothetical. What conclusions would we reach about the nature of death if we had to think about it from a secular perspective? What conclusions would we reach making use of only our own reasoning powers, as opposed to whatever answers we might be given by divinely revealed authority? If you do happen to believe in divine revelation, that's a discussion for another day. It's just not a debate that we're going to be engaged in here.

Finally, I need to explain what it means to say that this is an *introductory* book of philosophy: it means that it doesn't presuppose any background in the subject. But it doesn't mean that it's *easy*. Indeed, some of this material is rather difficult. Some of the ideas may be hard to grasp the first time around. The truth of the matter is that, if you had the time to do it, reading some of the following pages through a second time would often be a helpful thing to do. Of course, I don't really expect you to do that, but still, consider yourself warned: philosophy can be hard stuff to read.

I should also emphasize that this book is introductory in a second sense as well, namely, that there is *more* that can be said about each of the topics that we will be discussing. Every single subject that we discuss here could be pursued at considerably greater length; there are always further arguments beyond the ones that we will consider here. And many of those arguments rapidly become extremely complicated—too complicated to discuss in a book of this sort. That's true for each of the topics that we'll be examining.

So please don't come away thinking that whatever it is that I've said here is the last word on the subject. Rather, it's something more like first words. But, of course, first words can be an excellent place to start.

CHAPTER 2

Dualism versus Physicalism

Asking the Question

The first question we want to discuss has to do with the possibility of surviving death. Is there life after death? Is there at least the possibility that I might still exist after my death?

Now on the face of it, at least, it seems that if we are going to answer this question we'll need to get clear on at least two basic issues. The first is this: what, exactly, *am* I? What *kind* of a thing am I? Or generalizing—because, of course, we want to know not just about my own chances of surviving death, but everyone's—what kind of a thing is a *person*? What are we made of? What are our parts?

It certainly seems plausible to think that before we could answer the question "Do I survive?" we need to know how I'm built. And so the first thing we're going to spend a fair bit of time on is trying to get clear about the fundamental "building blocks" of a person. We need to decide what a person *is*.

The second thing we have to get clear on is this: what exactly is it to *survive*? If we want to know about the possibility of my surviving my death, we had better get clear about the very concept of surviving. What exactly is it for something that exists in the future to be *me*?

Now this question—about the nature of survival, or continued existence over time—is something that can be discussed in quite general terms. We can ask it about chairs, and tables, and trees, or just about anything. We

6

can ask: what is it for the very same thing to continue to exist over time? Or, put even more abstractly, what is the nature of persistence of identity over time?

But since we're especially interested in beings like us, people, we are especially interested in getting clear on what it takes for a given *person* to continue to exist over time. Philosophers call this the problem of *personal identity*—meaning the problem of identity of persons over time (being the same person at two different times). Next week, for example, there will be several people living in my house. I fully expect one of them to be me. But what, exactly, *is* it for one of those people next week to be the very *same* person as me, the person who is sitting here now at this desk? What makes *that* person the same person as *this* person? In short, what is the nature of personal identity? Or, if we prefer to raise the question in the language of survival: what does it take for a person to survive at all?

So on the face of it, at least, to get clear on the question of whether I do, or might, survive my death, it seems that we need to know what a person is, and we need to get clear about the nature of survival, or (more particularly) personal identity across time. Unsurprisingly, then, we are going to spend several chapters investigating these issues with some care.

But before we get started, there's an objection to the whole enterprise that we should consider. We're about to spend a lot of time asking the question: is there life after death? Or, *could* there be life after death? *Might* I survive my death? And according to the objection that I've got in mind, this whole complicated investigation is misconceived; it's based on a confusion. Once we see the confusion—the objection says—we can see what the answer to our question *has* to be. Could I survive my death? *Of course not!*

If that's right, that would certainly simplify our discussion. But is it right? Here's how the objection goes.[1]

One way of stating the question we are trying to ask is this: is there life after death? But what does this question mean? Suppose we start by asking, what does it mean to say that somebody has *died*? A natural definition of "death" might be something like "the end of life." But if that's right, then to ask, "Is there life after death?" is just asking, "Is there life after the end of life?" And the answer to *that* ought to be pretty obvious. Obviously enough, the answer to that is *no*. Asking whether there might be life after death is just a confusing way of asking whether there is still any more life after you've *run out* of life. Well, duh! Of course not! That's like asking: when I've eaten up all the food on my plate, is there any food left on my plate? Or:

what happens in the movie after the movie ends? These are stupid questions, because once you understand what they're asking, the answer is just built in. It follows trivially.

So—the objection continues—although it has seemed to people over the ages that the question "Is there life after death?" is one of the great mysteries, one of the great philosophical things to ponder, that's really a kind of illusion. In fact, once you think about it, you can see the answer has *got* to be no. There couldn't possibly be life after death. There couldn't possibly be life after the end of life.

Or suppose we ask the question in a slightly different way: might I *survive* my death? Well, what does the word "survive" mean? We say that somebody's a survivor if something has happened—an accident, perhaps, or an illness—and they haven't died. They're still alive. When there's a car accident, for example, you may remark that Mr. So-and-So died, but Ms. So-and-So survived. To say that she survived is just to say that she's still alive. So asking, "Might I survive my death?" is like asking, "Might I still be alive after my death?" And what's death? Death is the end of life. So asking whether I might survive my death is really just a way of asking: might I still be alive after I've stopped living? Might I be one of the people who didn't die when I died? And the answer to that, again, is: Duh! Of course not! You couldn't possibly survive your death, given the very definition of survival.

This objection always reminds me of a joke that I remember telling when I was little. You may have told it too. It seemed hysterical when you were seven. It sounds like a riddle: "A plane crashes exactly on the border of Canada and the United States. Exactly on the border. There are dead people everywhere. Where do they bury the survivors? Canada or the United States?" When you're seven you think, "I don't *know* where they bury them. Do they bury them in Canada? Do they bury them in America?" But the answer, of course, is: you don't bury the survivors! Survivors are people that haven't died yet! So asking, "Can I survive my death?" is like asking, "Could it be true that I haven't died yet—*after* I have died?" And the answer, of course, is no! If you *have* died, then obviously you *haven't* survived. So the question can't really get off the ground; it isn't really an open question. That, at least, is how the objection goes.

Now I don't mean to be utterly dismissive of this objection. That's why I spent a couple of paragraphs trying to spell it out. But I think there's a way to respond to it. We just have to get clearer about what precisely the question is that we are trying to ask. Here, then, is one attempt to make the question a bit more precise, and—crucially—make it a question that's genuinely an open question, a question we can legitimately raise.

As I will remind you on several occasions over the course of this book, I'm a philosopher. What that means is: I don't really know a whole lot of facts. So I'm about to tell you a story where I wish I knew the facts; but I don't. To do this properly, therefore, I would now invite a guest author, some distinguished physiologist, to provide us all with the facts that I don't really know. Instead, I am just going to fake it. I am going to say "blah, blah, blah" and fudge the details at the point where I should bring in our guest physiologist. No matter. For our purposes I think the details just aren't all that important.

Consider what happens when a body dies. No doubt, you can kill people in a lot of different ways. You can poison them, you can strangle them, you can shoot them in the heart. And they can die of natural causes—of a heart attack, or a stroke, or cancer. The causal paths that result in death may start in rather different ways, but I presume that typically they converge and you end up having a certain set of events. What are those events? This is exactly where I don't really know the details, but I take it it's something like this. Because of whatever the original input was, eventually the blood's no longer circulating and oxygen isn't making its way around the body. So the brain becomes oxygen-starved. Because of the lack of oxygen getting to the cells, the cells are no longer able to carry on their various metabolic processes. Because of this, they can't repair the various kinds of cellular damage the way that they need to, or create the amino acids and proteins they need. So decay begins to set in and the cell structures begin to break down; cells don't get repaired as they would normally. Eventually we have breakdown of the crucial cell structures and—boom!—the body is dead. Now as I say, I don't really know whether that's accurate, this little rough story I just told, but some story like that is probably right.

I've drawn that story for you here. And those events that take place in the body when it dies, the ones that I don't really know the details of? We can just call them B_1, B_2, B_3, up through B_n. ("B" for "body.") Before B_1 begins, you've got the body working, functioning in its normal, bodily way—respirating, reproducing cells, and so forth and so on. And at the end of the process, by B_n, the body's dead. B_1 through B_n: that's what death is. At least, that's what death of the *body* is. As I say, it's the sort of thing that somebody from a medical school or a biologist or a physiologist could describe for us. (See Figure 2.1.)

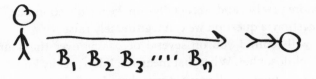

Fig. 2.1

Suppose we call that process "death of the body." Call what has oc-curred by the end of that sequence of events "bodily death." Now here's a question that we can still ask—at least it looks as though we can still ask it. Might I, or do I, still exist after the death of my body? Might I still exist after bodily death? I don't mean to suggest in any way that we yet know the answer to that question, but at least that's a question that it seems as though we can coherently raise. There's no obvious absurdity in asking, might I still exist after the death of my body? The answer could turn out to be no. But at least it's not *obviously* no. It's going to take some sustained argument to settle it one way or the other. The answer could turn out to be yes, for all we know at this point. This just brings us back to the thought that whether or not I could still exist after the death of my body looks like it should depend on what I *am*. So in a minute, that's the question that we're going to turn to.

But it's a bit cumbersome to be constantly asking, might I still exist after the death of my body? Having clarified the question that we're try-ing to ask, I think that no real harm will be done if we allow ourselves to restate it in a few different ways. Instead of insisting that we always ask whether I can continue to exist after the death of my body, we can allow ourselves to sometimes state the question this way: will I *survive* the death of my body? No harm done. Or we can even ask it this way: will I survive my *death*? Here, too, there is no real danger. Indeed, we can just stipulate that when I talk about "my death" in the context of this sort of question, what I mean to be talking about is the death of my body. So ask-ing, "Will I survive my death?" is just shorthand for asking, "Will I sur-vive the death of my body?" As I say, no harm done. For that matter, no serious harm will be done even if we ask it this way: is there life after death? Here too, we can safely assume that when I ask a question like this I am just trying to ask whether I will still exist even after the death of my body. That does seem to be a perfectly legitimate question. So let's try to answer it.

Two Views

As I have already suggested, if we want to answer the question whether I could continue to exist after the death of my body, we first need to get clearer about what I *am*. After all, it's reasonable to think that whether or not a person can survive the death of their body should depend (at least in part) on how they're "built"—what they're made of, what their parts are. We need to know what kind of a thing a person is. In philosophical jargon, this is a question about the metaphysics of persons.

So let me sketch for you two basic positions on this question. Both of them, I imagine, are fairly familiar. What we're going to have to do is try to decide between them. To be sure, they're not the only possible positions on the question of the metaphysics of the person. But they are, I think, the two most prominent positions; they are definitely the ones most worth exploring for our purposes.

The first possible position is this. A person is a combination of a body and something else—a mind. But the crucial thing about this first view is that the mind is thought of as something separate from, and distinct from, the body. To use a common enough word, it's a *soul*. So people are, or people have, or people consist of, bodies and souls. The soul is something, as I say, *distinct* from the body.

Now I take it that the idea of a *body* is a perfectly familiar one. In my own case, for example, my body is this lump of flesh and bone and muscle that's currently sitting in front of my computer screen, that I sort of drag around with me as I go through the day. You've got one too, that you too "drag around" with you. It's the sort of thing that we can put on a scale and prod with a stick and biologists can study. It's made up of various kinds of molecules, atoms, and so forth. So one thing people have is a body. But on this first view, we also have something that's *not* the body, something that's not a material object, not composed of molecules and atoms. It's a soul. It's the house of, or the seat of, or the basis of, consciousness and thinking, perhaps personality. In any event, the crucial point is that the proper metaphysical understanding of the mind is to think of it in nonphysical, nonmaterial terms—that is, as a *soul*.

We can call this first view the *dualist* view—because, of course, it posits two basic components for the person, a body and a soul. And in what follows I am going to try to reserve the word "soul" for this kind of dualist view, according to which the soul is something immaterial, something nonphysical. In contrast to the body, which is a material substance, the soul is an *immaterial* substance. That's the dualist view.

That, as I say, is the first basic view. I'll say more about it in a moment. But first, let me sketch the other basic view.

The alternative view that we're going to consider is not dualist but monist. It says there's only one basic kind of thing that goes into making up a person: there are just bodies. So what's a person? A person is just a certain kind of material object. A person is just a body. We'll call this second view *physicalism*, because it says that a person is just a body, just a particular kind of physical object.

On this second view, a person is just a material object, a physical thing. Of course, it's a very fancy kind of material object. Indeed, it's a rather amazing material object. After all—according to this second view—people are physical objects that can do things that most other physical objects can't do. We can talk. We can think. We can sing. We can write poetry. We can fall in love. We can be afraid. We can make plans. We can discover things about the universe. According to the physicalist view, a *person* is just a body that can *do* all of those things: reflect, be rational, communicate, make plans, fall in love, write poetry. That's the physicalist view.

So we have two basic positions. There's the dualist view, according to which people are bodies and souls. And there's the physicalist view, according to which there *are no souls*. There are no immaterial objects like that. There are only bodies—though properly functioning bodies like ours (the physicalist says) can do some pretty amazing things. Dualism and physicalism are the two basic views that we'll be considering.

From a logical standpoint, I suppose you might have a third possible view as well. If we've got the monist who says there are bodies but no souls, you could also imagine somebody who says there are souls but no bodies! For example, there could be a metaphysical view according to which there *are* minds (indeed, immaterial minds: souls), but there aren't really any *material* objects at all. All that exists are minds and their ideas. Perhaps talk of "physical objects" is just a convenient way of talking about the *ideas* the mind has, or something like that. Thinking about physical objects in terms of *matter* might be a kind of illusion that we easily fall into, a metaphysical mistake. In philosophy, this sort of view is known as *idealism*.

Now idealism is actually a position that has a very long and distinguished history in philosophy, and in a more complete survey of metaphysics it would be worth taking a fair bit of time to consider it more carefully.

But for our purposes, I think, it's simply not a contender. So I'm just going to put it aside.

There are still other possibilities. For example, there are views according to which talk of mind and body are just two different ways of looking at the very same underlying reality, where that underlying reality is fundamentally neither physical *nor* mental. That view—*neutral monism*—might also be worth taking seriously in a metaphysics book. But for our purposes, I mention it only to put it aside as well.

In this book, then, we aren't going to consider all the various exotic philosophical positions that one might take concerning the metaphysical nature of persons. Instead, we are going to focus on the two views that I take to be the most serious contenders, physicalism and dualism. Note that both of these views *accept* the existence of the body—just as, I imagine, you do. They simply differ about whether or not we *also* need to accept the existence of immaterial souls. Dualists say yes: people have, or are, souls as well as bodies. Physicalists say no: *all* we have, or are, are bodies.

Dualism

Let me say something more about the dualist position. First, and most importantly, according to the dualist the mind is an immaterial substance. We could call that substance by different names. Indeed, no harm would be done if we just *called* it a "mind." But when discussing dualism I will typically talk about a *soul*, to try to flag the crucial point of the dualist view, that the mind is based in, or just is, something nonphysical, something nonmaterial.

Second, the body and the soul interact. On the one hand, the soul can direct and give orders to the body. Right now, for example, my body is typing letters on a keyboard. It is doing this, according to dualism, because of the orders given to it by my soul. My soul can make my body stand up, sit down, or run around the room. So in various ways the soul can *affect* the body. But, on the other hand, the soul can also be *affected* by the body, for the body generates input that eventually gets sensed or felt by the soul. If you take a pin and you stick it through the flesh of my body, for example, I will feel pain in my soul, in my mind. So the interaction works both ways: the body can affect the soul, and the soul can affect the body. Of course, as is always the case with philosophy, there are more complicated versions of dualism where the interaction doesn't actually work both ways, but let's just limit ourselves to good old-fashioned, two-way interactionist dualism. My soul controls my body, and my body can affect my soul. Of course, despite this interaction, the body and the soul are separate things. But normally, in any event, there's this very tight connection.

Although it isn't really crucial for our purposes, it may be worth taking a moment to ask about the *location* of the soul. If there are souls, where *are* they? Indeed, do souls even have locations? I don't think the answer is at all obvious. On the one hand, we often talk as though souls do have locations. We say that the soul is in the body. Of course, it's not as though we think that if you start opening up the body you'd find some particular spot where the soul is located. But it does seem natural to think of souls as having at least a rough location. After all, I am viewing the world from *here*, just as *you* are viewing the world from a *different* particular location. So maybe your soul is located, more or less, in the vicinity of your body.

At least, maybe that's true as long as your body is working properly. Maybe at death the soul gets liberated from the body and is able to wander about more freely. In fact, perhaps this sometimes happens even while we are alive. Some people report out-of-body experiences, where they seem to leave their body behind and wander about without it. Maybe during these unusual times the soul moves away from the body, and later comes back to it. Of course, even if all of that is true and out-of-body experiences are possible, the soul would still be located *some* place or the other at any given time, even if it is not necessarily located precisely where the body is.

On the other hand, maybe that's all an illusion. Maybe the soul doesn't have any location at all. Maybe the *feeling* that I have a location is really just an illusion created by the fact that I'm normally getting all of this sensory input from my body. Imagine somebody who was locked in a room in New Haven, where all he can see are the images being displayed on the screen from the remote-feed television camera located in *Chicago*, and all he can hear are the sounds being picked up on the remote-feed microphone, which is also located in Chicago, and so forth and so on. If that was all that he had ever experienced, you could understand why he might fall into the error of thinking of *himself* as located in Chicago, what with all the sensory inputs coming from Chicago. So maybe that's how it works with the soul as well. We get lulled into thinking that we are where our bodies are. But maybe it's really just a metaphysical illusion: maybe souls don't have locations at all.

The truth of the matter is, I don't know. I know very little about how immaterial objects are supposed to work. (Can immaterial entities even *have* locations? I don't know.) As I have already explained, I don't myself believe in souls. I don't actually think the dualist position is correct. So I can leave this question—about whether souls are spatially located or not—to be worked out by those who do believe in them. Happily, for our purposes, I think it won't really matter. If you want to say that souls have a location, perhaps you'll be content to say that they are (normally) located more or less where the corresponding body is. But if you prefer to say that, on the contrary, souls don't actually have any locations of their own at all, that shouldn't really be a problem either.

What *is* important—for our purposes—is the dualist's claim that there *are* souls, and that they are distinct from the bodies that are normally connected to them, that they are immaterial substances. For if there is a soul as well as a body, and the soul is something immaterial, then even when the body dies, the soul might continue to exist!

Here's someone's living body. Sadly, it gets sick. We have B_1 through B_n. By the end of B_n, the body stops repairing itself. Decay sets in. The death of the body occurs. We all know the sad story: the worms crawl in, the worms crawl out. At the end of the day—well, maybe it takes longer than a day—the body has decomposed. Yes, all of that bespeaks the end of the *body*. But if the soul is something immaterial, something nonphysical, then that could *continue* to exist, even after the destruction of the body. That's the attraction, or at least one of the attractions, of the dualist view. The belief in the soul gives you something to continue to exist after the end of your body.

So what's death? Well, if normally there's this super tight connection between my soul and my body, death might be the severing of that connection. The body breaks and is no longer able to give input to the soul. The soul is no longer able to control the body and make it move around. But for all that, the soul might continue to exist. At least, that's a possibility. The possibility that I'll survive my death is one worth taking very, very seriously if we are dualists.

But here's a worry. According to dualism, the person is a combination of the body and the soul: a kind of body and soul sandwich. But if the person is the combination, if the person is the *pair*—soul plus body—then won't it still be true that when you destroy the body, you've destroyed the *person*? After all, isn't it true that when you destroy one *part* of a pair, the *pair* itself no longer exists either? So if a person is a pair—soul plus body— and the pair no longer exists, then the *person* no longer exists! And won't that mean that I can't really survive the death of my body after all, not even if we assume the truth of dualism?

Luckily, however, there are at least two possible replies that can be made by the dualist. One possibility is for the dualist to insist that, strictly speaking, a person isn't a soul *plus* a body; strictly speaking the person is *just* the soul. On this approach, I am just my soul, and nothing more. On this view, obviously, the destruction of my body doesn't really involve the destruction of even a *part* of me. Of course, I have a very tight connection to my body. But destroying that body simply doesn't destroy a part of me at all. (Here's an analogy. I have a particularly close connection to the house I live in. But in and of itself, destroying my house doesn't involve destroying a part of *me*.)

So that's one possible position that the dualist can take. The person is, strictly speaking, only the soul. The soul has a very intimate connection with the body, but the person is not the soul *and* the body. The person is *just* the soul. So even if that intimate connection gets destroyed, the person, the soul, could continue to exist.

That's *one* way the dualist can go, but she doesn't *have* to go that way. Instead, the dualist can insist that although my body is a genuine part of me, it isn't an *essential* part of me. Perhaps, instead, my body is a part that I can lose, while still continuing to exist. After all, things lose parts all the time, without necessarily being destroyed by that loss. For example, my car used to have a hubcap on the front right tire, but it no longer does. That hubcap was certainly a genuine part of my car, and yet for all that, my car did continue to exist even after the loss and destruction of the hubcap: the hubcap was *part* of my car, but not an essential part. (Indeed, my car continues to exist even though the hubcap has never been replaced!) Similarly, then, even though a person is—while alive—composed of a body and a soul, perhaps the person can continue to exist even after the destruction of the body. The body is part of the person, but not an *essential* part.

I won't try to decide which of these two answers is the better one for the dualist to adopt. Suffice it to say that both answers seem acceptable. Accordingly, one way or the other, I think it really is true that the dualist can hold out at least the *possibility* that I might survive the death and destruction of my body.

I emphasize the point that the dualist only holds out the *possibility* of surviving death, because of course the mere *existence* of an immaterial soul doesn't in and of itself guarantee that the soul *does* survive the death of the body. Perhaps there *are* souls, but they die when the body does!

So there are really two distinct questions that interest us here. The first question is whether there really are immaterial souls. Is it indeed the case that the mind is to be understood in terms of an immaterial substance, the soul? Is it truly the case that there are two distinct kinds of things, bodies and souls? That's the first question. But second, we also want to know whether the soul—assuming it does exist—*survives* the destruction of the body. After all, it could be that the soul is something separate from the body and yet, for all that, it too gets destroyed when the body gets destroyed.

That's why I've tried to say that if there are souls, at least that *opens the door* to the possibility that I will survive my death. But it doesn't guarantee it, because absent further argumentation there's no guarantee that the soul survives the death of the body. Even if it's separate, it could be that it gets destroyed at the very same time that the body's being destroyed. Remember, after all, that we are examining what I called *interactionist* dualism. There is this very tight causal connection between the body and the soul. When you prick my body, that bodily process results in various other events—the experience of pain!—that take place in my soul. Similarly, then, perhaps when my body dies—when the physical processes B_1 through B_n take place—they set up some parallel processes in my *soul*—call these S_1 through S_n—and these other processes result in (or constitute) the *destruction* of my soul. So as my body dies, my soul dies too!

Here's a picture of what I have in mind. (See Figure 2.2.) It's similar to our earlier figure, which showed the death of the body. But now I've added the idea that as the body dies, it causes the simultaneous death of the soul as well. (Of course, it isn't clear how to draw a picture of a soul, so I've just drawn little faces with halos.)

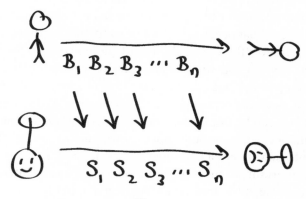

Fig. 2.2

At this point, however, one might want to raise an objection. The very idea of the soul that we're working with here is that of an immaterial substance. It's not made of ordinary, atomic matter. But if the soul is immaterial, doesn't it follow automatically, trivially, that the soul *cannot* be destroyed by a material process? The death of the body—B_1 through B_n—was obviously a physical process. And isn't it obvious that the soul, an *immaterial* entity, can't be destroyed by a material, physical process?

Sadly, however, I don't think that this is, in fact, obvious. For as I have just reminded us, we are here examining *interactionist* dualism, according to which bodies are able to affect the soul in a wide range of different ways. Right now, for example, light of various wavelengths is bouncing off of my eyes, and because of that, my soul is having various visual experiences concerning the different objects—computer, desk, telephone—in front of me. Right now, sound waves of various intensities are bouncing off my ears, and because of that my soul is having various auditory experiences of the different members of my family who are in the next room. Right now, gastric juices are building up in my stomach, and because of that my soul is having the experience of feeling hunger. In short, there are all sorts of physical processes taking place in my body which are causing all sorts of changes in my soul. But once we have admitted that on this kind of dualist picture the material body can influence what happens in the immaterial soul, then it doesn't seem that we have any grounds for shutting the door to the possibility that the right physical process, B_1 through B_n, might set up this horrible soul process, S_1 through S_n, which results in the destruction of the soul. It certainly seems to be a possibility. It's going to take further argument to rule it out.

In short, even if we do decide that there *are* souls, that doesn't yet guarantee that we survive the deaths of our bodies. That turns out to be a further claim, one that needs to be backed by further arguments.

In fact, however, there's actually a third question that we'll want to think about as well. Suppose that the soul does survive the death of the body. How *long* does it survive for? Does it continue to exist *forever*? Are we immortal?

Most of us would certainly like that to be true. We want there to be souls so that we can be immortal. And so we have to ask not only whether the soul is distinct from the body, not only whether it survives the death of the body, but also whether it continues to exist forever. That last question—about the immortality of the soul—was one that especially interested Plato. We'll turn to some of his arguments in Chapter 5. But first, we need to decide whether we should believe in the existence of souls in the first place.

Physicalism

According to dualism—our first basic view about the nature of persons—a person has (or is) an immaterial soul. I take it that this view is a perfectly familiar one. You may well believe in souls yourself. Even if you don't, you have probably been at least tempted by the belief. And in any event, I'm sure that at the very least you *know* people who believe in this view. It's a very familiar picture. But, of course, the question we're going to have to ask ourselves is, is it right? Is there reason to believe it's correct?

Before trying to answer that question, however, let's take a closer look at physicalism, our second basic view about the nature of persons. According to this view, a person is just a body. People are just material objects, the sorts of things biologists poke and prod and study.

Of course it is crucial to be clear about what's being said here. When the physicalist says that a person is just a body, just a physical object, they certainly aren't claiming that a person is just *any* old body! It's not as though there aren't important differences between different physical objects. Some physical objects can do things of a far more interesting sort than other physical objects.

On my desk I've got a pencil. It's just a physical object of sorts. What can it do? Well, not a whole lot. I can write on a piece of paper with it. I can break it in two. If I pick it up, and let it go, it drops down. It's not a particularly interesting physical object. I also have a cell phone. It's also just a physical object. It's not the most interesting physical object in the world either, but it's a whole lot more interesting than the pencil. It can do all sorts of things a pencil can't do.

And if the physicalist is right, then here's another physical object for you—me, Shelly Kagan. I'm a pretty impressive physical object. Now arrogant as I may be, I don't mean to suggest I'm any more impressive than you are. Each one of us, according to the physicalist, is just a body that can do some amazing things. We are bodies that can think. We are bodies that can plan. We are bodies that can reason. We are bodies that can feel. We are bodies that can be afraid and be creative and have dreams and aspirations. We are bodies that can communicate with each other. We are bodies that are—well, here's a word for it: we are bodies that are *people*. But on the physicalist view, a person is just a body. Nothing more.

According to physicalism, then, a person is a body that has a certain set of abilities, a body that can do a certain array of activities. People are bodies that can think, communicate, reason, plan—feel things, be creative, love and dream—and so forth and so on.

If we wanted to, we could argue about what exactly belongs on the best list of those abilities. For our purposes, however, I think that won't be crucial. So even though I will sometimes talk about this set of abilities, I won't actually try to produce a canonical list. Just think of it as the set of abilities that *people* have, the things that we can do that other physical objects—pencils, radios, cars—can't do. Call these the abilities that make something a *person*. To introduce a piece of jargon, we could call these the P abilities ("P" for "person"). According to the physicalist, then, a person is just a body that has the various P abilities. Equivalently, we can say that according to the physicalist a person is just a body that has the ability to fulfill the various *P functions* (reasoning, thinking, feeling, communicating, loving, and so on). And we can talk, then, about a person as a P functioning body. Or we could say that a person is a body that is P functioning.

Once again, it's important to see that the idea is that although a person is just a body, it's not just any old body. Indeed, it's not just any old human body. After all, if you whip out your gun and shoot me in the heart and I bleed to death, you will still have a human body in front of you. But it won't be a P functioning body. It won't be a body that's able to think, a body that's able to plan, to communicate, to be creative, to have goals. So the crucial thing about having a person is having a P functioning body.

Now what, exactly, is a *mind* on this view? On the physicalist view, it's still perfectly legitimate to talk about minds. But from the physicalist perspective, talking about the mind is just a convenient way of talking about these various *mental abilities* of the body. When we talk this way, we nominalize. We talk about the abilities using a noun, the "mind." But talk of the mind is just a way of talking about these special abilities that the body has when it's functioning properly.

This is similar, let's say, to talking about a smile. We all believe that there are smiles. But what is a smile? Well, a smile is just a way of talking about the ability of the body to do something—that characteristic thing we do, curling up our lips, exposing our teeth, and so forth. But it isn't an extra *part* of the body. If you were to list the parts of the body, you would list the teeth, you would list the lips, you would list the gums, you would list the tongue—but you wouldn't list the smile.

So should we accept some sort of *dualism* here? Should we conclude that smiles are extra, nonphysical things, things that have a special intimate relationship with bodies? You could imagine a view like that. But it would be rather a silly view. Rather, talking about a smile is just a way of talking about the body's *ability* to smile. There is no extra thing—the smile.

To be sure, we have a noun—the "smile"—and if you are not careful, that very fact might lull you into thinking that there must be a thing, the smile. And then you would have all of these metaphysical conundrums.

Where is the smile *located*? It seems to be in the *vicinity* of the mouth. But the smile isn't the lips. The smile isn't the teeth. So it must be something nonphysical!

But as I say, that would just be a silly way to think about smiles. Talk of smiles is just a way of talking about the ability of the body to smile, to form a smile. That's an ability that we have, that our bodies have.

Similarly, then, according to the physicalist, talk of *the mind* is just a way of talking about the abilities of the body to do various things. Talk of the mind is just a convenient way of talking about the fact that our body can think, can communicate, can plan, can deliberate, can be creative, can write poetry, can fall in love. Talk of all of those things is what we *mean* by "the mind," but there's no extra thing, *the mind*, above and beyond the body.

That's the physicalist view. Physicalists don't deny that there are minds. Just like we don't deny that there are smiles. But talk of minds, like talk of smiles, is just a convenient way to talk about things the body can do.

In particular, then, it's important to understand that from the physicalist's point of view, the mind is *not* the brain. You might think, "Look, according to physicalists, minds are just brains." And I have to admit that this wouldn't be a horrendously misleading thing to say, because according to the best science that we've got, the brain is the part of the body that is the underlying structure that gives us these various abilities. These P functions are functions that we have *by virtue of* our brain. So that might tempt you into saying that the mind on the physicalist view is just a brain.

But we probably shouldn't say that. Suppose, after all, that you have killed me. There's my corpse lying on the floor. There's my brain. (Let's not get too grisly: suppose it's still in my skull.) The *brain* is still there—but for all that, it seems pretty clear that the *mind* has been destroyed. So I think that we probably shouldn't say that the brain *is* the mind. At least, when there's the need to be careful we should say, instead, that talk of the mind is a way of talking about the P functioning of the body. Admittedly, our best science suggests that a well-functioning body can think and plan and fall in love *by virtue of* the fact that the brain is working properly. But strictly speaking, talk of the mind is really just a way of talking about the P functioning. That's the physicalist view of the mind.

And what is the physicalist view of death? On the *dualist* view, of course, death is the permanent separation of the mind—the immaterial soul—and the body, given the destruction of the body. But for the physicalist, there is no extra entity, the soul, which may or may not survive the death of the body. The mind is just the proper P functioning of the body. So when the ability of the body to function in that way has been destroyed, the *mind* has been destroyed. Roughly speaking, then, death is just the end of that kind of functioning.

As I say, that's a bit rough. In Chapter 11 we'll spend a while trying to clean this idea up, and make it somewhat more precise. But still, there's nothing mysterious about the basic idea. There's nothing particularly mysterious about death from the physicalist point of view.

I've got a stereo. Suppose I hold up my boombox for you and it's playing music. That's one of the things it can do. But I drop it on the ground, smashing it. It no longer can function properly. It's broken. There's no mystery why it can't function once it's broken. From the physicalist's point of view, death is basically just like that. It's the breaking down of the body, so that it no longer functions properly.

There is one other point worth emphasizing. As I have already explained, physicalists don't deny that there are minds (just as the rest of us don't deny that there are smiles). Still, talk of our minds is just a way of referring to some of the things that our bodies can do—the fact that they can think, and love, and plan. But it isn't as though the physicalist view is that we are just bodies that have some *illusion* of thinking. No, we are bodies that really *do* think. We are bodies that really do love. We are bodies that really do plan. So there really are minds. And we could, if we wanted to, call these minds *souls*—even on the physicalist's view of things.

After all, just as, from the physicalist's point of view, there is nothing wrong with talking about minds, there is nothing wrong with talking about souls. Usually, when we talk about souls, we aren't doing metaphysics, we aren't presupposing a particular metaphysical view. I am a physicalist, but in most contexts I am perfectly comfortable talking about a person's soul: "he's got a good soul," "she's a bad soul," "how the soul soars when one reads Shakespeare," and so forth.

There's nothing upsetting or improper about the *language* of "the soul"—not even from the physicalist's point of view. It is a perfectly appropriate way to talk. But as I have already remarked, in *this* book, just to try to keep us from getting confused, I'm going to save the *word* "soul" for when I am talking about the dualist position.

Perhaps I can put the point this way. We are going to use the term "mind" in a neutral fashion, in a way that doesn't commit us, one way or another, as to what a mind is. So we can all agree that people have *minds*— the house or seat of our thoughts and personalities. But the hard question remains: what *is* a mind? The dualist position, of course, is that the mind is a soul and the soul is an immaterial object. And in this book, when I use the word "soul," I will try to reserve it for that particular metaphysical view, according to which souls are something immaterial. In contrast to that, of course, we've also got the physicalist view. Physicalists also believe in minds. But according to physicalists, minds are just a way of talking about the abilities of the body. Physicalists certainly do *not* believe in immaterial souls of the sort that dualists believe in. So just to keep things clear, I will say that physicalists do not believe in souls at all. They believe in minds, but not in souls.

Our question, then, is this: who should we believe, the dualist or the physicalist? Are there souls, or not?

CHAPTER 3

Arguments for the Existence of the Soul

I've introduced two basic positions concerning the nature of persons: the dualist view and the physicalist view. Both, I take it, are familiar views, regardless of which one you accept. Just as we all know dualists, people who accept the existence of an immaterial soul, we also all know physicalists, people who deny the existence of souls and insist that people are just bodies. Both positions are familiar. But the question we need to ask is: which of these two views should we *believe*?

In choosing between these two views, the crucial issue, obviously enough, is whether we should believe in the existence of a soul. For both sides believe in the existence of *bodies*. The dualist, after all, doesn't deny the existence of bodies—she just believes in the existence of souls *as well as* bodies—and the physicalist obviously doesn't deny the existence of bodies either. So the existence of the body is common ground between these two views. Where they differ, rather, is over whether to accept souls in *addition* to bodies. So what we need to ask is this: is there good reason to believe in the *soul*?

How might one go about trying to prove the existence of a soul? Well, perhaps we should start by asking, how might one go about trying to prove the existence of *anything*? For example, how do we prove the existence of ordinary things, like chairs and tables, birds and trees?

For lots of familiar, everyday objects, of course, the answer is fairly straightforward. We prove the existence of these things by using our five senses. We just see them, or hear them, or feel them. How do I know that there are chairs? Well, here are some chairs in front of me. I open my eyes, and I just see them. How do I know that there is a desk? I can see it, touch it, feel it. How do I know that there are trees? I can see them (I see some out my window right now). How do I know that there are birds? I can see them, hear them. How do I know that there are apples? I don't see any right now, but I have seen them in the past. I have tasted them, touched them. And so forth and so on, for all sorts of ordinary everyday objects.

But that approach pretty clearly isn't going to work for souls! A soul is supposed to be something immaterial. It isn't something we see. It's not something we taste or touch or smell or hear. We don't directly observe souls with our five senses.

Of course, it is conceivable that someone might insist that although we can't observe souls with our five *outer* senses, we can nonetheless observe them using our *inner* sense, in the same way that I can use my inner sense to observe my thoughts, my emotions, the pain in my left foot, or the fact that right now I seem to be sensing a patch of blue. I cannot see these things using my outer senses, but for all that I can directly observe all these things in myself using my inner sense. Similarly then, someone might claim, I can also directly observe my own soul, using my inner sense.

If someone does try to argue in this way, I can only say that such a claim seems wrong to me. And I believe that if you think about it, you will see that it seems wrong to you, too. Try introspecting for a moment. Turn your mind's eye inward and ask, do you see a soul inside you? I don't think you will. Like me, you may observe various sensations in your body; you may observe various thoughts and feelings. But you won't observe a soul.

So even if you believe in a soul, I'll bet you agree with me that it isn't the sort of thing we can "see"—regardless of whether we are using outer sense *or* inner sense. Souls cannot be *observed*. Accordingly, if there *are* souls, we need some other way to prove their existence.

Inference to the Best Explanation

How can we prove the existence of things we can't see (or hear or taste, and so on—and, for that matter, can't observe using inner sense either)? What is probably the most important method goes something like this. Sometimes we justifiably posit the existence of something that we can't see, so as to explain something else that we all agree takes place.

For example, why do I believe in the existence of atoms? I certainly don't see individual atoms. Why am I justified in believing in the existence of particles so small that I can't see them? Because atomic theory *explains* things. When I posit the existence of atoms with certain structures and certain ways of interacting and combining and building up—when I posit atoms—suddenly I can explain all sorts of things about the physical world. So I infer the existence of atoms based on the fact that doing that allows me to explain things that need explaining.

This is a kind of argument that we use all the time. Why do I believe in x-rays, even though I don't see them? Because doing that allows me to explain how there can be photographic images of the insides of objects (for example, the bones in your hand). Why do I believe in certain planets too far away to be observed directly through a telescope? Because positing them allows us to explain things about the blinking of the star's light. We make inferences to the existence of things we can't see when doing that helps us to explain something we can't otherwise explain. This pattern of argument is ubiquitous. Philosophers call it *inference to the best explanation.*

I should emphasize that what's relevant here is inference to the *best* explanation. What we're justified in believing in are those things that we need, not simply when they would offer us *some* kind of explanation, but when they offer us the *best* explanation that we can think of. For example, why am I justified in believing in germs—various kinds of viruses or bacteria that I can't see? Because doing that allows me to explain why people get sick. But there are other things that would allow me to explain that as well. How about demons? I could believe in demons and say, "Why does a person get sick and die? Because of demonic possession." So why aren't I justified in believing in the existence of demons? It's certainly a *possible* explanation. But what we're justified in believing is not just any old explanation, but the *best* (available) explanation.

With regard to disease, then, we've got two rival explanations. We've got germ theory and we've got demon theory. And we have to ask ourselves, which of these does a better job of explaining the facts about disease? Which better explains who gets what kinds of diseases, how diseases spread, how they can be treated or cured? And the fact of the matter, of course, is that demon theory doesn't do a very good job of explaining disease, while germ theory does do a good job. It's the better explanation. So we're justified in believing in germs, but not demons. It's a matter of inference, not just to any old explanation, but to the *best* explanation.

All right, then, so what about the soul? We can't *observe* souls, but now we may have a possible way for the dualist to argue for them anyway.

What the dualist needs to do is point to something about us that the physicalist cannot explain, or can only explain badly. She needs to point to some mystery or puzzle about people, where the physicalist just draws a blank, but where we *can* explain these features if only we become dualists.

But are there such features? Are there things that need to be explained that we *could* explain if we posited something above and beyond the body, something immaterial, the soul? Are there things that the existence of a soul could explain, and explain better than the explanation that we would have if we had to limit ourselves to bodies? Suppose there was a feature like that, feature *F*. Then we'd say, "Look, although we can't see the soul, we have reason to believe in the soul, because positing the existence of a soul helps us to explain the existence of feature F, which we all agree we've got."

Suppose, for example, that it was true that you couldn't explain *love* from the physicalist perspective. We all know that people do fall in love—but suppose that physicalists couldn't explain that. And suppose that positing souls *would* allow us to explain that. Boom, we'd have an argument for the existence of a soul. It would be an example of inference to the best explanation.

Now the crucial question, of course, is what's the relevant feature F? *Is* there some feature that the physicalist can't explain, or can only do a rotten job of explaining—and so we need to appeal to something extra-physical to explain it? A feature where, if we were to appeal to something nonphysical, we would do a *better* job of explaining it? If we could find the right F, and show that the physicalist can't explain it, or does a bad job of explaining it, and that the dualist does a better job of explaining it, we would have some reason to believe in the soul. Like all arguments in philosophy, of course, it would only be a tentative argument. We might have to give up belief in the soul if some even better explanation for F eventually came along. But until that time came (and of course it might never come), we would have at least *some* reason to believe in the soul.

So what I want to ask is this: what might feature F be? *Is* there any such feature? Are there things about us that we can only explain well if we appeal to the soul?

We are actually going to consider a number of different possible proposals. Each will have to be examined separately, for each proposal points to a distinct potential argument. After all, inference to the best explanation is not the name for a single, unique argument for the existence of the soul; rather, it's the name for a certain *kind* of argument. Depending on what F you use to fill in the blank, what pet feature or fact you're trying to explain by appealing to the soul, you get a different argument. And the truth of the matter is there are several arguments of this sort that are worth taking seriously.

I hasten to add, however, that even though I think these various arguments are worth taking seriously, that doesn't mean that I think any of these arguments actually *work*. Indeed, I've already told you that I don't myself believe in the existence of a soul. Accordingly, it shouldn't surprise you to learn that as we run through each of these arguments I am going to go on to say that I'm not convinced, and here's why. And since I believe that these various arguments for the existence of the soul are unsuccessful, I hope that when you think it over, you will eventually come to agree with me. I hope that you too will conclude that the arguments don't really work after all.

But what's even more important to me is that you at least *think* about each of these arguments. Is this a convincing argument for the existence of a soul, or not? If you think it is, what response do you want to offer to the various objections that I'll be giving? Alternatively, if you agree that this or that particular argument doesn't work, is there another argument for the existence of a soul that you think is a better one?

Everyday Phenomena

Very well, we are going to consider a number of different candidates for feature F, something that (so it is claimed) we can explain properly only if we believe in the soul. We can divide these various proposals into two broad groups. One set focuses on ordinary, familiar, everyday facts about us. The fact that we love, the fact that we think, the fact that we experience emotions—these are ordinary features of us, and conceivably some of them need to be explained in terms of a soul. I'm going to start with those. Eventually, I'll turn to another set of things that might need explaining, things we might think of as extraordinary, supernatural facts. Maybe there are supernatural events, like communication from the dead or near-death experiences, that need to be explained in terms of the soul. We'll get to those later. But we can start with ordinary, everyday, humdrum facts about us. Even though they're ordinary and familiar, it still could turn out that we need to appeal to souls in order to explain them.

Let's start with the familiar but important fact that you can have a body that's *dead*. If all you have is a corpse, after all, that's clearly not a person. It's not a living being. It doesn't do anything; it just lies there. In contrast, of course, your body, your living body, is *animated*, just as *my* body is animated. I move my hands around; my mouth goes up and down. I walk from one part of my office to another, and so on. Maybe we need to appeal to the soul in order to explain what *animates* the body.

The thought would be this: when the soul and the body have been separated—or so the dualist explains—the soul loses its ability to give commands to the body. So the body is no longer animated. Here, then, we have a possible explanation of the difference between an animate and an inanimate body. It turns on whether the soul is in the right sort of contact with the body. That's certainly a possible explanation. The dualist might continue by claiming that, in contrast, the physicalist *can't* explain why some bodies are animated while others are not. After all, even when you have a corpse, all the physical parts are still there—at least if it's a fresh corpse, before decay has set in. So we need to appeal to something extra, we need to appeal to the existence of a soul, in order to explain the animation of living bodies like the ones that you and I have.

From the physicalist's point of view, however, all of this is way too quick. Remember the idea that, according to the physicalist, to have a person you have to have a P functioning body? Similarly, then, but more generally, to have an animated body at all, you have to have a *functioning* body. Simply having a body isn't enough; it has to be *functioning*. It's true, of course, that when you've got a fresh corpse, you've got all the parts there, but clearly they're not functioning properly. But all that shows us, says the physicalist, is that the parts are broken.

Remember my stereo? Suppose that I drop my boombox. It falls on the floor and doesn't work anymore; it stops giving off music. But all the parts might still be there: the CD, the batteries, the CD drive, the buttons, the wires. It's all still there, but of course now the whole thing is *broken*. Perhaps a wire has been ripped, or the power button's been smashed. Perhaps the parts aren't connected to each other in the right way anymore. The energy is not flowing from the batteries through the wires to the CD drive. I don't need to know the details to know that there's nothing mysterious about the idea that a physical object can *break*. It's certainly not as though we need to say that previously there was something *immaterial* there! Although we need to offer a story about what makes the parts work when they're connected with each other and interacting in the right way, there's no need to appeal to anything beyond the physical to explain the difference between a working stereo and a busted one.

Something similar will do, says the physicalist, when it comes to bodies. Here too we need to recognize that merely having all the right parts isn't enough—they have to be in working order, otherwise the body won't function properly, it won't be animated. When you have a corpse, the body is no longer in working order, so it isn't animated. And here too, you don't need to know the details to reasonably believe that we can explain all of this in physical terms. There's no need to appeal to an immaterial soul.

Of course, the dualist may try to refine the argument. She might say that we need to appeal to the soul in order to explain not just the bare fact that the body moves around, but the more particular fact that the body acts *purposefully*. There has to be something "pulling the strings," something *directing* the body. That's where the soul comes in—or so says the dualist.

In response, the physicalist will certainly admit that it's true that human bodies don't just move around in random patterns. So we do need something to direct it. But the physicalist asks, why can't that just be one particular *part* of the body? Why can't one part of the body play the part of the command module?

Suppose I've got a heat-seeking missile which tracks down airplanes. As the plane tries to dodge it the missile corrects its course. It's not just moving randomly, it's moving purposefully. There had better be something that explains and controls the motions of the missile. But for all that, it could just be—it just is—a particular piece of the missile that does that. More gloriously, we could imagine building a robot that does a *variety* of tasks. It's not moving randomly, but the tasks are all controlled by the CPU within the robot. Similarly, then, the physicalist says we don't need to appeal to anything as extravagant as a soul in order to explain the fact that bodies don't just move randomly, but rather move in purposeful, controlled ways.

You could imagine the dualist coming back and trying again. She might point out that in the case of the heat-seeking missile, or the robot for that matter, although it's doing things, and behaving purposefully, it is just obeying orders. And the orders were given to it from something *outside* itself. Something programmed the robot or the missile. So don't we need there to be something outside the body that programs or commands or controls the body? That could be the soul.

This new version of the argument raises an interesting question. *Must* there be something outside the body that controls the body? Suppose we think the answer is yes. Does that show that we must have immaterial souls? Not at all! Why not say, instead, that people are just like robots, getting our commands from something completely outside of us, not a part of us at all. On a familiar religious view, after all, God built Adam out of dirt, out of the dust. Perhaps Adam is just a certain kind of robot then. God breathes into Adam. That's like turning the robot on. Maybe people are just robots commanded from outside by God. But that doesn't mean that there's anything *more* to us than there is to a robot. We might still just be physical things.

That's one possible response. A slightly different possible response, of course, is to say that the instructions (or at least, the initial set of instructions) might simply be *built in*, just as a robot might have its instructions built in. How did that come to pass? Instead of telling a religious story, we might prefer to tell a rather more complicated story about evolution and biology. We would need to throw in stuff about genetics, evolutionary advantage, and reproduction, ultimately ending up with an account of how certain innate psychological programs get passed along. The details are pretty complicated, but the basic idea is simple enough: there are various physical processes that result in babies being born with some built-in instructions, an innate psychology that gets us started learning and adapting—moving purposefully. So even if we need (initial) instructions of some sort, all of this might still simply be the result of some complex physical process.

The argument quickly becomes very, very messy. Undoubtedly, the fan of the soul wants to protest: "Look, we're not just robots! We're not just robots with some sort of program in our brain that we're following. We've got free will. Robots can't have free will. So there's got to be something more to us than there is to robots. We can't just be physical things."

That's quite an interesting argument, but I think it's a *new* argument. We started with the idea that you needed to appeal to souls in order to explain why human bodies move, or perhaps why we move in purposeful, nonrandom ways. But it's fairly clear that you don't need to appeal to souls in order to do *that*. Appealing to the idea of a properly functioning physical body suffices, I think, to explain the difference between animate and inanimate bodies, or why our bodies move in nonrandom ways. If the brain is our CPU, then we'll behave in deliberate, purposeful ways just like a robot will behave in deliberate, purposeful ways. So this initial argument, I think, is not compelling.

Still, we might wonder, what about this new argument? Instead of claiming that we need the soul in order to explain the animation of the body, what if we move to a new candidate for feature F? What if we claim that we need the soul in order to explain *free will*?

That's definitely an argument worth taking seriously, but I want to hold off on it for the time being. Let's come back to it later.

First, let's run through some of the other things that might be appealed to as candidates for feature F. Suppose somebody says, "Look, it's true that we don't need to appeal to souls in order to explain why bodies move around in a nonrandom fashion. But people have a very special ability that mere bodies couldn't have, and that physicalists can't explain. That's the ability to *think*. It's the ability to reason. People have beliefs and desires. And based on their beliefs about how to fulfill their desires, they make plans. They have strategies. They reason about what to do. And this tightly connected set of facts about us—that we have beliefs, desires, reasoning, strategizing, planning—well, you need to appeal to a soul to explain all of that. No mere machine could believe. No mere machine has desires. No mere machine could reason."

Now I take it that it's uncontroversial that we do have beliefs and desires, that we do reason and think, make plans and carry them out. So the question is just whether it is really true that no mere machine could be like that. And it is easy enough to see why you might think that sort of thing when you stick to *simple* machines. It's pretty clear that there are lots of machines where it doesn't seem natural to ascribe beliefs or desires or goals or reasoning to the machine. My lawnmower, for example, doesn't want to cut the grass. Even though it does *cut* the grass, it doesn't have the relevant desires or beliefs. It doesn't think to itself, "How shall I get that blade of grass that's been eluding me?" So it's easy to see why we might be tempted to say that no mere machine could think or reason or have beliefs or desires.

But that argument is much less compelling nowadays than I think it would have been thirty or forty years ago. In an era of computers with quite sophisticated programs, it is, I think, much more natural to talk about machines—or at least, some machines—in terms of beliefs and desires, reasoning and planning.

Suppose, for example, that we've got a chess-playing computer. On my computer at home I've got a program that allows my computer to play chess. I, myself, stink at chess. This program can beat me blind. Imagine that I move my bishop and the computer moves its queen. What do we say about the computer? Why did the computer move its queen (or virtual queen)? The natural thing to say, I think, is this: it's worried about the fact that its king is exposed and it's trying to block me by capturing my bishop. That is what we say about chess-playing computers.

Think about what we're doing. We're ascribing desires to the computer. We're saying it's got an ultimate desire to win the game. It also has various subsidiary desires, such as to protect its king and to capture *my* king. Another subsidiary desire is to protect its various other pieces along the way. And it's got beliefs about how to do that—by blocking certain paths or by making other pieces on my side vulnerable. It's got beliefs about how to achieve its goals. Then it puts those combinations of beliefs and desires into action by moving in a way that's a rational response to my move.

So it looks as though the natural thing to say about the chess-playing computer is that it *does* have beliefs. It does have desires. It does have goals. It does reason. Of course, it's only rational to a limited extent. It's only able to play chess. But it's easy enough to imagine my computer—or perhaps a more powerful computer—running numerous other programs at the same time, expanding the range of things it thinks and reasons about. And as I say, it does seem natural to describe all of this in terms of the computer having beliefs and desires, as reasoning and strategizing. Yet we can explain all of this in strictly physical terms. We're certainly not tempted to say—are we?—that the computer has a nonphysical part! So it looks as though we don't really need to appeal to a soul after all, even to explain thinking and reasoning and planning.

Of course, it's perfectly open to you, as a dualist, to respond by saying, "Although we *personify* the computer—although we treat it as *though* it had beliefs and desires and so forth—it doesn't *really* have the relevant beliefs and desires, because it doesn't really have *any* beliefs and desires at all, because *no* physical object could have beliefs and desires."

But in response to that I just want to say: isn't that just prejudice? It is certainly true that if we simply *insist* that no physical object could really have beliefs or desires, and so forth, it will follow that when we are tempted to ascribe beliefs and desires to my chess-playing computer, we're falling into an illusion. That will follow once we assume that no merely physical object has beliefs or desires. But what reason is there for *saying* that it has no beliefs or desires? What grounds are there for *refusing* to ascribe beliefs and desires to the computer? That's far from obvious.

Here's a possibility. In typical cases, at least, *desires* seem to be very closely tied to emotions. When you're playing chess, for example, you get excited at the prospect of capturing my queen and crushing me. You get worried when your pieces are threatened. Similarly, of course, you get excited, your heart goes pitter-pat, when your girlfriend or boyfriend says they love you. And you have that sinking feeling in the pit of your stomach when you get a bad grade on a test, or you get a bad evaluation at work.

So maybe we should say that desires have two sides, two aspects. Admittedly, there's an aspect of desire that's purely behavioral. More generally, there's a side of our mental lives that can be cashed out in purely behavioral terms. That's the part that has to do with moving chess pieces around in a way that would make sense if you had the relevant goal. It's the part that has to do with accurately representing the way the world is, and responding rationally to it. And maybe machines can do that. But there's another aspect of our mental life, connected to our desires in particular—the *emotional* side— that machines can't have, but clearly we do have.

So if we find ourselves wanting to say that machines can't really think, can't really have a mental life, maybe what we really mean is that no machine could feel anything *emotionally*. So let's distinguish. Let's admit that there is a legitimate way of talking about beliefs and desires and reasoning which *can* be captured in behavioral terms. It's basically a matter of accurately representing one's environment, and then responding to that representation in a way that makes sense. Maybe computers and robots could do that. But there's clearly a *side* of our mental life, the emotional side, where we might reasonably worry whether a computer can feel anything at all. Could a robot feel love? Could it be afraid?

Remember, our question is whether there is something about us that we can explain only if we appeal to souls. The physicalist says no; the dualist says yes. But we can now see that if the feature that we are asking about is that side of our mental life that can be captured in *behavioral* terms, where even a chess-playing computer probably has it (to a limited degree), then that won't give us a very compelling argument for dualism. The physicalist will plausibly insist that we can certainly explain the behavioral aspect of our mental lives in physicalist terms.

But we can sharpen (or maybe revise) the argument, making it clear that what we are really wondering about is the *emotional* side of our mental life. Could a purely physical being fall in love? Could it be afraid of things? Could it hope for something? Can a robot truly feel emotions? Perhaps not.

So now our argument looks like this: People *can* feel emotions. We love. We're afraid. We get worried. We feel elated. We get depressed. But if you think about it (or so the argument continues) it's pretty clear that no robot could do that. No merely physical thing could feel emotions. So there must be more to us than a merely physical thing.

Now in point of fact, I think it is very plausible to suggest that unlike the case of chess-playing computers, we don't yet have machines that do feel things. But the question isn't whether we *do* have such machines. The question is, *could* we? Could there be a machine that could feel something, have an emotion of some sort?

Let's go a little science-fictiony and think about some of the robots and computers that have been shown in science fiction movies or described in science fiction novels. When I was a kid there was a television show called *Lost in Space,* about a group of people marooned on another planet along with their talking robot. Since it was a TV show, every episode some new dramatic danger would arise. And the robot would start whizzing and binging, and shout out, "Danger, Will Robinson! Danger, Will Robinson!" It seemed as though the robot was *worried.*

Here's a more recent example. You may have read some of Douglas Adams's books, *The Hitchhiker's Guide to the Galaxy* and the sequels to that. There's a robot in those books, Marvin, who is, well, *depressed.* Marvin is very smart. He's thought about the universe, he thinks life is pointless, and he acts depressed. At one point he talks to another robot, and he depresses the other robot, too. (Indeed, the other robot becomes so depressed it commits suicide!) In thinking about this case, it seems natural—at least, it seems natural to me—to ascribe depression to Marvin, the robot. That's certainly how he behaves.

Or take my favorite example, the computer Hal in the movie *2001: A Space Odyssey.* (If you haven't seen this movie I should warn you: I am about to give away a central part of the plot. So cover your eyes.)

In *2001: A Space Odyssey,* we get an indication that there's life on another planet: a mysterious black object recently discovered on the moon sends an indecipherable radio signal of some sort to Jupiter. So we send a spaceship to Jupiter to investigate. Onboard, there is a computer program named Hal that helps run the ship while most of the human astronauts are hibernating during the long flight. Hal has the goal of making sure the mission is successful. But Hal thinks to himself—fairly plausibly, I suppose—that humans often really screw things up. And since this is such an important mission, Hal decides to *kill* the humans, to make sure that they don't. One of the astronauts, Dave, discovering the plot, attempts to stop Hal. He proceeds to do the only thing he can do to defend himself against Hal, which is to shut down the program, effectively *killing* Hal (if we can talk that way).

Meanwhile, while all this is going on, Hal and Dave are talking to each other. Hal realizes what's happening, and tries, unsuccessfully, to stop Dave. And as Dave begins to shut down Hal's circuits, Hal tells him, "I'm afraid. I'm afraid, Dave."

What's Hal afraid of? He's afraid of dying. It seems perfectly natural to ascribe fear to Hal. Hal is behaving in exactly the way you would expect him to behave, if he felt fear. Hal's got reason to be afraid. He's behaving appropriately. He's *telling* us that he is afraid. As I say, it seems perfectly natural to say: Hal is afraid.

You could continue to fill in examples like this. Of course, they're all science fiction. But it's not as though we have trouble understanding these examples, trouble imagining them. It's not as though we throw up our hands and say "What do you mean, Hal is afraid? What do you mean, Marvin was depressed? What do you mean, the robot in *Lost in Space* is worried?" We can, I suppose, simply insist that robots and computers just *can't* have emotions; but examples like these seem to show that they *could*.

But obviously, there is no particular reason to think there is anything nonphysical going on in these cases. All we have here are hunks of metal, wires, and circuits. These are all just physical objects. So it seems that what we should say is, "We don't need to appeal to souls in order to explain emotions and feelings. Mere physical objects could have emotions and feelings. So we still have no reason to posit the existence of a soul."

How should the dualist reply to this objection? I think the best response is to distinguish two different *aspects* of feelings, two aspects of emotions. First, again, there's the *behavioral* aspect. Take fear, for example. The behavioral aspect of fear is this: when you're aware of something in the environment that poses a danger to you—that might harm you or destroy you—you respond in appropriate ways. You take steps to oppose the threat. You try to disarm the danger, to neutralize it. Roughly speaking, that's all just a matter of having the relevant beliefs, goals, responses, and planning— the sort of thing that we already saw the chess-playing computer can do, in a very limited way. That's the *behavioral* side of emotion. And it seems pretty plausible to think that robots could do *that*. Physical objects could do that.

But—and here's the crucial part of this dualist response—there's *another* side of emotions and feelings. There's the *sensation*: what it *feels* like. That's why we call them *feelings*, after all. There is something that it feels like on the *inside*, as it were, while all of this behavioral stuff is going on.

When you're afraid, for example, you have this familiar clammy feeling. Your heart is pounding, your blood is racing. I can't describe it all that well, but of course you're already familiar with what I'm talking about. There's a *feeling* that goes along with being afraid. And the same is true, of course, for being in love, or being worried, or being depressed. There are feelings that go along with each of these emotions. We could put it this way: there are certain characteristic *experiences* that go along with having any given emotion. (The word "experience" is ambiguous, though. Sometimes we use it to refer to the external situation that is creating the inner experience. Here, though, I am using it to refer only to the resulting inner mental state.)

So there is an experience that goes along with each emotion. There's what it feels like to you when you're afraid, what it feels like to you when you're worried or depressed or joyful or in love. And the thought—and I think this is a pretty powerful thought—is that even if the robots are behaving appropriately, even if they've got the behavioral side of the emotions down, they don't have the *feeling* side, the experiential side, at all.

Notice, however, that once you start thinking in these terms, there's no need to restrict yourself to worrying about emotions. We'll have the same worry in all sorts of humdrum cases as well. Right now I am looking down at the legs of my jeans. They're some shade of blue. Find something blue yourself, and look at it. Now think about that. Think about what it's like to see blue, what it's like to have the sensation of seeing blue. Think about how it differs from having the sensation of seeing red, or not having the sensation at all.

Of course, here too, we've got to distinguish between what I'll continue to call the *behavioral* side of seeing red or blue and the *experiential* side of seeing red or blue. After all, it's easy enough for us to build a machine that can *distinguish* red from blue. It just checks to see what light frequencies are bouncing off the object. We can, for example, build a machine that could sort red balls from blue balls. In fact, my son has a little robot that can do that.

But ask yourself, what's going on "inside" the machine? What does it *feel* like to be the machine, while it's looking at the red ball? Does it have the sensation of seeing red? Does it have the experience of seeing color at all? And I imagine that what you want to say—certainly what *I* want to say—is no, it doesn't have that sensation at all. The machine is sorting things based on their light frequencies, but it doesn't have the experience of seeing red. Indeed, it doesn't have any *experiences* at all (in that sense).

What we're trying to get at here can be pretty elusive, but I imagine that you are already familiar with the idea. It's the sort of thing you wonder about when you ask yourself, "If somebody was born blind, could he possibly know what it's like to see color?" He might be a scientist and know all sorts of things about how light works, and what colors different objects are. You hand him an apple and he'll say, "Oh, it must be red." Maybe he points his little light detector at it and the detector announces, "This is reflecting light at such and such a frequency," and so he says, "Oh, this is a very red apple, much redder than that tomato over there." But for all that, we've got the notion that not only is he not seeing red, he can't even *imagine* what it's like to see red, never having had these experiences.

Once you start to see things in these terms, you realize of course that our life is *filled* with this aspect of things. Things have colors. Things have sounds. Things have smells. And we experience all of this. This is the *qualitative* aspect of our experience. That's the side of experience that we're trying to get at when we ask ourselves, "What's it like to see red? What's it like to smell coffee or to taste pineapple?" Our experiences have qualitative properties. Indeed, philosophers sometimes use the term *qualia*, for just this reason, when trying to focus on this qualitative aspect of experience.

Just as a blind person might wonder what it's like to see red, you might wonder what it feels like to have a migraine ("what does that particular pain feel like?"), or you might wonder what it feels like to be tickled. And of course, to return to the point where we began, it seems that our emotions have a qualitative aspect as well: there are the characteristic sensations of fear or joy or depression.

Our mental life is shot through with this aspect, this qualitative aspect of experience. But a natural enough thought is this: no merely physical object can *have* this. No mere machine can feel pain, see red, or feel joy. Machines can do the behavioral stuff, but no merely physical object can have this *qualitative* aspect of experience. But *we* have it. So we are no mere physical objects. We are no mere machines.

That's the argument. And I think it is a pretty good one. It's certainly the best argument we've had for dualism so far. So we need to ask: what, if anything, can the physicalist say in response? Now the *best* possible response would be for the physicalist to say, "Here's how to do it. Here's how to build a machine that can have experiences in exactly this sense." Just as we can explain in physicalist terms how to build a machine that has desires and beliefs, a machine that gets all the *behavioral* stuff down right, it would be great if we could offer a physicalist account of the *qualitative* aspect of experience too. It would be nice if the physicalist could give us at least the outlines of that kind of story.

But the truth of the matter, I think, is this. We really don't have any idea *at all* about how to tell that story. Suppose we use the word *consciousness* to refer to this qualitative aspect of our mental life. Then I think we have to admit that from the point of view of the physicalist, consciousness remains a pretty big mystery. We really don't know how to explain it in physicalist terms. And it is because of that fact that I think we shouldn't be dismissive of the dualist, if the dualist says that we've got to believe in souls in order to explain consciousness.

We shouldn't be dismissive. But that's not to say that I think we should be *convinced*. Because it's one thing to say we don't yet know how to explain consciousness in physical terms. It's another thing to say we won't ever be *able* to explain consciousness in physical terms. I certainly agree that if we knew that no merely physical object could see red, taste honey, or feel pain, then we'd have to conclude that we are not merely physical objects, since *we* can see, taste, and feel. But I don't think we're yet in a position to know that. I think the simple fact of the matter is that we don't yet know enough about consciousness to *know* whether or not it can be explained in physical terms.

When I think about this situation, an analogy always occurs to me. Imagine that it's the fourteenth century, and we are trying to understand life—for example, the life of plants. We ask ourselves, "Could it possibly be that life can be explained in material terms?" That's going to seem very unlikely to us. How could it possibly be? After all, think for a moment about the kinds of machines that we would have had available to us in the fourteenth century. What would someone in the fourteenth century picture to herself, when she entertains the possibility that a plant might just be a machine? When I try to think in those terms, I have this little mental image of a plant made out of gears and pulleys. The gears begin turning, and the bud opens, or the flower turns toward the sun. The person's obviously going to say, "My god! That machine certainly wouldn't be *alive!*" Indeed, it's going to seem pretty obvious that *no* machine could possibly be alive. No merely material object could be *living*. In order to explain life (we're going to conclude), we have to appeal to something more than physical matter. Life requires something immaterial—something above and beyond matter—to explain it.

That would have been an understandable conclusion to come to in the fourteenth century, but it would have been *wrong*. We didn't have a clue back then how to explain life in material terms. But that didn't mean it couldn't be done.

I'm inclined to think the same thing is true right now for us and consciousness. I know there are physicalist theories of consciousness out there. (I won't try to describe them.) But my best take is that we're pretty much in the dark, just like we would have been in the fourteenth century thinking about life. We don't really have a clue yet, or at least not much of a clue, as to how you would even *begin* trying to explain consciousness in physical terms. It's not so much that we don't yet have the *details* worked out. Rather, we can't even begin to paint the picture in broad strokes.

But not seeing how something is possible is not the same thing as seeing that it's *impossible*. If the dualist comes and says, "Can't you just see that it's not remotely possible, it's not even conceivably possible, for a purely physical object to have experiences, to have *qualia*?" what I want to say is, "No, I *don't* see that it's impossible. I admit I don't see how to do it, but I don't see that it's impossible." So I don't feel forced to posit the existence of a soul.

To be sure, the fan of the soul can come back and say, "But that's not fair. We dualists don't have to claim that it's *impossible* to offer a physicalist explanation of consciousness. We only have to claim that we have a *better* explanation. So let's compare. Right now, at least, you physicalists can't offer any kind of explanation of consciousness at all! But we dualists can already do that. How is consciousness possible? Simple: we have souls. Souls are really very different from physical objects, and so they can be conscious. Since dualism offers the better explanation of consciousness, right now at least there is reason to prefer dualism over physicalism."

But I think it's important not to be too quick in granting the dualist her claim that she really does have an explanation of consciousness. That isn't at all obvious to me. When the dualist says, "Oh, I can explain consciousness. Consciousness is housed in the soul, not in the body"—just how much of an explanation *is* that? Suppose we ask the dualist: how exactly *is* it that a soul can be conscious? What does the dualist answer? "Well, um . . . er . . . ah . . . it just can." Obviously, that's not really much of an explanation! I don't feel I've got any sort of account going here as to how consciousness works, even if I *become* a dualist.

Of course, things would be different if the dualist were to start offering us some elaborate theory of consciousness: "Well, there are these various different sorts of soul structures, and this type creates these sensations and that type creates those sensations," and so forth and so on, actually giving us a *theory*. If the dualist were to do that, I'd begin to take dualism seriously as an explanation. But if all the soul theorist is saying is just, "Nyah, nyah. You physicalists can't explain consciousness, but I can—because immaterial souls can be conscious," then I find myself wanting to say that that's not really any better. That's no explanation at all.

Now it might seem that I am using a double standard here. It might seem that I'm defending the physicalist by saying, "Don't blame us. Physicalism might be true, even though we don't yet know how to explain consciousness in physicalist terms." So why, then, aren't I allowing the dualist to say the same thing? Why isn't the dualist *also* entitled to say, "Don't blame us. Dualism might be true, even though we don't yet know how to explain consciousness in terms of *souls*"? But that would be to misunderstand my point. I'm not letting one side off the hook while condemning the other side for failing to explain consciousness. My point, rather, is that it's a *tie*. Physicalists don't have a good explanation of consciousness; but then again neither do dualists. As far as I can see, *nobody* has a good explanation of how consciousness works. It's a mystery for both sides.

But notice that if it's a tie, then that doesn't give us what we were looking for. What we were looking for, after all, was some reason to believe in souls. And if the best the dualist can say is, "I can't explain consciousness and neither can you," then that's *not* a reason to believe in souls.

Remember, we already believe there are bodies. We already know bodies can do some pretty amazing things. What we're asking is whether there is good reason to *add* to our list of things there are. In particular, is there a good reason to add the soul? And if the best that the soul theorist has is, "Maybe we need this to explain consciousness, since I don't see how you physicalists can explain it. Maybe bringing in souls would help somehow, though I can't quite see how"—well, that's not a very compelling argument.

So I'm inclined to think that with regard to consciousness, the jury is still out. Presumably, we will continue to give it our best shot. We'll *try* to explain consciousness in physical terms, but perhaps, eventually, we'll decide that it can't be done, or can't be done well. And maybe we'll begin to work out some alternative theory of consciousness that does explain things in terms of immaterial substances. So maybe, at the end of the day, we will decide that if we are going to explain consciousness, or have the best explanation of consciousness, we do need to believe in souls. Maybe. But right now, at any rate, I don't think the evidence supports that conclusion.

Still, there are other possibilities, other candidates for feature F. Consider creativity. We can construct a new argument, one that still appeals to inference to the best explanation, but this time suggests that the feature that needs explaining in terms of souls is *creativity*. Here's how the argument would go: People can be creative. We write new pieces of music. We write poems. We prove things in mathematics that have never been proven before, or we find new ways to prove old theorems. We paint pictures that have never been seen before. We dream up new inventions. In any number of ways, then, we can be *creative*. But no mere machine can be creative at all. So we must be something more than a mere machine.

But if that's the new argument, then our next question has to be, is it really true that no merely physical object could be creative? And for what it's worth, I'm inclined to think that the answer is that physical objects of the right sort *can* be creative. Indeed, I think we have already mentioned an interesting example of this sort of thing: the chess-playing computer. When it comes to playing chess, computers can be very creative indeed.

That's probably not true for the simple chess-playing program that I have running on my computer at home. But I think it is a quite plausible thing to say when it comes to the very best chess-playing computers, the sort that can nowadays beat even the very best human players. These computers sometimes make surprising moves, playing in a way that often cannot be anticipated, not even by the very people who designed the programs. When one of the very best programs plays against a grandmaster, or a world chess champion, it may play in some particular way that, for all we know, no one has ever played before. In short, chess-playing computers *can* be creative. Or so it seems to me.

And computers can do other things of this sort as well. For example, there are mathematical theorem-proving programs. Now, some of these programs can prove things that are mathematically way over my head, but let's take something simple, like the Pythagorean theorem (the square of the hypotenuse of a right triangle is equal to the sum of the squares of the two adjacent sides). In school, you probably learned how to prove the Pythagorean theorem. Starting with the various axioms of Euclidean geometry, we derive various subconclusions, one after the next, until, finally, we arrive at the Pythagorean theorem itself.

Now it turns out that there are a number of different ways of proving the Pythagorean theorem, each of which takes its own distinct path from the axioms to the conclusion. And the interesting fact (for our purposes, at least) is this: computer programs can come up with proofs that, so far as we know, have never been seen before. Other than prejudice, then, what would stop us from saying that the computer program was being *creative*?

We see similar creativity in other areas too. There are, for example, computer programs that can write music. And I don't just mean throw out some random assortment of notes. I mean, there are programs that compose pieces that we recognize as being *music*—pieces that have melodic structure and develop themes and resolve. Now these are pieces of music that nobody's heard before. So shouldn't we say that a computer that composes such a piece of music is being creative? Other than prejudice, what would stop us from saying that?

In short, if the argument for dualism is that we need to posit the existence of a soul in order to explain creativity, I can only say that such an argument just seems wrong.

The argument appealing to creativity may not work, but there's a different argument that it immediately suggests that may be more persuasive. Even if we can build a computer—or, someday, a robot—that can be creative, that can do things that nobody's thought of before, all the computer or robot will be doing is just mechanically following its program—a series of commands written in code. So even if we are smart enough someday to build robots that can, by mechanically following the program, do things we've never thought of, still, all the robot will be doing is mechanically (necessarily, automatically) following the program's instructions. It won't have any choice about the matter. It won't have free will.

But *we* have free will. So, here's a new argument for the existence of the soul. People have free will. But no merely material object—no robot, no computer—could have free will. So, since we do have free will, we must be something more than a merely physical object. There must be something extra, something immaterial about us, the soul. Perhaps that's why we need to believe in souls: in order to explain free will.

I think a lot of people will find this a very compelling argument indeed. So we certainly need to think harder about it. Unfortunately, the subject of free will is a very, very complicated one. Many long and difficult books have been written about it. Meanwhile, I am going to spend only a few pages discussing it. So please don't misunderstand me. I certainly am not going to tell you everything you need to know about free will. Instead, I simply want to point out enough about the subject to help you see why I don't think an appeal to free will provides a slam-dunk argument for the existence of the soul.

The argument appeals to the thought that no merely physical object can have free will. But why does that seem so obvious? What exactly is the argument for that crucial claim? I suspect that the thought here is something like this. When a computer, say, is carrying out its operations, it just follows the laws of physics. And the laws of physics are *deterministic*. (In philosopher's jargon, we can say that the computer is a deterministic system.) What does that mean? Roughly, this: if the computer is initially in a given state, then, necessarily—given the laws of physics, and the way the computer is programmed, and the nature of its hardware, and so forth—such and such circuits will open or close until, inevitably, the computer will be in its next state. And then, given that it is in that new state (and given the laws of physics, and so forth), it will inevitably move to its third state. And so forth and so on. The computer simply has no choice about the matter.

More generally, then, given deterministic physical laws, for every physical event that happens, there was some earlier physical event that caused that later event to happen, such that given that earlier event (the cause), that later event (the effect) *had* to follow. That's what it is to accept a deterministic picture of how physical systems work.

Here's another way of thinking about this same idea. Suppose you set up a physical system, subject to deterministic laws, in some particular way. Given that initial setup, it will cause an effect of some sort. And the crucial point is this: given that initial setup, that very effect *had* to follow. It is determined by the laws of nature that an effect of precisely that sort will follow from a cause of precisely that other sort. Accordingly, if you were to rewind the tape (as it were) to the beginning, back to the initial setup, and press "go," the very same sequence of results would follow, one after the other, with causal inevitability. The results will always be identical. Each time you set things up exactly the same way, and then see what it all causes, you will inevitably move through the very same sequence of changes and transformations, ending up with the very same final effects. That's what it is for determinism to be true of something.

But given all of this, it is natural to think that there must be a kind of incompatibility with being free and being determined. You can't have free will *and* be subject to determinism. After all, the idea of free will seems to be that when I make a choice, it is nonetheless true that I *could* have chosen differently. Even if I was in the very same spot again—the very same situation, facing the very same choice—I could choose something else. So I wasn't determined to make the particular choice that I did. In short, if I really do have free will, then it can't be that I am subject to deterministic laws. Putting this same point the other way around, nothing subject to deterministic laws can have free will. The two are incompatible. (This view is sometimes known as *incompatibilism*, for obvious reasons.)

That's why the dualist thinks that an appeal to free will shows that there must be more to us than merely being physical objects. After all, from the physicalist's point of view we're just a kind of robot. Admittedly, we're able to do all sorts of things that most robots in science fiction movies can't do, but still, strictly speaking, we're just glorified robots. And robots, the objection goes, must follow their programs. More generally, robots are subject to deterministic laws, because they are just physical objects and the laws of physics are deterministic. But free will and determinism are incompatible: you can't have free will if you are a deterministic system. Therefore, since we *do* have free will, it can't really be true that we are mere robots. More generally, it can't really be true that we are mere physical objects. There must be something more than the purely physical to us.

In short, when we try to spell out the current argument for dualism, it ends up looking like this:

(1) We have free will.
(2) Nothing subject to determinism has free will.
But (3) all purely physical systems are subject to determinism.
So (4) we are not purely physical systems.

That's the argument we've just been considering, boiled down to its essential steps. The first premise asserts that we have free will. The second premise tells us that nothing subject to determinism has free will. Put one and two together and it follows that we're not subject to determinism. Suppose we then add premise three, that all purely physical systems *are* subject to determinism. It follows, then, that we are *not* purely physical systems. And that's what the conclusion of the argument, four, tells us: we are not purely physical systems.

Now this argument—the argument from free will—is certainly valid. That's philosopher's jargon for saying that *given* the premises, the conclusion really does follow. So the interesting question is, are the three premises really true? Note, importantly, that they *all* have to be true. To get the conclusion, we need all three premises. For example, if we give up the first premise, the claim that we've got free will, then it just won't follow that there is anything nonphysical about us. After all, even if something that did have free will would have to be more than physical, it wouldn't follow that *we* are more than physical objects. So the argument certainly needs the first premise. And something similar is true for each of the three premises of the argument. Give any one of the premises up, and the conclusion won't go through.

And the interesting thing is, each one of these three premises can be plausibly challenged. Unfortunately, however, I can't take the time here to discuss any of these potential challenges in depth (as I have already noted, the subject of free will is an extremely complicated one). So I am going to have to content myself with some quick comments.

First of all, then, as I have already explained, the argument from free will needs the first premise. If we are going to prove that we have a soul by appealing to the fact that we have free will, it had better be the case that we do indeed have free will.

But that assumption—natural and widespread though it may be—can be challenged. There are philosophers who have said that while we certainly *believe* that we have free will, it's just an illusion. Why do they think that? For precisely the sorts of reasons that are pointed to by the rest of the argument! These philosophers sometimes argue that since we are physical objects, we are subject to determinism. And since determinism is incompatible with having free will, we don't really have free will! Of course, they recognize that we *believe* that we have free will. But they think that this belief is just a mistake. We are, in effect, physical objects that labor under the *illusion* that we have free will.

That's not a silly position to take. After all, free will isn't something you can just see! You can't just peer into your mind and *see* that you've got free will. So yes, we've certainly got the sense that we could have acted differently, but maybe that's just an illusion. That, at any rate, is the position of some philosophers; and as we have already seen, without the assumption that we really do have free will, we no longer have a sound argument for the existence of a soul. Still, I might as well mention that while this is certainly one way to resist the argument from free will, I do not myself favor this particular reply. I don't think the belief in free will *is* a mere illusion.

But there are, of course, two other premises in the argument. Consider premise three: all purely physical systems are subject to determinism. We need that premise as well if the argument is going to work. For even if we accept incompatibilism, and agree that it can't be true that we both have free will and are subject to deterministic laws, and even if we agree as well that we do have free will—it *still* could be the case that we are merely physical objects, if it isn't really true that all purely physical systems are subject to determinism. Thus, if the appeal to free will is going to establish the truth of dualism, we need to claim that the laws of physics are deterministic ones. We need premise three.

Now it may seem that premise three is pretty secure. After all, isn't it true that the basic laws of physics are deterministic? But the answer, somewhat surprisingly, is that it is not at all clear that they are! Which is just to say, premise three can be challenged as well.

Of course, premise three is a claim about empirical science. What we want to know is, what does our best theory tell us about the laws of nature? Are they deterministic or not? So let me remind you: I am a philosopher, not a scientist, and I am certainly no authority on this sort of empirical question. And in particular, I am no kind of authority at all (believe me!) on quantum mechanics, our best theory of fundamental physics. Still, here's what I'm told: according to the standard interpretation of quantum mechanics, despite what many of us might have otherwise believed, the fundamental laws of physics are *not*, in fact, deterministic.

What does that mean? Suppose we've got some sort of radioactive atom, which has a certain chance of decaying. It might have, say, an 80 percent chance of "breaking down" in the next twenty-four hours. This means that 80 percent of the atoms just like this do break down in any given twenty-four hour period, and 20 percent of them don't. Now according to quantum mechanics under the standard interpretation, that's all there is to say about it. If you have an atom like that, there's an 80 percent chance that in the next twenty-four hours it will break down and a 20 percent chance that it won't.

Suppose it does break down. Can we say why it did? Sure! We can say that there was, after all, an 80 percent chance that it would. Or take an atom that after twenty-four hours still hasn't broken down. Can we say why it hasn't? Sure. There was a 20 percent chance that it wouldn't. Can we explain why the ones that do break down break down and the ones that don't break down don't break down? No, we *can't* do that. All we can say is, there was an 80 percent chance it would and a 20 percent chance it wouldn't; so most do, and some don't. That's as deep as the explanation goes. There is nothing more.

Of course, when we've got our deterministic hats on, we think to ourselves, "There's *got* to be some underlying causal explanation, some feature about the breakdown atoms that explains why they break down, a feature that is missing from the non-breakdown atoms and thus explains why they *don't* break down. Surely if you set up the atoms in *exactly* the same way, they've always got to do exactly the same thing." But, as I say, that's just us assuming that determinism *must* be true. And according to the standard interpretation of quantum mechanics, that's not how it works. Rather, all there is to say is: some of these atoms are going to break down, and some of them won't.

According to the standard interpretation of quantum mechanics, the fundamental laws of physics are *probabilistic*. Determinism is not true at the level of fundamental physics. That's what I'm told. Believe me, I'm in no position to say, but that's what I'm told. And of course, if that's true, then premise three is false. It just isn't true that all purely physical systems are subject to determinism. So even if it does turn out that you can't have free will and determinism, that doesn't rule out the possibility that we are purely physical objects, because not all purely physical systems are subject to determinism. If determinism isn't true of us at the fundamental level, then even if you couldn't have both determinism and free will, we could still have free will, and yet, for all that, still be purely physical systems.

While I'm busy pointing out ways in which the argument from free will doesn't succeed, I also want to take a moment and mention that premise two is also subject to criticism. Premise two, you recall, was the incompatibilist claim that nothing subject to determinism has free will. You can't combine free will and determinism; they're incompatible. Now, incompatibilism, I take it, is probably the commonsense view here. It is probably the view that you yourself believe. But here too, it's worth noting that it can be challenged. There are philosophers who believe that, in fact, free will is *not* incompatible with determinism. I'm one of them. So even if determinism were true of us, that wouldn't rule out our having free will, because you can—appearances to the contrary notwithstanding—have both determinism and free will. They're compatible. Unsurprisingly, this view is known as *compatibilism*.

It would, of course, be very helpful if I now tried to explain this position to you in turn, show you why free will—once it is properly understood—is actually compatible with determinism after all. Unfortunately, I can't do that here. It would take *way* too long. (As I said, it's a very complicated subject.) I just want to point out that, surprising as it may seem, compatibilism is also a live possibility; it is a respectable philosophical position.

If we do accept compatibilism, we'll be able to say: even if determinism *is* true of physical systems, and even if we *do* have free will, we can *still* be merely physical objects—since determinism and free will are compatible.

Think of it this way. Suppose that the standard interpretation of quantum mechanics is wrong somehow, and determinism is true. Or suppose that even though determinism is false at the *atomic* level, somehow it all washes out by the time we get up to the *macro* level, so that for midsize objects (like human bodies) determinism is true after all. Even if determinism *were* true at this level, it just wouldn't matter. For if compatibilism is true—if something can be subject to deterministic laws and still have free will—then even if we *are* subject to determinism, we can still have free will *and* be merely physical objects. So if compatibilism is true, the argument for dualism will once again be in trouble.

Mind you, I haven't said anything at all to try to convince you of the *truth* of compatibilism, nor am I going to try to do that. My point here is only to say that we shouldn't be so quick to think that we have to believe in the existence of a soul in order to explain our having free will. It takes *all* of the premises of the argument to get the conclusion that the soul exists, and *each* of the premises can be challenged. There are reasonable philosophical or scientific grounds for worrying about each one of the premises. That doesn't prove that the argument from free will fails, of course. But it does mean that you're going to have your work cut out for you if you're going to use this route to arguing for the existence of a soul.

Supernatural Phenomena

All right. Let's recap. We've been considering different kinds of arguments for the existence of a soul, each of which appeals to some feature about us— our creativity, our ability to feel, the fact that our experience has a qualitative aspect, our ability to reason, what have you—some fact about us that calls out for explanation. The claim on the part of the dualist was that we couldn't explain the given feature without appealing to a soul. And I've been sharing with you my reasons for thinking that these various arguments are not as compelling as one might initially suppose.

But notice that all of the considerations I've pointed to so far are what we might think of as everyday, familiar features about us. It's an everyday occurrence that we can think and reason and feel and be creative, or that we have free will.

Maybe we would find better arguments for the soul if we were to focus not on the everyday but on the unusual, on the supernatural. We can still offer arguments that make use of inference to the best explanation, but perhaps the dualist would do better if she argues that what needs explaining in terms of the soul are various supernatural phenomena. For example, maybe we need to posit the soul in order to explain ghosts. Maybe we need to posit the soul in order to explain ESP (extrasensory perception). Maybe we need to posit the soul in order to explain near-death experiences, or séances, or communications from the dead. For any one of these phenomena (whatever it is, exactly, that they come to), we could imagine an argument where the dualist says, "Look, here is something that needs explaining. And the best explanation appeals to the soul."

Now, I'm going to be considerably quicker in discussing this new family of arguments, but I do want to make at least a few comments. Let's start with near-death experiences. The basic idea here is probably a familiar one. The following thing happens to people now and again. Someone may have a heart attack, or die on the operating table, but after a few minutes they are brought back to life. And at least sometimes, when we question these people about it afterwards, they've had a very striking experience while they were dead. (Were they really dead? That's hard to say. But it often appears so.)

One of the things that's striking is how similar the experience can be from person to person, and from culture to culture. People often report having had the experience of leaving their body. Perhaps they begin to view their body on the operating table—from above, as though they were floating up above it. Eventually, perhaps, they have the experience of leaving the operating room altogether, and they have a feeling of joy and euphoria. They may have an experience of going through a tunnel, seeing some white light at the end of the tunnel. Perhaps at the other end of the tunnel they begin to communicate with or see some loved one who has died previously, or perhaps some famous person from their religious tradition. They have the sense that what has happened is that they have died and gone to heaven. But then suddenly they get yanked back, and they wake up in the hospital room. They've had what we call a *near-death* experience. (Perhaps, though, it would be better to say that they've had a *death* experience, but then have been brought back to life.)

Okay. When you survey people, you find that a certain number have had these experiences. And so we have to ask ourselves, what explains this phenomenon? And here's a perfectly straightforward and obvious explanation. These people died. They died and they went to the next world. They went to heaven. But then they were yanked back. Of course, during all of this, their bodies were lying there on the operating table; their *bodies* weren't in heaven. So something nonbodily went to heaven. That's how the explanation goes. It's a natural, straightforward explanation of what's gone on here. Accordingly—says the dualist—we need to posit the soul. We need to posit something immaterial that survives the death of the body, that can leave the body and go up to heaven. Of course, in cases of near-death experience, the tie between the body and the soul is never completely broken. The soul gets yanked back (somehow) and "reconnected" to the body, and the person wakes up.

To use a kind of analogy, it's as though there are two rooms. Think of this world, this life, as being one of those rooms. And what happens in near-death experiences is that your soul leaves this room and goes into a second room, the room of the next world or the next life. But for various reasons, it isn't allowed to stay in the next room. It gets yanked back to this room.

Well, that's a possible explanation. And in a moment, I'll ask whether it's the best possible explanation. But before we do turn to that question, there is an objection to this entire way of looking at things that's probably worth considering first. (The objection is similar to one that we considered at the very start of this book, when we asked whether there could be any genuine question about surviving death: "Could there be life after there is no more life? Duh, of course not!")

According to this objection, this two room idea has *got* to be mistaken. It *can't* be that what's going on in near-death experiences is that people are reporting what it's like to be dead because—so the objection says—they *never really died*! After all, twenty minutes later (or whatever it is), there they are, lying in their hospital beds, clearly alive. So it follows that they never really died. Or, if you want, you could say that maybe they died, but since they obviously didn't die *permanently* (after all, they were brought back to life), how could they possibly tell us what it's like to be permanently dead? How can we take their experiences as veridical reports of the afterlife? What we want to know is what it's like to be permanently dead, and these people were never permanently dead. So whatever unusual experiences they may be having, they are not reports of the afterlife. That's how the objection goes.

Now my own view is that this is not, in fact, an objection that we should take all that seriously. Suppose we were to agree that, strictly speaking, these people didn't die. At the very least, they certainly didn't die permanently. Does it follow from this that their experiences should not be taken as evidence of what the afterlife is like? I think that's really a misguided objection.

Suppose somebody tells us that they have spent twenty years living in France but have now come back to the United States, and they want to tell us what it's like in France. Now imagine that someone else objects, "You know, you never really moved to France permanently. So your experiences in France, whatever they are—interesting as they may be—can't really cast any light on what it would be like to move to France permanently." We would think that this was a ludicrous objection! It would be true, of course, that the first person hadn't moved to France permanently. Still, she would have some experience of France—indeed, a great deal, after twenty years. And so she can give us a pretty good idea of what it's like to live in France, even if she didn't move there for the rest of her life without ever coming back. Of course, if you've only been in France for a couple of days before coming back, you can't say nearly as much. But still, you can say something relevant.

Indeed, suppose you never went into France at all. Suppose all that happened was that you stood right on the border and peered into France, talking to some people *in* France. They were on the French side of the border and you were on the other side, but you talked to them for a while. You never went in. But for all that, you might have something helpful to say about what it's *like* in France.

If that's the right thing to say about the France case, then why not say the same thing about the case of near-death experience? Even if these people didn't *stay* in the second room—they didn't *stay* dead—they had some experience of *being* dead. Isn't that relevant to what it would be like to be dead? And even if we prefer to say that, strictly speaking, these people didn't *die* at all, they were just on the border of the next world looking in, what of it? They were on the border looking in! To suggest that these experiences can't be relevant evidence about death is like saying I can't tell you anything interesting about what's going on in the hallway right now, because after all I'm not in the hallway; I'm here in my office. So what? Even though I'm here in my office, I can see *into* the hallway and tell you what's going on in it.

So I think that attempts to dismiss the appeal to near-death experiences on what we might call "philosophical" grounds are misguided. Still, that doesn't mean that we should *accept* the argument for the existence of the soul from near-death experiences. Because the question remains, what's the *best* explanation of what's going on in near-death experiences? One possibility, as I suggested, was what we might call the "two room explanation." There's the room of this life, and there's the room of the next life, and people who have near-death experiences were either temporarily in the second room or else at least were glancing into it. That's one possible explanation. But of course, there's a different possible explanation: the *one* room explanation. There's just one room, life in this world, and as you come very close to the wall of the room, things end up looking and seeming and feeling rather different than they do in the middle of the room.

Doubtless, the one room metaphor isn't perfect, because it immediately prompts the question: what's on the other side of the wall? And of course the physicalist's suggestion is that there isn't *anything* on the other side of the wall. So maybe a better way to talk about it would just be this: Life is a biological process. And we are all familiar with that process in its *middle* stretches. But in its closing stretches, some fairly unusual biological processes kick in (unusual in the sense that they don't normally occur in the middle of life; they are, of course, quite common at the *end* of life). In rare but not unheard of cases, some people begin to undergo these unusual biological processes but then they return to the *normal* biological processes, and so they can talk about what was happening during the *unusual* biological processes. All of which is just to say, we need to offer a biological/physical explanation of what goes on in near-death experiences.

Of course, that's not yet to offer the physical explanation; it's just a promissory note. But at least we now have the *outlines* of two rival explanations: the dualist explanation, that the person went into the other world, and the physicalist explanation (or promissory note) in terms of biological processes. Admittedly, we don't really have very much of a physical explanation until we begin to offer scientific accounts of each of the various aspects of near-death experience—the white lights and the feeling of euphoria, seeing your body from a distance, and so forth. But this is, in fact, an area on which scientists work, and we may have the beginnings of a biological explanation. So, for example, when the body is in stress, as would likely happen toward the end of the biological processes of life, certain endorphins get released. Perhaps that explains the feelings of euphoria. Similarly, when the body is in stress, the sections of the brain responsible for vision get stimulated in unusual ways, and perhaps that explains the white light or the feeling of compression in the tunnel.

Now, again, I'm not any kind of scientist, and so I'm not in any position to say, "Look, here are the details of the explanation." But as I say, scientists have begun to offer explanations of near-death experiences in biological terms. So you have to make a judgment call. Does it seem more plausible that we can explain these experiences in terms of the traumatic stress that your body and brain are going through when you are near dying? Or is it more plausible to suggest that what's happening here is that the soul is being partly released from its normal connection with the body? For my money, I find the beginnings of the scientific explanation fairly persuasive and compelling. So I don't find the claim that we need to posit the existence of a soul so as to explain near-death experience an especially persuasive one.

Of course, there are various other "supernatural" occurrences we might appeal to instead. So far, I've only discussed near-death experiences. What about, for example, séances? How are we to explain the fact that some people seem to be able to communicate with the dead? How are we to explain the fact that the person who's conducting the séance knows things about your history that only your dead uncle would know?

The dualist presumably can explain these things by appeal to souls. The soul of your departed uncle is communicating with the person conducting the séance. That's how she knows things that only you and your uncle should know.

How does the physicalist explain things like that? The short answer is, I don't know. I'm not the kind of person who makes it his business to try to explain away those things in physicalist, scientific terms. But there are people who do make it their business. And they are often eager to explain. Don't ask *me* how the person conducting the séance manages to do the amazing things she does. You're wasting your time asking somebody like me. The person to ask is a magician, somebody whose profession it is to fool people and make it look like they can do things with magic! Now there are, in fact, professional magicians who make it their business to debunk people who claim to (truly) be in contact with the dead. They regularly explain how various standard magicians' tricks can be used to "read minds" and make it appear that one is in contact with the dead.

Of course, that doesn't prove the dualist is wrong. It could be that there really are genuine séances. It could be that there really is communication with the dead. As always, you've got to decide for yourself what strikes you as the better explanation. Is the supernatural, dualist explanation the more likely one? Or is the physicalist explanation the more likely one?

Or suppose you have a dream where your dead mother has come back to talk to you. One possible explanation, the dualist explanation, is that the ghost of your mother, immaterial soul that she is, is communicating with you—while you're asleep. But there's a second possible explanation, the physicalist explanation: it's *just* a dream. Of *course* you dream about your mother—you love her! You need to ask: what's the better explanation?

I can't take the space here to go through each purported type of supernatural phenomenon. But in principle, that's what we should do. We should look at each type of occurrence and review the various scientific explanations that have been offered for what's going on. (Sometimes, of course, it is even controversial what the bare facts are, that are in need of explanation.) I can't take the space to do that here. But speaking personally, when I review the evidence, I always come away thinking that there's no good reason to move beyond the physical.

So again, let's recap. One group of arguments for the existence of a soul says that we need to posit a soul in order to explain something, whether it's some everyday, utterly familiar fact about us, or something supernatural. In some of these cases, at least, I want to concede that the existence of a soul might well be the *beginnings* of a possible explanation. But the question is never, "Is that a *possible* explanation?" but rather, "Is it the *best* explanation?" And when I review these various arguments, I come away thinking that the better explanations are had by the physicalist.

Mind you, I certainly don't want to deny that there are some things that the physicalist has not yet done a very compelling job of explaining. In particular, as I've already conceded, I think there are mysteries and puzzles about the nature of consciousness, the qualitative aspect of experience—what it's like to smell coffee or taste pineapple or see red. It's very hard to see how you explain that in physicalist terms. So to that extent, I think, we can say the jury may still be out. But I don't think that what we should say is that the better explanation lies with the dualist. Because I think merely positing a soul doesn't really offer us much of an explanation either. It just holds out the promise of an explanation. So at best that's a tie, and therefore no compelling reason to accept the existence of a soul.

It would, of course, be a different matter if we could see that *no* conceivable physicalist explanation of this or that fact could possibly work. But I don't think we're in that situation. Rather, with regard to consciousness, and maybe some other things, we don't yet see how to explain it. But not yet seeing how to explain something in physicalist terms is not the same thing as seeing that it *can't* be explained in physicalist terms.

Similarly, if we already *had* a dualist explanation—whether of consciousness or some other mystery—with some details really worked out, maybe we'd be able to say that dualism offers us the *better* explanation. But it seems to me that dualism doesn't so much offer an explanation in the truly hard cases as just assert that we would be explanatorily better off—somehow!—if we posit something immaterial. And that, I think, is not a very compelling argument.

I conclude, accordingly, that the various arguments that we have been considering for dualism are unsuccessful, at least as they stand right now.

Of course, maybe someday that will change. Maybe someday we will decide that we really do need to appeal to a soul if we are going to explain (or offer the best explanation of) something that needs explaining. But right now, at any rate, as far as I can see, no appeal to inference to the best explanation provides us with a compelling reason to posit the existence of the soul.

CHAPTER 4

Descartes' Argument

Our various attempts to use inference to the best explanation so as to argue for the existence of the soul have been unsuccessful. Does that mean that we need to abandon dualism? Not quite. For there is a rather different type of argument for dualism that is also worth considering.

This "new" argument actually comes from the writings of René Descartes, the great seventeenth-century French philosopher (though I'll be spelling out the details of the argument in my own way).[1] One striking feature of the argument is that it is purely philosophical: it doesn't seem to have any significant empirical premises; it is based on philosophical reflection alone. Yet, despite being an example of pure "armchair" philosophizing, many people find this argument rather compelling.

The argument starts by asking you to imagine a story. I am going to tell that story in the first person. I'm going to tell it about myself and my morning. But you may find it more persuasive if you imagine it as being about you—you and your morning. Regardless, bear in mind that I am not at all claiming that the story I am about to tell really did happen. It certainly did not! But the crucial point here is simply that we can *imagine* this story happening. It seems *possible.*

I should probably say a word more about this idea, that the story I am about to tell is "possible." I don't mean to claim that it is empirically possible. I just mean to say that it is *logically* possible—it is a logically coherent story. We can imagine something like this happening. In the same sense, dragons and unicorns seem logically possible; we can coherently imagine them, even if, as it happens, they are *empirical* impossibilities. So the claim is only that the story I am about to tell is something we can coherently imagine happening.

Suppose, then, that I woke up this morning. That is to say, at a certain time this morning I look around my room and I see the familiar sights of my darkened bedroom. I hear, perhaps, the sounds of the cars outside my house, my alarm clock ringing, what have you. I move out of the room toward the bathroom, planning to brush my teeth. As I enter the bathroom (where there's much more light), I look in the mirror and—here's where things get really weird—I don't see anything! Normally, of course, when I look in the mirror I see my face. I see my head. I see the reflection of my torso. But now, as I'm looking into the mirror, I don't see anything at all. Or rather, more precisely, I see the shower curtain reflected behind me. Normally, of course, that's blocked by me, by my body. But I don't see my body. Slightly freaked out, I reach for my head, or perhaps we should say I reach for where I would expect my head to be, but I don't feel anything there. Glancing down at my arms, I don't see any arms. Now I'm really panicking! As I begin trying to touch my body, I don't feel anything. Not only can't I feel anything with my fingers, I don't have any sensations where my body should be.

We could continue this story—and no doubt a novelist could do a much better job of telling it than I just did—but I hope I have already said enough for you to grant that what we've just done is imagine a story in which I discover that my body doesn't exist. That, at least, was what I was *trying* to do. So let me be even more explicit: I am trying to get you to imagine a story in which my body really does not exist! It's not just that my body is there, but for some reason I can't detect it. No, I am asking you to imagine a story in which my body really isn't there at all! That seems possible, doesn't it?

Notice, however, that in the story I am telling, it is nonetheless true that my *mind* exists. After all, I am in the bathroom, thinking thoughts like this: "Why can't I see my body in the mirror? Why can't I feel my head? What's going on? Am I going *crazy*?" I am panicking, I am freaking out! We've got a story in which I am thinking all sorts of thoughts. So my mind clearly exists, and yet, for all that, my body does not. That's what I am asking you to imagine, and it does seem as though we can imagine something like this happening.

(Again, the claim is not that something like this could *actually* happen! It may well be *empirically* impossible for my mind to exist without my body existing. And indeed, if physicalism is correct, then it *is* empirically impossible for my mind to exist without my body. But still, even the physicalist should admit that it seems *logically* possible for my mind to exist without my body, in the sense that this is something I can coherently imagine. That's the point of telling the story, to help everyone see that!)

Now the brilliant thing about Descartes' argument is it goes from this simple thought—that it seems possible to imagine my mind existing without my body—to the conclusion that there must already be, *in fact*, a difference between my mind and my body. Here's how.

What we've just done is imagine that my mind exists but my body does not. What does that show? Descartes says it shows that the mind and the body must already be, in fact, two logically distinct things. The mind and the body cannot be the same thing. Because, after all, what I just did was imagine my mind existing without my body. How could I even *do* that, even in imagination? How could it even be possible to *imagine* my mind without my body, if talking about my mind is just a way of talking about my body? If mind and body are really, metaphysically speaking, the same thing, then you couldn't *have* one without the other after all, not even in imagination.

Consider a less controversial example. On my desk, right now, is a pen. Now try to tell a story in which that pen exists, but that pen also doesn't exist. You can't do it! After all, the pen is just one thing, the pen. And if it is just one thing, you can tell a story in which it exists, or you can tell a story in which it doesn't exist—but you can't tell a logically coherent story in which it both exists and doesn't exist.

In contrast, try to imagine a world in which your left hand exists but your right hand doesn't. That's easy to do! Why is it so easy? Because there are two different things that we're thinking about. Of course, that doesn't mean that in the real world one of them does exist and the other one doesn't. (I do hope that in the real world, you have both of your hands.) But it does show that in the real world your hands are two different things. That's why I can imagine a world with one but not the other.

In short, if I can tell a (logically coherent) story in which A exists and B doesn't exist, it's got to follow that A and B are not, in fact, the same thing. Because if "B" was just another word for, another way of talking about, A, then to imagine A existing but B not existing would be imagining A existing but—well, since B is just A—A not existing. But of course, you can't imagine a world in which A exists but A doesn't exist!

Put the same point the other way around. If I can imagine A without B, then A and B have to be logically distinct things. They cannot be identical. But since I *can* imagine my mind existing without my body, it follows that my mind and my body have to be logically distinct things. They cannot be identical. Talking about my mind cannot just be a way of talking about my body. Physicalism must be wrong, and dualism must be right.

Now, that's a very cool argument. Philosophers *love* this argument. And I've got to tell you, to this day there's a debate in the philosophical community about whether this argument works or not.

But it's important not to *misunderstand* the argument. In particular, the argument is not saying that if something is logically possible, if I can imagine it, it must be true. That's obviously false! After all, I can imagine unicorns, but that doesn't show that unicorns exist. But that's not what the argument is saying. The argument is only making a much more specific claim: if I can imagine one thing without the other, they must be *different* things. After all, you can't even *imagine* one thing without the other, if there is really only one thing that you are thinking about! So if I really *can* imagine something existing while something else does not, they really must be two different things, not just one.

Of course, it could still be that in the real world the one thing cannot *exist* without the other. There may be some sort of metaphysical connection that ties the two things so tightly together that you'll never actually get one without the other. That's not the question. The point is just that if I can at least imagine the one thing without the other, they must in fact *be* two separate things. And since I *can* imagine my mind without my body, it must be the case that my mind is something separate and distinct from my body. Otherwise, how could I imagine it existing without the body? (I can't imagine the body existing without the body!) If the mind is just a way of talking about the body, how could I so much as *imagine* the mind without the body? But since I *can* imagine the mind without the body, it follows that they're separate. So the mind is not the body after all. It's something different. It's the soul.

Try to imagine a world in which somebody's smile exists but their body doesn't. You can't do it. You can't have a smile without a body. And, of course, there's no mystery about that. It's because the smile isn't really some separate thing from the body. Talking about smiles, as we've noted before, is just a way of talking about what a certain area of the body can do.

You can *try* to imagine a smile without a body. But you won't succeed. In *Alice in Wonderland*, the Cheshire Cat disappears and all we have left, the last thing that disappears, is the smile. But of course, when you imagine the Cheshire Cat only having the smile there, you're still imagining the cat's lips, teeth, and maybe tongue. If you try to imagine a smile with *no* body at all, it can't be done. Why? Because the smile isn't something separate from the body.

But when Descartes tells us to try to imagine your *mind* existing without your body, it is very easily done. From which it follows that your mind and your body must not be one thing. They must, in fact, be two things. That's why it's possible to imagine the one without the other.

Descartes' argument seems to show us that the mind is something separate from, distinct from, the body. It's not just another way of talking about the body; it's something extra, above and beyond the body. It's a soul. That's what Descartes argued. And as I say, to this day, philosophers disagree about whether this argument works or not.

Speaking personally, I don't think that it does work. In a moment I'll give you a counterexample. More precisely, what I'm going to give is an example of an argument just like it, or at least an argument that seems to be just like it, where we can pretty easily see that the second argument doesn't work. And so something must go wrong with Descartes' original argument as well.

Here's the counterexample (it's not original to me). You have probably heard of the Evening Star. Roughly speaking, the Evening Star is a heavenly body that (as it happens) is the first one visible in the sky as it gets dark, at least at certain times of the year. And you have probably also heard of the Morning Star. The Morning Star is a heavenly body that (as it happens) is the last heavenly body that's still visible as dawn comes in and it begins to get light. So, roughly speaking, the Evening Star is the first star that's visible and the Morning Star is the last star that's visible at the right times of the year. The world that we live in has both the Evening Star and the Morning Star.

Now try to imagine a world in which the Evening Star exists, but the Morning Star does not. That seems like a fairly straightforward matter. I get up in the morning as dawn is approaching. I look around, and the Morning Star is not there. There is no star where the Morning Star should be (or where people have claimed it would be). But the *Evening* Star still exists. When I go out as sun sets and dusk falls, there is the Evening Star.

So, as I say, it's a trivial matter to imagine a world in which the Evening Star exists and the Morning Star does not. And so we can now construct a

Descartes-like argument. We can say, "If I can imagine the Evening Star without the Morning Star that shows that the Evening Star and the Morning Star must be two different heavenly bodies." That's how the argument would go. If we can imagine A without B, then A and B must be distinct things. And since we can imagine the Evening Star without the Morning Star, they must be distinct as well.

But in point of fact, that's not so! The Evening Star and the Morning Star are actually the very *same* heavenly body. Actually, it's not a star at all. It's the planet Venus. But the important point is that there's only *one* thing—Venus—not two. The Morning Star and the Evening Star aren't two different things, they're just one thing, namely, Venus, that we happen to view at different times of the day. In fact, the sentence *"They* are one thing" is slightly misleading. It would be more precise to say that *it* is just one thing, Venus.

And that means, of course, that the Descartes-like argument that we just considered is unsound. To begin with, most obviously, we know that the conclusion of that argument is wrong: the Evening Star and the Morning Star are not two, but one. But that means that the *argument* for the conclusion that they are two must go wrong as well: some step in that argument must go astray.

(Actually, some people may be tempted to say that the conclusion of the argument is right! These people may think that the Evening Star and the Morning Star really *are* two different things—since the one is seen in the evening and the other is seen in the morning. But I think that this view can't be right. The Evening Star, for example, doesn't exist only in the evening. It doesn't stop existing at other times of the day! In the actual world, the Evening Star is that very same heavenly body—Venus—that we also see in the morning, when we *call* it "the Morning Star." There is just *one* heavenly body—with two *names*.)

Now here's the really important point. If it's right that the Descartes-like argument goes astray (since it leads to a false conclusion), then that gives us reason to be suspicious of Descartes' own original argument as well. For the two arguments—Descartes' argument and our astronomical variation—do seem to be structurally *parallel* arguments. So if something is wrong with the Morning Star/Evening Star argument (and we do know that there *must* be something wrong with it), there is probably something wrong with the mind/body argument as well.

Now, that seems to me to be right. I think the original Cartesian argument does fail. And I think that the example of the Evening Star and the

Morning Star *shows* us that Descartes' original argument doesn't work. At least, that's how it seems to me. Still, as I say, there are philosophers who disagree. Some philosophers think that although our two arguments *look* parallel—they seem to be sufficiently similar so that if one fails the other must fail as well—perhaps, in fact, they're not. Perhaps there is some subtle but important difference between the two cases, and if we aren't looking carefully, we'll overlook it. As I say, the debate goes on.

One of the reasons the philosophical debate about Descartes' argument continues is that it is surprisingly difficult to pin down where, exactly, it goes wrong! It is, after all, one thing to decide that an argument must have a flaw someplace. It is quite another to show where, exactly, the flaw is located. Even among those philosophers who agree in rejecting Descartes' argument, there is more agreement that something goes wrong *somewhere* than there is about where, exactly, the mistake *is*.

Indeed, even in the case of the argument concerning the Morning Star and the Evening Star, it isn't particularly easy to say where, exactly, it goes wrong. We know it must go wrong someplace—since there aren't two different heavenly bodies here, but only one—but despite this fact, people still disagree about where, exactly, the mistake comes in.

Let's consider a few possible suggestions. If we can get clearer about where the astronomy argument goes wrong, maybe we can be in a better position to say whether Descartes' own argument goes wrong at the same place.

I think it is helpful to think of the astronomy argument as having three premises, from which the (mistaken!) conclusion follows:

(1) I can imagine a world in which the Evening Star exists, but the Morning Star doesn't.
(2) If something can be imagined, then it is logically possible.
(3) If it is logically possible for one thing to exist without another, then even in the actual world those two things must indeed be different things.
So (4) the Evening Star and the Morning Star must be different things (even in the actual world).

If the first two premises of this argument are correct, then it follows that it is logically possible for the Evening Star to exist without the Morning Star. But then, given the third premise, it would follow that even in the actual world, the Evening Star and the Morning Star must be different things.

Now we know that the conclusion of this argument is false. Yet the conclusion really does follow from the three premises. So one of the premises must itself be false. Which one is it?

The first premise says that I can imagine a world in which the Evening Star exists but the Morning Star doesn't. And it certainly does seem as though I can imagine this. But one possible diagnosis of how the argument goes wrong is to suggest that, appearances to the contrary notwithstanding, I can't actually imagine it after all. I *thought* I was imagining a world with the Evening Star but without the Morning Star, but in fact I haven't done that at all. I have misdescribed what it is that I have imagined.

That's not a silly thing to say about the astronomy case. Maybe that's the right diagnosis. Maybe I *haven't* really imagined a world where the Evening Star exists and the Morning Star doesn't. To be sure, I have imagined a world in which there is no heavenly body that is uniquely visible early in the morning. But is that a world in which the Morning Star doesn't exist? That's not clear. After all, "Morning Star" is just a name for a particular heavenly body—Venus. Maybe all I have done is imagine a world in which that particular heavenly body, Venus, isn't *visible* in the morning. But perhaps we should say that, strictly speaking, that's not really a world in which the Morning Star doesn't exist. Of course, we wouldn't *use* the name "Morning Star" in a world like that—but that doesn't show that the Morning Star doesn't exist in that world, only that we wouldn't call it by that name. Since the Morning Star *is* Venus, so long as Venus is around, the Morning Star is too—even if it isn't visible in the morning. So maybe I haven't really imagined a world in which the Morning Star doesn't exist (but the Evening Star does); maybe I have only imagined a world in which the Morning Star isn't visible in the morning, even though it does exist (along with the Evening Star).

If that *is* the right thing to say about the astronomy case, can we say something similar about Descartes' original argument? Can we say that I didn't really imagine a world in which my mind exists but my body doesn't? Consider the little story I told about waking up and not seeing myself in the mirror, and so forth. Should we say that I *thought* I was describing a world in which my mind exists and my body doesn't, but I wasn't really doing that at all? That despite my best attempts, I can't really imagine a world like that after all?

Maybe that *is* what we should say. But the simple fact of the matter is that most people find that suggestion very hard to take seriously. It really did seem as though I was imagining a scenario in which my mind exists, but my body doesn't. It's difficult to see why we should accept the suggestion that I haven't actually done this—that I unwittingly misdescribed what it was that I was really imagining.

(Note, incidentally, that if I haven't managed to imagine the relevant scenario in the astronomy case, but I have managed to do that for the mind/body case, then even if the astronomy argument fails—as we know it must—it could still be the case that the mind/body argument succeeds! It is complications like this that keep the debate about Descartes' argument alive.)

Suppose we decide that this first suggestion is mistaken, and I really have imagined a world where the Morning Star doesn't exist even though the Evening Star does. If so, then the first premise of the astronomy argument is correct. But we still know that the conclusion is false! So where else might the argument have gone wrong?

Some people prefer to challenge the second premise. Even if I did imagine a world in which the Morning Star exists and the Evening Star doesn't exist, maybe that doesn't show that such a world is truly a logical possibility. Maybe imagining something doesn't really show that it is logically possible.

But it is important not to misunderstand what the second premise is saying. It isn't claiming that imagination is a good guide to what is *empirically* possible. We already know that that's not so. I can, for example, easily imagine a world with dragons, but that doesn't mean that they are, in fact, physically possible. As we have already noted, however, the relevant kind of possibility here is only *logical* possibility. The second premise is only claiming that if I can imagine something then it must at least be a *logically* coherent possibility. And here, it does seem as though imagination is a good guide. We all think, for example, that even if dragons are physically impossible, they are nonetheless logically possible. And why are we so confident about this? Precisely because we can so easily imagine them! Our imagination seems to be a very fine guide when it comes to logical possibility.

Still, maybe it is not an infallible guide. Maybe there are cases where our imagination leads us astray. Maybe there are cases where we can imagine something that is nonetheless logically *impossible*.

It is hard to know whether there really are cases like that or not. Take something impossible—say, a round square. Can you imagine one? Try it! In certain moods, I sort of feel I can just begin to imagine it. If so, then maybe imagination really *is* a flawed guide to possibility. Maybe sometimes it just steers us wrong about what is logically possible.

If so, then we might reject the second premise. In the astronomy argument, we will be able to say that even if we can imagine the Evening Star without the Morning Star, nonetheless this may not be a genuine logical possibility. Maybe it isn't really logically possible for the one to exist without the other. In which case, of course, it won't follow that the two are different things. Our Descartes-like argument will fail because its second premise is mistaken.

And if we do say that, then of course that will mean that Descartes' original argument will fail as well. For it too moves from a claim about what we can imagine (my mind existing without my body) to a claim about what is logically possible (my mind existing without my body). But if imagination is a *fallible* guide to possibility, then Descartes won't yet have shown that it really is logically possible for my mind to exist without my body. In which case, of course, he won't be in a position to prove that the two are different things. His argument will fail, because it too relies on the second premise, and the second premise is mistaken.

That's what we can say if we do decide that imagination is a flawed guide to possibility. But should we say that? I can't decide. I am not sure if there really *are* any cases where imagination leads us astray in that way. Consider the example of a round square once again. That really does seem logically impossible, but the truth of the matter is, I am not at all sure I can imagine one after all. Most of the time, it seems to me that I can't—and the obvious explanation is that I can't imagine one precisely because they're logically impossible. So maybe premise two is actually correct after all: maybe imagination is a reliable guide to what's logically possible.

But if the first premise and the second premise of the astronomy argument are both correct, where else could the argument go wrong? Well, perhaps we should challenge the *third* premise. Maybe we should say that even if it is *logically* possible for one thing to exist without another, nonetheless in the actual world those "two" things might still be one single thing. If so, then, in particular, even if it is logically possible for the Evening Star to exist without the Morning Star—so that in the world we are imagining they are not the same thing—nonetheless it might still be the case (and indeed, it is the case) that in the actual world the Evening Star and the Morning Star are actually just *one* thing (the planet Venus).

To reject the third premise in this way is to claim that identity can be *contingent*. It is to say that whether A and B are two things or one can vary from one logically possible world to the next. It might be, for example, that in one logically possible scenario A and B are distinct, not at all identical to one another, and yet, for all that, in some other logically possible scenario A and B *are* identical to one another, so that they are not truly two things but only one single thing. In particular, then, it might be that in the actual world A and B are one and the same thing—one thing, not two—even though in some other perfectly coherent, logically possible scenario, A and B "come apart" and are two things, not one. To reject the third premise is to say that it's a mistake to assume that if A and B are the very same thing, then A must *always* be the very same thing as B, no matter what.

Suppose we do reject the third premise. Then we will have explained where the astronomy argument goes wrong: it mistakenly moves from the fact that the Morning Star and the Evening Star are different in *some* logically possible worlds, to the (false!) conclusion that they are different—two things, not one—in *this* world too, the *actual* world. And having said this, we will now be in a position to conclude that Descartes' original argument must fail as well. All that Descartes will have shown is that in *some* logically possible world there are minds that are not identical to bodies—or perhaps, more specifically, that in some logically possible world *my* mind is something distinct from my body—but for all that, nothing will follow about minds and bodies being distinct in *this* world. Descartes' proof of dualism— that my mind is distinct from my body in *this* world—will have failed.

That, at least, is what we can say if we reject the third premise and accept the idea of contingent identity. But I have to say that this notion of contingent identity is a rather puzzling one. After all, if A really is B—if they are one and the same thing, not two things but one—then how *could* they "come apart"? How could it be that in some other logically possible world, "they" are two things, not one? After all, if A and B really *are* identical, one single thing, then there is, indeed, only one thing there. There is nothing to come apart! There is just A—which is the very same thing as B. How can that single thing possibly be two? In short, rejecting the third premise is not an option that everyone is going to find appealing either.

So where, exactly, does the astronomy argument break down? Where does it go wrong? Is it that I'm not really imagining what I thought I was imagining? Is it that imagination is not really an adequate guide to possibility? Or is it that identity is somehow contingent? The interesting thing about the Descartes-like argument is that although it is easy to see that it must go wrong someplace (since the Morning Star and the Evening Star are one, not two), it is not at all a trivial matter to decide *where*, exactly, it goes wrong.

Still, it does go wrong someplace, and so that gives us at least some reason to be skeptical about Descartes' original argument as well. At the very least, the astronomy example shows that it is easy to be misled by arguments like Descartes'. Of course it remains a possibility that Descartes' own argument is a sound one, even though the Descartes-like argument is not. Perhaps a fuller examination of these issues would show that the astronomy argument makes a mistake that Descartes' original argument somehow avoids. That's certainly a possibility. But my own view is that *both* arguments are flawed, and that Descartes' attempt to establish the distinctness of the mind from the body—brilliant and fascinating though it may be—is ultimately unsuccessful.[2]

Think about where that leaves us. We've spent the last two chapters examining various arguments for the existence of the soul. Several of these arguments have been tempting, but none of them, I think, have been particularly successful. Indeed, my own view is that the same thing would be true even if we continued this part of our discussion, examining still other arguments for dualism. As far as I can see, *all* attempts to establish the existence of a soul—an immaterial object, the house of consciousness, separate and distinct from the body—all of these arguments ultimately fail. The conclusion I reach, then, is a skeptical one: we simply do not have good reason to *believe* in the existence of a soul. We should reject dualism and embrace physicalism.

I recognize, of course, that this is a matter concerning which reasonable people can disagree. Perhaps you think that I have been unfair to some of the arguments that we've been considering, and they're more persuasive than I have acknowledged. Or maybe you think there are better arguments than the ones I have discussed. Ultimately, of course, this is a question you will have to decide for yourself. But if you do believe in the soul, I hope that isn't simply because you find the idea a comforting one. If you do believe in the soul, you need to ask yourself: what's the *argument*?

CHAPTER 5

Plato on the Immortality of the Soul

When I first introduced the idea of dualism (in Chapter 2), I noted that even if one accepts the existence of a soul—an immaterial substance, distinct from the body—it doesn't yet follow that the soul is immortal. Indeed, it doesn't even follow that the soul can so much as *survive* the death of the body. It might be, instead, that when the body dies, the soul is destroyed as well.

Of course, I have been arguing that we have no compelling reason to believe in souls in the first place. And obviously enough, if the soul doesn't even exist, it cannot possibly be immortal. So there is a clear sense in which we don't really need to ask about the *immortality* of the soul at all. Still, the simple fact is that many people do believe in souls, and so it is probably worth asking about immortality as well. Suppose, then—if only for the sake of discussion—that there *are* souls. Is there any reason to believe that our souls could *survive* our deaths? In particular, is there any reason to believe in *immortality*?

I want to explore this question by looking at Plato's dialogue, the *Phaedo*. (Plato wrote his philosophy in the form of dialogues, that is to say, *plays*, in which the various characters argue about philosophical questions.) This particular dialogue is set just before the death of Plato's teacher Socrates, on Socrates' very last day. As I'm sure you know, Socrates was put on trial and condemned to death for "corrupting" the youth of Athens (he was arguing philosophy with them). Socrates is given hemlock to drink. He drinks the poison and dies.

Now, this is a historical event. Socrates really did have a circle of friends and disciples that he would argue philosophy with. One of his disciples was Plato. Plato then grew up and wrote philosophical works. But Plato does not appear in his own dialogues. (In fact, the *Phaedo* explicitly mentions that Plato wasn't there with Socrates on the day that Socrates dies.) So, how do we know, then, when we're reading one of Plato's dialogues, which position in the play represents *Plato's* position? The short answer is that Socrates almost always represents Plato's own views. That is to say, Plato, the *author* of the play, uses Socrates, the *character* in the play, to state *Plato's* views.

If this were a book on ancient philosophy, we'd have to complicate that answer, especially if we were trying to reconstruct the actual views of the *historical* Socrates. But for our purposes there is no need to do that. We can simply assume that every view that Socrates endorses in the *Phaedo* is a view that *Plato* accepts. Accordingly, I will sometimes say that "Plato holds" such and such a view, and sometimes I'll say that "Socrates argues" for such and such. But I won't bother trying to sort it all out—because for our purposes it's all the same.

The *Phaedo*, as I say, is set on Socrates' last day. At the end of the dialogue he drinks the hemlock and he dies. Unsurprisingly, then, what he does with his friends up until that moment is this: he argues about the immortality of the soul. That's the question that's driving the discussion in the *Phaedo*. Do we have any good reason to believe that the soul survives the death of the body? And more particularly still, do we have good reason to believe it's immortal? Socrates believes in the immortality of the soul. And so he attempts to *defend* this position, to justify it to his disciples who are worried that it may not be true.

You might think that Socrates would start by trying to prove that the soul exists. But the fact of the matter is, although there are points raised in the dialogue that might be relevant for trying to offer such a proof, that isn't centrally what Plato is up to. For the most part the existence of the soul is simply taken for granted in the dialogue; it's pretty much just *assumed*. The question that gets all the attention is not, "Is there a soul?" but rather, "Does the soul survive the death of the body? Is it immortal?"

Plato's Metaphysics

Since this is Socrates' last day on earth, you would expect him to be pretty upset. You'd expect him to be sad. But one of the most striking things about the dialogue is that Socrates is actually in a very happy, indeed jovial, mood. He's not worried about the fact that he's going to die. Indeed, he welcomes his death. Why is that? First of all, of course, because he thinks there is a soul, and it will survive the death of his body. But beyond that, Socrates thinks that when he dies he is going to go to a sort of heaven. He believes in a realm that's populated by gods and other kindred souls. And if you have lived your life properly here on earth, then when you die, your soul will go to this heavenly realm. Socrates thinks he's done that, and so he faces the prospect of death with excitement and anticipation.

Why does Socrates believe all of this? To answer that question, we're first going to need a crash course in Plato's metaphysics. Obviously, what I can say here will have to be rather quick and superficial; but it should be enough to give us at least some of the basic ideas.

Let's start with beauty. There are all sorts of beautiful objects in the world, some more so than others. But Plato suggests, plausibly, that there's nothing in the world that's *perfectly* beautiful. And yet for all that, we can think about perfect beauty itself. We might put it this way: ordinary, humdrum, everyday physical objects are *somewhat* beautiful. They're partially beautiful. As Platonists sometimes put it, these objects "participate" in beauty; they partake of beauty to varying degrees. But none of them should be confused with beauty itself.

Or take justice. Different social arrangements can be just or unjust to varying degrees. Different people can be just to varying degrees. But presumably we would all agree that no society in the world and no person in the world is *perfectly* just. So whatever perfect justice *is*, it's not one more thing to be found in the everyday, empirical world. Justice is obviously something that things in the empirical world can *participate* in or partake of to varying degrees. But for all that, we shouldn't confuse the physical things which can *be* just—the people or societies that can be just to one degree or another—with perfect justice in itself. Still, even though perfect justice is never realized in this world, there *is* such a thing as perfect justice, and the mind can *think* about it. Perfect justice is something that the mind can think about and study, even though we don't find it in the everyday world.

Or take being round. The mind can think about perfect circularity. But no physical object is perfectly circular. There are only things that are circular to a greater or lesser degree. Yet here too, we can think about perfect circularity, even though it can't be found in the everyday, empirical world.

Clearly, the mind has a special ability—an ability to think about, to grasp and understand, these nonphysical "things" that we have been talking about: beauty, justice, circularity. And of course, there are many, many other similar "things" that the mind can think about when it wants to, even though they can't be found anywhere in the ordinary, everyday world.

We need a word for this kind of "thing." And Plato gives us a word: *eidos*. Sometimes this Greek term is translated as "Idea"—to mark the fact that the mind can grasp these things. But in English, at least, the term "idea" suggests something that is merely "in the head"—something with no external existence, independent of our minds—and that's certainly not Plato's view about these things at all. So I will use the alternative translation, "Forms," which nicely carries the suggestion that these things provide the ideal template, or the standard, against which ordinary objects can be measured.

Whatever we call them, the crucial point is this. According to Plato, these Forms are perfectly real. We can think about them, study them—learn things about justice, or health, or beauty, or goodness. But the Forms are not themselves *part* of the ordinary, everyday, empirical world. To be sure, ordinary, humdrum things can *participate* in the Forms to varying degrees; they can participate in perfect justice, beauty itself, perfect health, or goodness itself, and so on. But ordinary material objects should not be confused with the Platonic Forms themselves, for the Forms are not *part* of this world, they are not *in* this world. And yet, for all that, even though we don't bump into the Platonic Forms in this world, we can think about them. Our mind has a kind of grasp of them.

The problem is, we're distracted by the comings and goings, the hurly-burly of the ordinary everyday world. And so we don't have a very good grasp of the Platonic Forms. We're able to think about them, but we're distracted. So what the philosopher tries to do, according to Socrates, is to free himself from the distractions that the body poses—the desire for food, the craving for sex, the concern with pleasure and pain. All of these bodily cravings get in the way of thinking about the Platonic Forms. What the philosopher tries to do, then, so as to better focus on these ideal things, is to disregard the body, put it aside, separate his mind as much as possible from his body. That's what Socrates says he's been trying to do with his own life. And so, because of that, he's got a better handle on these ideal Forms. Accordingly, he believes that when death comes and the final separation of the mind and the body occurs, his soul will go up to this heavenly realm (instead of being pulled back down by bodily desires). Philosophers nowadays sometimes talk about "Plato's heaven"—the otherworldly realm where the Platonic Forms are to be found. What Socrates believes, in effect, is that when he dies, his soul will go to Plato's heaven, where he can have more direct contact with the Forms.

Now, I don't have the space here to say enough to try and make it clear why at least the basic elements of this Platonic metaphysical view are worth taking seriously. (Indeed, not only is the idea of a Platonic Form worth taking seriously; to this day, many, many philosophers think that something like this must be *right*.) But let me mention one example that may give you a feel for the idea. Think of math. Think of some simple mathematical claim like $2+3=5$. When we say that $2+3=5$, we're saying something about numbers that our mind is able to grasp. But what *are* numbers anyway? They're certainly not physical objects. It's not as though someday you're going to open up an issue of *National Geographic* where the cover story is going to say that "at long last, explorers have discovered the number two." It's not as though the number two is something that you see or hear or taste or could bump into. Whatever the number two is, it's something that our mind can grasp but isn't actually in the physical world.

Most of us are *Platonists* about math. We believe that there *are* numbers. The mind can think about them, and things can "partake" of them. If I were to hold up two pencils, for example, there's a clear sense in which the pencils would be participating in "twohood." But of course, the pencils themselves are not the number two itself! If I were to snap the pencils, destroying them, I wouldn't be destroying the number two. So the number two is some sort of Platonic "abstract object" that doesn't exist in space and time. And the same thing is true, obviously, about the number three, or the number five, and all of the other numbers as well. None of them are physical objects, to be found in the physical world. And yet, for all that, they are perfectly real, and the mind can think about them. They are Platonic Forms.

That, at least, is the idea. And it's not a silly idea. It seems like a very compelling account of what's going on in mathematics. Numbers are not physical objects. Numbers are not part of the empirical world. We don't do empirical experiments to see whether one plus two equals three. Rather, we use our minds to grasp the truths about these particular Platonic Forms.

But Plato's thought is that *everything* is like that. It's not just math. Justice itself, for example, is like that. There are just or unjust things in the world, but they are not justice itself. Perfect justice is clearly something the mind can think about, but it's not here in the world. It's another abstract entity, a Platonic Form. And the same thing is true for goodness itself, or health itself, or beauty itself, and so on. All of these things are Platonic Forms.

That's the picture. Plato's idea is that if we start doing enough metaphysics, we can see that there must be this realm of Platonic Forms, a realm that exists distinct from and in addition to the ordinary, physical world that we're all familiar with. And yet, even though the Forms are not a part of the everyday world, we are able to think about them, to study them. How do we do that? Through the *mind*. This can't be a job that the *body* does, because the body is limited to using the five senses. It is limited to contact with things in the physical world. It is the *soul* that can think about Platonic Forms.

So one important difference between ordinary physical objects and the Forms is the fact that the Platonic Forms don't exist in the empirical world, but rather in a distinct realm, out of space and out of time. Here's another: unlike ordinary objects, there is something *perfect* about the Forms. They are eternal; they never change. Circular *objects*, for example, may come and go, but circularity itself can never be destroyed or altered. The nature of circularity itself is always precisely the same, never changing. It is eternal. Similarly, the number of geese may rise or fall, but the nature of the number *seventeen*, say, never changes. It is always an odd number, always exactly one more than sixteen. (It is an eternal truth that $17 = 16 + 1$.) And so on, similarly, for the various other Forms.

In contrast, physical objects are constantly changing. Something might be short at one point and become tall at another point, ugly at one point and then beautiful. Think of the Ugly Duckling, from the tale by Hans Christian Andersen: it starts out ugly, but then it becomes a beautiful swan. (And later, no doubt, it dies and stops existing altogether!) But beauty itself never changes. Perfect justice never changes. Perfect goodness never changes. Unlike the things in the empirical world, the Forms are eternal and beyond change. In fact, the more you start thinking about the everyday world from the perspective of this perfect Platonic realm, the more the world we live in just seems crazy. It is almost insanely contradictory.

Plato thinks it really *is* crazy, in just the way that a dream is. When you're caught up in a dream, you don't notice just how insane it all is. But if you step back and reflect on it, you can see it. "Well, let's see, I was eating a sandwich and suddenly the sandwich was the Statue of Liberty, except the Statue of Liberty was my mother. And she's flying over the ocean, except she's really a piece of spaghetti." That's how dreams are. When you're *in* it, it sort of all makes sense. You're caught up in it, never noticing the contradictions. But when you step back properly, you can see the contradictions and you say, "That's just insane." Plato thinks that the empirical world has something of that kind of insanity, something of that kind of contradictoriness, built right into it, although we don't ordinarily notice. "He's a basketball player, so he's really, really tall. Except he's only six feet. So he's really, really short for a basketball player. This is a baby elephant, so it's really, really big—except it's a *baby* elephant, so it's really, really small."

The world is constantly *rolling*—that's a Platonic expression—rolling between one Form and the other. And it's hard to make sense of. In contrast, the mind is able to get a firm grip on the Platonic Forms: they're stable, they're reliable, they're lawlike. They don't change. They're eternal. That's the Platonic picture.

Now, it's not my purpose here to try to argue for or against Platonism with regard to these kinds of abstract entities. As I suggested in talking about the example of math, it's not a silly view, even if Platonism is not a view that we all take automatically. So let's simply suppose—if only for the sake of argument—that Plato was *right* about the Forms. We still need to ask, what follows?

Plato thinks that what's going to follow is that we have some reason to believe in the immortality of the soul. And beyond that, given that the soul *is* immortal, we have reason to be concerned about what will happen *after* we die.

I have, of course, been emphasizing the point that the mind—the soul—is able to grasp the eternal Platonic Forms. It must be admitted, however, that typically at least, most of us don't spend all that much time thinking about the Forms. We're distracted by our *bodies*, by the desire for food, drink, sex, sleep, and so on. But Plato believes that by distancing oneself from the body, the soul is able to better concentrate on the Forms. And if you're good at that, if you practice this while you're alive, separating yourself from the cravings of your body, then when your body dies, your soul is able to go to this Platonic heavenly realm and commune with gods and other immortal souls and think about the Forms. On the other hand, if you haven't separated yourself from your body while alive, if you're too enmeshed in its concerns and desires, then upon the death of your body your soul will get sucked back in, reincarnated in another body. If you're lucky, you'll be reincarnated as another person; if you're not so lucky, you'll be reincarnated as a pig or a donkey or an ant, or what have you.

So your goal in life, Plato says, should be to practice *death*—to separate yourself from your body as much as possible. Socrates thinks he's done a decent job of this. And because of that, even though he's facing death, he isn't distressed at the prospect but happy. He's happy that the final separation will take place and he'll be able to go to heaven.

The *Phaedo* ends, accordingly, with Socrates' death. He drinks the hemlock and dies with equanimity. It is one of the great death scenes in Western literature, and I am always moved when I read it. For as the very last sentence of the dialogue reports about Socrates, "Of all those we have known, [he was] the best, and also the wisest and the most upright."[1]

A great deal goes on in the *Phaedo* before that last bit. Some of the dialogue is an attempt to explain and defend the theory of the Forms. Some of it is an attempt to criticize rival attempts at metaphysics. And just before the very end, just before the death scene, there is a long myth, whose purpose seems to be to express the idea that most of us are rather mistaken about the nature of reality. (If you've read Plato's later dialogue *The Republic*, this should remind you of the allegory of the cave.)

But our concern, in any event, is going to be with some of the arguments that make up the center of the dialogue. It is there that Socrates defends his belief that he is going to live forever, that his soul is immortal. Socrates' friends and disciples are understandably worried that this may not be true. And so the heart of the dialogue consists of a series of arguments in which Socrates attempts to lay out his reasons for believing in the immortality of the soul. That's the part I want to focus on.

Even here, however, I have to be selective. To discuss all of Socrates' arguments properly would take far too many pages.[2] Instead, I am going to focus on two of the most interesting ones. (Some of the others would require even more background in Plato's metaphysics than we already have; and at least one turns on some rather technical distinctions in what philosophers nowadays call modal logic. Let me assure you, though, I don't think any of the arguments I am passing over are successful.)

The Argument from the Nature of the Forms

Okay. We've got this nice Platonic picture. Socrates has been telling his disciples that the mind can grasp the eternal Forms, but it has to free itself from the influence of the body to do that properly. And so, the philosopher—who has trained himself to disregard his bodily cravings and desires—will welcome death, because at that point he'll make the true and final break from the body.

And the obvious worry that gets raised in the dialogue at this point is this: how do we know that when the death of the body occurs the soul doesn't get destroyed as well? That's the natural worry to have. Maybe what we need to do is to separate ourselves as much as possible from the influence of our body without actually going *all the way* and breaking the connection. If you think about it like a rubber band, maybe the more we can stretch the rubber band, the better; but if you stretch too far and the rubber band snaps, that's not good, that's bad. It could be that we need the body in order to continue thinking at all. We want to free ourselves from the *distractions* of the body, but we don't want the body to *die*, because when the body dies the soul dies as well. For as we have noticed before, even if we are dualists—even if the soul is something different from the body—it could still be the case, logically speaking, that if the body gets destroyed, the soul gets destroyed as well.

And so, Socrates' friends ask him, how can we be confident that the soul will *survive* the death of the body? And more particularly, how can we be confident that the soul is immortal? That's what prompts the series of arguments.

Now, the first argument I want to consider I dub "the argument from the nature of the Forms." And the basic thought is fairly straightforward. As we have already seen, the Forms—justice itself, beauty itself, goodness itself—these things are not physical objects. Justice is not a physical object. The number three is not a physical object. Goodness itself is not a physical object. Perfect roundness is not a physical object. But Socrates thinks it follows fairly straightforwardly from this that the mind must itself be something nonphysical. For if the Forms are not physical objects, then Socrates thinks it follows they can't be grasped by something physical, like the body. Since the mind *can* grasp the Forms, it follows that the mind must itself be something nonphysical. That is, it must be a soul.

But although Socrates certainly believes all of this, that doesn't yet give us what we want. Even if it is true that the mind must be a soul—must be nonphysical—in order to grasp the nonphysical Forms, it doesn't yet follow that the soul will survive the death of the body. To get that crucial last step, we need to bring in not just the fact that the Forms are nonphysical, we also need to bring in the fact that they are *eternal*. It is the eternal nature of the Forms, Socrates thinks, that establishes the immortality of the soul.

Here, then, is the argument, spelled out a bit more fully:

(1) Forms are eternal and nonphysical.
(2) The mind can grasp the Forms.
But (3) the eternal and nonphysical can only be grasped by the
     eternal and nonphysical.
So (4) the mind must be eternal and nonphysical.
And so, in particular, (5) the mind must be nonphysical—that is,
     it must be a soul.
And (6) that soul must be eternal.

Platonic metaphysics, let us suppose, gives us the first two premises. From these it follows, of course, that the mind can grasp something eternal and nonphysical. If we then throw in premise three, that things that are eternal and nonphysical can only be grasped by something that is itself eternal and nonphysical, this will give us the main conclusion (stated in 4) that the mind must be both eternal and nonphysical. And from this of course, we get the two further subconclusions, first, that the mind must be a soul, since it is nonphysical, and finally, second, that the soul must itself be eternal, immortal.

Since we are simply granting Plato premises one and two (if only for the sake of argument), the crucial premise for our purposes is premise number three. Is it or isn't it true that those things that are eternal and nonphysical can only be grasped by something that is itself eternal and nonphysical? For it really does seem that if we give this to Plato as well, his conclusions really will follow: that which grasps the Forms, the mind, will itself be nonphysical, it will be a soul; and that soul will be immortal, since, like the Forms themselves, it will be eternal. All of that will follow from Plato's views about the Forms, *once* we give Plato premise number three.

Of course, Plato never states premise three in just those terms. But I think it is clear that he has it in mind. As Socrates puts it at one point, "The impure cannot attain the pure." Bodies are corruptible, destroyable, physical, passing (they exist for a brief period, and then they cease to exist). These impure objects cannot attain, cannot grasp, cannot have knowledge of the eternal, changeless, nonphysical Forms. "The impure cannot attain the pure."

What's more, premise three is based on a pretty familiar idea. If we were to state premise three in more contemporary language, I suppose that what Plato is saying is simply that it takes one to know one. Or to use slightly different language that Plato himself uses at various points, "Likes are known by likes."

In a nutshell, then, Plato's argument boils down to this: "What is it that we know? We know the eternal Forms. But it takes one to know one. So we must ourselves be eternal." Thus, given Plato's metaphysics (premises one and two), the conclusion that the soul is immortal follows pretty quickly, once we give Plato premise three. That's the crucial premise.

Unfortunately, as far as I can see, there's no good reason to *believe* premise three! Despite the popularity of the claim that it takes one to know one, I have to say that this claim just seems to me to be false. Consider some examples. A zoologist, say, might study cats. If it takes one to know one, it would follow that the zoologist must herself *be* a cat! Well, that's clearly false. You don't have to be feline to study the feline. Or suppose someone argued that you can't be a Canadian and study Mexicans, because it takes one to know one. That would clearly be a dumb thing to say. Of *course* the Canadians can study the Mexicans, just as the Germans can study the French. To understand truths about the French, you do not yourself need to be French; it does *not* take one to know one. Or take the fact that some doctors study dead bodies. Aha! If it takes one to know one, then to study and grasp things about corpses, you must yourself be a corpse. But that obviously isn't right either. Thus, once we start looking at examples, once we start asking whether it really does take one to know one, the answer is, at least as a general claim, that it's just not true. Normally, at least, it *doesn't* take one to know one.

Strictly speaking, that doesn't prove that premise three is false. It could still be that although normally you don't have to be like the thing that you're studying in order to study it, nonetheless, in the particular case of nonphysical and eternal objects, you *do* have to be eternal and nonphysical to study them. That is to say, it could be that even though the general claim "it takes one to know one" is false, the particular claim "eternal and nonphysical things can only be grasped by the eternal and nonphysical" is true. And it is, after all, only the particular claim that Plato needs to make his argument go through.

Fair enough. But still, all I can say is: why should we *believe* premise three? If, as I have just argued, the barrier between Xs and non-Xs can normally be crossed, so that non-Xs can study Xs, why should that barrier suddenly become uncrossable in the particular instance at hand, where we're dealing with Platonic Forms? Why couldn't it be the case that souls are *mortal* and yet, for all that, capable of grasping the eternal Forms? (For that matter, why couldn't physical bodies be capable of grasping the nonphysical, eternal Forms?) We need some reason to *believe* premise three, but as far as I can see, Plato doesn't actually give us any. Accordingly, even if we grant Plato the existence of the Forms, and even if we grant as well that the soul exists and can think about them, we haven't yet been given any good reason to believe that the soul must be *immortal*. Thus Plato's first argument—the argument from the nature of the Forms—is, I think, unsuccessful.

The Argument from Simplicity

Plato himself may well have recognized the inadequacy of that first argument, because he has Socrates go on to offer others. Or maybe Plato *didn't* recognize the shortcomings of that first argument and simply thought that he had some others that were worth mentioning as well. In any event, let's consider a rather different argument for the soul's immortality. (By the way, if Plato did recognize the inadequacies of the first argument, why did he bother offering it? Perhaps because he hoped that his readers would come to recognize the weaknesses of the argument on their own. Plato may well have intended his dialogues as a kind of teaching device, a tool to help the reader get better at doing philosophy.)

Our worry, of course—voiced repeatedly by Socrates' disciples in the *Phaedo*—is that even if there is a soul, that doesn't yet show us that the soul is immortal. Perhaps it dies with the body; perhaps it too faces destruction. In an attempt to put this concern to rest, Socrates turns to a metaphysical discussion of the *kinds* of things that can be destroyed. He thinks about examples and tries to extract a general principle from those examples. And then, armed with this principle, he tries to convince us that the soul is indestructible and thus immortal. All of this makes for a quite interesting argument. I call it "the argument from simplicity."

It is an obvious enough point that lots of things can be destroyed. Here, for example, on my desk, is a piece of paper. It can be destroyed. Indeed—I am writing this next sentence a moment later—I have just ripped it into shreds. Why was it that the sheet of paper was the sort of thing that could be destroyed? The obvious and straightforward answer is that the paper had *parts*. And in breaking it, in destroying it, I literally ripped one part from another. To destroy the piece of paper, I took its parts apart. Here's a pencil. The pencil, too, can be broken; it can be destroyed. If I do that, what am I doing? I am taking its parts apart. More generally, then, the kinds of things that can be destroyed have parts. They are composite. They are composed of their parts. A body can be destroyed because you can take a sword to it and chop it into pieces. Composite things can be destroyed. Things that have parts can be destroyed.

What kind of things *can't* be destroyed? It won't surprise you to learn that when Plato looks for an example of something that's eternal and indestructible, his mind immediately starts thinking about the Platonic Forms. Take the number three. The number three can't be destroyed! Even if a nuclear explosion took place and somehow (think of the kind of monstrous chain reaction that is always being shown in science fiction movies) everything on Earth got atomized and destroyed, the number three still wouldn't be touched. It wouldn't be fazed. It would still be true that three plus one equals four. You can't hurt the number three. Similarly, you can't alter or destroy perfect circularity. You can't destroy beauty itself. Why not? Because these things don't have any parts. That's Plato's thought. The Platonic Forms are eternal, and Plato's view is that the reason that they are eternal, changeless, and indestructible is because they are *simple*—"simple" here being a term for the metaphysical notion that they're not composed of anything. Take anything that's built up out of parts, and you could, at least in principle, worry about the parts *coming* apart—and, thus, the thing being destroyed. But for anything that's simple, it *can't* be destroyed in that way. It has no parts to *take* apart.

So the kinds of things that can be destroyed are the things with parts. And what kinds of things are those? Why, the things that can *change*. Even if something isn't destroyed, what is a sure tip-off to the fact that it is composite? The fact that it changes. Suppose I take a bar of metal and I bend it. I haven't destroyed it, but I have changed it. I'm able to change it by rearranging the relationships between the various parts. Similarly, of course, my body is constantly changing because the relationships between my arms and legs and my head and so forth are constantly changing. You rearrange the parts, and the thing changes. Putting the same thought the other way around, if it changes, it's got parts. And if it's got parts, it can—in principle, at least—be destroyed.

So we've got some nice generalizations. Things that change have parts; things with parts can be destroyed. And what *are* the kinds of things that you can change and (in principle) destroy? The familiar empirical objects that we can see: pieces of paper, bodies, pencils, bars of metal.

In contrast, on the other side, you've got things that are invisible, like the Forms. These things never change. Take the number three. Nobody sees the number three. (We can think about it, but we can't *see* it.) And the number three never changes. It was an odd number yesterday, and it will be an odd number tomorrow, and the day after that. It's not as though there is some chance that perhaps tomorrow it will be even. It is eternally an odd number. And similarly, of course, three plus one equals four today, yesterday, and forever. These facts about the number three will never change. The number three is changeless. And the same thing is true for all of the other Forms as well. They are invisible; they are eternal; they are changeless. The Forms are simple, and simple things can't be destroyed, they never change.

These are the sorts of thoughts that Socrates assembles in this stretch of the dialogue. And when you put them all together, they make for a rather interesting argument. Here's my best attempt at stating it exactly:

(1) Only composite things can be destroyed.
(2) Only changing things are composite.
(3) Invisible things don't change.
So (4) invisible things can't be destroyed.
But (5) the soul is invisible.
So (6) the soul can't be destroyed.

The first two premises say that only composite things can be destroyed, and only changing things are composite. Putting these two together, it follows that only changing things can be destroyed. Suppose we now add premise three, invisible things don't change. It follows of course that invisible things can't be destroyed, which is what we are told in four. That's the metaphysical principle that Socrates has arrived at by thinking about cases. And that's the crucial subconclusion for the overall argument, because then Socrates invites us to think about the soul. Is the soul visible or invisible? Plausibly enough, he tells us (in premise five) that the soul is *invisible*. But if invisible things can't be destroyed, and the soul is invisible, then the soul can't be destroyed. It must be immortal.

That's my best attempt at reconstructing Plato's argument from simplicity. Of course, it's not as though Plato himself spells his argument out like this, with numbered premises and conclusions and so forth, but I do think that this is fairly faithful to the kind of argument he means to put forward. In essence, the argument is that the soul is invisible, and so simple, and thus not the sort of thing that can be destroyed.

In a moment I'll turn to evaluating whether this is a *good* argument or not. But first, I have to make a confession: Socrates doesn't actually conclude his argument in quite the way I have said he does. In my statement of the argument from simplicity, the conclusion—given in (6)—is that the soul can't be destroyed. But Socrates doesn't say this. His actual conclusion is this: "And so the soul is indestructible or nearly so."

That's rather an odd qualification: "or nearly so." The conclusion that Socrates reaches from his examination of change and invisibility, compositeness and simplicity, and so on, is that "the soul is indestructible or *nearly* so."

Adding that qualification opens the door to a worry. The worry gets raised by Cebes, one of Socrates' disciples, who points out that even if we grant that the soul is *nearly* indestructible, that's not good enough to get us immortality. And he gives a very nice analogy of a man and his coats. Someone can go through many coats over the course of his life. In that sense, compared to any given coat, his body may be far more nearly indestructible. But for all that, the body isn't immortal. Eventually it too wears out. So if all we have is the conclusion that the soul is "nearly" indestructible, that it takes a whole lot more work to destroy it than it takes to destroy a body, that's still not enough to give us the *immortality* of the soul. (Perhaps the soul goes through many bodies, as a result of repeated reincarnation, but eventually it too is destroyed.)

That's the objection that Cebes raises. And one of the oddities of the dialogue is that, as far as I can see, Socrates never directly *responds* to that objection. Plato *raises* this objection, through Cebes (the character), but he never answers it. Socrates—the character Socrates—never answers the objection on Plato's behalf. Instead, he tries to defend the immortality of the soul by offering yet another argument.

It's hard to say what exactly is going on. It might be that Plato is worried that he hasn't really succeeded yet in showing that the soul really is immortal. Maybe this argument from simplicity isn't nearly as good as it needs to be, and that's why Plato eventually goes on to offer a new argument. But *I* want to say, on Plato's behalf, or at least on behalf of the argument, that Socrates should never have concluded the argument with this odd qualifying phrase, that the soul is "indestructible or nearly so." He should have simply concluded that the soul is indestructible, full stop.

After all, if we have premises one, two, and three—that only composite things can be destroyed, that only changing things are composite, and that invisible things don't change—then you are entitled to reach the subconclusion I gave above in (4)—that invisible things can't be destroyed. You don't get the more modest conclusion, "invisible things can't be destroyed or it's a whole lot harder to destroy them." No, if we've got premises one, two, and three, then we're entitled to the bold conclusion: "invisible things can't be destroyed, period." But then, if (5) is true as well, if the soul really is invisible, we're entitled to conclude with (6) that the soul can't be destroyed, *period*. Not: the soul can't be destroyed, or if it *can* be destroyed, then it's very, very hard to do so, and it takes a very, very long time. We are, rather, entitled to the bolder conclusion: that the soul can't be destroyed. Full stop, period, end of the discussion.

So despite the fact that Socrates draws this weaker conclusion, it seems to me that the argument he's offered us, if it works at all, entitles us to draw the bolder conclusion. Not that the soul is indestructible or nearly so, but that the soul is indestructible. Well, maybe Plato realized that; maybe that's the reason why he doesn't bother giving an answer to Cebes. Maybe it's an invitation to the reader to recognize that there's a better argument here than even the characters in the drama have noticed. I just don't know. I don't know what Plato had in mind.

But at any rate, our question shouldn't be, "What was Plato thinking?" but, "Is the argument any *good*?" It certainly seems that if the soul can't be destroyed it is immortal. So do we now have a sound argument for the immortality of the soul? Is the argument from simplicity a good one or not?

Let's approach that question by thinking about a different objection. This one gets raised by Simmias, another of Socrates' disciples. Simmias says that we're not entitled to conclude that the soul is indestructible (or nearly so, or whatever), because we shouldn't believe the subconclusion given in (4), that invisible things can't be destroyed. On the contrary, Simmias says, invisible things *can* be destroyed. And if that's true, then of course we no longer have an argument for the indestructibility (or near indestructibility) of the soul at all. For even if the soul *is* invisible, as premise five asserts, if, nonetheless, invisible things *can* be destroyed—contrary to what Socrates was claiming—then maybe the invisible soul can be destroyed as well.

Simmias doesn't merely assert, baldly, that invisible things can be destroyed. He offers an *example* of an invisible thing that can be destroyed: harmony. In particular, the harmony that gets produced by a stringed instrument, such as a lyre (a kind of harp). In fact, he says, this is a particularly apt example for us to think about, because some people have suggested— Simmias reports—that the mind is *like* harmony. It's as though the mind is the harmony of the body. A bit more fully, harmony is to the lyre as the mind is to the body.

I'll say more about this analogy later. But right now, at any rate, the central point is this: harmony is invisible, and yet harmony can be destroyed.

Thus, on the one hand, harmony certainly does seem to be invisible: you can't see it. And yet, at the same time, it also seems clear that harmony can be destroyed. Here's the lyre, making its melodious, harmonious sounds. But then you take an ax to the lyre, destroying it, and now the harmony's been destroyed as well. So even though it's invisible, you can destroy harmony by destroying the musical instrument on which it depends.

Now if you *accept* the analogy between harmony and the mind, then you're going to be particularly worried at this point. For if the mind is like the harmony of the body, and you can destroy harmony by destroying the instrument on which it depends, then maybe you destroy the *mind* when you destroy the body upon which the mind depends. So when the body dies the mind will die as well. Obviously enough, that's a pretty serious worry.

Still, the crucial point, right now, is that thinking about harmony provides us with a counterexample to the generalization that invisible things can't be destroyed. Harmony is invisible, yet it can be destroyed. So it seems that Socrates is *wrong* when he says that invisible things can't be destroyed. Thus even if we grant that the soul is invisible as well, it might just turn out that the soul is one of the invisible things that *can* be destroyed.

That's a great objection. It's an objection worth taking very seriously. And the oddity is, Socrates doesn't respond to it in the way that he should have, in the way that he needed to. Instead, Socrates spends some time worrying about whether the mind (or soul) *is* really like harmony. He spends a fair bit of time criticizing the analogy between harmony and the mind.

In the next section I'll ask whether Socrates' criticisms of the analogy are good ones or not. But the essential point to notice is this: even if they are good criticisms, that won't be enough to help Socrates' argument. After all, even if we were to say that the mind *isn't* very much like harmony at all, that the analogy is a poor one, what of it? The argument from simplicity will still be in trouble. For all that Simmias needs—if he is to cause problems for Socrates' argument—is the claim that harmony is invisible and harmony can be destroyed. As long as *that* is true, we can't continue to believe that invisible things can't be destroyed.

So what Socrates needs to do, if he is going to save his argument, is to say either that harmony can't be destroyed or that it isn't invisible. I'm not saying that doing this would be easy, but if he can *defend* either one of these claims—if it turns out that harmony can't really be destroyed or isn't really invisible—then we would no longer have a counterexample to the claim that the invisible can't be destroyed. And then the argument from simplicity could proceed as before.

So that's what Socrates should have done. He should have said, "You know what? Harmony is not really invisible," or maybe "It can't really be destroyed." But there's not a whiff of that, as far as I can see, in the dialogue. Socrates never says, for example, "Simmias, here is where your objection goes wrong. Harmony can't really be destroyed. So we don't really have a counterexample." Instead, he gets hung up on the question of whether harmony is, in fact, a good analogy for thinking about the nature of the mind. But as I have been explaining, even if it isn't a good analogy, even if the mind is nothing at all like harmony, that still won't save Socrates' argument, so long as harmony really is invisible, and really can be destroyed.

To reject Simmias' purported counterexample, we need to claim either that harmony isn't really invisible or that it can't really be destroyed. The latter option, I think, isn't very attractive. It does seem clear enough that if we destroy the lyre, then the harmony coming out of the lyre is destroyed as well. Accordingly, I think that if we are to have a chance of answering Simmias' objection, we'll need to focus instead on the first alternative, claiming that harmony is not, in fact, invisible. Can that claim be plausibly defended? Perhaps.

Suppose we ask the following question: when we say that "invisible things can't be destroyed," what, exactly, do we mean by "invisible"? It seems to me that there are at least three different possible interpretations of the notion of invisibility. And so, depending on which we have in mind, there are at least three different ways of interpreting Socrates' argument.

Here are the three things we might mean:

Invisible =

1. can't be seen (by the eyes)
2. can't be sensed (by any of the five senses)
3. can't be detected (by any method at all)

On the first interpretation, to say that something is invisible simply means that it can't be seen, that it is invisible to the eyes. On the second interpretation, to say that something is invisible means that it can't be sensed at all, regardless of which of the five senses is used. And on the third interpretation, to say that something is invisible means that there is no way to detect it at all, no matter how we try.

Let's be clear about how these meanings differ. Some things (such as colors) can be seen, and others (such as smells) cannot. But some things that can't be seen—and thus are invisible in the first sense of the word—can still be sensed in some other way. So, for example, although the smell of coffee can't be seen, it can still be sensed. More generally, then, smells are invisible in the first sense of the term, but they are not invisible in the second. Similarly, sounds can't be seen, and so they're invisible in the first sense of the word; but for all that, of course, they too can be sensed—we can hear them—so they are not invisible in the second sense of the term either. In contrast, individual radioactive atoms are invisible even in the second sense: we can't see them, or taste them, or hear them, and so on. But for all that, we can *detect* them—using a Geiger counter, which gives off a click when such an atom decays—and so they are not invisible in the third sense of the term. But the number seventeen, as I suppose, is invisible, even in this broadest sense of the term. It can't be detected in any way at all: it leaves no causal trail behind, by which we might detect its existence.

Without getting hung up, then, on what, precisely, the English word "invisible" means, let's just notice that there is a difference between saying "it can't be seen through the eyes," "it can't be observed through *any* of the five senses," and "it can't be detected at all." And what we have to ask ourselves is this: when Socrates puts his argument forward, which of these different possible meanings did he have in mind?

The most natural way to start is by interpreting Socrates in terms of the first possible meaning. On this first interpretation, then, when Socrates says, "Invisible things don't change" (in premise three), what he means is that things that you can't see don't change. If we then continue to interpret the term "invisible" in the same way in line four, then what Socrates is arguing is that "If you can't see it with your eyes, it can't be destroyed."

The trouble with this interpretation of the argument is that harmony shows that that's just not so. Harmony is indeed invisible in the first sense of the term. You cannot see it with your eyes. But for all that, it can be destroyed. So if what Socrates means by invisibility is the first notion—something that can't be seen with your eyes—then the argument's not any good. Harmony is a pretty compelling counterexample.

But maybe that's not what Socrates *means* by invisible. Instead of the first meaning, perhaps he has the second meaning in mind. When he talks about the soul being invisible, and about invisible things being indestructible, maybe he means things that can't be observed through *any* of your five senses. In point of fact, I think that this *is* what he meant. Socrates has been talking about the differences between visible things—like trees, stones, horses, and clothes—and invisible things, like the Forms. And then he says, "These latter [trees, horses, and the like] you could touch and see and perceive with the other senses, but those that always remain the same [the Forms] can only be grasped by the reasoning power of the mind. They are not seen but are invisible." So I think it's pretty clear that when Socrates starts talking about what's visible versus invisible, he doesn't mean to limit himself to vision; he means to be talking about all of the five senses. So when he says, "Invisible things can't be destroyed," he means the things that you can't see *or* touch or hear or smell or taste. *Those* are the things that can't be destroyed.

Notice, however, that if *that's* the way we interpret his argument, then harmony no longer works as a counterexample. Harmony counted as invisible when we meant definition number one, something that can't be seen. But it's not invisible if we mean definition number two, something that can't be sensed. For harmony *can* be sensed—through the ears—in which case it's not really a counterexample to the relevant claim after all. And so, when Simmias says that harmony is an example of something invisible that that can be destroyed, what Socrates *should* have said is that harmony is not in fact invisible in the relevant sense of invisible. It may not be visible to the eyes, but for all that, it *can* be sensed. So for all we know, it could indeed be true that invisible things—in the relevant sense of invisible—are indestructible.

And then Socrates could have continued by pointing out that the soul *is* invisible in this sense of the term. You don't see the soul; you don't taste the soul; you don't touch it, hear it, or smell it. So if we understand the argument in terms of the second possible interpretation of "invisible," it looks as though the argument still goes through. Simmias' counterexample fails. Harmony is not invisible in the relevant sense, and so it could still be true that invisible things can't be destroyed. And since the soul is invisible in that sense of the term, it might still follow that the soul can't be destroyed.

Unfortunately for Plato, however, even if Simmias' particular counterexample—harmony—fails, that doesn't yet mean that we should accept the argument from simplicity. Because even if Simmias' own attempt at a counterexample is unsuccessful, there might still be others that are more worrisome. Suppose, for example, that we think not about harmony but about radio waves. Radio waves, I take it, are invisible in the second sense of the term. They cannot be sensed. You don't see a radio wave. You can't touch a radio wave; you can't smell or taste a radio wave. And interestingly enough, you can't even *hear* radio waves. But of course, for all that, they can be destroyed. So even if we grant that what Socrates meant by invisible was "cannot be sensed," we still have to say, with Simmias, "You know, premise

four is just not true. Some invisible things can be destroyed." Radio waves
can be destroyed even though they're invisible in the relevant way.

Of course, radio waves are not very much like the Forms, and it is clear
that the particular invisible things that Socrates has in mind are the Forms.
But that observation—true as it may be—is not enough to save Socrates' argument. Radio waves *are* invisible, just as the Forms are. But unlike the Forms,
they can be destroyed. And that's precisely why we still have to worry about
the soul. Apparently, some invisible things (the Forms) can't be destroyed,
but others (radio waves) can be. But if that's right, then even when we point
out that the soul, too, is invisible, we won't have any good reason to conclude
that it is one of the invisible things that cannot be destroyed. The argument
for the immortality of the soul will be undermined.

I do hope it is obvious that my purpose here is not to say, "Oh, you idiot,
Plato! Why didn't you think of radio waves?" Our question is not whether
Plato was overlooking something that he should have thought of. (I don't
think he should have thought of radio waves!) Rather, our question is, does
Plato's argument work or not? Is it *true* that invisible things can't be destroyed? And it seems to me that some things that are invisible in the relevant sense *can* be destroyed. Radio waves are an example of that. So even
though the soul is also invisible in the relevant sense, maybe it can be destroyed as well.

The only answer I can imagine Plato giving at this point is to say,
"Look, I need a different definition of invisible. Don't use definition number two, use definition number three. Don't talk about what we can sense;
talk about what we can detect." Suppose Plato did say that. Then we would
have to admit that for all we have seen so far, it might indeed be true that
things that are invisible in the relevant sense—the third sense—are indestructible.

After all, radio waves are *not* invisible in this third sense of the term.
They *can* be detected. All you have to do is turn on a radio! If a radio wave
is passing by, and you turn on your radio and properly tune it, you will detect it! The radio will turn the radio wave into various sounds that we can
hear. Thus, we can detect radio waves—on the basis of their effects on radios, among other things.

In short, even though radio waves can be destroyed, this will have no
bearing on Socrates' argument, once we decide that the relevant sense of
invisibility is the third sense, not the second. For all we know so far, it might
indeed be true that things that are invisible in this third sense are indestructible. Indeed, thinking about the Forms may well support our endorsement

of this claim. The Forms, after all, cannot be detected in any way at all. There is no Geiger counter to tell you that the number seventeen is nearby, or even that it exists. The Forms leave no causal traces by which we may detect their presence. And as we have already several times noted, the Forms are indestructible. So perhaps we really should agree that invisible things—in the third sense—cannot be destroyed.

So if Plato were to adopt the third definition of invisibility— undetectability—perhaps he would still be entitled to embrace claim (4). Perhaps things that are invisible in *this* sense really *are* indestructible. At the very least, I don't myself have any further counterexamples to offer.

But if this is the relevant sense of invisibility, then it is no longer clear to me that premise *five* is true. *Is* the soul invisible? It certainly was, if by invisibility we meant can't be seen (the first definition). And it was, if by in- visibility we meant can't be tasted, or touched or heard, and so on (the sec- ond definition). But is it still invisible, if what we mean by invisible is "can't be detected"? Is it *true* that the soul can't be detected?

I've got to say, that doesn't seem right to me. Once we interpret invis- ibility in this way—as undetectability—then I think it turns out that the soul is *not* invisible in the relevant sense; I think that the soul *can* be de- tected, in something like the way that radio waves can be detected. If you hook a radio wave up with a radio, you can tell the radio wave is there be- cause of what the radio is doing: giving off sounds. Similarly, then, if you hook a soul up to a body, you can tell the soul is there by what the *body* is doing: discussing philosophy with you. You detect the presence of your friend's soul through its effects on your friend's body.

But that means the soul isn't really undetectable. And if the soul's not really undetectable, it's not really invisible in the relevant sense. And if it's not really invisible (in that sense), then even if there is a kind of invisibility, such that things that are invisible in that sense can't be destroyed, the soul's simply not invisible in that sense. Once again, then, we are forced to con- clude that Plato's argument for the immortality of the soul is unsuccessful.

In effect, the problem is this. There are notions of invisibility (the first two definitions) where it really does seem plausible to claim that the soul is invisible. But as we have seen, things that are invisible in these senses of the term can still be destroyed. And there is a notion of invisibility (the last) where it doesn't seem implausible to claim that invisible things (in this sense) cannot be destroyed. But as it turns out, the soul is not invisible in this particular sense. So regardless of how we understand the relevant no- tion of invisibility, the argument from simplicity is unsuccessful.

As it happens, there are still other problems that might be raised for this argument. Plato is trying to convince us that the soul is invisible, because he thinks this means it can't be destroyed. But why does he believe that? He believes it because he thinks there are deep metaphysical connections between being invisible, being changeless, being simple, and being indestructible. I've been arguing that we should be suspicious of attempts to move from the first part of this chain (the soul's invisibility) to the last (its indestructibility). But in point of fact, there are more particular questions that might be raised about several of the intervening links as well.

For example, Plato apparently wants us to believe that the soul is changeless. After all, its invisibility is presumably supposed to indicate its changelessness, which in turn should indicate its simplicity. But it is far from obvious that the soul really *is* changeless. In fact, if you think about it, on the face of it at least, the soul does indeed change. On some days, after all, you believe that it's cold. On others, you believe that it's hot. On one day, you believe that Alcibiades is a nice person; on the next, you decide he's not. Today you want to learn to play the piano; tomorrow you may give up on that goal. Your beliefs, your goals, your intentions, your desires—all of these things are constantly changing. And so, at least on the face of it, it looks as though we might well want to say the soul is changing as well (provided, of course, that we want to talk about souls at all), in terms of what thoughts and beliefs it's housing.

So we should have been skeptical right away, when the argument invites us to conclude, on the basis of the invisibility of the soul, that it is changeless. It certainly doesn't *seem* to be changeless. Furthermore, we should be, or at least we might well be, skeptical of the claim that the soul is *simple*. Indeed, Plato himself, in other dialogues, argues *against* the simplicity of the soul. (Of course, that doesn't mean that he's right in the other dialogues, but at least it suggests that we shouldn't be too quick to *accept* the simplicity of the soul.) In *The Republic*, famously, Plato goes on to argue that the soul has at least three different parts. There's a rational part that's in charge of reasoning; there's a spirited part that's like the will; and there's a part that has to do with appetite (desires for food, drink, sex, and what have you). Thus Plato elsewhere argues that the soul is not simple at all. So perhaps it shouldn't shock us that the argument that he's sketching in the *Phaedo* for the simplicity of the soul—based on the supposed changeless, invisible nature of the soul—doesn't really succeed after all.

Finally, we might well wonder whether it is really true that if Plato *could* establish the simplicity of the soul, it would follow that the soul was indestructible. To be sure, in introducing the argument from simplicity, I tried to show why this was a plausible enough idea. If the soul doesn't have parts, then you obviously can't destroy it by taking it *apart*. Nonetheless, I now want to register the thought that, despite this point, it isn't actually obvious that simples cannot be destroyed.

It is, of course, obvious that simples can't be destroyed by the particular method of destruction we have just mentioned—taking things apart. Since simples don't have parts, you can't take them apart. But for all that, it still seems conceptually possible for a simple to be destroyed in the following sense: it goes out of existence. After all, where did the simples come from in the first place? From a logical point of view, at least, it seems as though there's no difficulty in imagining that at one point a given simple didn't exist, and then at the next point it just popped into existence. At the beginning of Genesis, God says, "Let there be light." So maybe he also says, "Let there be simples." At a given moment, the simples weren't there; the next moment, they were. That seems possible. But if so, then maybe after a while, God gets tired of the simples. Maybe God says, "Let the simples no longer exist." At a given moment, there they were; and then, the next moment, they no longer exist.

That seems like a coherent possibility as well. Suppose it is. Then even if we *agree* that the soul is simple—even if we grant everything else in Plato's argument up to this point and agree that the soul really is simple—it still won't follow that it's immortal. We'll still have to worry about the possibility that the simple soul might simply pop out of existence at a given point, perhaps the very point when the body gets destroyed. Simplicity alone doesn't guarantee immortality. So here too, I think, we have reason to conclude that Plato's argument for the immortality of the soul does not succeed.

Mind as the Harmony of the Body

Before we leave the *Phaedo*, there's a piece of unfinished business. Recall Simmias' suggestion that the soul is like the harmony of the body. We've already examined at some length the question of whether harmony provides an adequate counterexample to Socrates' argument (since harmony is invisible, yet can be destroyed). But we haven't yet considered the analogy in its own right. Is it *plausible* to think about the mind in this way? What would it *mean* to say that the soul (or perhaps, less contentiously, the mind) is like the harmony of the body?

My own view is that this is a very interesting analogy indeed. In fact, I think we should think of it as a very early attempt to describe something like the *physicalist* conception of the mind. Just as harmony is something that gets produced by a well-tuned instrument, the soul or the mind is something that gets produced by a well-tuned body. And that, as I say, is not a bad account of how the physicalist thinks about the mind. After all, according to the physicalist, talk about the mind is just a way of talking about the body. Or, more carefully, it's a way of talking about certain things that the body can do when it's functioning properly—when it's well-tuned, as we might put it. And so, in a way, according to the physicalist, the mind is indeed something *like* harmony. Just as the production of harmonious, melodious sounds is one of the things that a lyre can do when it's functioning properly, just so—according to the physicalist—the production of thought and feelings and other mental states is one of the things that a human *body* can do, when it too is functioning properly. In short, the mind is like the harmony of the body.

So the harmony analogy, I think, is an attempt—and not a bad attempt—at gesturing toward the way that physicalists think about the mind. Of course, when I first tried to get you to grasp the physicalist account of the mind, I used examples concerning computers and robots and the like. But it's hardly surprising that *Plato* doesn't use those kinds of analogies. He doesn't have computers; he doesn't have robots. Still, he has physical objects that can do things, and the ability to do those things depends on the proper functioning of the given physical object. Thus, I think that Plato can see that there's an important alternative to his dualism. He can see that you could be a physicalist and say that the mind is dependent on the body, that the mind is just a way of talking about what the body can do when it's working properly. It's dependent in just the same way that—well, for example, harmony is dependent upon the physical instrument.

So I think that what Plato is offering us here is a rather impressive attempt to discuss the physicalist alternative to his own dualism. Accordingly, I want to end our discussion of the *Phaedo* by taking a quick look at his objections to that way of thinking about the mind. As I have already remarked, Socrates spends a fair bit of time *criticizing* the harmony analogy. If he can convince us that the soul is *not* like the harmony of the body, then maybe that will give us reason to doubt the physicalist's view. After all, even if Plato's arguments for the immortality of the soul are unsuccessful, he might still have some good arguments against the alternative, physicalist position.

But in thinking about these objections, it's important to bear in mind that the harmony analogy is only meant as just that—that is, as an *analogy*. The claim isn't, or at least it shouldn't be, that the mind literally *is* harmony. The idea, rather, is that the mind is *like* harmony. Just as a well-tuned, properly functioning instrument can produce melody and harmony, a well-tuned, properly functioning body can produce mental activity. *That's* the suggestion. And so even if it turns out that there are some ways in which the mind isn't *exactly* like harmony, that won't yet show us that the physicalist view is wrong.

So let's take a look at Plato's objections. The first one is this. Socrates points out that harmony clearly cannot exist before the existence of the instrument on which it depends. That's clearly correct: the melodiousness of the lyre can't exist prior to the physical construction of the lyre. And so, if mind were the sort of thing that was produced by the proper functioning of the physical body—as the physicalist claims—then pretty obviously the mind could not exist prior to the creation of the physical body. However, in an earlier part of the dialogue (that we didn't discuss), Socrates has already argued that the soul *does* exist prior to the existence of the body. If that's right, if the soul really does exist before the body, then the mind obviously can't be like harmony. Physicalism has clearly got to be false.

Obviously enough, this first objection crucially depends on the claim that the soul exists before the body does. And in fairness to Plato, I have to admit that we haven't looked at that argument, and so I haven't shown you where I think it goes wrong. Nonetheless, I will have to content myself with telling you that I do not think that the earlier argument is successful: I don't think that Plato does give us compelling reason to believe the soul exists before birth. Accordingly, this first objection is not one that I think that we need to dwell upon.

In a second objection, Socrates points out that harmony can vary. An instrument can be harmonious to varying degrees, and in different ways. But it doesn't seem as though *souls* come in degrees. Either you've got a soul, or you don't. Either you have a mind, or you don't. And if that's right, then whatever the mind is, it's not quite like harmony.

But I'm not so sure we should agree that the mind can't come in degrees. At the very least, it does seem as though the various aspects of the mental can come in different kinds and different degrees. We can have varying degrees of intelligence, for example, or varying degrees of creativity; varying degrees of reasonableness, or varying degrees of ability to communicate. So just as we can say that a well-functioning lyre can produce different kinds of harmony, and be harmonious to varying degrees, similarly, I think, we can say that a well-functioning body can produce different types of mental activities, and display those activities to varying degrees. So the analogy still seems to me to be a good one, and this second objection doesn't seem to me very compelling.

In his third objection, Socrates points out that the soul can be good or it can be wicked. Now when the soul is good, when you have someone who is virtuous, we might speak of her as having a harmonious soul. Yet if the soul were to the body like harmony is to the instrument and the soul can be harmonious, it would seem as though we'd have to be able to talk about harmony being harmonious. That is, if the soul is like the harmony of the body, then just as we can talk about the harmony of the soul, we'd have to be able to talk about the harmony of the harmony. But we *don't* talk about the harmony of the harmony.

I'm not quite sure what to make of this objection. Perhaps this is a point where it would be good to remind ourselves of the fact that the suggestion was never that the soul (or mind) just literally *is* harmony. It's just supposed to be *similar* to harmony, in certain ways. In particular, says the physicalist, the mind is similar to harmony in that both get produced by the appropriate well-functioning physical object. We can accept this idea, embracing the analogy between harmony and the mind, without having to say that *everything* that's true of the mind is true of harmony and everything that's true of harmony is true of the mind.

Still, I think that there's a bit more that we can say in response to this objection. Just as it is true that we can talk about minds or souls as being good or wicked, we can talk about different *kinds* of harmony. Certain harmonies are sweeter than others; some of them are more jarring and atonal or discordant. Although we might not normally talk about how harmonious the harmony is, it does seem as though harmonies can come in different sorts and different kinds. But if that's right, then it turns out we really do have a point of analogy to the mind here after all. Both harmony and the mind can come in different sorts and different kinds. So I think this third objection isn't really compelling either.

Finally, Socrates raises one more objection. He points out that the soul is capable of directing the body—of bossing it around—and, indeed, of *opposing* the body. To give a familiar example, your body might want to eat a piece of chocolate cake, but your soul can disagree, saying, "No, no. You're on a diet. Don't eat it!" Your soul can *oppose* your body. But if the soul was just the harmony of the body, how could it possibly do that? After all, Socrates argues, the harmoniousness of the lyre can't affect what the lyre itself does. All of the causal direction is one way, as we might put it. In the case of the lyre, it is the physical state of the lyre that causes the harmony to be the way it is; but the harmoniousness of the lyre doesn't ever change or alter or direct the lyre itself. In contrast, not only can the body affect the soul, the soul can affect the body. So that suggests that the relation between mind and body can't really be like that between harmony and the lyre after all.

I think that's a pretty interesting objection. Since we do think that the mind can affect the body, how can the physicalist view possibly be correct? If talk about the mind is just a way of talking about what the body can do, how can the abilities of the body affect the body itself?

As I say, it's an interesting objection. But I think it can be answered. The physicalist should say that when we talk about the soul or mind affecting the body, what's really going on is that certain physical parts of the body— the parts that underwrite the proper mental functioning of the body—are altering *other* parts of the body.

Look at it this way. Right now, I'm typing. I'm telling my body to wiggle my fingers on the keyboard in various ways. My mind is giving instructions to my body. How does that happen on the physicalist view? Roughly, like this: when my mind gives those instructions ("wiggle my fingers"), that's just one part of my body, my brain, giving instructions to *another* part of my body, the muscles in my fingers. So, when we talk about the mind altering the body, strictly speaking what's going on is that one part of the body is affecting another part.

Can we have something like that with a lyre? Maybe not. Maybe a lyre's just too simple a machine to have one part of it affect another part of it in that way. Even if that were true, of course, that wouldn't give us reason to reject the physicalist conception. It would just give us reason to think the lyre is not *very* much like the mind and the body. Thinking about the lyre and harmony is just the beginning of a physicalist picture, not the whole picture.

Still, even if we think about the lyre and harmony, I think we can see something analogous. Suppose I pluck a string on my lyre, producing a certain note. As we know, the vibrations of one string can set other strings vibrating as well (these are the overtones). And so, suddenly, what's happening in one part of the lyre affects what's going on in other parts; one set of vibrations results in *different* vibrations. Admittedly, that won't be a precise analogy to what happens when the mind directs the body. But it does suggest that the analogy may indeed hold, at least in rough terms, even here.

I conclude, accordingly, that Plato's various objections to the harmony analogy are unsuccessful. For all that he has shown, the mind may indeed be like harmony, just as the physicalist claims.

Nonetheless, I want to give Plato a lot of credit for taking the physicalist view seriously enough to try to criticize it. Given that, when he was writing, there weren't the kind of complicated thinking machines that we've got nowadays, it's certainly no criticism of Plato that he used simple machines like musical instruments to try to think about what a physicalist picture would look like. Indeed, it is a sign of Plato's brilliance that he saw the need to *argue* against the physicalist alternative at a time when no one could do anything more than merely gesture vaguely in the direction of an adequate physicalist account. So I want to give him credit. But at the same time, I also want to suggest that the various objections that Plato raises against the physicalist position are unsuccessful. At the end of the day, it seems to me, Plato hasn't given us sufficient reason to abandon physicalism.

CHAPTER 6
Personal Identity

Plato offered us a series of arguments for the immortality of the soul. But I have claimed that although some of these arguments are worth taking seriously, none of them are successful. And I hardly need remind you that our discussion of Plato came on the heels of two previous chapters in which I argued that attempts to establish the very *existence* of an immaterial soul were unsuccessful as well. As far as I can see, then, the various arguments that might be offered for the existence of an immaterial soul, let alone an immortal soul, simply don't succeed.

It's not that the *idea* of a soul is in any way silly; it certainly isn't that dualism isn't worth considering. It's just that when we ask ourselves, "Do we have any good reason to believe in an immaterial soul?" and then actually try to spell out what those reasons might be—we find, as we look more carefully, that the arguments are not very compelling.

So I'm prepared to conclude that there *are* no souls. There simply isn't any good reason to believe in them. Or perhaps I should say, somewhat more guardedly, there isn't good *enough* reason to believe in them. Either way, I conclude that there are none.

At any rate, that is the position that I'm going to be assuming for the rest of this book. I'm going to have us continue to think about death, but now think about death from the physicalist perspective. We're going to think about death given the assumption that the body is all there is, that talk about the mind is just a way of talking about the ability of the body to engage in certain special mental activities. There are no *extra* things beyond the body, no immaterial souls.

Disproving Souls?

It wouldn't be unreasonable at this point to accuse me of having a double standard, one for dualists, and another for physicalists. After all, think about what I've done. I've put the entire burden of proof on those who *believe* in souls. I've told the dualist, "Give me some reason to believe your position." And I've said that the arguments on behalf of dualism aren't very convincing. But in fairness, then, don't I now need to do the same thing to the physicalist? Shouldn't I turn to the physicalist and say, "Give me some reason to believe that *physicalism* is true"? Since I asked the dualist to give me reasons to believe in the existence of souls, and then complained when those reasons turned out to be not very compelling ones, don't I also need to turn to the physicalist and ask him to give me reasons *not* to believe in souls? Shouldn't I demand that the physicalist prove that souls *don't* exist? Isn't that what fairness to both sides requires?

So let's pause and ask ourselves, how do you go about proving that something doesn't exist? And for that matter, when do you *need* to prove that something doesn't exist? When we have examples of things whose existence we don't believe in, how do we decide when we're justified in *disbelieving* them?

Take something like dragons. I am going to assume that you, like me, don't believe in the existence of dragons. Of course, there could have been dragons—they're not logically impossible. It's just that we happen to believe that there aren't any. But don't you need to *disprove* the existence of dragons, before you continue on your way, not believing in them? Yet how could you possibly do that? How can you (or anyone) *prove* that there aren't any dragons?

Or take the Greek gods. I imagine that nowadays nobody believes in the existence of Zeus. So don't we have an obligation to prove that Zeus doesn't exist? But how could you do that? How could anyone *disprove* the existence of Zeus?

Unsurprisingly, perhaps, I don't actually think that you *do* have an obligation to disprove the existence of these things. Of course, that doesn't mean you don't have any intellectual obligations here at all. We just have to be very careful about stating what the intellectual obligations come to. Take the case of dragons. What do we need to do here, to justify one's skepticism

about dragons? The most important thing you need to do, I think, is to re-
fute all of the arguments that might be offered on *behalf* of dragons.

My son's got a book about dragons with some very nice photographs
and other pictures. So, one of the things I need to do in order to justify my
skepticism about dragons is to "explain away" the photographs and drawings. I need to explain why it is that we have pictures of dragons, even though
there really aren't any. It's not a particularly difficult job. Some of the pictures are just drawings, after all, and it is a familiar point that people often
draw things out of their imagination. But even the "photographs" are easily
explained. Nowadays, with computer-generated graphics and photo-altering
software, it is easy to make pictures that look just like a photograph, even
though the things *in* the photographs don't really exist.

Or take unicorns. How do I prove there aren't any unicorns? Well, I
look at the various reported sightings of unicorns and I try to explain them
away. I might offer some historical conjectures about how the belief in unicorns first arose. ("Think about the first time Europeans saw a rhinoceros.
Perhaps it looked like a horse with a big horn. And maybe that's where the
various reports of the unicorn came from.") I examine—or read reports by
experts who have examined—the various "unicorn horns" that have been
found in various collections. Unsurprisingly, they always turn out to be
horns from other sorts of animals (narwhal horns, and so forth). In short,
you look at each bit of evidence that gets offered on behalf of the unicorn
and you debunk it. You explain why it's not compelling.

And when you're done, you're entitled to say, "You know, as far as I
can tell, there aren't any unicorns. As far as I can tell, there aren't any dragons." It's not as though you've got some obligation to look in every single
cave anywhere on the surface of the Earth and say, for example, "Nope. No
dragons in there, no dragons in there, no dragons in there." You are pretty
much justified in being skeptical about the existence of dragons once you've
undermined the arguments *for* dragons.

Now, there *might* be something more that you could do. In at least
some cases, you can go on to argue that the very idea of the kind of thing
you're talking about is impossible. Take the example of dragons, once again.
It's not just that there are no good reasons to believe in dragons. Arguably,
the very idea of a dragon may be scientifically incoherent. After all, dragons
are supposed to breathe fire. So does that mean that they've got fire in their
belly? But how does the fire continue to exist in their belly in the absence of
oxygen? And why isn't the fire in the belly busy burning and destroying the

membranes of the stomach? You could, I suppose, try to prove that dragons were scientifically impossible. And if you did, then you'd have an extra reason to not believe in them.

But it's not as though you *have* to prove that something's impossible to be justified in not believing in it. I don't think unicorns are impossible. I just don't think there are any. Surely, there could be horses with a single long horn growing out of their forehead. There just aren't any.

Armed with these ideas, let's come back to the discussion of souls. Do I, as a physicalist who does not believe in the existence of souls—immaterial entities above and beyond the body—do I need to *disprove* the existence of souls? ("Well, there's no soul here, no soul there.") No. What I need to do is to look at the arguments that get offered *for* the existence of a soul and rebut them—explain why those arguments are not compelling. I don't need to prove that souls are *impossible*. I just need to undermine the case *for* souls. If there's no good reason to believe in souls, that actually constitutes a reason to believe that there *are* no souls.

If you want to, you could go on and try to prove that souls are impossible, in the same way that maybe dragons are impossible. But speaking personally, I don't find such impossibility claims especially persuasive. I don't *believe* in the existence of souls, but that doesn't mean that I find the idea of an immaterial entity like the soul impossible.

Of course, someone might argue that it violates science as we know it, perhaps physics in particular, to posit the existence of something immaterial. So isn't there good scientific reason to deny the existence of souls? But science is constantly coming around to believe in entities or properties that it didn't believe in previously. Maybe it just hasn't gotten around to believing in souls yet. Alternatively, if current science rules out the possibility of souls, maybe we should just say, "So much the worse for current science."

So I'm not somebody who wants to say that we can *disprove* the existence of souls. Indeed, I don't think that we *can* disprove their reality. At any rate, I certainly don't think the idea of a soul is in any way incoherent. To be sure, there are philosophers who have thought that. But I'm not one of them.

But the crucial point is this: I don't think I need to disprove the existence of a soul to be justified in not believing in them. Unicorns aren't impossible, but for all that, I'm justified in thinking there aren't any. Why? Because all the evidence for unicorns just doesn't add up to a very convincing case. Similarly, then, *souls* are not impossible, but for all that, I think

I'm justified in believing there aren't any. Why? Because when you look at the various arguments that have been offered to try to convince us of the existence of souls, those arguments just aren't very compelling. Or so it seems to me.

Accordingly, from this point on out, I'll assume that we are justified in accepting the physicalist view. I will assume that the physicalist view is the *correct* one. Of course, that doesn't mean that we are going to stop discussing souls altogether. I will, from time to time, stop and ask how a dualist might think about some issue or the other. But typically, at any rate, when I do this, my goal will be to better understand the physicalist's alternative perspective. Thus, as we turn to our various questions about death, our primary concern will be with asking how to best understand these different issues from the physicalist's point of view.

That is all well and good, I suppose, if I have convinced you of the truth of physicalism (or you were already inclined to accept it). But if you do still believe in souls, what then? I suppose that you will have to take much of the discussion that follows as a sort of sprawling subjunctive conditional: if there *were* no souls, then here's what we would have to say about death. In short, if you haven't yet become convinced of the truth of physicalism, so be it. I've given it my best shot. But I do hope that you will at least find it of more than passing interest to see what we would need to say about death if we *were* to decide—with the physicalist—that people are basically just bodies.

Personal Identity

You will recall that at the very start of this book I suggested that if we want to think properly about the question of whether I could survive my death, there were two things we needed to get clear on. First, we need to know: what *am* I? What are my parts? Am I just a body? Or am I, instead, a combination of physical body and immaterial soul? (Or perhaps *just* a soul?—albeit one associated with a particular body.) Having looked at that question, we are now going to turn to the second basic question: what does it take to *survive*? What is it for a thing like *that*—a thing like *me*—to continue to exist? And in particular, of course, given our special concern with death, we'll want to know: what would it be for a thing like me to survive the death of my body? Can it even make *sense* to talk about a person surviving the death of his body?

You might reasonably think that the answer to that last question must be no. At least, it may seem that it must be no if we are physicalists. For if I am just my body, doesn't it follow trivially that the idea of my surviving the death of my body is an incoherent one?

As I say, this seems like a reasonable enough conclusion. But in fact, as we shall see, matters are significantly more complicated than they may at first appear. I don't think it at all obvious what the best answer to our question should be.

In any event, before we try to address the particular question of whether my surviving the death of my body is so much as a coherent possibility, I think we should first try to get clear about a much more basic question: what is it for me to survive *at all*? What is it for me to *continue* to exist?

Consider this simple example. Here I am, today—Thursday—sitting at my desk, typing these words. And no doubt, *somebody* is going to be here, at my desk, typing even more words, come Monday. The question about survival can be asked even about this very simple case. Is the person who will be sitting here typing words on Monday the very same person as the person who is sitting here now, typing the words you are reading this moment? Will the person who is typing now survive the weekend?

I certainly *expect* to survive the weekend. But what *is* it to survive a weekend? What does survival *consist* in?

We do, of course, already have the beginnings of an answer. For me to survive until Monday, presumably, is for there to be somebody, some person, alive on Monday, and—here's the crucial part—for that person on Monday to be the very *same* person as the person typing these words today, on Thursday. After all, if I were to be killed in a plane accident this weekend and someone else took over writing my book for me on Monday, there would be *somebody* alive writing words at my desk on Monday. But, of course, that wouldn't be *me*. So the question we want to get clear on is this: what *is* it for somebody on Monday to be the *same* person as the person sitting here typing on Thursday?

We can ask the question more grandly, about larger expanses of time. Suppose there's somebody alive forty-odd years from now, in the year 2055. Could that be me? To ask whether I will survive until 2055 is to ask whether that person who will be alive in 2055 is the very *same* person as the person who's sitting here now, typing these words. But what *is* it for somebody in the future to be the very same person as this person who's here now today? That is what we need to get clear on.

Philosophers call this the problem of personal identity, since it asks what it is to be the very same person (the numerically identical person) at two different times. What we want to get clear on, then, is the nature of personal identity across time.

But in thinking about this question, it's important not to make a certain tempting mistake. You may find yourself tempted to say, "Look, the person who was typing the book on Thursday had at least a fair bit of his hair. He had a beard. But let's suppose that the person alive in 2055 is bald and bent over, and has no beard. So how could they be the *same* person? One's got hair, one doesn't. One's got a beard, one doesn't. One stands straight, one's crooked. It just can't be the *same* person."

That's the mistake that it's important for us to avoid making. It really *could* be me, alive, in 2055, even if "he" is bald, while I am not. It's a mistake to think otherwise.

But it is a very tempting mistake, and it is easy to get confused about this point. So I want to consider the issue rather carefully. I want to start by considering some cases involving identity where we're not likely to be particularly puzzled about what to say. Indeed, I'm going to start with some examples that don't even involve people—or, for that matter, time—at all. Once we have worked our way through these easy cases, we can make our way back to more complicated cases, cases that do involve both people and time.

Suppose, then, that you and I are walking along and we see a train. (See Figure 6.1.) As we are walking, getting closer to the train, I point to the caboose (imagine that we are approaching from the left) and I say, "Look at that train." And we're walking along, we're walking along, we're walking along. We come to the end of the train and I point to the locomotive and I say, "Wow! Look how long that train is! That's the very same train I pointed to five minutes ago. We've been walking along it all this time."

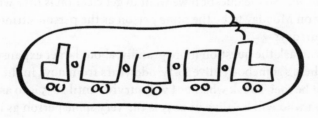

Fig. 6.1

Now, imagine that you reply, "This isn't the *same* train as the train we pointed to five minutes ago. After all, right now what you're pointing to is a locomotive, whereas five minutes ago what you pointed to was a caboose. A caboose isn't the same thing as a locomotive. How could you possibly say it's the same thing? Who could possibly make a mistake like that? The locomotive has got smoke coming out of it, the caboose doesn't, and so forth and so on. There are a lot of differences between the two. How could you make such a silly mistake?"

Of course, you wouldn't ever actually say anything as stupid as this, but imagine that you did. Then what I would want to point out to you, of course, is that it was actually you, not me, who was making a mistake. I would agree with you, obviously, that a locomotive is not the same thing as a caboose. But I wasn't claiming that it was. Rather, initially, when we started our walk, I pointed to a caboose, but by pointing to the caboose, I picked out a *train*. I said, "Look at that train." And what I was referring to wasn't just the caboose, but the whole, long, extended-through-space object, the train, of which the caboose was just a part. And now, at the *end* of our walk, when I point to the locomotive and say, "Look at that train," by pointing to the locomotive I am once again picking out a train, an entire train—a long, extended-through-space object—of which the locomotive is just a part. So when I say, "This train that I'm pointing to now is the very same train as the train I pointed to five minutes ago," I'm not saying something that is certainly and obviously false. In particular, I'm not saying that the locomotive is the same thing as the caboose. Rather, what I'm saying is that the entire extended-through-space train that I'm pointing out now is the same train as the entire extended-through-space train that I picked out five minutes ago. And that claim, far from being false, is true.

Now, as I say, none of us would ever actually make that mistake. But it's a mildly tempting mistake, I suppose, if you're not being careful. And that same mistake, in any event, can seem much more attractive when we start thinking about cases of identity across time. But let's continue with the train for a bit longer.

Suppose, as we're taking our walk, part of the train isn't visible. There's a large warehouse that's blocking the view. (See Figure 6.2.) We're walking along the way. We see a caboose. I say, "Ha! There's a train." Then for a while we're walking, but we don't see anything because all you can see is the warehouse. And then, after we get past the warehouse (a very long warehouse), I see a locomotive and I say, "Hey look. There's a train." And I ask you, "Do you think that this is the same train as the train we pointed to before?"

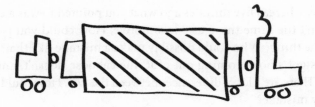

Fig. 6.2

Again, it's important not to misunderstand that question. I'm not asking whether the locomotive that we're pointing to now is the same as the caboose that we pointed to earlier. Of course it isn't! The locomotive is not the same as the caboose. But that's not what I'm asking. Rather, earlier, when I pointed to the caboose and I started talking about a train, I was picking out some entire extended-through-space train. And right now, in pointing to a locomotive and talking about a train, I'm picking out an entire train, some entire extended-through-space train. So I'm not really asking about the locomotive and the caboose at all. Rather, I'm asking about the *trains* that I pick out by *means* of the locomotive and the caboose. Are they the *same* train? Or are they *different* trains? And the answer is, "I don't know; I can't tell. The building is blocking the view."

Suppose we had x-ray vision and could see through the building. Then we would give one of two different answers, depending on what we saw. If the situation is like the one shown in Figure 6.3, then of course the answer would be that we *do* have one single train: the extended-through-space train that I picked out at the end of our walk is the very same train as the extended-through-space train that I picked out at the beginning of our walk.

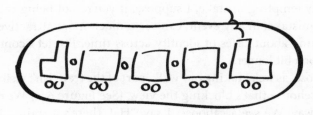

Fig. 6.3

But it might not turn out that way. It might turn out if I had x-ray vision, what I'd see is the situation shown in Figure 6.4. Then the answer would be that there isn't one train here but two: the extended-through-space train that I'm picking out when I point to the locomotive turns out to be a different train from the extended-through-space train that I picked out when I pointed to the caboose.

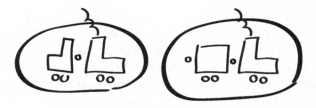

Fig. 6.4

Of course, the fact of the matter is, I *don't* have x-ray vision. So I don't know which one of these two different metaphysical hypotheses is the correct one. But still, we understand perfectly well what it takes for one answer or the other to be correct. We know how identity works (in these cases, at least) with trains.

Now let's talk about something not a whole lot more complicated: cars. I used to have a car that I bought in 1990. In 1990 my car was new. It was sparkly. But I drove it for some years and it got some dents and scratches. By 1996 or 2000, it wasn't looking so good. The sparkle had gone. It had some rust spots. That was the car in 2000. By 2006, it had a lot of dents, and there were engine problems. Indeed in 2006, my car finally died. (See Figure 6.5.)

Fig. 6.5

I take it that we all understand the claim that the car I had in 2006 was the very same car as the car I had in 1990. Of course, here too, you've got to be careful not to misunderstand what's being said. We all know that by 2006 the car had a lot of scratches and had gotten banged in on one side; in 2006 it was pretty sorry looking in terms of the scrapes and the paint job and the rust. In contrast, the car in 1990 was new and shiny and smooth. You might say the 2006 car "stage" is obviously not the same thing as the

1990 car stage. That's a little like pointing out that the locomotive is not the same thing as the caboose. But when I say it's the same *car*, I don't mean to be talking about car *stages*. I mean to be talking about a single thing that was extended through time.

There I am, proud owner of my new car in 1990, and I say, "This is a car. It's a car that will exist for more than a few minutes. It's a car that will exist for years and years and years" (though at the time I didn't realize it was going to last sixteen years or longer). When I refer to my *car*—as opposed to what we could dub the car stage or the car slice—when, in 1990, I refer to the *car*, I mean to be talking about the entire extended-through-time object. Similarly, in 2006, when I point to that sad heap and say, "I've had that car for sixteen years," I'm obviously not talking about a car stage or a car slice. I haven't had that car *stage* for sixteen years! That car stage or that car slice—if we want to talk about it that way—has only been around for a few months at best, or a year (or maybe just a few moments—it depends on how thin we make the "slices"). But when I talk about the *car*, I'm not picking out just the current slice or the current stage of the car, but the entire extended-through-time object. When I say, "That's the very same car I've had for sixteen years," I mean, "Think about the long-lasting extended-through-time object that I'm picking out by pointing to the current slice. That's the very *same* extended-through-time object that I picked out sixteen years ago by pointing to what was then the current slice." The *slices* obviously aren't the same; but the *car* is. It's the very same car.

Next, let's imagine a somewhat more difficult case. At the end of 2006, my engine failed. I sold the car to a junk dealer. Suppose, though, that in 2010 I see a car in the junk lot and it looks familiar to me. (See Figure 6.6.) I say, "Whoa! That's my car." Well, is it, or isn't it my car?

Fig. 6.6

This is sort of like the case we discussed earlier, with the factory blocking the view. But this time, instead of it being a building that's blocking the view, it's the mists of time. For sixteen years, from 1990 to 2006, I saw the car every day; it was easy to keep track of it. But now, in 2010, four years have gone by, and I just don't know what the facts are. So I ask, is this the same car or not?

By this time, I imagine, you don't really need to be warned about how to properly understand my question. But let me spell it out anyway, just to be safe. I am *not* asking whether the 2010 car stage is the very same car stage as the 2006 car stage (the last I saw of my old car). Obviously, it isn't. Rather, by pointing to the 2010 car stage, I mean to be picking out an entire extended-through-time entity—a *car*. And what I am asking is whether *that* car, that particular extended-through-time entity, is the very *same* car as the car (a particular extended-through-time entity) that I used to own. *That's* what I want to know. And the answer is, I don't know! The mists of time are blocking my view.

I don't know the answer. But I know what the possibilities are. One possibility is that it is, indeed, the very same car. Somehow my car has made it from the junk dealer to this new lot. It may be a little worse for the additional years, but it is the very same car. (See Figure 6.7.)

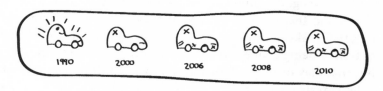

Fig. 6.7

But there is a different possibility as well. It could have been that after I sold my car to the junk dealer, he crushed it, turning it into a heap of metal, and that was the *end* of my car. If so, then the car I'm seeing on the dealer's lot in 2010 must be some other car with its own history. (See Figure 6.8.)

Fig. 6.8

Let's introduce a piece of jargon. Take another look at Figure 6.7, which shows my car—my one single car—extended through space and time. I've drawn a circle around the different stages, to drive home the fact that although the stages are distinct, what we have here is indeed one single object, extended through space and time. The whole thing looks a bit like a worm. So philosophers say that I've drawn a picture of a *space-time worm*. That's just a colorful way of making the point that the car itself is something that extends through space and time.

What I want to know when I see a car (in 2010) that looks a bit like my old car (last seen in 2006) is this: am I dealing with one space-time worm, or two? Is the space-time worm that makes up *this* car the *same* space-time worm as the one that made up my old car? Of course, we don't know the answer. We don't know the facts. But at least that's what the question is.

Now there are, in fact, somewhat different ways of trying to describe some of the metaphysical issues that we've begun to discuss. Think, for example, about trains. It certainly does seem plausible to say that a train is made up out of the various cars—the locomotive, the caboose, and so on—which get linked together. A train seems to be a bit like a *sandwich*. Metaphysically speaking, the fundamental things seem to be the caboose, the locomotive, and the intervening cars. If they're "glued" together in the right way, they make up a train. And what's the right kind of metaphysical glue for trains? Being connected with those little coupling locks.

But that may or may not be the right way to think about what I've been calling car stages or car slices. On some metaphysical views, to be sure, the situation is indeed just like that with the train. The car *stages* are the metaphysically fundamental things, and a car, something extended through time, is glued together like a sandwich from the car stages. And then, of course, if we accept this view, we have to ask about the relevant metaphysical glue. (Unlike the cars of a train, the various car stages that make up a car aren't coupled together; so what *is* the relevant metaphysical glue?) But on other metaphysical views, what's really metaphysically prior is the car *itself*, and talk about car stages is just a convenience, one way of "chopping up" the fundamental thing, the car. On this view, we shouldn't think of the car as being like a sandwich—it's more like a *salami* that you can slice. For certain purposes it may be useful to talk about (or create) slices, but the metaphysically fundamental thing is the entire salami.[1]

In thinking about cars, then, should we say that the fundamental things are the car stages and that, metaphysically speaking, they get put together like a sandwich to make cars? Or should we think that the fundamental thing is the car itself, extended through time, something that can be "sliced up" (for the purpose of certain philosophical discussions) to make car stages? Happily, for our purposes, I think we don't have to try to settle this question. It shouldn't really matter. As long as we're comfortable talking about entire space-time worms—the cars—and also comfortable talking about the slices or stages, we won't have to ask which is metaphysically prior. Either view should do.

I hope to sidestep other metaphysical controversies as well. For example, I've been implicitly helping myself to the suggestion that we should think about extension over time analogously to the way we think about extension over space. That's why I started with a spatial example, the train, and moved to a temporal example, the car. There are philosophers who think that this is *exactly* the right way to think about this matter (things have temporal parts, in exactly the way that they have spatial parts). But there are also philosophers who think that if we take the analogy between space and time too far it can become misleading (since—they say—when an object is extended over time, the entire object is right there at every single moment, but when it is extended over space, only a part of it is at any given location). These are interesting and difficult questions. But again, for our purposes, I don't think we need to explore them.

In any event, I will continue to help myself to this language of space-time worms, of objects that extend not only over space but also over time. And I will continue to distinguish the entire worm from the various slices or stages that either make up the worm or that we could slice the worm into. And given all of this, one way to state the point I have been emphasizing is this: you shouldn't confuse the stages that make up the worm with the entire worm itself. The stages will differ from one another—at the very least numerically, and perhaps qualitatively as well—even when they compose a single worm.

But what, exactly, does it take for different stages to go together to form a space-time worm? What's the relevant metaphysical glue? In the case of trains, as we saw, it's fairly easy to describe what's needed to glue a locomotive, a caboose, and other cars together so as to form a single train: they need to be coupled together in the right way. But that was a case of spatial parts, not temporal parts. What should we say about gluing "stages" or "time slices" together? Take my car. What makes the 1990 car stage a stage in the very same car—the very same space-time worm—as the 2006 stage? What's the metaphysical glue that glues these stages together? What does it take for these two slices to be slices of the very same car?

The answer, I take it, is this: it's the very same car if it's the very same hunk of metal and plastic and wires. After all, what is a car? A car is just some metal and plastic, rubber and wires. That's certainly all that my car was. There was a particular such hunk that was my car, and that very same hunk continued to exist from 1990, through 2000, and on into 2006. The glue, the key to identity across time for cars, is being the same hunk of stuff. (Of course, it doesn't suffice if the hunk has been smashed and is no longer a *car*! What it takes for my car to survive is for there to be a *car* that is the same hunk.)

That doesn't mean that everything has got to be the same *atom for atom*. We know that's not true. Think about my steering wheel. Every time I grabbed the steering wheel to drive, I wore away thousands of atoms. It seems clear that you can lose some atoms and still have the very same steering wheel. You can lose those atoms and still have the very same car. Similarly, every now and then I'd replace the tires on my car. But for all that, my *car* continued to exist, despite these changes. Why? Because it was the same overall hunk of stuff.

Obviously, this raises an interesting and important question. What kinds of changes in the constituent parts can you have and still have the same hunk of stuff? If this were a book on the general topic of identity across time, that would be a problem that we'd have to face head on. But since we are only looking at enough of the problem of identity to get to the question that we really want to think about, the nature of personal identity across time, I'm not going to pursue this question any further. I just want to flag the thought that you can have the very same hunk of stuff, even if some of the constituent atoms have changed along the way. And you can have the same hunk of stuff even if you have replaced some of the bigger parts (for example, the headlights or the tires). That's certainly what happened in the case of my car. My car continued to exist from 1990 to 2006 (at the very least), because it was the same hunk of stuff. And when I see a car on the junk dealer's yard in 2010 and ask, "Is that my car or not?" the answer turns on whether the hunk in front of me is the very same hunk as the hunk that used to be my car. I don't *know* if it's the same hunk of stuff or not. But that's the key. That's the relevant metaphysical glue.

And so, finally, we can turn to the case we really wonder about, the case of personal identity. Here I am, Shelly Kagan, typing these words in 2011. Now imagine that there is someone alive in 2055, and you ask, is *that* Shelly Kagan? We don't know the answer yet, so just to play it safe, let's give this person stage his own name. We'll call him "Mr. X." (See Figure 6.9.) You point to Mr. X and you ask, is that the same person as Shelly Kagan or not?

Fig. 6.9

By this point, I trust, you're not going to be tempted by the mistake I've been warning us about. You understand full well what the question really means. We are *not* asking whether this person stage, Mr. X, is the same person stage as the person stage you might have pointed to in 2011. Let's call that earlier stage "SK 2011." (Sounds like a computer, doesn't it? "Get me an SK 2011!") Obviously enough, Mr. X is not the same stage as SK 2011. After all, SK 2011 has hair, has a beard, and stands up more or less straight. Mr. X, in contrast, is bald, doesn't have a beard, and walks a little bent. We're not asking whether person stage Mr. X is the same stage as person stage SK 2011. Rather, what's going on is this: you are asking about how many *people* there are here—long-lasting, extended-through-time entities. What you want to know is whether the person that Mr. X is part of is the very same *person* as the person that SK 2011 is part of.

The person *stages* are obviously different. But by looking at the stages we manage to pick out an entire space-time worm that makes up a person. And what you are asking is whether *that* particular space-time worm (the one you pick out when you look at Mr. X) is the same space-time worm as the one you picked out previously (when you looked at SK 2011).

The answer, presumably, is going to be that it *depends*—it depends on whether the various stages are glued together in the right metaphysical way. So part of what we need to know is just what it *takes* for two person stages to make up or be part of the very same extended-through-time person. What's the key to personal identity? What's the relevant metaphysical *glue*? If we could get clear about the answer to that question, we'd at least know what we needed to find out to tell whether we have one person or two.

Ultimately, of course, what we want to know is whether I can survive my death. But let's go back, for a moment, to an easier case: can I survive the *weekend*? What would *that* take? To survive the weekend, there's got to be somebody who's alive on Monday, and that person has to be the very same person as the person who is writing these words today, on Thursday.

Or, to put the same idea in terms of stages, there has to be a person stage alive on Monday, and that stage has to be part of the very same space-time worm as this current stage (the one that's here right now, at my desk, on Thursday). The stages have to be glued together in the right way.

Of course, we can't tell whether that's really true or not, until we know what the relevant glue is. But I anticipate—more than anticipate, I fervently hope!—that it will be true. I assume that there *will* be a person stage here on Monday that is glued together, in the right way—whatever that turns out to be—with the person stage that is sitting here, right now, at my desk.

Suppose, then, that I ask: will I survive my death? Let me be optimistic. Let me assume that I am going to make it to 2040. In 2040 I won't even be ninety yet! That's not too wildly optimistic. (It's optimistic, but not wildly optimistic.) And now let us imagine that, sadly, in 2041 my body dies. And so I ask, could I survive my death in 2041—that is to say, the death of my body? What would it take for that to be true? Well, there would have to be a person alive in, say, 2045, and that person would have to be the very same person as I am. Or, to put the same point in the language of person stages and space-time worms, there would have to be a person stage in 2045 that is part of the very same space-time worm as the person stage who is sitting here, right now, at my desk, in 2011. (See Figure 6.10.)

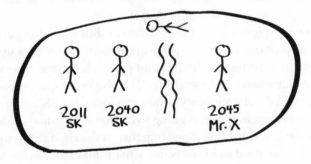

Fig. 6.10

That's all well and good, as far as it goes. But is it *possible*? *Could* there be someone who is the very same person that I am, even after the death of my body? Is that really possible? Unfortunately, we can't answer that question yet—not until we get clearer about what it takes to have personal identity across time. When it's a *person* that we are dealing with—not a train, not a car, but a person—what's the relevant metaphysical glue? What's the key to *personal* identity? Until we get an answer to that question, we can't say whether surviving one's death is so much as possible.

The Soul View

Suppose we believed in souls. Then there would be a natural proposal to make at this point: the metaphysical key to personal identity is having the very same soul.

So if I were a dualist, I might say this: "Sitting here, right now, at this desk, is a particular body. But connected to that body, in a special and intimate way, is a particular soul, the soul of Shelly Kagan. And what makes it true that the person who will be working on this book next Monday is also Shelly Kagan is the fact that it will be the very same soul. As long as this very soul is here at work again on Monday, then that will still be Shelly Kagan. If, however, there is a *different* soul writing those words, then that *won't* be Shelly Kagan."

That's the natural thing to suggest if we believe in souls. As it happens, it's not the *only* option available to dualists. But it is certainly the most obvious proposal for the dualist to make. The key to personal identity is having the very same soul. Same soul, same person. Different soul, different person. Let's call this *the soul theory of personal identity*; or *the soul view*, for short.

Imagine, then, that God, or a demon, or what have you, for whatever perverse reason, severs the ordinary connection between my body and my soul and then reconnects the wires, as it were, so that there's a different soul animating and controlling this body on Monday. And then imagine that, for whatever perverse reasons, maybe to make some sort of philosophical point, that person decides to come to my office on Monday anyway and work on my book. According to the soul view, it won't be *me* writing those words on Monday. Why not? Because we've just stipulated that it's not the same soul. It's a different soul. And according to the soul theory of personal identity, the *key* to personal identity is having the same soul.

According to this view, then, when I ask myself, "Will I survive the weekend?" what I'm asking is, "Will my soul still be around come Monday?" As long as my soul still exists and is functioning, it's still me; I've survived. In fact—peeking ahead a bit—even if my body *dies* this weekend, so long as my *soul* continues to exist, *I* continue to exist. The key to personal identity, after all, is having the same soul. As long as my soul continues to exist, it's still *me*, whether or not my body's still alive.

It's precisely for this reason, of course, that belief in souls holds out at least the possibility of surviving death. We merely need to combine belief in the existence of souls with belief in the soul theory of personal identity. We may not *know* that the soul will continue to exist after the destruction of the body; but at least it seems like a real possibility. So even if I can't *prove* that my soul will continue to exist after my body dies, at least I'll be able to say this: I *might* be able to survive the death of my body.

In contrast, the prospects for surviving the death of my body don't look so promising if we don't believe in dualism. If we agree with the physicalists that a person is just a P functioning body (see Chapter 2), how could it possibly be that after the death of his body *he's* still around? That still seems like a rather incoherent view.

We'll say more about the options available to physicalists later. For the time being, though, let's go back to the soul view. On this view, as we've seen, it's me as long as it is the same soul. If it is a *different* soul, then it just isn't me. So consider the following possibility. Suppose that over the weekend, at 3:00 A.M., early on Sunday morning, God replaces my soul (while I'm asleep) with a different one. He hooks that new soul up to my body, and he gives that soul, that replacement soul, all of my memories, all of my beliefs, all of my desires, all of my intentions. Suppose that God does all of this. What's going to happen next? Well, *someone* is going to wake up Sunday morning and say, "Hey, it's a great day. It's a great day to be alive. A great day to be Shelly Kagan. A great day to get to work." But something is wrong here. He *says* he's Shelly Kagan. But he's not. According to the soul view, that's not *me*. Because according to the soul theory of personal identity, to be me that person's got to have my soul. And in this story, he doesn't *have* my soul. My soul got *destroyed*, let's suppose, at 3:00 A.M. Sunday morning. A new soul got created. So it's not me. There's a *person* there, all right. It's a person that doesn't have a very long history. Maybe he'll go on to have a long history. But he's a different person than the one who is writing these words right now—me, Shelly Kagan. Because, according to the soul view, to be *me* it's got to have the same soul as *I* have, and we just stipulated that it's not the same soul.

Think about what that means. If God were to replace my soul Saturday night (and destroy the original), I die. The person that wakes up Sunday morning isn't me. Of course, he'd *think* he was me. He'd think to himself, "I'm the very same person who was writing about philosophy last week." But he'd be wrong. He isn't the same person, because it's not the same soul. He'd be wrong and—this is an especially important point—there would be *no way at all* that he could tell. He can check his beliefs. He can check his desires. He can check his memories. But that's not the key to personal identity, according to the soul view. The key to personal identity, according to the soul view, is having the very same soul. You can't check that. You can't see the soul to see if it's the same one. So if this were to happen, the person who woke up on Sunday morning wouldn't *be* Shelly Kagan, the person who'd been writing about philosophy last week. But there would be no way at all that he could know that.

And now the question you would need to ask yourself is this: how do you know this didn't happen to *you* last night? You woke up this morning thinking, I'm the very same person—Joe, Laura, Sally, whatever it is—the very same person who was reading this book yesterday. But how do you know? How could you possibly know? If God replaced that person's soul with a new one, destroyed the old one, and gave the new one all the old memories, beliefs, desires, goals, and so forth, then the person who was reading this book yesterday *died*. The person who's reading this book now hasn't been around twenty years, forty years, what have you. You were born a few hours ago. And there'd be no way at all that you could possibly tell.

How do you know, not only this didn't happen to you last night, how do you know something like this doesn't happen every single night, every hour on the hour, every minute, every second? God whips out the old soul, destroys it, puts in a new one. Maybe souls only last for a minute and a half! If that's what's happening, then—according to the soul view—people don't last very long. Bodies may last 20 years, 50 years, 80 years, 100 years, but people would only last an hour or—if it's a substitution every minute—a minute. And you would never be able to tell.

These worries were raised by John Locke, the great seventeenth-century British philosopher, and he thought that this is too big a pill to swallow.[2] This is too big a bullet to bite. We can't take seriously the suggestion that there's no way at all to tell whether it is still me from one day to the next, from one hour to the next, from one minute to the next. That's just not plausible. It's not that there's anything *incoherent* about this view. It doesn't say anything logically contradictory. You just have to ask yourself, "Could this really be what personal identity is all about? That there would be no way at all to tell whether I've survived from one minute to the next, from one hour to the next?" Locke thought the answer was no, that you can't possibly take the soul view seriously if you think about what it implies.

Notice, incidentally, that this is not an argument that souls don't *exist*. If you find this argument convincing, what it's an argument for is the claim that even if souls do exist, they may not be the key to personal identity. It's not an argument against *dualism*; it's an argument against the soul theory of *personal identity*. And so what we have to ask ourselves is, what's the alternative? What better suggestion is there? What else can we point to as the metaphysical glue, the key to personal identity?

The Body View

The natural alternative is to say that the key to being the same person is not having the same *soul*, but rather having the very same *body*. Call this *the body theory of personal identity*, or *the body view* for short. And notice: even if you *do* believe that souls exist, nothing stops you from accepting the body theory of personal identity; nothing about dualism rules out the possibility that having the very same *body* is the key to being the very same person over time. Thus even if you *believe* in souls, you can accept the body view. On the other hand, it certainly looks as though if you *don't* believe in souls, you *have* to accept the body theory of personal identity.

As it turns out, that appearance is deceptive. There's an alternative to the body view that is also open to the physicalist. We'll consider that alternative in a few pages, but first, let's take a closer look at the body view.

On this theory, of course, the secret to being the same person is having the same body. Now as I am sure you remember, earlier in this chapter— when I was discussing the question of what it would take for me to survive the weekend—I kept pointing out that it was Thursday. But that was yesterday. As I write the particular words you are reading right now, it's a new day, Friday. So let's ask, a bit more guardedly, am I *right* to describe the situation in the way I just did? Am I right to say that I am the same person as the person who wrote those other words on Thursday?

According to the body view, the answer turns on whether the particular body—the particular lump of flesh and bone—that is writing these words right now is the very same body as the body that wrote those other words yesterday. If it is (and by the way, it is!), then it's the same person. So I am the person who was writing yesterday about personal identity, because it's the very same body. That's what the body view says.

And unlike souls, where it's all rather mysterious how you could tell whether soul swapping was taking place or not, it's not all that mysterious how we check to see whether the same *body* has been around. Even though you didn't do it, you could have snuck into my house, and watched my body go to sleep and then get up in the morning. You could have followed the body around until it sat down and began typing these words. You could have *tracked* that body through space and time and said, "Hey look. It's the very same body as the one that was writing on Thursday." In the same way that we are able (at least in principle) to track cars, our earlier example, and say that something is the same hunk of metal and wire, rubber and plastic, we can say whether something is the same body, by tracking it through space and time. And if it is the same body, then it's the same person. That's the body theory of personal identity.

Now suppose we accept the body view and turn to the question, could I survive my death? Could I survive the death of my body? At first glance, it looks as though the answer's going to have to be, "Well, of course not." Because when my body dies, it begins to decay. It decomposes, turns into molecules which get absorbed into the soil, or what have you. It may take years or decades or even centuries for my body to *completely* decompose, but pretty soon after the death of my body, my *body* no longer exists. And so how could I *survive* the death of my body, if for me to survive there's got to be somebody who's me, where being *me* requires having the same body? For me to survive the death of my body, my body would have to still be around. But it's not! So I can't survive. That's certainly what it looks like at first glance.

But at second glance, it seems as though there's at least a logical *possibility* of surviving the death of my body. All it takes is for my body to be put back together: bodily resurrection. Now I'm not going to pursue here the question of whether we should believe that bodily resurrection really does or will occur. I'll merely note that there have been religious traditions that have taught and believed in this possibility. In particular, it is probably worth mentioning that early Christians believed in something like the body theory of personal identity and believed that bodily resurrection would happen on, or just before, Judgment Day. But in any event, we can certainly *understand* the possibility that God would perform a miracle, put the relevant molecules back together, and turn my body back on. And so: same body, same person, come Judgment Day. That's the possibility. So it's at least worth emphasizing the fact that even if we *don't* believe in souls, we could still believe in the possibility of surviving one's death, the death of one's body, if we're willing to believe in bodily resurrection. At least, that's how it looks.

But let's take a harder look. Talking that way assumes that when God puts the body back together on Judgment Day that's still *my* body. Is that right? I'm inclined to think it *is* right. If God gathers up all the particular molecules that had composed my body, reassembles them in the right order, putting this calcium molecule next to that hydrogen molecule and so forth and so on, then it seems like that should be my body. (Of course, it's crucial that God reassemble the molecules in the right way; if what he makes out of my body's molecules is an *automobile*, then that's obviously not my body.)

Here's an analogy to give you a sense of what's going on. Suppose I take my watch to the jeweler because it stopped working. And in order to clean and repair it, the jeweler takes it apart. He takes the rust off of the gears. (Are there still gears in watches? Imagine it's an old pocket watch.) He cleans all the pieces, buffs them and polishes them, and then he reassembles the whole thing. A week later, I come back and ask, "Where's my watch?" And he hands it to me. So far, so good.

Now imagine that I say to the jeweler, "Wait a minute, buster. Not so quick. That's not my watch. Admittedly, it's composed of all the very same pieces that made up my watch. Admittedly, all those pieces are in the very same order as my watch, but still, that's not my watch." That seems to be the wrong thing to say. On the contrary, it seems to me that the right thing to say about our example is that it *is* my watch. (Of course, my watch was disassembled for a period of time. Perhaps—I'm not sure—we should say that my watch didn't exist *during* that period of time. But happily, it got put back together. And given that it did, that's my watch.)

If that's the right thing to say about the watch—and it does seem to me to be the right thing to say—then God could presumably do the same thing on Judgment Day. He could take our molecules, which have been scattered around the globe, put them back together and say, "Ha! That's your body." And if the body theory of personal identity is right, well, that would be me. Or so it seems to me.

But there's a different example that we have to worry about as well, one which argues against this idea—the idea that a body could decompose and then be recomposed. This is an example that's due to Peter van Inwagen, a contemporary metaphysician.³ Suppose that my son builds an elaborate tower out of wooden blocks. It's very impressive. And he says, "Please show it to Mom when she comes home," and then he goes to bed. Later, after he goes to bed, I'm cleaning up the house and—oops!—I knock over the tower. I say, "Oh my gosh, he's going to be so angry. I promised him I'd be careful." So what I do is I take the blocks and I put them back together, building a tower in the very same shape and with the very same structure as the tower that my son had built. And in fact, I'm so careful—perhaps the blocks are numbered—I'm so careful that every block is in exactly the same position as it was when my son first built the tower.

All right, I build (or rebuild) this tower and my wife comes home and I say, "Look what our son built. This is the tower that our son built." Hmm. That doesn't sound right. That's *not* the tower that our son built. That's a tower that *I* built. This is a *duplicate* tower. To be sure, if my son were to wake up and I didn't tell him, he wouldn't know that it was a duplicate. But when you take a wooden block tower apart and then put the pieces back together, piece for piece, you don't have the very same tower that you started out with. That's what van Inwagen says, and I've got to admit that it sounds right to me. If I were to point to that tower and say, "My son built that," or "That's the very same tower that my son built," I'd be saying something false.

So, van Inwagen concludes, if you have an object and you take it apart and then put it all back together again, you don't have the very same object that you started out with. So even if Judgment Day were to come, and God were to reassemble the molecules and resurrect the body, it's not the very same body that you started out with. And if having the very same body is the key to personal identity, it's not the same person. Come Judgment Day, we've got a *duplicate* of me, but we don't have *me*. That's what van Inwagen would say, if that's the way bodily resurrection would work.

I have to confess: I don't know what to say about these metaphysical questions. When I think about the tower case, I do find myself inclined to say, with van Inwagen, that it's not the tower my son built. But when I think about the watch case, I find myself saying that it *is* the very same watch. So all I can do is invite you to think about these two cases and ask yourself, what should we say here? Of course, for those people who think it really is the same tower, there's no problem. Then we can say that in both cases—the watch *and* the tower—it's the very same object when it's reassembled. And so, presumably, if we reassemble the body, that will be the very same body as well. Similarly, of course, there isn't really a problem for anyone who thinks that van Inwagen was *right* about the tower, and who concludes on the basis of this that he was right about the watch as well—that the reassembled watch isn't the very same watch. Such people can simply hold that bodily resurrection does not result in the very same body. So that wouldn't be me waking up on Judgment Day.

But what if you're like me, wanting to say one thing about the watch and a different thing about the tower? Can we find some relevant *difference* between the watch case and the tower case, something that allows us to say that when you reassemble the watch, it is the same watch, but when you reassemble the tower, it's not the same tower? Obviously, it's not good enough to just *say* that there's a relevant difference—we would need an *explanation* of why those two things should work differently in the reassembly cases. And then, of course, we'd have to further investigate the case of bodily resurrection. When you reassemble a body, is it more like the watch case, or is it more like the tower case?

I just have to confess, I don't know what the best thing to say about these cases is. I find myself *inclined* to think: reassembled watch, same watch; reassembled tower, different tower. Maybe there's a difference there. I don't know. I certainly don't have a good theory as to what the difference is. Since I don't have a good theory as to what the difference is, I'm not in a good position to decide whether a reassembled body would be the same body or a different body. I just don't know. So there's metaphysical work to be done here by anybody who's interested in getting the theory of identity worked out properly.

Still, it does seem at least *possible* that when we work out our metaphysical theory, we will be able to say that a resurrected body would be the very same body. So I suppose there's still at least the *possibility* that bodily resurrection would result in me.

So what should we say if we accept the body view? Could there be life after death? Could I survive the death of my body? As far as I can see, that does still seem to be a possibility, even though there are genuine puzzles here that I don't know how to see my way through. Mind you, that's not to say that I believe that there *will* be a Judgment Day, and that on that day God will reassemble the bodies. But at least it seems like a coherent possibility.

Let's refine the body view. According to this view, to have the same person you need to have the same body. But of course, as we know from thinking about familiar, everyday objects, you don't need to have every single piece of an object stay the same to have the same thing. As I have already noted, every time I drive I rub off some atoms from the steering wheel of my car. But that's okay. It's still the very same physical object. Having the same steering wheel is perfectly compatible with losing some of its parts. And the same thing is true for bodies, of course. When you get sunburned, your skin peels, and you lose some atoms in your body. But it doesn't really matter. It's still the very same body. So if the body is the key to personal identity, we don't have to worry about the fact that we're constantly gaining and losing atoms.

Now consider someone who loses a huge amount of weight. She feels different. People treat her differently. She may even feel rather differently about herself. We might even say, speaking loosely, that it's as though she's "a whole new person." But strictly speaking we don't think she literally *is* a whole new person. It's not as though we say, "Poor Linda died when she entered the spa and dropped those 50 pounds. Somebody else who remembers all of Linda's childhood, some imitator, came along." We don't say "different person." We say, "same person, who's lost a lot of weight."

Obviously, that's not a problem for the body view, because on the body view the question is only whether it's the *same* body. And it still is Linda's body, even after she has lost all that weight. Similarly, it's still your body after you've eaten dinner, even though some new molecules have now been absorbed into your body that weren't there before. There can be *changes* in your body that are compatible with it still being the *same* body.

Of course, it's not as though *every* change is acceptable. Suppose that Linda goes to bed, and in the middle of the night we atomize her body and put some new body there. That's a 100 percent change, and that's clearly too much. But certain smaller changes do seem acceptable. The change in the body that results from eating a meal isn't a problem. The somewhat larger change resulting from losing a fair bit of weight doesn't seem to be a problem either.

Which changes make for a different body and which changes make for the same body? And in particular, how should we think about this issue, if we are viewing the body as the key to personal identity? In answering that question, I think we're going to want to say that not all parts of the body are equally important. For example, if you lose a fair bit of weight, some fat from your gut, that's not a problem; it's still the same body.

Here's another example, one of my favorites. In the *Star Wars* movies, Darth Vader whips out his light saber and slashes off the hand of Luke Skywalker. "Luke, I am your father," intones Darth Vader. "No!" screams Luke. Zip, goes the hand. But in the very next scene—this always amazes me—in the very next scene Luke's got an artificial hand that's been attached to his body. And they never even mention it again! No one says, "Oh, poor Luke. He died when Darth Vader cut off his hand."

It seems pretty clear that not all parts of the body matter. You can lose a hand and still survive. It is, after all, the same body, except now without a hand. Suppose that Darth Vader had aimed a little higher and cut off Luke's entire arm. It would still be Luke. It would still be Luke's body. Or suppose, even worse, that Darth Vader slices off both arms and both legs. It would still be Luke because it would still be Luke's body, though now without arms and legs.

What part of the body, if any, is essential? Well, here's a proposal. It seems to me we'd say something rather different if what happened was that Luke's *brain* got destroyed. Suppose that Darth Vader uses the force—the dark side of the force, of course—to turn Luke Skywalker's brain into pea soup. Now I think we might want to say, "Alas! No more Luke." And even if they drag out some artificial brain, some replacement brain, and somehow hook it all up, that's still not Luke.

So here's a possible version of the body view. According to this version, the crucial question in thinking about personal identity is whether it's the same body—but not all parts of the body matter equally. The most important part of the body is the *brain*. Why the brain? No surprise there: it is because (as we now know) the brain is the part of the body that is the house of what we might call your *personality*—your beliefs, your desires, and your memories, your fears, your ambitions, your goals. That's all housed in the brain. And so that's the part of the brain that's the key part of the body for the purpose of personal identity.

That's what I'm inclined to think is the best version of the body view. And we find examples of this thought—that the brain is the key—in odd places. Let me share one with you. This is something from the Internet that my brother sent to me some years ago. It purports to be from a transcript from an actual trial in which a lawyer is cross-examining a doctor. I don't know whether it's actually true or not, or whether somebody just made it all up. But it purports to be true.

> Q: Doctor, before you performed the autopsy, did you check for a pulse?
> A: No.
> Q: Did you check for blood pressure?
> A: No.
> Q: Did you check for breathing?
> A: No.
> Q: So then it is possible that the patient was alive when you began the autopsy?
> A: No.
> Q: How can you be so sure, doctor?
> A: Because his brain was sitting on my desk in a jar.

Q: But could the patient have still been alive nevertheless?
A: It is possible that he could have been alive and practicing law somewhere.

The reason that this is funny, of course, is that it shows that the lawyer is an idiot. But why is it so clear the lawyer's got to be an idiot? Because, of course, we think, "Lose a hand, and the guy could still be alive. Lose an arm, or lose a leg, he might still be alive. But lose the *brain*, and he's certainly not alive." Now this is hardly philosophical proof, but it does show that we're readily drawn to the thought that the key part of the body is the brain.

Think about the implications of holding that view. Suppose we adopt this version of the body view. Imagine that I get a liver transplant. Here I am, and we take out my liver and we put Jones's liver inside. I've gotten a liver transplant. It's still me. Or suppose we rip out my heart and put Jones's heart in there. I've gotten a heart transplant. It's still me. Or suppose we rip out my lungs and put in Jones's lungs. Now I've gotten a lung transplant. But it's still me. Finally, suppose we rip out my brain, put in Jones's brain. Have I gotten a *brain* transplant? No! What's happened is that *Jones* has gotten a *body* transplant. Or, to be a bit more precise, a *torso* transplant. If we accept this version of the body view, then we are saying that the crucial part of the body for personal identity is not sameness of torso; the crucial part of the body is sameness of brain. Just as we can say "follow the soul" if we believe in the soul theory of personal identity, if we believe in the *brain* version of the body theory of personal identity, we can say "follow the brain." Same brain, same person. Different brain, different person.

As I've said, I think that may be the best version of the body view. But not all body theorists agree. Some body theorists, for example, think that the key part of the body is the *torso*.[4] So if you want to follow the person, you need to follow the torso, not the brain. I'm inclined to say no. At least, in those moods when I *accept* the body theory, I'm inclined to think you should follow the brain. So even though a torso theorist would say that when you get a brain transplant you really *have* gotten a brain transplant, because it's the same torso, I myself think it is more plausible to say that when you get a so-called brain transplant, what's really happened is that someone else has gotten a torso transplant. If you want to follow the person, follow the brain.

How *much* of the brain is required? Do we need all of it? Perhaps not. After all, as we've already seen, we don't have to follow the parts of the body that aren't essential for housing the personality. So we might ask ourselves, do we need the *entire* brain to house the personality?

Scientific research suggests that there's actually a fair bit of redundancy in the brain. You can certainly lose portions of the brain and still have a perfectly functioning person. In particular, there is a fair bit of redundancy between the two *hemispheres* of your brain. So does that mean that an entire hemisphere of your brain could be destroyed without having you lose any of your functioning, without losing any of your personality? Sadly, not quite. It seems that we don't actually have *complete* redundancy in the two hemispheres.

But suppose that we did. Let's be science-fictiony. Suppose that, as a kind of backup security device, evolution has produced so much redundancy in the brain that either half of the brain would suffice. And now, let's think about brain transplants a bit more.

Version one. There's been an accident involving Smith and Jones. Jones's torso gets destroyed, but his brain is fine. Smith's *brain* has gotten destroyed, but his torso is fine. We take Jones's brain and we put it in Smith's torso. We hook up all the wires, as it were, and someone wakes up. Who *is* it? Well, follow the brain. It's Smith's torso, but it's Jones's brain—so it is *Jones* that wakes up.

Version two. Another horrible accident. Jones's torso has once again been destroyed, just like in version one, but this time the left half of his brain has been destroyed as well. Happily, however, the *right* half of his brain is still in good shape. Smith's torso is fine, but his entire brain has been destroyed. We take the right half of Jones's brain, put it into Smith's torso, hook up all the wires the right way, and someone wakes up. Who is it? It's Jones. Follow the brain. More particularly, follow however much of the brain it takes to still have *enough* of the brain to give you the personality— the various memories, beliefs, desires, and so forth and so on. It probably isn't true, sadly, that half a brain is enough to do that, but if it *were* enough, then half a brain would be enough. It would be Jones that wakes up.

So *one* thing that a physicalist can say is this: "The key to personal identity is the body. Having the same person is a matter of having the same body." And then—I'm inclined to add—the *best* version of the body view is the *brain* view. That's certainly a position that a physicalist can embrace. And for that matter, it's a position that a dualist can embrace as well. After all, even if there *are* souls, that doesn't force us to say that they're the key to personal identity. Maybe sameness of *body* (and in particular, sameness of brain) is the key to personal identity, *despite* the existence of souls.

That's something a physicalist or dualist *can* say. But as I suggested earlier, that's still not the only view available to physicalists (or, for that matter, dualists). Even if there are no souls, we don't have to say that the key to personal identity is the sameness of the body. We could instead say that the key to personal identity is the sameness of the *personality*.

The Personality View

Go back to Locke's worries about the soul theory of personal identity. He asked us to imagine a case in which the soul is constantly changing, even though the memories, beliefs, desires, goals, ambitions, and fears all stayed the same. It seems very hard to believe in such a case that this isn't the same person, even if the soul *is* constantly changing. Why does it seem so clear that it is the same person? Roughly speaking, because it's the same personality.

Or think a bit more about the body view. I suggested that the very best version of the body view was the brain view. But why did that seem plausible? Why *didn't* we say that Luke Skywalker died when he lost his hand? Obviously enough, because the brain is the part of the body that houses the personality. Indeed, I even suggested that you might not need the *entire* brain, just *enough* of it. But how much is enough? Enough to keep the personality.

But if we think that what's really important here is the personality, why don't we just say that directly? Why not say that the key to personal identity is *personality*? Why not just say that it's me provided that there's somebody who's got the same set of beliefs, desires, goals, memories, and so on? In a word, the same personality. So the secret to personal identity on this new proposal isn't sameness of body, it's sameness of personality. Let's call this view *the personality theory of personal identity*, or *the personality view* for short. (Just to be clear, in stating the view this way, I am of course using the word "personality" as a bit of jargon—as a convenient way of referring to the overall collection of beliefs, desires, memories, goals, and so on.)

Now, it's important to bear in mind that this new view—the personality view—is perfectly compatible with being a physicalist. After all, we're not saying that in order to have personalities you need to have something nonphysical. As physicalists, we can still say that the basis of any given personality is that there is a body that is functioning in certain ways. But for all that, the key to being the same person could have to do with having the same personality rather than having the same body. Of course, normally the way you get the same personality is by *having* the same body. Still, if we ask, "What's doing the metaphysical work here? What's the key to being the same person?" we can say that even though sameness of body gave us the same personality, it was sameness of personality that made it be the very same *person*.

Could there be some *other* way to get sameness of personality? Some way to have the same personality *without* having the same body? Maybe. Suppose that I have a terrible disease. The doctor tells me the horrible news that I have some disease that's eventually going to turn my brain into pea soup. But luckily, just before that happens, they can take all of my personality and put it into an artificial replacement brain. Just like you can have artificial hearts, artificial livers, or artificial kidneys, suppose that you can have artificial brains, which can get imprinted with the relevant personality. So just before my brain turns to soup, they will take an artificial brain and give it my personality. It will have all the same memories, beliefs, desires, fears, and goals.

Obviously, we can't actually do anything remotely like that—at least not today. This is a science fiction story. But it allows you to see how the body and the personality *could* come apart. In principle, at least, it seems as though we could have the same personality without having the same brain. And if personality really is the key to personal identity, then that would still be me.

In any event, the point I was trying to emphasize was that even if we are physicalists, we can still accept the personality theory of personal identity. As physicalists, of course, we will want to insist that there is some physical explanation—normally, having to do with the body—that explains why we have the personality that we do. But for all that, the key to personal identity is having the same *personality*.

It is also worth noticing that even a *dualist* can accept the personality view. Locke, for example—the father of modern personality theories—believed in souls. He just didn't think that they were the key to personal identity. So you might think that the physicalist is *wrong* when he says that personality is housed in or based in the body. You can be a dualist and think that personality is housed in an immaterial soul. And yet, for all that, dualists can consistently say that having the same soul is not the key to personal identity. Rather, having the same personality is the key. And so, to revert back to Locke's example one more time, even if God *replaces* my soul every ten minutes, as long as he does it in such a way as to imprint the very same personality on the replacement soul, that will still be me. (The fact that the soul is being replaced doesn't matter any more than it does if God also replaces some of my atoms.) In short, the personality theory of personal identity can be accepted by dualists *as well as* by physicalists.

Just to keep score, then, right now we've got three basic theories of personal identity on the table. There's the soul view, the body view, and the personality view. We haven't yet tried—or tried all that hard—to choose between them, and eventually that's something we will need to do. We'll do that in the next chapter. First, though, let's refine the personality view a bit.

We all agreed, I trust, that you can have the very same body even though some of the parts come and go. Atoms get added, other atoms get knocked off; Luke Skywalker loses a hand, Aunt Sally gets a hip replacement. Not every change in the body results in a *new* body. (Of course, it may not be qualitatively identical after the change, but it will be numerically identical—the very same body.)

We should say something similar when it comes to *personalities*. You can have the very same personality, even if some of the elements in your personality change. After all, I defined a "personality" as a collection of beliefs, memories, desires, goals, and so forth. But those things are constantly changing. I have all sorts of memories now that I didn't have when I was ten. I have memories of getting married, for example. I certainly wasn't married when I was ten. Does the personality theorist have to say, "Uh-oh, that's a different personality. So the person who was once a kid no longer exists. That person died. He got married and the memories changed and he died." If we do have to say that, we have very, very short lives. Because, after all, right now I've got some memories that "I" didn't have two hours ago. I have some memories that "I" didn't have twenty minutes ago, or even fifteen *seconds* ago. If every time you get a new memory you have a new personality—and we accept the personality theory when it says that having the same personality is the key to survival—then *none* of us survive more than a few seconds.

Presumably the answer is going to be that the *best* version of the personality theory doesn't require having *all* of the very same beliefs, memories, desires, and so forth. Instead, it's satisfied if there is enough of an overlap. Change is permitted, so long as it is gradual.

Your personality can change and evolve over time. So here I am as a ten-year-old child. I've got certain desires, certain memories, certain beliefs. As the years go by, I get some new memories, and I lose some of my old ones. I change my mind about some things—I gain new beliefs while losing others. And my goals change as well. For example, when I was ten, I wanted to be a trash collector when I grew up. (That was my first chosen profession!) But at some point along the way, I gave up that goal; I didn't want to be a trash collector anymore. Similarly, when I was ten, I had pretty vivid memories of kindergarten. Now I have very sketchy memories of kindergarten. Still, it wasn't abrupt. It was gradual. So my memories, my beliefs, my desires, these things were always changing, but—and this is the crucial point—they all changed *gradually*. I've lost a lot of memories over my life, for example, but it's never been all at once. There was this slow evolution of my personality over the years. And so when personality theorists say that the key to personal identity is having the same personality, they don't mean having literally the very same set of beliefs and desires and so on. They mean, rather, the same slowly evolving personality.

Here's an analogy. Suppose that I have a rope that stretches from one end of the room all the way across to the other end. It is, of course, one single rope, the very same rope at this end as it is at that end. Now what makes up a rope? As you know, ropes are basically bundles of fibers, very thin fibers that have been woven together in a certain way. But the interesting thing is, the fibers themselves aren't actually all that long. They might be a couple of inches long, or at most a foot or so. And so no single fiber stretches all the way across the room. Or even if some few fibers did do that, most of the fibers don't. Does that force us to say, "Ah, so it's not the very same rope at the end as at the beginning"? No. We don't have to say that at all. What we say, rather, is that it's the same rope as long as there's this pattern of overlapping fibers. At any given spot, certain fibers end, but most of the fibers continue. Some new fibers get introduced. They continue for a while, too. Eventually maybe those fibers end as well, but in the meantime some new fibers have been introduced. We can have old fibers ending, and new fibers starting, and it will still be the same rope as long as it's not abrupt. Imagine, on the other hand, that I take my scissors and cut out a foot in the middle. Then we'd have to say that there *isn't* the right kind of pattern of overlap and continuity. We really would have two ropes: one rope here, one rope there. But if, in contrast, there is the right pattern of overlap and continuity— which is, after all, what we have if I haven't cut the rope—then it is the *same* rope, all the way across the room, even if no single fiber makes it all the way across.

Something analogous needs to be said by the personality theorist. Even if I have few or no memories identical to the ones that I had when I was ten, that's okay. We can still say it's the same personality, the same evolving personality, so long as there's a pattern of overlap and continuity.

New memories get added, some memories get lost. New goals get added, some goals get lost. New beliefs get added, some beliefs get lost. There might be few, if any, beliefs, desires, or goals that make it all the way through. But as long as there's the right pattern of overlap and continuity, we have the same personality. And according to the personality view, it is having the same *personality* that is required to have the same person. We don't have to keep any particular beliefs, desires, or memories.

CHAPTER 7

Choosing between the Theories

Two Cases

In the last chapter, I introduced three rival theories about the key to personal identity: the soul view, the body view, and the personality view. But which one is right? Since I don't myself believe in souls, it's hardly going to surprise you to learn that I don't think the soul theory of personal identity is right. For me, it boils down to a choice between the body theory of personal identity and the personality theory of personal identity. Of course, in real life, they go hand in hand. In ordinary cases, at least, if we have the same body, we have the same personality, and vice versa, so both theories are going to say it's the very same person. And for what it's worth, if you believe in souls, you are likely to think that in such cases it's the same *soul* as well. In ordinary cases, then, you have the same soul (if there are souls at all) if and only if you have the same body, if and only if you have the same personality. In short, in ordinary cases the three views are likely to agree about whether you have the same person.

So if we want to think about which one of these is the *key* to personal identity, we need to think about cases—maybe somewhat fantastical, science-fiction cases—in which they come apart. We need cases in which bodies and personalities go their own separate ways, as it were. (Since I don't believe in souls, I won't worry about where *they* are going.)

So here's what I'm going to do. I'm going to tell you a story in which your body ends up one place and your personality ends up someplace else.

And I'm going to invite you to think about which of these two resulting end products is you. Once you decide which one's you, that will tell you whether you accept the body view or the personality view.

What's going to be your guide? Rather gruesomely, I'm going to torture one of the two end products. (Not in real life! This is a science fiction story.) I'm going to ask you, which one do you want to be tortured? Or to put the point more properly, which one do you want to *not* be tortured? Because I'm going to assume that it's important to you that you not be tortured! Thus, by seeing who you want to keep safe, this will help us see which one you think is you.

Of course, I've got to be sure that you're thinking about this in the right way. I don't know you, but very likely you are a decent, compassionate individual, and you don't want *anybody* to be tortured. If I were to say to you, "Ah, I'm about to torture Linda over there," very likely you would say, "No, no. Don't torture Linda." You are, as I say, a decent enough person. But still, if I were to say to you, "I'm about to torture *you*," you'd undoubtedly say, "No, no! Don't torture me!"—and there'd be some extra little something in your voice when you said that. Right?

I want to invite you to keep that extra little something in mind as I tell the story and I ask, "Okay, who do you want to be tortured, this person or that?" I want you to think about this question from that special egoistic perspective that we're all familiar with. If *someone's* got to be tortured, who do you want it to be? Which person is the one you *really* care about? That's going to be our guide to deciding between our rival theories.

So please, just bracket any moral concerns you may have about torturing other people or agreeing that somebody else should be tortured. For our purposes, right now, the relevant idea is just this: if I dragged you and some complete stranger to my hidden laboratory and asked you which one you want tortured—you or the stranger?—the answer you should be giving me is to torture the *stranger*. "Let *that* person be tortured" should be your answer: "Don't let it happen to *me*." That's the way I want you to think about the story I am about to tell.

Actually, though, I am going tell this story about *me*—Shelly Kagan. That will make it easier for me to get into the part. But as usual, I want to invite you to think about the story as though it's being done to *you*. That may make it easier to evoke the relevant intuitions.

All right, then. Here's case number one.[1] The mad scientist has kidnapped me and he makes the following speech: "As you can see, I've got you imprisoned. And if you look over there, at the other end of the lab, you'll see that I also have a second prisoner, Linda. Why have I kidnapped the two of you? Because I've been working on mind transfer machines, and I am ready to put them to work. I'm going to hook you both up to my machines and swap your minds. More precisely, what I'm going to do is this: First, I'll read off the memories and beliefs and desires (and so forth) from *your* brain, and then I will 'scrub' the brain completely clean, leaving no trace of your earlier beliefs and desires. Then I will read off the memories and desires and beliefs (and so forth) from *Linda's* brain, before scrubbing *that* brain clean. And then I'm going to electronically transfer Linda's memories and beliefs and so forth over *here* and implant them onto *this* brain, your brain. And then I'll take your memories and beliefs and so forth and implant them over *there*, onto Linda's brain. Of course, I'll knock you both unconscious before I do this procedure—what do you think I am, a monster?—but then, later, when you wake up, you will wake up over *there*, in Linda's body."

The mad scientist continues: "Think about what will happen when you wake up over there, at the other end of the lab. At first you will be confused. You'll say, 'What am I doing in this new body? What happened to my beard? Why am I speaking in this high, female voice?' But eventually it will come back to you. You'll say, 'Oh, right, the mad scientist kidnapped me and he swapped our minds. And sure enough, here I am, Shelly Kagan, inhabiting Linda's body. I guess the machines really do work!' Oh, how glorious that moment will be for me!"—the mad scientist chortles—"All my hard work will have been vindicated."

The mad scientist pauses for a moment while I take this all in. But eventually I get the picture. Two people will wake up after the operation. The person over here will have my body—Shelly's body—with Linda's personality. That person will be thinking "How did I—Linda—end up over here? What am I doing with a beard? How did I end up in Shelly's body?" And the person over *there*, at the far end of the lab, will have Linda's body but *my* personality—Shelly's personality. *That* person will be thinking, "Oh, I guess I—Shelly—really did get transferred into Linda's body after all."

Once the mad scientist is confident I understand all of this, he concludes: "Now once the transfer is complete, I am going to torture one of you. I am, after all, not just a mad scientist, but an *evil* mad scientist. So I am going to torture one of you. But because I am a *generous* evil mad scientist, I am going to give you a choice. Tell me, which one should I torture? You choose."

Now, when I think about this—and again, I'm inviting you to think about this story in the first person, so all of this is happening to you—I find myself wanting to say, "When the swap is over, torture the one that ends up over *here* (with Shelly's body, but Linda's personality)." For it seems pretty clear to me that *I* am going to end up over *there*—in Linda's body, horrified at what's been going on, horrified that Linda's being tortured, but at least happy that it's not happening to *me*. That's the intuition I've got when I think about this case.

After all, suppose he *does* torture the person who ends up over there. That person will be thinking, "I'm Shelly Kagan. However did I get into this bizarre situation? I wonder if he can really—*Oh, the pain, the pain! Stop the pain! Make it go away!*" I certainly don't want that to happen to me. Whereas, in contrast, if the person over *here* is being tortured, terrible as that may be, at least nobody is thinking to themselves, "I'm Shelly Kagan, and I am in horrible pain." So I want the person over *here* to be tortured.

Think about the implications of that intuition. I seem to be saying that I, Shelly Kagan, will end up over *there*. For it is the person who will be over *there* that I want to keep safe from torture after the operation. So that's the one that I think will be *me*. Notice, however, that that's not the person who ends up with my old body. That person ends up with *Linda's* old body. Shelly Kagan's old body stays over *here*. So the body isn't the key to personal identity. Rather, *personality* is the key to personal identity. For the person over *there* will have my personality—Shelly Kagan's personality—my memories of growing up in Chicago and becoming a philosopher, my thoughts about what I want to have happen to my children, my fears about how I'm going to explain what's going on to my wife, and so forth. In short, if the person over *there* is the one that's going to be me—and that's certainly what my intuition tells me—then it isn't the body view, but the personality view, that gives us the right account of personal identity.

Do you share that intuition? Or rather, do you share the corresponding intuition when you tell this story about *yourself*? Most people, I think, do. If you are one of them, then that suggests that what you find intuitively plausible is the personality theory of personal identity.

Now let's tell a *different* story. It's another example for us to think about. Once again the mad scientist kidnaps me, along with Linda. And he tells me, "Shelly, I've got some news for you. I'm going to torture you." I say, "No, no! Please don't do it to me! Please, please, don't torture me!" He thinks it over and replies, "Well, you know, I'm in the mad scientist business. This is what I do. So I am going to torture you. But because I'm a *generous* mad scientist, before I torture you I'm going to give you amnesia. I'm going to completely scrub your brain clean so that you won't remember that you're Shelly Kagan. You won't have any memories of growing up in Chicago or of deciding to become a philosopher. You won't remember getting married or having children. Indeed, I will wipe out not only your memories but all your desires, beliefs, goals, and fears. The whole thing will be completely wiped clean. You will have total, perfect amnesia before I torture you. Don't you feel better?"

No, I don't feel better. I'm still going to be tortured—only now we've added insult to injury. I'm going to have amnesia as well as being tortured. No comfort there. "Well," he says, "I'll make the deal sweeter for you. After I give you amnesia, but before I torture you, I will drive you insane and make you believe that you're Linda. I've been studying Linda. There she is at the far end of the lab. I've been looking at her brain waves, studying her psychology, and now I know every single belief, every desire, every memory she has. I'm going to give them all to you. I'm going to *delude* you into thinking that you *are* Linda. You'll have Linda's memories of growing up in Pennsylvania, and you'll remember Linda's family and, like Linda herself, you will want to be a deep sea diver, and so forth and so on. You will think to yourself, 'Oh, here I am, Linda, in another messy situation.' And then, after all of that, I will torture you. Are you happy now?"

No, I'm not happy now. First of all, I am still going to be tortured. Second, I'm being given amnesia. And now, third, he's going to drive me crazy and delude me into thinking that I'm Linda. No comfort there. "Okay," he says, getting somewhat exasperated, "You're not being very reasonable. Here's my last offer. After I drive you crazy and make you think you're Linda, I'm going to do the corresponding thing to Linda. I'm going to give *her* amnesia and then I'm going to drive *her* crazy and make her think that she's Shelly Kagan! I'll give her all of *your* memories and beliefs and desires. *Now* is it okay that I'm going to torture you?"

No. It isn't okay. It was bad enough that I was going to be tortured and given amnesia and driven insane. It doesn't really make it any better that he's *also* going to give amnesia to someone else and drive *her* insane as well. In any event, I still don't want him to *torture* me! If he's got to torture somebody, then I would much prefer that he do it to *her*. I know, that's not a very nice thought, but in my noncompassionate mood that's certainly my reaction. Don't do it to me, do it to her. Don't torture me, the person over *here*—do it to the person over *there* who will, sadly, insanely believe she is Shelly Kagan.

That's my intuition, when I think about this second case. And I am guessing you will have the same intuition (or rather, the corresponding intuition) when you tell this story about yourself. But think about the implications of this for the theory of personal identity. I don't want the person who is going to end up over *here* to be tortured, because I think it's *me*. But if it's me, then what's the key to personal identity? Not personality—because, after all, the person over here won't end up with my personality, Shelly Kagan's personality. No, Shelly Kagan's personality is going to end up over *there*. What stays here isn't Shelly Kagan's personality but rather Shelly Kagan's body. So if I don't want the person who ends up over here to be tortured, that suggests that I must believe in the *body* theory of personal identity. So to follow the person, you need to follow the body, not the personality. (Even though the mad scientist will swap our personalities, it's still *me* he's torturing.) That's the intuition I have when I think about this second case.

Well, we really are in a bit of a pickle now, from the philosophical point of view. Because when we thought about the first case, the intuition seemed to be that *personality* is the key to personal identity. But when we think about the second case, the intuition seems to be that *body* is the key to personal identity. So our intuitions seem to be in conflict with one another. At least mine are, for those really are the intuitions I have when I think about these cases. So I've got a philosophical problem: two different cases give us two different, diametrically opposed answers to the very same question. And if you are with me—if you share those intuitions—then you've got a problem too.

But the problem is even worse than that. Because if we are careful and think about it, we can see that we don't really have *two* different cases here at all. Rather, there's just one case. It's the very same story, being told twice. In both cases, after all, after the various mind-scrubbing and mind-swapping operations take place, but before the torture starts, we end up with Shelly Kagan's body over *here* with Linda's personality, and Linda's body over *there* with Shelly Kagan's personality. And we're being asked, which one of those two "end products" do you want to have tortured? It's the very same setup. I simply told the story two different times, emphasizing different elements so as to manipulate your intuitions. But it's the very same case.

Obviously enough, then, it can't be that in one of these stories we should follow the body, while in the other we should follow the personality. That can't possibly be right! Not if they really are the very same story!

It is very difficult to know what to make of all of this. Is there some reason to trust *one* of our conflicting intuitions here more than the other? But which one? And why?

Here's an interesting suggestion: I've been acting as though in these two stories the body view and the personality view come apart, because the bodies stay put, while the personalities get swapped. But maybe that's not right. After all, I suggested previously that the best version of the body view may be the brain theory, where the crucial question isn't what happens to the *torso* but what happens to the *brain*. And someone might suggest that when the mad scientist puts my personality into Linda's body, he has to *modify* Linda's brain, making it more like my brain than hers. Perhaps, then, at the end of the process, it really is *my* brain over there, in Linda's torso! If so, then both the personality theory *and* the body view (at least in the brain version of the body view) should agree that I end up over *there*—with my personality *and* my brain. That might then give us reason to embrace the conclusion that I move in *both* cases—since in both cases both my brain and my personality are moved—vindicating the first intuition over the second. In effect, the suggestion is that when I think about the second case I get too hung up on the location of my *torso* and don't pay enough attention to the location of my *brain*. That's why we're entitled to dismiss the intuition from the second case.

As I say, that's an interesting suggestion. But I think it's mistaken! I don't think it's correct to say that my brain has moved. Suppose you ask me: after the operation, where are Shelly Kagan's legs? The answer is, they're still here. Where's my heart? Still here. Similarly, then, where's my brain? Still here, too. After all, it's not as though what the mad scientist does is open up my skull and take my brain out. No, the whole thing is done electronically. He hasn't *replaced* Linda's brain; he's just *reprogrammed* it.

An analogy here might be helpful. Think of the difference between a computer and the programs and files that are saved on that computer. Someone's personality is a bit like the particular collection of programs and data files. What the mad scientist does, in effect, is to completely wipe out Linda's hard drive and then download the various programs and files from the Shelly Kagan computer. But it's still the very same central processing unit, the same hard drive. Or so it seems to me.

Of course, it is true that after the operation Linda's brain will be *similar* in certain important ways to Shelly Kagan's brain (from before the operation). But still, if we ask where Shelly Kagan's brain ends up, the answer is over *here*, where it has been all along. Not over there.

So we really do have a story where the body (including the brain) stays put, while the personality moves. And so our two theories of personal identity—the body view and the personality view—really do disagree about which one of the end products is me. But the trouble, of course, is that when I think about this story, I find myself reacting to it in two different ways, depending on how, exactly, I tell it—despite the fact that metaphysically speaking it seems to be the very same story.

The upshot is this. In my own case, at least, thinking about this "pair" of cases doesn't really help all that much. If we're going to decide between the body view and the personality view, perhaps we need to consider a different kind of argument.

Duplication

A rather different approach to choosing between the rival theories begins with a particular objection to the personality view. The idea is that the personality view seems to have an implication that we cannot possibly accept. If that's right, then we should reject the personality view and embrace the body view instead.

Here's the objection (it may have already occurred to you). According to the personality theory, whether somebody is me depends on whether he's got my beliefs, memories, and so forth—for example, the belief that I'm Shelly Kagan, professor of philosophy at Yale University. Of course, I'm not an especially interesting fellow. So let's make it more dramatic and think about Napoleon. Perhaps you've read about this sort of thing: every now and then there is a crazy person who thinks he's Napoleon. Imagine that right now there's somebody in an insane asylum in Michigan who's got the thought "I am Napoleon." Well—the objection goes—clearly this guy is just *insane*, right? He is *not* Napoleon. He's David Smith, who grew up in Detroit. He just insanely *believes* that he's Napoleon. Yet according to the personality view he really *is* Napoleon, because he's got the beliefs of Napoleon. He's got Napoleon's personality. And so—the objection concludes—since that's obviously the wrong thing to say about this case (he's *not* Napoleon), we should reject the personality view.

But not so quick. The personality view doesn't say that anybody who has any elements at all of my personality is me. One belief in common is obviously not enough to do the trick. Look, we all believe the earth is round.

That's not enough to make somebody else *me*. Of course, the belief "I am Napoleon" is a much rarer belief. I presume that you don't have it. I certainly don't have it. And sure enough, Napoleon had it and David Smith in Michigan has it. But so what? One belief, even one very unusual belief, is not enough to make somebody Napoleon according to the personality theory. To be Napoleon, you've got to have the very same overall *personality*, which is a very big, complicated collection of beliefs and desires and ambitions and memories.

David Smith doesn't have that. David Smith in the insane asylum in Michigan does not remember being crowned emperor. He doesn't remember conquering Europe. He doesn't remember being defeated and exiled to Elba. He doesn't have any of those memories. What's more, Napoleon spoke French, but David Smith doesn't! And so forth, and so on, for all of Napoleon's other memories, beliefs, desires, aims, and intentions. In short, David Smith doesn't really have Napoleon's *personality*.

So the David Smith case isn't really bothersome. It's not really a *counterexample* to the personality theory. For the personality theory says that to be Napoleon you've got to have Napoleon's *personality*. And David Smith doesn't actually have that. Consequently, we can all agree that despite the fact that he *thinks* he's Napoleon, David Smith is *not* in fact Napoleon. Even fans of the personality view can agree to that. So this case doesn't really pose any sort of problem for the personality view.

But we could tweak the case, revising it. Some foe of the personality theory could ask us to imagine that the guy in Michigan really *does* have Napoleon's personality. He's got the memories of being crowned, and of conquering Europe, and of being defeated, and so on. He speaks French fluently. He has all the right beliefs and desires, aims and fears. In fact, while we are at it, since we are trying to imagine a case in which this person really does have *Napoleon's* personality—and not some strange mixture of Napoleon's personality and David Smith's personality—we had better stipulate as well that the person in the asylum does *not* have any of *David Smith's* old memories, ambitions, or goals. For example, he doesn't have any memory of growing up in Detroit, and so forth and so on. (How could Napoleon have memories of growing up in Detroit? Napoleon grew up in France!) The objection then says that even if this guy *did* have Napoleon's exact personality, he still wouldn't *be* Napoleon. So the personality view must be mistaken.

This time around, we've told the story right. This time around, the personality theory really does have to say that this guy is Napoleon. But now I am not so confident anymore that that's the wrong thing to say!

Let's try to imagine the case from the point of view of Napoleon. There he was, in the 1800s, being crowned emperor, conquering Europe, and ultimately being defeated. He's exiled on Elba; he dies on St. Helena. The real Napoleon has memories of all of this, memories of getting sick and becoming deathly ill. The light begins to fade; he loses consciousness. And then he wakes up—or at least let's try to describe it that way—he wakes up in Michigan. He thinks to himself, "Allo. Je suis Napoleon!" I'm going to write the rest of these thoughts in English, but imagine that he's thinking all of this in French: "I am Napoleon! What am I doing in the Michigan territory? The last thing I remember, I was going to bed from my dreadful illness on the Island of St. Helena. How did I get over here? I wonder if there's any chance of reassembling my army and conquering the New World."

You get the picture. Keep filling in all of the details like this. Here's the guy in Michigan, but now he's got a personality that in *all* the relevant ways is continuous with and overlapping with the personality of Napoleon. If that happened, it isn't at all clear to me that it would be wrong to say that he *is* Napoleon! I mean, it would be totally bizarre. Things like this don't really happen. But my own suspicion is that if something like this *did* happen, we might well say that somehow Napoleon had been reborn or reincarnated. By some sort of process of "possession" (as we might call it) Napoleon has taken over the body of the former David Smith. It was David Smith before, but now it's Napoleon. I find myself thinking that maybe that would be the right thing to say.

Of course, at this point, one might worry that we've moved too quickly. Is it really true, for example, that this guy has Napoleon's memories? That's far from obvious. After all, Napoleon—the real Napoleon—had the experience of being crowned emperor. But this guy didn't have the experience of being emperor. Maybe what we should say is he *thinks* he remembers the experience of being crowned emperor, but it's a fake memory. It's an illusion, or maybe a delusion—a *quasi-memory*, if you will—but in any event, he doesn't really have the genuine memory. To have the genuine memory, he has to have *been* crowned emperor. And *he* wasn't crowned emperor; Napoleon was.

Well, that's what we *might* say, but we *shouldn't* say it until we decide that he's *not* Napoleon. After all, if he really is Napoleon, then these aren't mere quasi-memories, these are genuine memories. If you are ready to insist that they aren't genuine memories, but rather mere illusions, then it must be that you think he isn't the real Napoleon. In which case, what you're discovering is that you don't really believe the personality view after all. (To be careful, however, perhaps we should state the personality theory in terms of having the relevant quasi-memories, and so forth, so that we don't have to first decide who someone *is*, before deciding whether he has the relevant personality.)

Why *isn't* he the real Napoleon? If you think he's a mere deluded imposter, and not the real Napoleon, it must because you think the crucial point is that he simply doesn't have Napoleon's *body*. That, at any rate, is what the body theorists are hoping you'll say. We can make the personality as much like Napoleon's as we want, but that just won't do the trick. To be Napoleon, you have to have Napoleon's body.

But as I say, I'm just not sure that that's right. Suppose that the guy in Michigan has a memory (or quasi-memory, if you prefer to put it in that more guarded way), a memory from Napoleon's life that as far as we know Napoleon never shared with anyone, one that he never wrote down in his diary, never mentioned in any speech. The guy in Michigan thinks to himself, "I remember playing as a lad in France, burying my little toy saber." Suppose we start digging up in France, and sure enough—there's the saber! Suppose this guy knows *all sorts* of things that only Napoleon would know. I find myself thinking, well, maybe it *is* Napoleon.

Or suppose that something like the Napoleon case was an everyday occurrence. Every few days, someone's body gets "possessed." A new personality takes over. No trace of the old personality remains, and the process is never reversed. Imagine that there were some elaborate physical explanation for the whole thing. What would we say? If it happened frequently enough, I think we might well say that a "new" person—the person whose personality is now in place—had taken over the body previously occupied by someone else. We wouldn't follow the body, I suspect: we'd follow the personality.

So speaking personally, I don't find the Napoleon objection a telling one. To be sure, I'm not confident enough about the various intuitions I've just been expressing to be prepared to *endorse* the personality view on the basis of those intuitions. But be that as it may, thinking about this case certainly doesn't leave me feeling that the personality view has to be *rejected*.

But we can tweak the Napoleon case even further! There was Napoleon, back in France, with his memories and beliefs and so forth. Death comes, and he loses consciousness. A moment ago I tried to tell you a story in which he wakes up in Michigan, or at least his personality somehow gets transferred to Michigan. But if it could happen in Michigan, I suppose it could happen instead in New York. And if it could happen in New York and it could happen in Michigan, I suppose it could happen in both New York *and* Michigan. So let's imagine that right now there are *two* people with Napoleon's personality, one of them in Michigan, and one of them in New York.

Whoa! What should we say now? What is the personality view going to say about *this* case?

I think it may help to sort our options out if we draw some pictures. Let's start with a picture of the case where Napoleon's personality travels to Michigan and Michigan alone. I'm not really sure how to draw a personality, so the diagram actually shows some little stick figures; but I mean these to be *personality stages*, not body stages. (See Figure 7.1.) In the left half of the diagram, we've got the continuing, evolving, personality of Napoleon while he is in Europe. Just before the line, let's suppose, we have his personality just as it was on his deathbed. And then to the right of the line we have the Napoleon personality continuing—only now we find it in Michigan!

Fig. 7.1

There is a point I should probably mention, since I haven't been explicit about it before. Immediately to the right of the line, when Napoleon's personality first appears in Michigan, the personality stage will of course be very similar indeed to the personality stage just to the left of the line, on the deathbed. The memories, beliefs, aims, and so forth will be almost identical; the "overlap" between these two stages of the personality will be almost complete. But as time goes on, of course, the personality will continue to change and evolve. The person in Michigan will continue to learn new things, get new memories, gain new goals. Over time, then, the personality stages of the person in Michigan will be less and less like the personality stages of Napoleon back in Europe. But that's not any kind of threat to the claim—embraced by those who accept the personality view—that the *person* in Michigan to the right of the line is, and continues to be, Napoleon. After all, the actual, historical, Napoleon also had a constantly evolving personality. The point to bear in mind, of course, is that we need to think of personalities as things that are allowed to evolve over time. Change is permissible, so long as it isn't too abrupt—as long as we have the familiar pattern of overlap and continuity.

Since we are imagining that we *do* have this pattern of overlap and continuity in the example we are discussing, it is appropriate to say that the person in Michigan to the right of the line has the same evolving personality as Napoleon had, to the left of the line. And that means, of course—if we accept the personality view—that it really is *Napoleon* there, to the right of the line, and not just to the left. That's why I've drawn a circle around all of the different personality stages, both to the left of the line and to its right—to mark the fact that we have one single person here, Napoleon.

Next, let's imagine our new version of the Napoleon example where, in addition to having someone with Napoleon's personality in Michigan, we also have someone in New York with Napoleon's personality. (See Figure 7.2.) What do we want to say about *this* case?

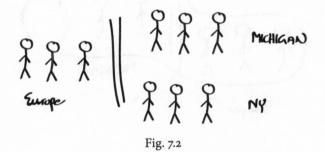

Fig. 7.2

Of course, if the Michigan guy weren't *there*, what I would do—if I believed the personality view—is this: I would draw a circle around the various personality stages in Europe and New York, marking the fact that we have the same evolving personality on both sides of the line. I would say, "Oh look, Napoleon has been reincarnated in New York." That's what the personality view would say about the case—if the New York guy had been the *only* one to still have Napoleon's personality today.

The trouble, of course, is that the case as we are now imagining it *isn't* one where Napoleon's personality continues only in New York, nor is it one where it continues only in Michigan. Rather, we've got someone who has Napoleon's personality in Michigan *and* we have someone who has Napoleon's personality in New York. We have *two* copies of Napoleon's personality continuing past the death of his body in Europe. So what should we say *now*? How many people do we have here? One? Two? Three? It is because the answer isn't at all clear that I haven't drawn any circles here yet, to connect the relevant personality stages. It just isn't clear how many people we are dealing with in this case.

So what are our choices? What can we say? One possibility, I suppose, would be to say that the guy in *New York* is Napoleon, and the guy in Michigan isn't. The guy in Michigan is just an insane person who happens to have Napoleon's personality. You could say that. But that's a difficult answer to accept, because of course it seems that it would have been just as plausible to say the *reverse* and insist that it isn't really the New York fellow who is Napoleon, but rather the Michigan fellow who is. Obviously, there's no good reason to favor the New York fellow over the Michigan fellow, just as there's no good reason to favor the Michigan fellow over the New York fellow. So saying that *one* of them is Napoleon and the other one isn't doesn't seem like a very attractive answer. That position seems too hard to believe.

Well then, what's the alternative? Another possibility, I suppose, is to say that they're *both* Napoleon! (See Figure 7.3, where I have now drawn a circle so as to capture this view.) Somehow, bizarrely enough, Napoleon has split into two. Napoleon now has two bodies, and *both* bodies are parts of the one single Napoleon. Now it's very important to understand how bizarre this proposal would be. The claim is *not* that we now have two "Napoleons" who are, of course, not identical to each other (though perhaps they are very similar psychologically, for the time being). No, no, we've got a *single* Napoleon. A Napoleon who was in one place at a time in Europe, but who is now simultaneously in *two* places at the very same time in the United States. A single Napoleon, who will *continue* to be in two places at the same time, until one of the new bodies dies.

Fig. 7.3

That seems very hard to believe. This answer seems to violate one of our fundamental notions about how people work, metaphysically speaking. Surely, we want to say, people *can't* be in two places at the same time! But maybe that metaphysical claim just needs to be abandoned. Maybe we should say, instead, that under *normal* circumstances people can't be in two places at the same time, but under the right circumstances they can be. And so, in our example, the guy in Michigan is Napoleon, and the guy in New York is Napoleon and—hard as this may be to believe—the guy in Michigan is the very *same* person as the guy in New York. The guy in New York and the guy in Michigan are not in fact two people but one—a *single* person, Napoleon, who is currently bilocated. In real life, of course, things like this don't happen. But maybe they could. And if they did, maybe that is what we should say: that Napoleon is currently in two places at once. (On this view, then, all of the personality stages shown in Figure 7.3 make up only one single person. That's why the circle goes around all of them: there is only one person shown in our picture.)

Maybe that *is* what we should say. But normally, at any rate, I find that too big a price to pay. People can't be in two places. It's one thing to say that people are space-time worms extended through space and time. It's another thing to say that they can be *Y-shaped* space-time worms. It seems to violate one of our fundamental metaphysical beliefs about how people "work."

I've got to warn you, though, that *none* of the options here are all that attractive. So when I say, as I have been saying, "you don't want to say this, you don't want to say that," consider yourself warned: we're going to run out of possibilities. None of them are all that appealing. So maybe, at the end of the day, this is what you'll want to say after all.

In the meantime, though, saying that Napoleon is in Michigan but not in New York doesn't seem very attractive. And saying that he's in New York but not in Michigan doesn't seem very attractive. And saying that he's in both places at the very same time doesn't seem very attractive either.

But what other possibilities are there? If Napoleon is not one of these guys but not the other, and if he's not both, then the only other possibility is that he's *neither*. Given this situation, *neither* of these guys is Napoleon. (See Figure 7.4.) Instead, you've got three separate people. There's one person, Napoleon, a space-time worm who came to an end in Europe. And there are two additional people: one of them is a space-time worm currently located in Michigan, and one of them is a space-time worm currently located in New York. But neither of *these* people is Napoleon. That certainly seems to me to be the least unattractive of the options we've got available.

Fig. 7.4

But notice that if we say this—if we say that *neither* of these guys is Napoleon, *despite* having Napoleon's personality—then the personality theory of personal identity is false. It's rejected. We're giving up on it. Because the personality view, after all, said that if you've got Napoleon's personality, you're Napoleon. But here we are, saying that even though these people do have Napoleon's personality, they are *not* Napoleon. So if we say that neither person is Napoleon, then the personality theory ("follow the personality") is wrong. But, as we have just seen, saying that neither is Napoleon does seem to be the least unacceptable of the options. So the personality theory has got to be rejected.

And I think that's the right conclusion. The personality theory has to be rejected. At least, the personality theory as I have presented it *so far* has to be rejected. But that doesn't mean we couldn't revise it. Perhaps we can change it in a way that keeps the spirit of the original version, while somehow avoiding the particular problem we've just been looking at.

Here, then, is what I take to be the most promising way to revise the personality view. Fans of the personality theory should say that we were simplifying unduly—getting it wrong—when we said, "Follow the personality. If you've got Napoleon's personality, that's enough to make you Napoleon." In point of fact, that's not quite enough. We need to throw in an extra clause to deal with "branching" and "splitting" cases of the sort that I've just been talking about. Roughly speaking, we need to say that if there's somebody in the future who's got my personality, then that person is me—but only as long as there's only *one* person who's got my personality. If you have *multiple* copies—splittings, duplications—then nobody, none of them, is me. (Somewhat more precisely: if at some time in the future there are multiple person *stages* with equally good copies of my personality, and those person stages exist at the same time, then none of those stages are part of me.)

So where the original personality theory said that having the same personality is good enough for being the same person, the new version throws in a no competitors clause, a no branching clause. It says that having the same personality is good enough, but only if there's no branching; when there *is* branching, neither of the branches is me. (There are ways to refine this idea a bit more; but this should do for our purposes.)

If we accept the no branching clause, then we're able to say that in our original story (where someone in Michigan has Napoleon's personality, but no one in New York does), the guy in Michigan really is Napoleon, since he has the right personality and there's no relevant competitor. Similarly, had we had someone in New York, but not Michigan, with Napoleon's personality, then *that* guy would have been Napoleon, because he would have had the right personality and no competitor. But in the case where we've got branching, where we've got somebody with Napoleon's personality both in Michigan and in New York, that violates the no branching rule, and so we just have to say that *neither* of them is Napoleon.

As I say, that does seem to me to be the best available revision of the personality theory. But we still need to ask, can we possibly *believe* that revision? Can we possibly *accept* the no branching rule? Sadly, the no branching rule seems rather bizarre in its own right.

Think about an ordinary familiar case. I am, of course, the same person as the person that was working on this book last week. And according to the personality view or the revised personality view, that's because I've got the same personality. The guy last week thought he was Shelly Kagan and believed he was a professor of philosophy. *I* think I'm Shelly Kagan, and *I* believe I'm a professor of philosophy. The guy last week had all sorts of memories of his childhood. I've got the same memories. He had desires about finishing this book. I've got those same desires. And so forth and so on. It's the same personality. And so it's me. That's what the personality view says. So I conclude, hey, it's me. I know you were worried about whether I'd survive the weekend. Good news: I made it!

Or did I? Or perhaps I should ask, "Or did *he*?" Yes, there was someone here last week (Shelly Kagan), and there's someone here now, and yes, the person here now has got the same personality as the person who was here last week. But according to the no branching rule, we can't yet conclude that I'm the same person as the person that was writing this book last week. We can't conclude *that* until we know that there aren't any competitors, that there isn't anybody else around right now who *also* has the same personality. If I *am* the only one around today who's got Shelly Kagan's personality, then—happily—I am in fact the same person as the person who was writing this book last week: Shelly Kagan. But if, unbeknownst to me (and I presume unbeknownst to you), there's somebody in Michigan right now who also has Shelly Kagan's personality, then we have to say that it turns out I'm not Shelly Kagan after all! Neither is he. Neither of us is Shelly Kagan. Shelly Kagan died.

So am I Shelly Kagan or am I not Shelly Kagan? Sadly, we can't tell, until we know what's going on in Michigan! That seems very, very hard to believe. In deciding whether or not I am the same person as the person who was writing this book last week, facts about what's going on in Michigan right now just don't seem *relevant* (since I am writing these words in Connecticut). Intuitively, whether I am the same person or not should turn only on facts about the guy who was writing last week, and facts about this guy who's writing these words to you today, and maybe some facts about the relationship between that guy and this guy. But not on facts about what's happening in Michigan! (Alternatively, if we prefer to put it this way, questions about whether or not I am the same person should turn on facts about those earlier person stages and this current person stage, and the relevant relations between all those stages, but nothing more.)

How could the question of who I am possibly turn on what's happening in Michigan? How can whether I am the same person as the guy who was writing this book last week depend on what's happening in Pennsylvania, or Australia, or Mars? To use some philosophical jargon, the nature of identity seems like it should depend only on intrinsic facts about me—or, perhaps, only on facts about the relations between my various stages. But it shouldn't depend on extrinsic, external facts about what's happening someplace else! Yet if we accept the no branching rule, we're saying that whether or not we've got identity *does* depend on what's happening elsewhere. With the no branching rule, identity ceases to be a strictly internal affair; it becomes, in part, an external affair. That, as I say, is very, very hard to believe. But if you're *not* prepared to believe it, it looks as though you've got to give up on the personality view.

Fission

Let's quickly review the problem that has apparently brought the personality view to ruin. In a nutshell, the difficulty arises from the possibility of duplication. Personalities can be duplicated—we can have multiple copies of the very same personality existing at the very same time. What, then, should the personality view say about such cases? It seems as though the only plausible thing to say is that in cases of duplication, none of the duplicates is the same person as the original person—even though they have the relevant personality. So if we are to avoid abandoning the personality view altogether, we must revise it, so as to include a no branching rule. But the trouble with this proposal is that the no branching rule itself seems unacceptably counterintuitive, since it makes identity an external affair, rather than leaving it a strictly internal one. Accordingly, it seems, we really do need to reject the personality view after all; there's no acceptable way for personality theorists to deal with the problem of duplication.

Now as the personality view has been going through all of these desperate twists and turns, in the unsuccessful hope of dealing with the problem of duplication, fans of the body view have been having a grand old time. I always picture the body theorists standing there, watching all of this and laughing. "Ha!" they say, "You poor fools. The personality theory of personal identity is implausible *precisely* because of the possibility of duplication, precisely because personalities can be copied. (Indeed, if you can have two copies, nothing stops us from having 100, or 1,000, or more!) But *bodies* can't split! Bodies don't branch! So we neatly avoid the duplication problem altogether if we abandon the personality view and embrace the body view instead."

Think about it. Bodies don't split; they don't divide or branch. For example, there's no way that the body of your brother, say, split into two identical bodies overnight. So we simply avoid the problem that so plagued the personality view. Body theorists don't have to figure out what to say in the face of multiple copies of the very same body, because there can't *be* multiple copies. Of course, we could perhaps have another body that looked very *similar* to mine—for example, if I had a twin brother. But no matter how similar another body is to my own body, no one else can literally have my body: unlike my personality, my body can't be in two places at the very same time. Consequently, if we want to know whether someone in the future is the same person as me, all we need to do is to follow this single, unbranching body around, and see where it ends up. In principle, at least, that's a fairly straightforward matter.

So it seems as though we have a rather compelling reason to favor the body view over the personality view. The personality view can't come up with a plausible thing to say about duplication. But the body view doesn't even *need* to have anything to say about duplication, because bodies can't split.

That, at least, is what a body theorist might say. But is it really true? Is it really true that the body view doesn't face a duplication problem? Is it really true that human bodies don't and couldn't split? The crucial word here, of course, is "couldn't." After all, personalities don't *actually* split either. Although I've been discussing a science fiction case in which personalities do split (so that we end up with, for example, two perfect copies of Napoleon's personality), the example has indeed been just that—science fiction. And if it is legitimate to use science fiction to think about the possibility of a personality splitting, then it seems like it should also be legitimate to use science fiction to think about the possibility of *bodies* splitting as well. So let's try to do that.

Actually, we are already familiar—in real life—with some low-level examples of bodies splitting. After all, *amoebas* split. (Amoebas, of course, are a particular type of single-cell organism.) Suppose you've got a single amoeba. It's going along. At a certain point it starts to divide: it sort of pulls itself apart, as it were (I won't try to spell out the biological details). It pulls its two halves farther and farther apart until—boom!—you've got two cells where before you had one. The amoeba *splits*. (See Figure 7.5.)

Fig. 7.5

Human bodies, unlike amoebas, don't do that. But maybe there's nothing in biology that rules out the possibility. Imagine that I open up the *Yale Daily News* tomorrow and see that the Yale Center for Amoebic Studies has made this tremendous breakthrough and has discovered how to cause a *human* body to replicate and split in an amoeba-like fashion. It certainly seems like a coherent possibility. So we are entitled to ask the body view just how it plans to deal with this sort of case. What should we say about the problem of bodily branching?

However, instead of pursuing that particular example, let me introduce a slightly different case that has been discussed a fair bit in the philosophical literature. You'll recall that when we talked about the body view, I said that the best version of the body view doesn't actually require having the *entire* body. Rather, having the same brain is enough. ("Follow the brain.") But we pushed a bit further and suggested that we may not even need the entire brain, perhaps just enough of the brain (however much that turns out to be) to house the personality. Finally, I asked us to suppose— what does not in fact seem to be the case—that one hemisphere of the brain was enough. I want you now to make that assumption again. Imagine that there's enough redundancy in the brain so that even if your right hemisphere gets destroyed, your left hemisphere will suffice to leave you with all the same memories, desires, beliefs, and so forth. Similarly, of course, if your left hemisphere gets destroyed, your right hemisphere is good enough as well. Obviously, that means the story I am about to tell is just another science fiction story; but it's fascinating to think about anyway.

Suppose, then, that this coming weekend I end up in some horrible accident. My torso gets destroyed, but they keep my brain on life support, oxygenating it just long enough to do some radical transplant surgery with my brain and some spare torsos. (Where did the extra torsos come from? Perhaps there were some people—Smith and Jones—who had a very rare brain disease, and their brains suddenly liquefied. So now we've got some spare torsos.) Unfortunately, brain transplants have a very high failure rate, so as an extra precaution the surgeons divide my brain into two, transplanting each hemisphere into its own torso. They figure that this doubles my chances of surviving.

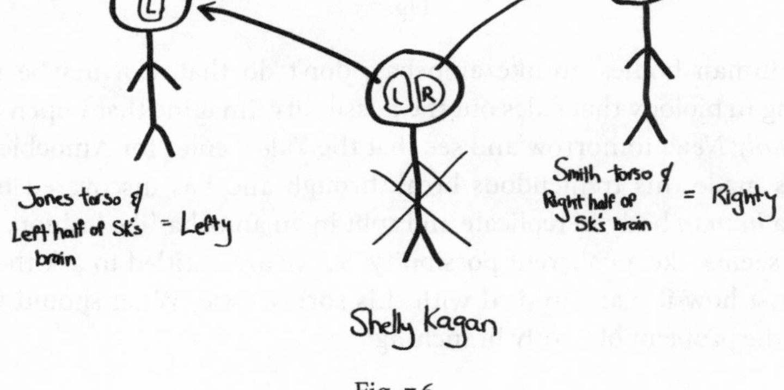

Fig. 7.6

Figure 7.6 should help us keep this all straight. In the middle of the picture is me, Shelly Kagan. There's a big X through most of my body to mark the fact that my torso has been destroyed. In my skull, of course, is my brain—at least, that's where it is before the hemispheres get transplanted. Okay, then: one team of surgeons takes my left hemisphere and they transplant it into Jones's torso. That's what we've got shown on the left. And at the same time, a different team takes my right hemisphere and they transplant it into *Smith's* torso. That's what we've got shown on the right. Both teams connect all the relevant "wires" (the neurons, veins, arteries, and so on), and then they wait.

Much to everyone's surprise, the operation is a complete success! Indeed it is a smashing success. *Both* "end products" wake up. The person that has Jones's torso with the left half of Shelly Kagan's brain wakes up. And the person that has Smith's torso with the *right* half of Shelly Kagan's brain wakes up as well. And now we need to ask, who is who?

We're going to need some neutral way of talking about these various people, so let's just give the two end products names that don't beg too many questions. Let's call the one that has the left half of Shelly's brain "Lefty," and the one that has the right half of Shelly's brain "Righty." And our job, of course, is to figure out who Lefty and Righty are!

After all, the operation is a complete success. Lefty and Righty both wake up. And given our assumption that either hemisphere of my brain is enough to support my personality, it follows that both Lefty and Righty have my personality! Thus, they both *think* they're Shelly Kagan. They both remember (or quasi-remember) growing up in Chicago. They both believe that they are married with three children. They both want to finish writing their next book. And so forth, and so on, for each element in my personality. Each of them *thinks* he is Shelly Kagan. But what we need to ask is this: according to the body view, which one *is* Shelly Kagan?

What are the possibilities? One possibility, of course, is to say that Lefty is Shelly Kagan and Righty is not. Righty is just a deluded imposter. But there's nothing in the body view to give us a reason to make that choice. It's certainly true that Lefty's got half of Shelly Kagan's brain and that's "good enough" (that is, good enough to have Shelly Kagan's personality). But it's also true that Righty's got half of Shelly Kagan's brain and that seems good enough as well. So there's no reason to say that Lefty is Shelly Kagan and Righty isn't. And similarly, of course, there's nothing in the body view to make us say that Righty is Shelly Kagan and Lefty isn't.

So what are the remaining possibilities? We could, I suppose, try to say they're *both* Shelly Kagan. And so Shelly Kagan continues merrily on his way, except now he's doing it in two places at the very same time. After all, the body theorist might say, *enough* of my brain continues, it's just that now it continues in two different places at the same time. But having enough of my brain is good enough to be me. And so, from now on, Shelly Kagan, that single person, is in two different places at the very same time. Suppose that Lefty goes to California, while Righty moves to Vermont. From now on, then, Shelly Kagan is bicoastal.

Well, we *could* say that, but it just doesn't seem right. Remember, the claim here is not that there are two people, very similar to one another (very much like the old Shelly Kagan) but not identical to one another. No, the claim being considered is that *both* Lefty *and* Righty are the very same person as Shelly Kagan—and so they are the very same person. According to this view, then, there is only *one* person who survives the accident: Shelly Kagan. It is just that Shelly Kagan can now be in two places at once. It's *that* view that seems rather hard to believe.

So what else can the body view say? Perhaps we should say that neither Lefty *nor* Righty is Shelly Kagan. Shelly Kagan died in that gruesome, horrible accident. Although it's true that we now have two people, Lefty and Righty, each of whom has half of Shelly Kagan's brain—and all of Shelly Kagan's memories, beliefs, and desires, for whatever that's worth—*neither* of them is Shelly Kagan. We certainly could say that. And once again, that seems the least unpalatable of the alternatives.

But if we do say that, then we've given up on the body view. Because the body view, after all, said that to be Shelly Kagan it suffices to have enough of Shelly Kagan's brain. And in the case we're imagining, both Lefty and Righty do seem to have enough of Shelly Kagan's brain. So if we decide that neither one of them is Shelly Kagan—and that does seem like the best thing to say—then we are abandoning the body view! Or rather, to be a bit more guarded, we're abandoning the body view as I have presented it so far.

You can probably see what's coming. As far as I can see, the best option for the body theorist at this point is to add—no surprises here—a no branching rule! The body theorist should say, "The key to personal identity is having the same body, to wit, the same brain, to wit, enough of the brain to keep the personality going—*provided* that there's no branching, no splitting, no perfect competitors. But if more than one person has enough of the brain, then neither is the original person." (Again, we can state this rule more precisely in the language of person stages; but I won't bother doing that here.)

The example we have just been discussing is known in the philosophical literature as the *fission* case (because it is a little like nuclear fission, where a big atom splits into two). Suppose, then, that the body view adds a no branching rule. Then we can say that in the case of fission the no branching requirement is violated—since the brain splits—and so neither Lefty nor Righty ends up being Shelly Kagan, despite the fact that both of them have enough of my brain.

Contrast that with the ordinary, humdrum case. Why am I the very same person as the person who was working on this book last week? Because the brain in my skull (I can't see it, but I know it's there!) is the very same brain as the brain that was in the skull of the person who was writing this book last week. The body view tells us to follow the body and, in particular, to follow the brain. In the ordinary case, that's good enough. But in the special case of fission—where splitting takes place—we're able to say that having enough of the brain *isn't* good enough. Neither Lefty nor Righty is me.

That's what the body view can say, if we amend it so as to include the no branching rule. But that just brings us back to the already noted problem, that the no branching rule just doesn't seem very plausible intuitively. If we accept the no branching rule, after all, then whether I am the same person as the person who was writing this book last week will depend on whether—unbeknownst to me—over the weekend someone removed half of my brain, stuck it in some other torso, and then sealed me all back up. But how could that matter? According to the no branching rule, if she removed half of my brain and then threw it away, I am indeed the same person as the one who was writing this book last week, but if she implanted it properly in a spare torso, I am not. How can that be? How can who *I* am turn on what happens to some part of a brain miles away from me? Identity should be an internal affair, shouldn't it?

But if you find the no branching rule unacceptable, then you're in trouble as a body theorist. Indeed, you're in exactly the same trouble as the personality theorist found herself in. Both views face a problem in cases that involve splitting. Both views can avoid that problem by adopting a no branching rule. And both views have to admit that a no branching rule just isn't all that attractive.

As it happens, the fission example provides not only a nice case of splitting on the body view, it actually provides a rather nice example of splitting in terms of the personality view as well. Here, before the accident, was Shelly

Kagan, somebody who had a certain collection of beliefs, desires, memories, goals, and so forth. And there, after the accident, you've got Lefty and Righty, both of whom have Shelly Kagan's memories, beliefs, desires, and goals. Splitting the brain shows how you could, in principle, split the personality as well. So the very same case raises the very same problem for both the body view and the personality view. And the only solution that I can see, at least the best solution that I can see, is to accept the no branching rule. If you don't like the no branching rule, it's not clear what your alternatives are. Or rather: it *is* clear what your alternatives are; it's just not clear which alternative would be any better.

During all of this—while we have been rehearsing problems for the body view and the personality view—the soul theorist has been having a field day. We can easily picture the soul theorist saying, "Look you guys, you found yourself needing the no branching rule—silly and implausible as that seems—because of the problem of splitting. As we've now seen, both personalities and bodies can split. But if you had only seen the light, and stuck to the *soul* theory of personal identity, all these problems could be avoided. Because unlike bodies and unlike personalities, *souls* can't split."

Of course, as you know, I don't actually believe in souls in the first place. So I can't really go and embrace the soul theory of personal identity. But forget that point for the moment. Suppose that there really were souls. Is it true that at the very least the soul theory has this advantage—that it avoids these problems of duplication and splitting? I'm not sure.

Let's ask what someone who accepts the soul theory of personal identity should say about the fission case. So here's the gruesome accident. My brain gets split apart. One half gets put into Jones's torso, one half into Smith's torso. After the operation, Lefty wakes up thinking he's Shelly Kagan, and Righty wakes up as well, also thinking he's Shelly Kagan. What should the soul theorist say about this case?

Remember that according to the soul view, the key to being the same person is having the same soul. In the humdrum case we keep discussing, for example, I am the same person as the one who was writing this book last week because I have the same soul. The soul animating the body that is typing these words today is the very same soul as the one that animated the body that was working on the book last week. That's why I am the same person.

But what does the soul theorist say about the *fission* case? I'm not quite sure, in part because the answer depends on a metaphysical question that we have touched upon before but haven't answered: can souls split? Fission raises a problem for the personality view and the body view, because in principle at least, both of those things can split. But what about souls? Can they, or can't they?

I don't know the answer to that, of course. So let's consider both possibilities.

Possibility number one: souls, just like bodies, and just like personalities, *can* split. Suppose that that's what happened in the fission case. We started *out* with a single soul here, Shelly Kagan's soul, but somewhere in the middle of this gruesome accident followed by this amazing operation, Shelly Kagan's soul *split*. So there's one of the Shelly Kagan souls over here in (or connected to) Lefty and there's one of the Shelly Kagan souls over there in (or connected to) Righty. Both Lefty and Righty have one of the now split Shelly Kagan souls. (And of course, these aren't just inadequate bits of a soul; no, each one is a complete, functioning Shelly Kagan soul.)

All right, so now we can ask ourselves, "According to the soul theory, which one is Shelly Kagan?" By this point, of course, you can probably run through all the possibilities yourself! We could say, for example, that it's Lefty that's the same person as Shelly Kagan, and not Righty. But there's nothing in the soul theory that supports that claim. Both Lefty and Righty have an equally good piece of the original Shelly Kagan soul. So there's no reason to say that Lefty is Shelly Kagan and Righty isn't. And similarly, of course, there's no good reason to say that Righty is Shelly Kagan and Lefty isn't.

Would it be better to say that they're *both* Shelly Kagan—that as long as you have one of the (post-splitting) Shelly Kagan souls you just *are* Shelly Kagan? But in that case, Lefty and Righty are *both* Shelly Kagan, and Shelly Kagan is now bicoastal, one part of him in California, one part of him in Vermont. Should we say that? That there's just *one* person here, Shelly Kagan, who now manages to be in two places at the same time? That doesn't seem very satisfying either.

But what's the alternative? The best alternative, it seems, is for the soul theorist to say that *neither* of them—neither Lefty nor Righty—is Shelly Kagan. But if neither of them is Shelly Kagan, then Shelly Kagan died. But how can we say that if we accept the soul theory? Both Lefty and Righty have (enough of) Shelly Kagan's soul—at least, that's what we're imagining. So if neither is Shelly Kagan, then having (enough of) Shelly Kagan's soul isn't good enough. In which case we have to reject the soul theory—or rather, we have to reject the soul view in the version we've been considering *so far*. If souls can split, and we are going to avoid abandoning the soul theory altogether, it seems that what the soul theorist would have to do at this point (you saw this coming, didn't you?) is to accept the no branching rule! "Ah," the soul theorist should say, "Follow the soul—unless the soul splits, in which case neither of the resulting people is Shelly Kagan."

The trouble, of course, is that we don't find the no branching rule very plausible. It seems counterintuitive. But at this point, you might begin to think, maybe we just need to learn to live with it! If the personality theory needs the no branching rule, and the body theory needs the no branching rule, and the soul theory needs the no branching rule, maybe we're just stuck with the no branching rule, whether we like it or not. And if we're stuck with it, of course, then it's not an objection against any one of the theories that uses it. At any rate, this is what we might say as soul theorists if we think souls can split.

But we still need to consider the possibility that souls *can't* split. Maybe the soul theorist has an alternative available to her that fans of the other theories don't have. Suppose Shelly Kagan's soul cannot split. What does that mean? It means that when my brain gets split, my soul is going to end up in Lefty or in Righty, but not in both. After all, if my soul can't split, it can't end up in both of them.

Why can't the soul split? Maybe because it doesn't have any parts! Maybe the soul is simple rather than composite. As we know, that's what Plato was arguing in the *Phaedo*. He didn't convince me, but let that pass. Maybe the soul is simple, and simple things can't split. If simple things can't split, and the soul really is simple, it would follow, obviously, that souls can't split.

This might be a good place for me to confess that I don't actually know whether it's true that simple things can't split. Metaphysically speaking, I'm just not sure whether that's a possibility or not. But let's just put that sort of worry aside. Let us suppose that for whatever reason—whether having to do with its simplicity, or something else—the soul simply cannot split. And now, armed with this assumption, let's ask, in the case of fission, which one is Shelly Kagan? Lefty or Righty?

The answer, of course, depends on which one ended up with Shelly Kagan's soul. Since the soul can't split, they can't both have my soul, so one of them will have it, and the other one won't. You want to know which one is actually Shelly Kagan? The one that actually ends up with my soul! If Lefty ends up with my soul, then Lefty is Shelly Kagan and Righty is a deluded imposter. Righty thinks he's Shelly Kagan, but he's not, because he doesn't have Shelly Kagan's soul: Lefty has it. On the other hand, of course, if Righty's got my soul, then Righty is Shelly Kagan and Lefty is the imposter.

Sadly, looking at the situation from the outside, you can't tell which one of the two really is Shelly Kagan, because, of course, you can't tell which one really has my soul. Presumably, one of them really does have my soul, and that one really is me. But there's no way for you to know which one that is.

Interestingly, and somewhat more surprisingly, even looking at the situation from the *inside*, we won't be able to tell either. Lefty will say, "Give me a break. Of course I'm Shelly Kagan. Of course I've got Shelly Kagan's soul. Of course I'm the one." But Righty will also say, "Give me a break. Of course I'm Shelly Kagan. Of course I've got Shelly Kagan's soul. Of course I'm the one." If souls can't split, one of them is mistaken. But there's no way for them to know which one is the one that's deceived.

Now, that may not be an implication that you're unwilling to swallow. As we've seen, all the views here have their difficulties. So maybe that's the particular difficulty you're prepared to accept. What's the right answer in fission? Maybe you just want to insist that it depends on who's got Shelly Kagan's soul. There's no way to tell, but for all that, that's the answer to the metaphysical question.

(What happens if *neither* of these two has Shelly Kagan's soul? Then they're *both* imposters. That's a little bit like the case from John Locke that we worried about when we first started thinking about the soul theory of personal identity. What if last night God destroyed my soul and put in a new soul? According to the soul theory, Shelly Kagan died. Similarly, then, according to the soul theory, if Shelly Kagan's soul does not migrate to Lefty or Righty, neither of them is Shelly Kagan. So what happened to Shelly Kagan? On the one hand, if the soul got *destroyed*, then Shelly Kagan died. And on the other hand, if the soul didn't get destroyed but simply moved somewhere else altogether, then maybe somebody else that we weren't even looking at is Shelly Kagan!)

So as I say, the soul theory can at least give us an answer that avoids the no branching rule. If souls are simples and simples can't split, there's no possibility of having two things at the same time with the relevant soul. So we won't need to amend the soul theory by adding the (counterintuitive) no branching rule. That would certainly be a potential advantage for the soul theory, if only we believed in souls. But at the same time, I need to point out that the fission case also raises a special *disadvantage* for the soul theory.

Suppose that God tells us a metaphysical secret—that it's Lefty that has Shelly Kagan's soul. Then of course, given the soul view, it's Lefty that is Shelly Kagan. Righty is a deluded imposter. Righty *believes* he's Shelly Kagan—he has all the memories, beliefs, and desires of Shelly Kagan—but he's *not* Shelly

Kagan, because he doesn't have Shelly Kagan's soul. Lefty happens to have it. That's a nice answer to the problem of fission, but notice the trouble it raises for many of the arguments for believing in souls in the first place.

In Chapter 3 we considered an important family of arguments for the existence of souls. These arguments were all examples of inference to the best explanation. The thought was that there is some familiar, ordinary feature of being a person that needed to be explained in terms of souls. Perhaps you need to believe in souls in order to explain why bodies are animated, or why people are rational, how they can be creative, or have free will, or be conscious. However exactly we fill in the blank, the claim was that you needed to believe in souls in order to explain all of that.

But if that's right, what's going on in Righty's case? Righty is conscious. Righty is creative. Righty has free will. Righty makes plans. Righty is rational. Righty's body is animated. According to many dualists, we need to believe in souls in order to explain how you can have a *person*. But Righty is a person—even though he lacks a soul! So how does the dualist explain that? (Did God create a new soul—and stick it in Righty? Maybe. But why did God bother? Why not just let Lefty wake up with my soul, and call it a day at that?)

So at the very same moment that positing the nonsplitting of souls seems to offer a nice answer to the fission case, that very same case yanks the rug out from underneath the soul theorist by undermining some of the most important arguments for believing in dualism in the first place. After all, if Righty can be a person—admittedly not Shelly Kagan, but a person—without a soul, then maybe the same thing is true for us as well, which is of course exactly what the physicalist says.

Let me mention one other possibility, because it's quite intriguing.[2] Suppose the soul theorist answers that last objection by saying, "Ain't ever going to happen." Yes, she admits, it would be a problem for believing in souls if Righty could wake up without one. But since we stipulated that Shelly Kagan's soul is going to end up in Lefty, Righty is not going to wake up. Alternatively, of course, it might have been that Righty woke up, but Lefty doesn't. Either one can wake up, but only *one* can wake up.

Indeed, suppose we did brain transfers all the time and the following thing always happened. Transfer the entire brain, and the patient wakes up. Transfer one hemisphere, the patient wakes up. Transfer both hemispheres, one patient or the other wakes up, but *never both*. If that happened, we'd have a great new argument for the existence of the soul. What could possibly explain why either hemisphere of the brain would *normally* be enough, as long as we don't transfer both? What could explain why, if we do transfer both, one hemisphere or the other will work, but never both? What could possibly explain that? *Souls* could explain that. If souls can't split, then any given soul can follow only one half of the brain, either half, but never both halves of the brain at the same time.

So if we found these kinds of results, that would provide a new empirical argument for the existence of the soul. Of course, that's a big "if." Please don't go away thinking that what I just said is, here's a new argument for the soul. We don't actually do brain transfers, let alone half-a-brain transfers. We don't have any experiments at all that suggest that if we did do such half-a-brain transfers only one half would ever wake up. All I'm saying is that if someday we did do this kind of brain transplant, and found this sort of result, then *at that point* we'd have a new argument for the soul.

Well, let me put away the soul theory once again. I was exploring it because it's interesting to think about its implications. But since I don't believe in souls, I want to choose between the body view and the personality view. And both of those theories, as we saw, seem to need some version of the no branching rule. If either theory is going to survive, it seems, we need to throw a no branching rule in. I don't see any plausible alternative.

Of course, that doesn't make the no branching rule any less bizarre. It still seems wildly counterintuitive. But if both views are stuck with it, well then, maybe *we* are just stuck with it. At the very least, it suggests that we can't try to decide between the personality view and the body view on the basis of concerns about splitting, duplicates, and branching. Both theories face corresponding problems here, and both theories deal with those problems in the very same way—by adopting a no branching rule.

So which of these two theories should we accept? The body view or the personality view? Which of these is the better theory of personal identity? My answer is, I'm not sure.

Over the course of my philosophical career, I have moved back and forth between them. There was certainly a long period of time in which I found the personality theory (with an appropriate no branching rule) to be the better and more plausible theory. And this approach certainly has any number of advocates on the contemporary philosophical scene. But at other times in my philosophical career, I have found the body theory (with an appropriate no branching rule) to be the more plausible theory. And it is certainly the case that the body theory has its advocates among contemporary philosophers as well.

For what it's worth—and I don't actually think that what I'm about to say is worth all that much—for some time now, I've been inclined to go with the body theory. I'm inclined to think that the key to personal identity is having the same body, as long as there's no branching, as long as there's no splitting. But it's certainly open to you to decide that you think that the personality theory is the stronger view. I can't settle the question. I don't have any more philosophical arguments on this issue up my sleeve.

But I do have one other point that's worth considering. Although I'm inclined to think that the body theory may be the best view about what's the key to personal identity, I'm also inclined to think it doesn't really matter!

What Matters

We've been asking the following question: what does it take for me to survive? But what I want to suggest now is that this may not really be the question we should have been thinking about! To be sure, I don't think we would have been in a position to see this until we had worked through the various main theories of personal identity. But now that we're here, we can finally raise a crucial question: should we be asking about what it takes to *survive*? Or should we be asking about what *matters* in survival?

In posing this new question, I am obviously presupposing that we can draw a distinction between the question "Do I survive? Is somebody that exists in the future me?" and the question "What was it that I *wanted*, when I wanted to survive? What was it that *mattered* in ordinary survival?" But I do think these are different questions. And more importantly, I think the answers can potentially come apart.

To see this, suppose we start by thinking again about the soul view. Suppose there are souls. I don't believe in them, but let's imagine. And suppose that souls are the key to personal identity. So somebody is me if they've got my soul. I *survive*, as long as there's somebody around with my soul. Will I still be around in a hundred years? Well, I will be if my soul is still around. That's what the soul theory says. And suppose it's the truth.

Now consider the following possibility. Suppose that people can be reincarnated. That is to say, at the death of their body, their soul takes over—animates, inhabits, gets connected to—a new body that's being born. But unlike the kind of reincarnation cases that get talked about in popular culture, where at least under the right circumstances you can remember your prior lives, let's imagine that when the soul is reincarnated, it's scrubbed completely clean, leaving no traces whatsoever of the earlier life. There is simply no way to retrieve any earlier memories; there is no underlying personality that will potentially reassert itself. There are no karmic similarities of personality from the previous life of any sort, or anything like that; the soul simply starts over from scratch, like a blank slate. Think of it like a blackboard that's been completely erased: we have the very same blackboard, but now we start writing completely new things on it. Imagine that that's the way reincarnation worked.

So if somebody asks you, "Will you still be around in 1,000 years?" the answer is yes. I will still be around because my soul will be reincarnated. In 1,000 years there'll be somebody that has the very same soul that's animating my body right now. Of course, that soul won't remember being Shelly Kagan. It won't have any memories of its prior life. It won't be like Shelly Kagan in any way in terms of Shelly Kagan's desires or ambitions or goals or fears. (Similarly, it won't be that the future personality emerges somehow through karmic cause and effect in any way that is a function of what I am like now, in this life.) That future person will be me—Shelly Kagan—because he will have Shelly Kagan's soul. But there will be no overlap of personality, memories, desires, anything.

When I think about this case, I want to say, who cares? The fact that I will *survive* under those circumstances doesn't give me anything that *matters* to me. It's no comfort to me to be told I will survive ("because after all, the soul is the key to personal identity"), if there's no similar personality, no memories, no beliefs, no retrievable elements from past lives. Given all this, who cares that it's *me*?

If you can feel the force of that thought, then you're seeing how the question "Will I survive?" can be separated out from the question "What matters? What do we *care* about?" Bare survival of my soul, even if that were the key to personal identity, wouldn't give me what I want.

It's no more comforting or satisfying than if you had said, "You know this knucklebone? After you die, we're going to do knucklebone surgery and implant that knucklebone in somebody else's body. And that knucklebone is going to survive." I would reply, "Oh, that's sort of interesting, that my knucklebone will be around 100 or 1,000 years from now. But who *cares*?" And if the knucklebone theory of personal identity got proposed and somebody said, "Oh, yes, but you see, that person now with that knucklebone will be *you*, because the key to personal identity is having the very same knucklebone," I would say, "All right, so it's me. Who cares?" Bare knucklebone survival does not give me what matters.

The knucklebone theory of personal identity is a very stupid theory. In contrast, the soul theory of personal survival is not a stupid theory. But for all that, it doesn't give me what I want. When we think about the possibility of bare survival of the scrubbed clean, erased soul, we see that survival wasn't really everything we wanted. What we wanted—at least what *I* want, and I invite you to ask yourself whether you want the same thing—is not just survival, but survival with the same *personality*. So even if the soul theory is the correct theory of personal identity, it's not enough to give me what *matters*. What matters isn't just survival. It's survival with the same personality.

Next, let's consider the body view. Suppose that the body theory of personal identity is correct. I'll survive, as long as there is someone in the future who has my body. Let's also suppose that the brain version of the body theory is the best version. And now, imagine that next year there's going to be somebody that's got my brain. But let's imagine that the brain has been scrubbed clean. All memory traces have been completely erased. We're talking complete irreversible amnesia, complete erasure of the brain's hard drive. Imagine that there are *no* traces of my personality. No memories, desires, intentions, or beliefs to eventually be recovered if only we do the right procedure (have the right surgery, undergo the right psychotherapy). No, it's all just *gone*.

The person that wakes up after this complete irreversible amnesia will no doubt eventually develop a new personality, a set of beliefs and memories. Suppose that nobody knows who he is, though. They find him wandering on the streets. They call him John Doe. John Doe will eventually have a bunch of beliefs about how the world works, make some plans, get some memories. And according to the body theory, that's me. If the body theory of personal identity is correct, then by golly it *is* me.

But when I think about this case, all I can say in response to the fact that it's me is, who cares? I survive, but so what? I'm not comforted by the thought that I will still be around fifty years from now, if the person that's me doesn't have my personality.

Mere bodily survival isn't enough to give me what I want. I want *more* than mere bodily survival. I want to survive with the same personality. So even if the body theory of personal identity is the *correct* theory of personal identity, what I want to say is, so what? The really crucial question is not "Do I survive?" but "Do I have what I *wanted* when I wanted to survive?" And the fact of the matter is, having the same body doesn't guarantee that I will. I don't just want to survive. I want to survive with the same personality.

The question we really need to get clear about, then, is this: what *matters* in survival? Of course, it is plausible to think that in the normal cases of survival, I do get what matters. That, after all, is probably the reason why we come to care about survival so much: because it normally provides us with what matters. But for all that, we can see that in unusual cases, mere survival—bare survival—may not actually be *enough* to give us what matters.

If there can be cases where I survive, but I don't have what I *normally* have when I survive, and so I don't have what matters, then in such cases I don't really have what I wanted when I wanted to survive. For all that, of course, it could still be true that in *typical* cases of survival I've got the extra thing that matters, whatever it is. But if we can think of cases in which I survive, but I *don't* have that extra thing, then I wouldn't have everything that matters to me. So perhaps we should say that mere survival or bare-bones survival doesn't really give me what matters. What I want is survival plus something *more*.

But what's the extra something? What's the "something more"? The examples we've been discussing so far suggest that what I want is to survive with the same *personality*. Is that the right conclusion? Is what matters in survival not just survival, but surviving with the same personality? I think that that's close—but not quite right.

To see that, let's take another look at the personality view. Suppose that the personality theory of personal identity were correct. Would that then guarantee that I have not only survival, but also what matters? I don't think it would.

Recall the fact that, according to the personality view, survival doesn't require that my personality never change. It's not as though I have to keep every single one of my beliefs, desires, and memories fixed. Because of course, if it did require that, then we would have to say that I am going to die as soon as I get a new belief! I'm going to die as soon as I forget any detail of what I was doing twenty minutes ago! Rather, according to the personality theory, what personal identity requires isn't that every single element of my personality stay the same, but that I keep the same evolving-over-time personality. I can gain new beliefs, new desires, new goals. I can lose some of my previous memories, lose some of my previous beliefs. All of that is okay, as long as it's the same slowly evolving personality, with the right pattern of overlap and continuity.

So consider the following case. Here I am, almost sixty. I've got a set of beliefs. For example, I believe my name is "Shelly Kagan" and I teach philosophy. I have a set of memories about growing up in Chicago, and marrying my wife, and so forth. And I have various desires—for example, I want to finish writing this book. But of course, I will get older, and my personality will change. I'll get some new beliefs, new memories; I'll have new desires and new goals. Imagine, then, that I get older and older and older. Suppose that I get very old indeed—very, very, very old. I get to be 100 years old, 200 years old, 300 years old, and more.

Suppose that somewhere around 200, my friends give me a new nickname. They call me Jo-Jo. Who knows why, they call me Jo-Jo. And eventually the nickname spreads. By the time I'm 250 years old, everybody calls me Jo-Jo. Nobody calls me Shelly anymore. Indeed, by the time I'm 300, 350, 400, I've forgotten that *anybody* ever called me Shelly. I no longer remember growing up in Chicago. Of course, I do remember some things from my "youth," when I was a mere lad of 150. But I can't go back to what it was like in the early days, from my twenties or thirties or forties, just like you can't go back to what it was like to be three or four. And imagine that while all of this is going on, while I'm getting older and older, my personality is changing in a variety of other ways as well. Along the way I lose my interest in philosophy and take up an interest in something I've never cared about before at all, perhaps organic chemistry. I become fascinated by the details of organic chemistry.

And my values change, too. Right now, today, I'm a kind, compassionate, warm individual who cares about the downtrodden. But around 300, I start to lose my compassion. At 400 I'm saying things like, "The downtrodden. Who needs them?" And by the time I'm 500, I'm completely self-absorbed: I'm a vicious, cruel, vile person. Here I am, 800 years old, 900 years old, more.

Methuselah, in the Bible, lives for 969 years. He's the oldest person in the Bible. So here I am, at the end of my life, 969 years old.

Let's call this the *Methuselah* case. And the crucial point about it is that we stipulate that at no point along the way was there a dramatic change in my personality. It was all gradual, slow, evolving, in just the way that it normally happens in real life. It's just that I live a very, very, very long time. And toward the end of it—let's say, somewhere around 700 or 800—I'm a "completely different person," as we might put it. Of course, I don't mean that literally. I mean that it's as *though* I were a completely different person—given how different my personality is.

Now remember, according to the personality theory of personal identity, what makes someone me is the fact that they've got the same evolving-through-time personality as I have. And I stipulated that it *is* the same evolving personality. So that's still *me* that's going to be around 600 years from now, 700 years from now. (In case you're a stickler for detail, let me also stipulate that the no branching requirement is satisfied as well; so it really is me.)

But when I think about the Methuselah case I say, "So what? Who cares?" When I think about that case, I find myself wanting to say that even if we just *stipulate* that this will be me in 700 years, that still doesn't give me what I want. That person is completely unlike me, as I am now. He doesn't remember being Shelly Kagan. He doesn't remember growing up in Chicago. He doesn't remember my family. He has completely different interests and tastes and values. I find myself wanting to say, "It's me, but so what? This doesn't give me what I want. It doesn't give me what matters."

When I think about what I want, it's not just that there should be somebody at the tail end of my evolving personality. I want that person to be *like* me, not just *be* me. (More precisely, of course, I want that person to be like me *now*—to be like this particular person stage. But I won't keep adding this qualification explicitly.) Sadly, in the Methuselah case, I end up not being very much like me at all. So that case doesn't give me what I want either—even though I survive with the same evolving personality.

In short, when I think about what I want, it's not just survival. And it's not just survival with the same evolving-through-time personality. Roughly speaking, what I want is survival with a *similar* personality. It certainly doesn't have to be identical, item for item. But it has to be close enough to be fairly similar to my personality now. Give me that, and I've got what matters in survival. Don't give me that, and I don't have what matters. Of course, you may find yourself wanting something different. I can only invite you to ask yourself what it is that you want, what matters to you in survival. But when I think about what *I* want, that's pretty much it.

Actually, though, I'm inclined to go a little bit further. Once you give me that there's somebody around in the future with a similar enough personality to my own, I think that may be *all* that matters here. So in a certain way, what I've been saying up to this point has been misleading. I've been saying that mere survival by itself isn't good enough: you need survival plus something more. But strictly speaking, it might be that *all* that matters is the something more. Perhaps, as long as I have that, I have what matters—even if I *don't* have survival.

Suppose, for example, that there really are souls. And suppose that the soul really is the key to personal identity. And suppose as well that the thing that Locke was worried about really does happen: every day at midnight God destroys the old soul and replaces it with a new soul that has the very same personality as the one before midnight—the same beliefs, desires, and so forth and so on. If I were to somehow discover all of these metaphysical facts I'd say, "Huh! It turns out that I'm not going to survive tonight; I'm going to die. But who *cares*? There will be somebody around tomorrow with precisely my beliefs, my desires, my goals, my ambitions, my fears, my values. That's good enough. I don't really care whether I'm going to *survive*. What I care about is whether there'll be somebody that's similar to me in the right way in terms of my current personality. And there will be."

So it might be that the whole question we've been focusing on, "What does it take to survive?" is misguided. The real question may not be "What does it take to survive?" but "What matters?" Of course, in ordinary circumstances, having what matters goes hand in hand with surviving. Survival is normally the only way that we can *get* what matters. But logically speaking, at least, the two things can come apart. And what really matters, or so it seems to me, isn't survival per se at all, but having a similar personality. (I trust it is obvious that I don't really mean that this is the only thing that matters in any way whatsoever! I simply mean, it's what matters when I am concerned about surviving.)

Imagine that tonight, while everyone is sleeping, God replaces my body with some identical-looking body, and he gives it a personality identical to my own from just before I went to sleep. Since I am inclined to think that the body view is the correct theory of personal identity, and since that new body obviously won't be *my* body, I believe that the person who will wake up tomorrow won't be me. I won't survive the night. I'm going to die. But that's okay. What matters to me isn't survival per se. Indeed, it isn't survival at all. It's having someone with a similar enough personality. That's good enough.

So imagine that when we die, what happens is this: God takes all the relevant information about my personality from the moment just before my death, and he creates a *new* body up in heaven (perhaps a new angelic body) with that very same personality. Since the body view is the correct view, I think that won't be me. (That's not my body up in heaven; *my* body is rotting here on earth.) It turns out, then, that we don't survive our deaths. But still, I find myself wanting to say, so what? Survival was never what really mattered anyway. Even though it won't be *me* up in heaven, this may still give me what matters.

In short, a physicalist need not despair. Despite what we might have initially thought, even a physicalist can believe that death doesn't rob us of what matters. On the one hand, as we have seen, if the physicalist accepts the *personality* view, then even the death of my body doesn't logically entail that I don't survive. There remains the possibility that my *personality* will continue, in which case *I* will continue as well. And on the other hand, even if the physicalist accepts the *body* view, so that upon the death of my body I cease to exist, there might still be someone with a personality similar enough to my own to give me everything that *matters*.

There is, then, at least a logical possibility that after the death of my body, I will still have what matters. Indeed, I might even survive, as well—if there is bodily resurrection, or if it is the personality view rather than the body view that gives the correct account of personal identity. But for what it's worth, I don't in fact believe that any of this is *going to happen*. In particular, as far as I can see, there is no good reason to believe that my personality will continue after the death of my body. And so, as far as I can see, there is no good reason to believe that I will still have what *matters* after the death of my body.

Of course, these questions are partly theological matters. And I'm certainly not trying to say anything here to argue you out of the theological conviction that God will resurrect your body or that God will transplant your personality into some new angel body. If you believe either of these things, so be it. It's not my goal here to argue either for or against these particular theological possibilities.

Still, the truth is, I do not myself believe in either one of these possibilities. I do not think that after my death my body will be resurrected, or my personality transplanted. On the contrary, I think that death really will be the end. The end of me, and the end of my personality. That, it seems to me, is the simple fact of the matter. Death will be the end.

CHAPTER 8

The Nature of Death

What Is Death?

According to the physicalist, a person is just a body that is functioning in the right way, a body capable of thinking and feeling and communicating, loving and planning, being rational and being self-conscious. A body that is *P functioning*, as I have sometimes put the idea. According to the physicalist, a person is just a P functioning body.

If we accept this idea, what should we say about death itself? What *is* it to die, on the physicalist account? That is the question I want to turn to next. And we can approach that question by thinking about a closely related one: *when* do I die?

The basic answer certainly seems like it should be straightforward enough. Roughly speaking, at least, the physicalist should say that I am alive when we've got a P functioning body, and so I *die* when we no longer have that—when the body begins to break and it stops functioning properly. That does, in fact, seem to me to be more or less the right answer from the physicalist's point of view. But as we'll see, we're going to need to refine it a bit.

First of all, then, we need to ask: *which* functions are the crucial ones in defining the moment of death? Think about a properly functioning human body—yours, for example. Your body is currently engaged in a wide variety of functions. Some of these have to do with merely digesting food and moving the body around, making the heart beat and having the lungs open and close, and so forth. Call those things the *body* functions, or *B functions* for short. In addition, of course, there are also a variety of higher-level cognitive functions, which I've been calling the P functions (person functions). Now, roughly speaking, I die when the body's functioning stops. But which functions are the *relevant* functions? Is it the B functions or the P functions—or both?

The answer to this question isn't obvious, because normally, of course, P functioning stops at the *same time* as B functioning. Science fiction examples aside, P functioning *depends* on B functioning. So normally we don't need to ask ourselves which type of functioning is the relevant *kind* for defining the moment of death. We lose both, more or less simultaneously.

That's the situation we have in Figure 8.1, where I've drawn a schematic history of my body, from the start of its existence (at the left) to the end of its existence (at the right). We can divide that history into three major phases, A, B, and C. During the first two phases—A and B—my body is functioning just fine. At least, it's carrying out its *body* functions perfectly well (digesting, breathing, moving, and so on). Initially, though, in phase A, that's *all* it's capable of. It can't yet engage in the higher cognitive processes we've been calling P functioning. For some initial period of time, the brain simply isn't sufficiently developed to engage in communication, rationality, creativity, self-consciousness, and the like. So we don't yet have P functioning. That doesn't start until phase B. Finally, in the last phase, C, my body can no longer P function or B function. It is no longer functioning at all. It's just a corpse. (Obviously, more fine-grained divisions would be possible as well; but these should suffice for our purposes.)

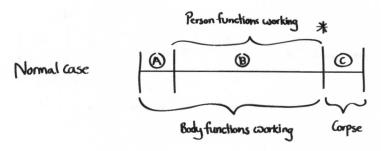

Fig. 8.1

So that's the *normal* case. The body begins to exist, and for a while, in phase A, it is capable of B functioning but not P functioning. But then, after a while, both B functioning *and* P functioning are going on. That's phase B. And then, after a considerably longer while, they both stop. Perhaps I'll be in a car accident, or have a heart attack, or die from cancer. Whatever the precise cause, my body will no longer be capable of B or P functioning. Of course, my body will still *exist*—for a while, at least. But it will be a *corpse*. That's phase C.

Now, when did I die? The natural suggestion is to say that I died at the very end of phase B, when my body stops functioning. So I've drawn a little star there, to mark that point. Since this is the normal case that we're thinking about, where both my body functions and my person functions stop at the very same time, it is, I suppose, uncontroversial that my death occurs at the moment marked by the star. That's when I die.

But we can still ask, which loss was the *crucial* one? The loss of P functioning or the loss of B functioning? Which loss is relevant for defining the moment of my death? You can't tell by thinking about the *normal* case, because the B functioning and the P functioning both stop at the same time. But suppose we draw an *abnormal* case. Imagine that I suffer from some horrible disease that will eventually destroy my ability to engage in any of the higher-level cognitive processes that we are grouping together as P functioning. However—and this is the crucial point—for some period of time after that (months or years), my body will still be able to carry out its B functions in the ordinary way. Eventually, of course, my body will lose its ability to B function as well. But in the case I've got in mind, the P functioning stops long before the B functioning does. That's what we've got in Figure 8.2.

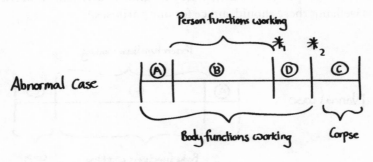

Fig. 8.2

This time, I've divided the history of my body into *four* phases. Once again, in phase A the body is capable of B functioning but not yet capable of P functioning, in phase B it is capable of both, and in phase C it is capable of neither. But now there is a new phase, phase D. That's the period where the ability to P function has been lost, but the body is still engaged in *B* functioning. (Obviously, the phases are no longer in alphabetical order; but I introduced D in the middle so that the other phases could keep their old labels.)

In this case the loss of P functioning and B functioning come apart. Body functioning stops at the end of phase D, person functioning at the end of phase B. That much is clear. But when does *death* occur? When do I die? There are, it seems, two suggestions worth taking seriously, and I've marked each with a star. Either death occurs when person functioning stops, or it occurs when body functioning stops. And interestingly enough, which answer seems more plausible may depend on whether we accept the body view or the personality view.

Suppose we accept the personality view. Then for someone to be *me*, they've got to have the same evolving personality as I have. And this means, of course, that for me to *exist*, my personality has to be around as well.

One fairly straightforward implication of this view, then, is that in phase C, I don't exist. After all, during phase C, there's *nothing* with my personality. Nobody thinks they're Shelly Kagan. Nobody has my memories, beliefs, desires, and goals. Pretty clearly, then, on the personality view I don't *exist* at phase C. Of course, if we're speaking loosely, we can say that I am just a corpse. But that's potentially misleading, insofar as it suggests that I still exist—*as* a corpse. Strictly speaking, however, that's just not true. It would be more accurate to say that all that is *left* of me is a corpse. In phase C, I no longer exist.

But what about phase D? Here, at least, my body is still functioning. Or rather, more precisely, it is engaged in B functioning. But for all that, my personality has been destroyed. Nothing exists with my beliefs, memories, desires, fears, or ambitions. But according to the personality theory, for me to exist at a given time there has to be something at that time that *has* my personality. And that's just not true during phase D. So I don't exist during phase D either. In short, since my personality ended at the close of phase B, it seems that those who accept the personality theory should say that I *died* at the end of phase B as well. The moment of my death is the one marked by the first star, the moment where my body loses the ability to P function.

All of that is reasonably straightforward. But there is a complication. Suppose that instead of asking whether I exist or not, we ask whether I'm *alive*. Phase D now seems a bit more puzzling.

Presumably, we're all agreed that my *body* is still alive in phase D. After all, it's fully engaged in B functioning. But what about *me*? Am *I* alive? That's rather hard to believe. Think about what we would be saying: I don't *exist*, but I'm *alive*! That seems like a very unpalatable combination of views. How can I be alive if I don't even exist? So it looks like we're going to have to say that I am *not* alive during phase D. Not only don't I exist, I'm not alive either.

Yet even though *I'm* not alive, my *body* is. So the personality theorist needs to draw a distinction between *my* being alive, on the one hand, and my *body* being alive, on the other. In the normal case—Figure 8.1—my body stops being alive at the very same moment that *I* stop being alive. The two deaths occur simultaneously. But in the abnormal case—Figure 8.2—the two deaths come apart. The death of my body occurs at the second star; *my* death occurs at the first.

That, at least, is what we should say if we accept the personality view. But what if, instead, we accept the body view? Now things really get interesting.

According to the body view, for me to exist at a given time there's got to be somebody around with my body at the relevant time. They don't have to have my personality; having my body suffices. ("Follow the body.") So consider phase C. All that's left of me is a corpse. But what *is* a corpse? It's a body, and indeed, my corpse is *my* body. Since my corpse is still around, that means that my body is still around. And so—given the body view—that means that *I'm* still around. I'm *dead*, of course, but I still *exist*.

(Why does the body theorist agree that in phase C I'm *dead*? Unlike the personality theorist, the body theorist has no need to distinguish between *my* being alive and my *body's* being alive. Since my body is not alive in phase C, the body theorist reasonably holds that I am not alive either.)

Think about the question with which this book began. Can you survive your death? Will you still exist after you die? According to the body view, there's good news and there's bad news. The good news is, you will exist after your death. The bad news is, you'll be a corpse. That seems like a bad joke, but if the body view is right, it's not a joke at all. It's the literal truth.[1] After I die, I will continue to exist, at least for a while. Eventually, of course, my body will decay, turn into atoms, decompose. At that point my body will no longer exist, and *I* will no longer exist. But at least for a while, during phase C, the body theorist should say, "Yes, Shelly Kagan still exists. He exists, but he's not alive."

This just reinforces the point I was making in the last chapter, that the crucial question is not survival per se. The crucial question is, what do you *want* out of survival? And one of the things I want out of survival is to be *alive*. Admittedly, according to the body view, I will still *exist* during phase C. But I won't be *alive*. And so I won't have what *matters*. That, I take it, is what a body theorist should say. (In contrast, of course, on the personality view, I don't even *exist* when all that's left is my corpse.)

And what should the body theorist say about phase D? Something similar. Here too, of course, I exist, since my body exists. What's more, in phase D, unlike phase C, I am alive—since my body is alive. Sadly, however, I am still not a person. My body cannot P function. Thus, it is still the case that I fail to have what *matters*. It isn't enough to exist, and it isn't enough to be alive. Rather, I want to be a living *person*—and we only have that in phase B.

In short, according to the body view, I *die* at the moment marked by the second star, when my body is no longer alive. But I lose what *matters* at the moment marked by the *first* star, when I stop being a *person*.

"When I stop being a person." That's an odd and rather surprising turn of phrase. Most of us, I imagine, think that being a person is the sort of thing I cannot stop being until I stop existing altogether. In the jargon of philosophy, being a person is one of my essential properties: it is a property I must have if I am to exist at all. But it seems that if we accept the body view, we will have to say that being a person is *not* one of my essential properties. I can stop being a person and yet continue to exist.

I am, of course, *in fact* a person, but according to the body view that won't *always* be true of me. When I am a corpse, I will cease to be a person, but I will still exist. And if I end up in one of the abnormal cases—where my body continues to digest, pump blood, and respirate, but it is no longer capable of thinking and reasoning and so forth—then there too we will have to say that I exist, indeed I am alive, but I am not a person.

On this view, then, being a person is something you can "do" for a period of time and then stop doing, without going out of existence. It is like being a child, or being a professor. These are things that you can be, for a while, and then stop being, without ceasing to exist. I was a child once, and I no longer am; but I still exist. Being a child was just a "phase" I went through. Similarly, then, on the body view, being a person is just a phase that I—that is to say, my body—can go through. Being a person is something that my body can do for a *while*. It wasn't doing that during phase A. It certainly won't be doing that in phase C. And if I find myself in one of the abnormal cases, then it won't be doing that in phase D either. Being a person isn't something that I am *essentially*; rather, I am a person for only part of my existence—and, indeed, for only part of my life. That, at least, is what the body view says. (For the personality view, in contrast, it seems that being a person is indeed one of my essential properties. I cannot exist at all, unless I exist as a person.)

Notice, incidentally, that if we do adopt this sort of position, then there is something somewhat misleading about the standard philosophical label for the set of problems we've been thinking about for the last few chapters. We've been worrying about the nature of personal identity—that is to say, what it is for somebody to be me. But notice that this very label, "personal identity," seems to have built into it the assumption that whatever it is that's me is going to be a *person* (and so the relevant question is only whether a given person is the *same* person as me or not). But now, it turns out, this assumption—built right into this standard label—may well be false. On the body view, something could still be *me* without being a person at all. Perhaps, then, philosophers shouldn't call our topic the problem of personal identity after all, but simply the problem of identity. (Earlier parts of our discussion of personal identity may have been misleading in just the same way. For example, in Chapter 6 I said that I will survive provided that there is some *person* in the future who is the same *person* as me. As we now can see, however, that may be more than what my bare survival actually requires.)

In addition to the questions we have been asking about the end of life, there are, of course, corresponding questions concerning the *beginnings* of life. In particular, what should we say about phase A, when the body is engaged in B functioning but the brain has not yet gotten to the stage at which it is capable of P functioning? Do I exist during that phase or don't I? Presumably, if we accept the body view we should say that I do exist in phase A. Admittedly, I am not yet a person in phase A, but no matter; as we have already seen, according to the body view I can exist without being a person. In contrast, if we accept the personality view, then we should say that I do not yet exist in phase A, even though my body does, since my evolving-through-time personality has not yet begun. There are further complications even here (for example, when exactly does my body begin to exist?), but since the *start* of life is not, strictly, our topic, I am going to have to leave these fascinating and difficult questions aside.

Instead, let's think a bit more about phase D. Imagine that my body's ability to P function has been destroyed, but its ability to B function continues unabated. So there's my body, lying in the hospital bed: the heart's pumping, the lungs are breathing, it is able to digest food, and so forth, but it will never again be able to think, to reason, to communicate, to love or be aware.

Next, imagine that you have someone who needs a heart transplant. Tissue compatibility tests reveal that my body is a suitable donor. So what you need to know now is, is it morally permissible to take the heart out of my body or not?

In the *normal* case, of course, when thinking about whether it is morally permissible to remove someone's heart from their body, all we need to ask is, "Is the potential donor still *alive*?" After all, if she *is* alive, and you remove her heart, she'll end up dead; you will have killed her. And obviously enough, that's morally forbidden: people have a right to life, which certainly seems to include (among other things) a right not to be *killed*.

But thinking about the abnormal case helps us realize that things are actually somewhat less straightforward than we might otherwise recognize. Suppose, for example, that we accept the personality view. Then, as we have seen, the correct thing to say about phase D seems to be that *I* am no longer alive, but my *body* is. And this means, of course, that even if you remove my beating heart from my chest, you won't actually kill me—after all, I am already dead—you will only kill my body. And it isn't at all obvious whether doing something like *that* is morally impermissible or not.

Most of us, no doubt, would feel uncomfortable—to say the least!—in taking a beating heart out of a living body. It just seems horrendously immoral to even contemplate doing something like that. But perhaps that is just confusion on our part, brought on by our failure to think the issues through sufficiently carefully.

What we need to decide, presumably, is who or what it is that actually *has* the right not to be killed. Do *I* have the right to life, or does my *body* have the right in question? (Or are there, perhaps, two such rights—one had by me and one had by my body?) On the one hand, if my body has a right to life, then it is indeed immoral to take my heart, even though I am already dead! But on the other hand, if it is just me that has a right to life—if the *person* is the rightholder, not the body—then it may well be permissible for you to remove my heart after all (perhaps after getting my family's consent), even though this will kill my body, since doing so won't actually violate *my* right to life at all. Admittedly, accepting the personality view doesn't settle this question (we'd need to turn to a lengthy discussion in moral philosophy to try to do that), but it is striking to realize that it at least opens the door to saying that it is permissible to kill the body, so long as doing so doesn't actually kill the *person*.

And what if it is the body view that we accept, rather than the personality view? According to the body view, of course, I am still *alive* in phase D. So it may seem obvious that here, at least, we do indeed need to say that it would be wrong to harvest the heart, since doing so would kill my body, and thus kill me. Surely, we may find ourselves wanting to say, if *anything* violates my right to life, removing my beating heart while I am still alive does that, and thus is morally forbidden.

But even here, things are not so simple. As we have already seen, being alive is not all that it's cracked up to be! In terms of getting what matters, the important question is not whether I am alive or not, but whether or not I am a *person*. And in phase D, even though I am still alive, I am not a *person* anymore. Conceivably, then, sufficient reflection on this sort of case might eventually persuade us that the so-called right to "life" is somewhat misleadingly named. Maybe it's not so much that I have a right not to be killed, as that I have a right not to be "depersonified"—a right not to have my personality destroyed. If that's the real right, then here too there would be nothing unacceptable about removing my heart, given that my personality has already been destroyed. To be sure, in the normal case killing someone does destroy their personality, and so is impermissible. But in the abnormal case, where I am still alive though no longer a person, perhaps killing me can be morally justified after all.

I hope it is obvious that these are all important and difficult questions. But we don't have the space to pursue them properly here. And so, having merely gestured in the direction of some possible answers, I am going to put these further questions aside as well.

Ability

As we have seen, if we accept the personality view then the moment of death should be defined in terms of P functioning, rather than B functioning. Roughly speaking, I am alive only as long as my body is a P functioning body. If it *isn't* still P functioning, then even though my *body* may still be alive, *I* am no longer alive: I am dead.

Surely *something* along those lines is what we are going to want to say about death, given the personality view. But it can't be quite right as it stands. To see this, think about last night. Let me suppose that last night, at 3:20 A.M., you were fast asleep; indeed, let's suppose you were in a deep, *dreamless* sleep. You weren't thinking. You weren't reasoning. You weren't communicating. You weren't remembering. You weren't making plans. You weren't being creative. You weren't engaged in any form of P functioning at all.

But if we accept the idea that when your body stops P functioning you're dead, then we have to say—unacceptably—that you were dead last night at 3:20 A.M.! Indeed, since you doubtless went through various cycles of dreamless sleep followed by dreaming, we'll have to say that you were dead and then alive and then dead again, on and off and on and off all through the night. That's clearly not the right thing to say. So we are going to have to be a bit more careful in defining the idea of death. We cannot simply say that if your body isn't P functioning, you're dead. We need a more subtle approach.

One natural suggestion for the personality theorist to make is to say that it's okay if you aren't P functioning, as long as your failure to P function is *temporary*. If your body has been P functioning in the past (and so you already are a person) *and* it will P function again in the future, then you are still alive, even if it isn't P functioning now. That nicely handles our case of dreamless sleep, since even though you weren't P functioning at 3:20 A.M., you did indeed resume P functioning later; so we are able to say, appropriately, that you remained alive even during dreamless sleep. According to this suggestion, then, death requires more than the lack of P functioning: P functioning has to have stopped *permanently*.

But this revision won't quite do either. It still misclassifies certain examples, calling some people dead that intuitively we take to still be alive, and calling other people alive that intuitively we take to be dead. For an example of the first sort, consider a modification of our example of dreamless sleep. Imagine that Frank was in a period of dreamless sleep last night, from 2:00 A.M. until 2:30 A.M., and then, tragically, at 2:30 A.M. he had a heart attack and died in his sleep, never regaining consciousness, indeed never resuming P functioning of any sort. According to our current proposal Frank died at 2:00, since it was at 2:00 that he stopped P functioning for the very last time. Intuitively, however, that seems to be the wrong answer. Frank was still alive, albeit in dreamless sleep, at 2:15. He didn't die until 2:30, when he suffered the heart attack. So the mere fact that P functioning has stopped, never to resume, is not sufficient for death.

Nor is it necessary. That is to say, in at least some imaginable cases a person can be *dead* despite the fact that P functioning will eventually *resume*! Suppose, for example, that come Judgment Day, God will resurrect the dead. In particular, then, after the resurrection there will be someone (and only one someone) who has the very same personality as you had just before your death. According to the personality view, as we know, that postresurrection person will be *you*. You will be alive; you will have been resurrected. And the same thing is true, let us suppose, for everyone: everyone who has ever died will once again be alive.

That's what we want to say. But according to our current proposal, to say this is a mistake—for despite what we may have thought, none of these people were ever really dead in the first place! After all, after the resurrection all of these formerly "dead" people will be P functioning. And that means, of course, that despite the fact that P functioning had stopped—in some cases for hundreds or thousands of years—it never stopped *permanently*. The break in P functioning was only temporary, like when we are in dreamless sleep, only for a much longer period. So all these people were alive all along; they never died at all.

That's what the current proposal has to say, and it just doesn't seem right. On Judgment Day, God resurrects the *dead*. It's not that he simply wakes up those in a deep, deep "sleep." So the current proposal—that death is a matter of permanent (rather than temporary) cessation of P functioning—doesn't seem quite right either.

Here's a different proposal, one that I think is probably closer to the right account. It starts with the important observation that when you are asleep, even if you are not actually engaged in P functioning, nonetheless it remains the case that you are *capable* of P functioning. For example, when you are sleeping you are not doing your multiplication tables. And yet, for all that, you *could* still do your multiplication tables. How do we know that? All we have to do is wake you up! We wake you up and we say, "What's three times three?" And after you stop swearing at us, you'll say, "Well, it's nine." Similarly, if you know a foreign language—French, let's suppose—then even though you aren't speaking it while you are asleep, it is still true of you while you are asleep that you can or could speak French. We could wake you up, ask you to conjugate such and such a verb, and you could do it. More generally, then, even if you are not engaged in P functioning while you are asleep, it is still true of you, even while asleep, that you have the *ability* to engage in P functioning.

Abilities aren't always actualized. Your P functioning is actualized now, because you're engaged in thought, but you don't lose the *ability* to think during those moments when you're not thinking. Suppose, then, that the personality theorist says that for you to be alive is for you to be *able* to engage in P functioning. And to be dead is to be *unable* to engage in P functioning. Why are you unable? Presumably because the cognitive structures in your brain that underwrite the ability to P function have been *broken*, so that they no longer work. When you are dead, your brain is broken. It's not just that you're not currently engaged in P functioning, it's that you're no longer *able* to engage in P functioning.

An account along these lines seems to handle our various cases properly. In dreamless sleep, you are still able to P function, even if you aren't actively engaged in P functioning, and so you are not dead. Even Frank, who tragically will soon die of a heart attack in his sleep, isn't dead *until* the heart attack, since during his last half hour of dreamless sleep he too is capable of P functioning (though he isn't engaged in any). So the account doesn't inappropriately misclassify the living as dead. Nor does it misclassify the dead as living. If God will resurrect the dead on Judgment Day, then it's true that at that point in the future they *will* once again engage in P functioning. But for all that, it isn't true right now, of those who have died, that they can engage in P functioning. On the contrary, right now they *can't* engage in P functioning; their brains are broken—or worse! So until God fixes them, until God resurrects them, the dead are indeed dead, just as we thought.

An account along these lines also gives us some helpful guidance when thinking about still other potentially puzzling cases. Take somebody who is in a coma, not engaged in P functioning. Their body, let's stipulate, is still alive. (The heart is still beating, the lungs are still breathing, and so forth.) But we wonder, is the *person* still alive? They are certainly not actively engaged in P functioning. But the relevant question, we now realize, is this: *can* they still engage in P functioning?

To answer that, of course, we will need to know more about the underlying physical situation. It will depend on the *details*. Are the relevant cognitive structures still there? Or have they been broken or destroyed? Think for another moment about what's going on in sleep. When someone is asleep, we need to do something to wake them up, something to turn the P functioning back on. The cognitive structures are still there, but the on-off switch is switched to off. Perhaps that's what it's like when someone is in a coma, or certain types of comas. Suppose, then, that the right way to think of the case is something like this, Coma Case One: the cognitive structures in the brain relevant for P functioning are still in place, it's just that the on-off switch is stuck in the off position (or perhaps, to shift the metaphor slightly, there's a lock on the switch). And so we can't turn the switch on in the normal way. Shaking the person in the coma and saying, "Wake up, Jimmy" doesn't do the trick. But for all that, although the on-off switch may be stuck in off, if the underlying cognitive structures of the brain are such as to still make it true that if we *were* to flip the on-off switch back to on, the person *could* still engage in P functioning, then maybe the right thing to say is that the person is still alive.

Contrast that with Coma Case Two. (I don't know if this would still qualify as a *coma* from a medical perspective, but that needn't concern us here.) Imagine that what's gone on is this: there has been decay of the relevant brain structures that underwrite cognitive functioning. So now it isn't simply that the on-off switch is stuck in the off position. Rather, the brain is no longer capable of engaging in the relevant higher-order P functions. The damage is too severe. Here, it seems, the right thing to say may well be that the person is no longer alive. Their *body* is still alive, but the *person* has died.

In short, if we accept the personality view, where death is to be defined in terms of the loss of P functioning, it seems that the most plausible thing to say is that death requires the loss of the ability to P function. The mere loss of P functioning itself—the mere fact that P functioning has stopped, even permanently—is not sufficient for death, as long as the *ability* to P function is retained.

But what if you accept the *body* view, rather than the personality view? Then, it seems, the moment of death should be defined in terms of B functioning, rather than P functioning. And so we will say—at least, as a first pass—that I am alive only as long as my body is a *B* functioning body. If it *isn't* still B functioning, then I am no longer alive: I am dead.

Does this account *also* need to be refined? Is it a mistake, here too, to think in terms of the loss of the relevant sort of *functioning* rather than the loss of the *ability* to carry out the functioning in question? Should the body theorist define death in terms of the loss of the *ability* to B function? Or does it suffice to say that death comes when the body *stops* B functioning? (In any event, we presumably won't want to say that death requires that B functioning stop *permanently*. For if we did say that, then we might have to say—unacceptably—that if God will genuinely resurrect our bodies on Judgment Day, then none of the "dead" are truly dead.)

It is difficult to know what to say here, in part because it is difficult to think of cases in which the body stops B functioning and yet retains the *ability* to B function. (There is no obvious analog of the dreamless sleep case for the body theorist.) If a body stops B functioning for more than a few moments, decay rapidly sets in, and soon enough the ability to B function is lost as well.

Of course it isn't difficult to think of cases where one or another B function has stopped while the others continue. Suppose that someone has a heart attack, and their heart stops beating for a few moments, until an electric shock is applied, and it starts up again. Were they *dead* during the intervening moments? Sometimes we talk that way, but I am not sure whether it is the right thing for the body theorist to say, especially given that various other B functions were going on during the relevant period. What we'd like to have is a case in which *all* B functioning is stopped, and yet, somehow, the ability to B function has not been destroyed.

How about this? Suppose we put somebody in a state of perfect suspended animation, cooling their body down so that the various metabolic processes come to a complete stop. Imagine, though, that if you heat them back up properly, they will start functioning again. We certainly can't do that yet, at least not with humans. But there's no obvious reason to think this must be impossible. So imagine that we eventually learn how to do this with humans, and we take Simon and put him into this state of perfect suspended animation. Is he *dead*?

To be honest, when I think about this case I am not sure *what* to say, nor is it clear to me what the body theorist should say. In some moods I find myself wanting to say that Simon is dead; in other moods, that he's still alive. (And in still other moods, I find myself thinking that maybe we need a third category to cover this case: perhaps Simon is neither dead nor alive; he's *suspended*.) I imagine that my confusion is shared by many others. In any event, let's consider the two (main) possibilities.

If we want to say that Simon is still alive while suspended, then presumably the body theorist should move to a definition of death according to which death requires the loss of the *ability* to B function. After all, it is a stipulation of the case that while he is in suspended animation no B functioning of any sort is taking place. So if the cessation of B functioning suffices for death, we would have to say that Simon is dead while suspended. (And so reanimation, heating him back up, brings him *back* to life—back from the dead.) In contrast, if we define death in terms of the loss of the *ability* to B function, then we may be able to say that Simon remains alive, even while suspended. After all, the relevant brain and other bodily structures (needed to underwrite B functioning) remain in place, undamaged, even while Simon is suspended. There is a clear sense in which suspended animation is like Coma Case One, where the on-off switch is stuck—literally frozen!—in the off position. Reanimating Simon, then, won't bring him back to life, for he will never have been dead. It will simply allow the B (and P) functioning to resume.

On the other hand, if we want to say that Simon is dead while suspended, then perhaps the body theorist should stick with the definition of death which holds that the cessation of B functioning is indeed sufficient for death. On this view, it won't matter that Simon's body remains, in principle, *capable* of B functioning. It *isn't* B functioning, and so, we can say, he is dead.

Note, incidentally, that the case of suspended animation can be puzzling from the perspective of the personality theorist as well. If I am right in suggesting that the personality theorist should define death in terms of the loss of the ability to P function, then it seems that we will have to say that Simon remains alive while suspended. For as I have just pointed out, it does seem as though there is a *sense* in which Simon's body retains its ability to carry out its various functions, including P functions, even while suspended. But what if the personality theorist wants to say instead that Simon is dead while suspended? Since the personality theorist cannot hold that actually engaging in P functioning is required to be alive (for if she did say that, then you are dead during dreamless sleep), she will presumably need to claim that in the *relevant* sense of ability, while Simon is suspended he no longer has so much as the *ability* to P function. He may—if reanimated—regain that ability; but while suspended he lacks it. Obviously, making out this last position will require still further work: we will need to distinguish different notions of ability, and we will need to explain why someone in a coma, say, may still have the relevant sort of ability, while someone in suspended animation does not. It does seem to me possible that the relevant distinctions could be provided and defended; but I won't try to investigate the question any further here.

In any event, aside from the question of how best to classify the case of suspended animation, it seems to me that once we become physicalists there is nothing especially deep or mysterious about death. A healthy human body is able to function in a variety of ways. As long as the relevant lower-level B functions are occurring (or, perhaps, able to occur), the body is alive. Of course, when all goes well, the body is also able to engage in certain higher-order cognitive functions, P functions. And then you've got a living person. Sadly, however, eventually the body begins to break. It loses the ability to P function. At that point, we no longer have a living person.

Eventually—perhaps at the same time, perhaps later—the body will break even further, losing the ability to B function as well. And that is the death of the body.

There may of course be a lot of details to work out from the scientific point of view. But from the philosophical point of view there is nothing mysterious going on here. The body works and then it breaks. That's all there is to death.

CHAPTER 9

Two Surprising Claims about Death

Not Believing I Will Die

Since my body will eventually break—like countless others have done before it—I am going to die. Indeed, I take it to be a commonplace and familiar observation that we are *all* going to die. We all know it, or so it seems. Yet sometimes this last idea—that we all know we are going to die—gets denied. Indeed, some have suggested that somehow, at some level, nobody *really* believes that they're going to die at all. That's a rather surprising claim. Is there any good reason to believe it?

Of course, having distinguished between what I have called the death of the person and the death of the body, we need to distinguish between two possible interpretations of this surprising claim. What exactly is it that's being proposed? Is it that no one truly believes they will cease to exist as a *person*? Or that no one truly believes that their *body* is going to die? Let's consider both possibilities. (Typically, no doubt, people fail to distinguish these two more particular claims, and so it isn't at all clear *what*, exactly, they mean to be suggesting.)

The most common argument for the claim that no one believes that they are going to cease to exist as a person—as a conscious, thinking being—takes the following form. The argument begins by suggesting that it is impossible to picture being dead. That is to say, it is impossible for me to picture *my* being dead, and it is impossible for you to picture *your* being dead. But if I can't picture being dead, I can't really imagine it. I can't, for example, imagine not existing. And so—the argument concludes—I can't really believe that I am ever going to cease to exist.

Clearly, the argument assumes that you can't believe in possibilities that you can't picture or imagine. So the first thing to point out is that this assumption can be challenged. Indeed, I think we probably shouldn't *believe* a theory of belief that says that in order to believe in something, you've got to be able to picture it in your imagination. I think that this view involves a misguided conception of what it takes to have a belief. But still, let's *grant* the assumption, if only for the sake of argument. Let's suppose that in order to believe in something, you've got to be able to *picture* it. What then? How do we get from there to the conclusion that I can't believe that I'm going to die, that I can't believe I am going to cease to exist as a person? The other premise of the argument, of course, is that I can't picture or imagine my being dead.

It's important here to draw some distinctions. I can certainly picture being ill. There I am on my deathbed, dying of cancer, growing weaker and weaker. I can perhaps even picture the moment of my death. I've said good-bye to my family and friends. Everything is growing grayer and dimmer. It's growing harder and harder to concentrate. And then—well, after that, there is no "more." I've died. So it does seem that I can picture my dying.

But that's not the relevant claim. The argument isn't saying that I can't picture being ill or dying. The claim's got to be that I can't picture *being* dead. Well, try it. Try to picture being dead. What is it *like* to be dead?

Sometimes people claim that it's a mystery. We don't know what it's *like* to be dead, they say, because every time we try to imagine it, we fail. We don't do a very good job. Suppose you set yourself the goal of trying to imagine, from the first-person perspective, what it's like to be dead. Perhaps you start by trying to strip off the parts of your conscious life that you know you won't have when you're dead: you won't hear anything, you won't see anything, and you won't think anything, and so on. And then, perhaps, you try to imagine what it's *like* to not think or feel or hear or see. And you don't do a very good job of it. So you throw your hands up and you say, "Oh, I guess I don't know what it's like to be dead. I can't imagine it. It's a mystery."

But that way of thinking about the issue is really confused. There is no mystery at all. Suppose I ask, what is it like to be my cell phone? The answer, of course, is that it's *not* like anything. Now it is essential not to misunderstand this answer. It's not that there is something that it's like to be a cell phone, but it's different from being anything else. It's not that there is a special type of experience, unlike any other and so impossible to describe, that's had by cell phones. No, that's not it at all. Cell phones simply don't *have* experiences. There is nothing to describe or imagine. There is *nothing* that it's like, on the inside as it were, to be a cell phone.

Suppose that I try to ask myself, what is it like to be my ballpoint pen? I might start by trying to imagine being really, really stiff—because you're not flexible when you're a ballpoint pen. You can't move. And I might imagine being really, really bored, because you don't have any thoughts or interests when you are a ballpoint pen. I might try to do all of that. But obviously that's completely the wrong way to go about thinking what it's like to be a ballpoint pen, because the simple fact of the matter is that there's *nothing* that it's like to be a ballpoint pen. There's nothing to describe, nothing to imagine. There is no mystery about what it's like to be a ballpoint pen, just as there is no mystery about what it's like to be a cell phone.

Similarly, then, I put it to you, there is no mystery about what it's like to be dead. It isn't like *anything*. And here too, it is important not to misunderstand that objection. I don't mean to suggest that being dead is like something, only something different from everything else. I mean, rather, that there is nothing there to describe. When you're dead, there's nothing happening on the inside to be imagined.

Suppose that that's right. Should we conclude, accordingly, that we now have the other premise needed by the argument? After all, if there is nothing to imagine, then of course I can't imagine it. And since we are already assuming—if only for the sake of argument—that what I can't picture or imagine I can't believe, shouldn't we conclude, in light of all of this, that the argument is sound, and you really can't believe you will ever be dead?

No. We shouldn't conclude that at all. To see that our argument must go wrong someplace, consider the fact that not only can't you picture, from the inside, what it's like to be dead, you also can't picture, from the inside, what it's like to be in dreamless *sleep*. After all, when you are in dreamless sleep you are not experiencing or imagining anything. There is nothing that it's *like* to be in dreamless sleep; so you can't picture it from the inside. Similarly, of course, it's not possible to picture or imagine what it's like to have fainted and be completely unconscious (with nothing happening cognitively). There's nothing there to picture or imagine from the inside.

So should we conclude, in light of this, that nobody really believes that they've ever been in dreamless sleep? That no one ever believes they have previously passed out? That, obviously, would be a silly thing to conclude. Of *course* you believe that at times you are in dreamless sleep. Of *course* someone subject to fainting spells realizes that sometimes they pass out. To suggest otherwise would be absurd.

From the mere fact that you can't picture it from the inside, it doesn't follow that nobody believes they're ever in dreamless sleep. From the mere fact that you can't picture it from the inside, it doesn't follow that nobody believes that they have ever fainted. Similarly, then, from the mere fact that you can't picture from the inside what it's like to be dead, it doesn't follow that nobody believes that they're going to die.

But didn't I start off by saying that I was going to grant the assumption (if only for the sake of argument) that in order to believe something you've got to be able to picture it? And haven't I just said, "Look, you can't picture being dead"? So aren't I taking something back? If I insist that you can believe that you're going to die, and yet agree that you can't picture it from the inside, haven't I taken back the assumption that in order to believe something, you've got to be able to picture it?

Not quite. Although I remain skeptical about the claim that belief requires picturing, I am going to continue granting this assumption for the sake of argument. What I want to claim, rather, is that you *can* picture being dead after all. It's just that you can't picture it from the inside. But that's not a problem, because you can still picture being dead from the *outside*.

Consider the case of dreamless sleep once more. I can picture my being in dreamless sleep quite easily. In fact, I am doing it right now: I've got a little mental image of my body lying in bed asleep, dreamlessly. Similarly, I can picture fainting, or having fainted, quite easily. I need only picture my body lying on the ground, unconscious. And similarly, of course, I can picture my being *dead* quite easily as well. It's a little mental picture of my body in a coffin, with no functioning of any sort occurring in my body. There. It is very easily done.

So even if it were true that belief requires picturing, and even if it were true that you can't picture being dead from the inside, it wouldn't follow that you can't believe that you're going to die. All you have to do is picture it from the outside. I conclude, accordingly, that of course you can and do believe that you're going to die.

But at this point, there is a common enough response to the argument I've just given. Someone might object in the following terms: "Suppose I try to picture, from the outside, my being dead. I try to picture a world in which I don't exist as a person. I am no longer conscious, I no longer experience anything. Perhaps, for example, I picture my own funeral. I can certainly try to do that. And yet, when I do try, I find myself *observing* the funeral.

I'm watching it, I'm seeing it. In short, I'm thinking. So I haven't really imagined a world in which I no longer exist after all, a world in which I'm incapable of thought and observation. I've smuggled myself back in as the observer of the funeral. Indeed, every time I try to picture myself being dead, I smuggle myself back in, existing as a conscious person, and thus not dead at all. I may succeed in imagining my *body* being dead, but I never truly imagine myself, the person, dead. From which it follows—given our assumption that belief requires picturing—that I don't really *believe* I'll ever be dead. I don't believe it, because I can't imagine it."

This argument shows up in various places. Let me mention only one example, the writings of Sigmund Freud. At one point, Freud says the following:

> After all, one's own death is beyond imagining, and whenever we try to imagine it we can see that we really survive as specta-tors. Thus the dictum could be dared in the psychoanalytic school: at bottom, nobody believes in his own death. Or, and this is the same: in his unconscious, every one of us is convinced of his immortality.[1]

So there's Freud, basically offering the argument I just sketched for you. When you try to imagine your being dead, he says, you smuggle your-self back in as a spectator. And so, Freud concludes, at some level none of us really believes we're going to die.

As it happens, I think that's a horrible argument. I certainly hope you're not persuaded by it. To see that it *must* be a bad argument, let's con-sider a less controversial example. Suppose you are a member of some club, and this afternoon there is going to be a meeting that you won't be able to attend. Ask yourself, do you believe that the meeting is going to take place without you? At first glance it seems obvious that you do, but now imag-ine someone making a Freud-like argument to show that you don't really believe this after all. Here's what they say: "Try to imagine that meeting, the one you are going to miss. Perhaps you have a little mental image of the room, and you've got a picture of people sitting around the table perhaps, discussing the business of the club. But wait! You are watching all of that in your mind's eye; you've smuggled yourself back in as a spectator. (If you are like me, you are probably picturing the room looking down from a corner or a wall, kind of a fly's perspective.) But that means that you *haven't* really pictured the meeting taking place without you being in the room. You just can't do it. And this means, of course, that you don't really believe the meeting is going to take place without you after all."

I trust you agree with me that this argument must go wrong someplace. It is clear that we all do believe that meetings take place all the time without us. But this shows that the mere fact that in *some* sense I have smuggled myself back in as an observer isn't enough to imply that I don't really believe in the particular possibility that I am trying to imagine. I can believe in meetings taking place without me, even if (in some sense) I smuggle myself back in when I picture them. Similarly, then, I can believe in the possibility of a world existing without me, even if (in some sense) I smuggle myself back in when I try to picture such a world.

But where, exactly, does the argument go wrong? There are actually two points that I think we need to keep in mind, if we are to understand the answer. The first point is that when you look at a picture you need to distinguish between the undeniable fact that you are indeed *looking* at the picture, and the further quite distinct question of whether you are yourself one of the elements represented *within* the picture. The second point is to bear in mind the fact that pictures always (or at least typically) represent a scene from a specific point of view, a particular location.

Suppose I hold up a photograph of a beach with nobody in it. Does the picture show me, too? In particular, does it show me as being on the beach? Of course not. We specified that the photo is of a beach with nobody at all on it, including me. To be sure, while I look at that picture—whether in reality or in my mind's eye—I must myself exist! I can hardly see or imagine a picture without at the same time existing. But for all that, to do this, I don't have to be one of the things *in* the picture; it doesn't have to be a picture of *me*. So part of where the argument goes wrong is that it invites us to move, mistakenly, from the undeniable fact that when I try to picture something without me (a beach, a meeting, or the world) I must of course exist right now, I must be observing that picture, to the quite distinct (and by hypothesis mistaken) conclusion that I am myself one of the things shown *in* the picture—that it is a picture of *me*. That certainly needn't be the case: I can easily picture a meeting taking place without my being in the picture in any way. And the same thing is true, of course, for picturing a world without me, after my death.

But why then is this mistake so tempting? I think perhaps that the second point is relevant here. A picture of a beach (or a meeting, or the world without you) is going to represent the scene from a particular point in space. It might be down the shore (or on the wall, or at the back of the funeral).

And so it is easy to start thinking that whoever is seeing that scene must be doing so from the relevant point in space. And then, since *I* am the one do- ing the seeing, it is easy to think that I must be imagining myself as being *at* the particular location in question, whether on the beach, or in the meeting room—or simply in the world, never having died at all. As I say, I suspect that something like this explains why it is so easy to get confused here. But confusion it is. It is, in point of fact, a trivial matter to imagine a world without me, so long as we do so from the outside. And thus, even if imagin- ing or picturing is indeed required for belief, it remains the case that all of us can easily imagine being dead.

At the start of this section I distinguished two possible interpreta- tions of the claim that nobody believes that they're going to die. So far, we've been discussing the first, according to which nobody believes they will ever cease to exist as a conscious, thinking being. As I've just explained, the most popular argument for this idea is unsuccessful. But what about the second possible interpretation, according to which nobody believes their *body* is going to die. Is there any better reason to believe the original claim when it is understood in this second way?

Let's start by pointing out how very odd it is to suggest something like this. People certainly do *seem* to believe that their bodies are going to die. After all, even if you believe, say, that your immortal soul will someday go up to heaven, so that you will continue to exist forever as a conscious, thinking being, you might still recognize what seems to be the undeniable fact that your *body* will eventually die. Surely we all recognize that our bod- ies will eventually cease functioning—that my own body, for example, will become a corpse that will need to be buried or cremated, and so forth.

Indeed, people engage in all sorts of behaviors that become very, very hard to interpret if they don't really believe that their bodies are going to die. For example, people take out life insurance. Why? Presumably because they believe (correctly!) that there's a decent chance that they will die—that is, that their bodies will die—within a certain period of time; and they want their children and family members to be cared for. If you didn't really be- lieve you were going to die (that is, undergo bodily death), why would you take out life insurance? Similarly, people write wills, explaining what to do with their assets after they die. If you didn't really believe you were going to die, why would you ever bother writing a will? Since many people do write wills, or take out life insurance and so forth, it seems as though the natural thing to suggest is that many people, probably most people, do recognize that they are going to die.

Why would we think otherwise? The reason for thinking otherwise—the reason for not being utterly dismissive of this suggestion—is that when people get ill, terminally ill, it often seems to take them by surprise. A famous literary example of this can be found in Tolstoy's novella, *The Death of Ivan Ilyich*. In that story, Ivan Ilyich falls and hurts himself. The injury doesn't get better. He gets worse and worse and eventually it kills him. The astonishing thing is that Ivan Ilyich is shocked to discover that he's mortal. And of course, what Tolstoy is trying to convince us of, what he's trying to argue through this example, is that *most* of us are actually in Ivan Ilyich's position. We give lip service to the claim that we're going to die, but at some level we don't really believe it.

Just to be clear, I want to emphasize the point that the relevant belief—or lack of belief—concerns the death of the *body*. That's the thing that surprises Ivan Ilyich. What takes him aback is the discovery that his *body* is mortal. For all we know, after all, Ivan Ilyich still believes in souls, still believes he is going to go to heaven. It is not the prospect of his death as a person that brings him up short; indeed, he may not *believe* he is going to die as a person. What surprises him, rather, is his *bodily* mortality. Tolstoy draws a highly realistic and believable portrait of somebody who is surprised to discover that he's mortal.

Of course, for all that, I presume that Ivan Ilyich had a will. And for all I know, Ivan Ilyich had life insurance as well. So we've got a puzzling situation here. Some of Ivan Ilyich's behaviors indicate that he really did believe that he was mortal after all, that he fully recognized the fact that he was someday going to die. And yet, at the same time, the shock and surprise that overcome him when he actually gets sick and has to face his mortality strongly suggest that he is reporting correctly when he says that he didn't really believe at all that he was going to die.

How could that be? There's a kind of puzzle here. Even before we move to the question of how widespread cases like this may actually be, it's puzzling how we can so much as *understand* what's going on in cases like this. How can anyone both believe and not believe in their own mortality?

Perhaps we need to distinguish between what someone consciously believes and what they unconsciously believe. Maybe at the conscious level Ivan Ilyich believed he was mortal, but at the unconscious level he believed he was immortal. Or maybe we need to distinguish between those things he gives a kind of lip service to and those things he truly and fundamentally believes. Maybe Ivan Ilyich only gave lip service to the claim that he was mortal. If you had asked him, "Are you mortal?" he would have said,

"Oh, of course I am." And he buys life insurance accordingly. But does he thoroughly and truly believe he's mortal? Perhaps not. At any rate, we certainly need *some* such distinction if we're going to make sense of Ivan Ilyich.

Now I take it that we find Ivan Ilyich a perfectly believable example. That is, we think it's conceivable that somebody could, at some level, not really believe he's going to die. But I also take it that Tolstoy means to be putting forward more than just a claim that there *could* be such a person. ("Look how bizarre he is. Let me describe him for you.") Rather, the suggestion is meant to be that Ivan Ilyich's case is quite typical. Maybe all of us are in his situation, or most of us. At the very least, many of us are. The case of Ivan Ilyich becomes more than an interesting oddity only if we have reason to agree that many of us are *like* him in this regard.

But what kind of evidence could be offered for a claim like that? Since most or all of us will presumably insist that we really do believe that we are going to die, what kind of argument could possibly be offered to suggest that we are mistaken?

What we would need, I think, is something like this. Suppose there were some kind of behavior that many of us engage in. And suppose as well that this behavior on our part calls out for explanation. And suppose, finally, that an adequate explanation of that behavior is to be had only if we agree that at some fundamental level we don't really believe what we normally claim to believe. If all that were true, that might well give us good reason to admit that we don't really believe what we say we believe; it is something to which we are merely giving lip service.

To see an argument of this sort at work, take someone who suffers from a compulsion that leads him to wash his hands over and over again. We ask him, "Are your hands dirty?" He might answer, "No, of course not." And yet, there he is, going back to the bathroom, washing his hands once again. Arguably, the only way to explain this behavior is to say that at some level he really does believe his hands are dirty, despite the fact that he says they're not. In the same way, then, if we could find some behavior on our part that calls out for explanation, where the best possible explanation would be that at some level we don't really believe that we're going to die, then that would indeed give us reason to think that we *don't* really believe we're going to die, even though we *say* that we believe it.

Suppose, for example, that if you really did believe, fundamentally, that you were going to die, the horror of that realization would lead you to start screaming and just keep screaming. (At a certain point in his illness,

Ivan Ilyich begins to scream, and from that moment on he screams and screams and screams, almost until his death.) If this really were true—if it were really true that if you took seriously the thought that you were going to die then you would be unable to stop screaming—then we would have an argument of the appropriate sort. For, of course, the fact of the matter is that most of us do not go around screaming. And so, if you really *would* be screaming if only you truly believed in your mortality, it would follow that we don't really believe in our own mortality after all. As I say, that *would* be a good argument—but only, of course, if it were really true that anyone who completely believes in her own mortality must be forever screaming. And obviously enough, there is no good reason to believe anything like that at all.

You might ask, though, whether there is some *other* behavior that might similarly support the suggestion that we don't really believe that we're going to die. Here is what I take to be the most plausible proposal. As we know, there are people who have brushes with death. They might, for example, be in an accident and come close to being killed but walk away without a scratch. Or they might suffer a heart attack and be on the operating table for some period of time and then, thanks to cardiac surgery or what have you, be resuscitated. Now when people have these near brushes with death, it's easy to believe that the fact of their mortality is more vivid to them. It's more before their mind's eye. It's something that they now really truly do believe. And the interesting point is that often enough, when people have this sort of experience, they say, "I've got to change my life. I need to spend less time at the office and more time with my family. I need to do the things that are important to me and spend less time worrying about getting ahead and making money. I need to tell the people that I love that I love them."

Let's suppose that something like that is true of all of us, or at least most of us. When we find the fact of our mortality is made vivid—when we fully absorb the fact that we're mortal—then we change our priorities and we stop devoting all our time and attention to trying to get ahead in the rat race; we spend more time with our loved ones, doing what's important to us. Suppose that that claim were true. Well then, armed with that claim we might then notice that most of us *do* spend a lot of time trying to get ahead, trying to earn a lot of money; we *don't* spend the bulk of our time doing the things that we really think are most important. We don't tell our friends and family members how much they mean to us, how much we love them. What, then, are we to make of that fact? Perhaps this. Perhaps the explanation is that although we give lip service to the claim that we're mortal, at some more fundamental level, we don't truly believe it. The belief's not vivid for us. We don't believe it "all the way down."

This argument, I think, has at least some chance of being right. Or so it seems to me. I am not at all convinced that it *is* right. But at least it doesn't seem to be a nonstarter. It does seem as though people who have brushes with death often change their behavior in significant ways. So the fact that we normally *don't* behave in those other ways gives us some reason to believe that perhaps at some level we don't completely or fully or fundamentally believe we're going to die. As I say, I'm not sure whether that argument's right. But at least it's an argument worth taking seriously.

Dying Alone

Let me turn now to a different claim that sometimes gets made about death. This is the claim that everybody dies alone. That is to say, although we are able to eat meals together, take vacations together, and listen to music together, death is something we all have to do by ourselves: we all die alone. That's the claim. If it's true, it seems to be offering a deep insight into the nature of death. It has an air of profundity about it. Everyone dies alone. It seems that this is telling us something deep and important and interesting about the nature of death.

As far as I can see, however, it's just not *true*. Of course, here too, it isn't altogether clear how the claim in question is to be interpreted. But however we interpret it, it seems to me, it just ends up being implausible, or simply false, or uninteresting. So I am going to give this claim a very hard time.

I'm going to give it such a hard time that sometimes I am not even sure it is worth discussing this claim. A few years ago, in fact, I had pretty much decided that I would *stop* discussing this claim in my course on death. I had decided that people *don't* really think that we all die alone—so why waste any time examining that view? And then, I kid you not, that very afternoon I came across a quote that seemed to express exactly that thought! And then, a day or two later, my daughter showed me another. And the fact of the matter is, once you start looking for it, you can find this idea expressed in all sorts of places. So I guess it really is a common enough idea after all, and it does deserve to be examined.

Here are the two quotes. The first one is from the folk singer Loudon Wainwright III, from his song "Last Man on Earth": "We learn to live together and then we die alone."[2] We die alone. That's undeniably an interesting claim. It seems to say something important about the nature of death. Here's another quote. This one is from the children's book *Eldest*, by Christopher Paolini. "'How terrible,' said Eragon, 'to die alone, separate even from the one who is closest to you.'" And the answer given to Eragon? "Everyone dies alone, Eragon. Whether you are a king on a battlefield or a lowly peasant lying in bed among your family, no one can accompany you into the void."[3] Everyone dies alone.

As I say, this is a common enough view. I've only given you two quotes, but I could certainly produce others. So the question we're going to ask is this: can we find some interpretation of this claim—that everyone dies alone—where this actually turns out to be *true*?

Actually, it is going to take a bit more than that to satisfy me. Suppose that by some bizarre coincidence people always die on Mondays. There is no reason why they couldn't die on some other day, they just don't happen to do that. That would certainly be a moderately interesting fact, but it wouldn't really tell us anything deep about the nature of death, not if people could just as easily die on Tuesday—if it is just an accident, as it were, that everyone dies on Monday. What we are looking for, I suppose, is some *necessary* truth about death. Similarly, then, it won't be enough if it just *happens* to be true that everyone dies alone. After all, if it just happens to be the case that everybody dies alone in a room, with no one else there at the moment of death, that would certainly be mildly interesting, and we might wonder what causes it. But it wouldn't be some deep insight into the nature of death if it is just an *accident* that no one else is ever there. So it's not enough for the claim to be true; it needs to be a necessary truth.

And a bit more: once we properly understand what the claim is asserting, it had better be saying something *interesting*! If when we interpret the claim that everyone dies alone, that just ends up being a slightly pretentious way of saying that everyone *dies*, we might respond by saying that even though that's true, and indeed a necessary truth, it isn't an especially *surprising* truth! It isn't some new, deep insight into the nature of death. We all know that everyone dies. If you take that familiar fact, and you wrap it up in misleading language and express it by saying that everyone dies alone, you are only pretending to offer us a deep insight into the nature of death.

Finally, when we say that everyone dies alone, this is supposed to be telling us something special about *death*. It had better not be the case that everyone does *everything* alone—whatever the relevant sense of "alone" turns out to be. Because, of course, if everyone does everything alone, then of course that might be interesting, it might be very important and insightful, but you're not saying anything especially interesting about *death* if it turns out that everyone also eats their *lunch* alone (in the relevant sense of "alone"). Admittedly, it might be asking too much to insist that the claim being made about death be utterly unique to death—perhaps there are other things that we do alone as well; but it had better not be true of just about everything.

I've been spelling out all of these conditions because I think that people fool themselves into thinking that they are saying something deep and profound—and true!—about death when they claim that everyone dies alone. But my own suspicion, on the contrary, is that there is no profound truth here at all. Indeed, I suspect that most people who make this claim haven't even thought very hard about what, exactly, they mean. Once you actually push people, try to pin them down, you end up with proposals that are either not true, not necessary, not interesting, or not particularly unique to death.

Here's a possible interpretation—the most natural, straightforward, literal, flat-footed interpretation I can think of. To say that somebody does something *alone* means they do it not in the presence of others. Consider somebody who lives by himself and goes to sleep. If there's nobody else in the bedroom, he's sleeping *alone*. On the most straightforward interpretation, then, to say that everybody dies alone is to say that it's true of each one of us that he or she dies not in the presence of others. If that was true, it would be sort of surprising. We might wonder whether it's a necessary truth or just an accident. But at least there'd be something interesting there.

But of course, it's not *true*. We all know full well that sometimes people die in the presence of others. Socrates, for example, drank the hemlock and died in the company of his friends and disciples; he didn't die alone. And of course, as we know, there are many, many other cases in which people die in the presence of their friends, family, and loved ones. So it's just not true— given this first interpretation of the claim—to say that we all die alone. If that's what the claim means, it's just false. The challenge, then, is to find some other interpretation of the claim that fares better.

Here's a second possible interpretation. Perhaps when people say that everyone dies alone they do not mean to deny that you may die in the presence of others. They mean to be saying, rather, that even if there are others with you, dying is something that you are *doing* alone. They aren't dying; only you are. Thus, for example, Socrates' friends and disciples were not dying. *He* was the only one dying. Perhaps, then, everyone dies alone in *that* sense.

This too would be an interesting claim, if it were true. But it's *not* true. There have been many battlefields, for example, where people have died along with others doing the same. There is Jones dying, but he's not dying alone: Smith is dying at the same time, right next to him. So if this is what people mean when they say that everyone dies alone, then that claim is clearly false as well. I can only assume that this is *not* what people mean. But then, what was it that they did mean?

We can do better. We might point out that even on the battlefield, when Smith and Jones are both dying "together," it's not like this is some sort of cooperative, joint undertaking. There is no coordination here, no planning. No one is dying in cooperation with anyone else. The situation is similar to what happens when you are walking down the sidewalk and Sylvia happens to be walking down the sidewalk at the same time. Even though you are both walking down the sidewalk, and doing this next to each other, there is a clear sense in which you are not walking down the sidewalk *together*. Of course, you *can* walk together with someone. You turn to Nathan and say, "Hey, let's go to the library." And then you walk down the sidewalk together. Walking is something you *can* do with others, in the sense that it can be a joint activity, a joint undertaking.

Perhaps, then, the claim is that dying is not something that can be done in that way as a joint undertaking. Even if you're in a hospital room or a battlefield where people are dying to your left and to your right at the same time as you, dying is not and cannot be something that is a joint undertaking.

That might well be what some people mean when they say that everybody dies alone. But if it is, then all I can say, again, is that it just seems to be false.

Admittedly, dying as a joint undertaking is far rarer than dying alone. But remember, we are looking for some deep insight into the nature of death. And we will have one only if dying as a joint undertaking is *impossible*. And it isn't. You could have, for example, some sort of suicide pact. Indeed, there have been cases, gruesome as they may be, in which entire groups of people drink poison together so as to not die alone, so as to die together as a group, part of a joint dying. Or—less gruesome but still sad— there have been couples in love who together jump off a cliff, committing suicide together, so that they may die, not alone, but with each other as part of a joint undertaking. I take it that cases like this actually do occur. They certainly seem possible. So if somebody comes along and says that dying as part of a joint activity of dying together is impossible, they simply seem to be saying something false.

Joint undertakings are a bit like playing chamber music with a string quartet. (Actually, that's a standard philosophical example of a joint activity.) It's something you are doing *with* others. It's not just a coincidence, after all, that the others are playing music at the same time. It's not as though all these people just happen to be playing the violin, the viola, or the cello next to you. No, no, they deliberately coordinated with one another so as to together produce this music. It seems possible in the case of string quartets. It seems possible in the case of joint suicide pacts as well.

Still, a fan of the claim that we all die alone might make the following reply: "In the case of the string quartet, although it is true that I am playing with others, somebody else could take my part. Somebody else could play the second violin part *for* me. In contrast, when I die, even if I'm dying with others, nobody can take my part." Perhaps, then, this is what it means to say that everybody dies alone: nobody can die your death *for* you; nobody can take your part.

Now if that is what people mean when they say that everyone dies alone, then at the very least I want to point out that they haven't been expressing themselves very clearly. It seems to me rather a stretch to think that when someone says "everyone dies alone," we should realize that what they mean is that "nobody can die for me, nobody can take my part." That seems to me a rather misleading, unhelpful way of making your point. But let's just bracket that complaint.

Is it *true* that nobody can take my part? People can certainly take my part in the string quartet. Is it true that nobody can take my part in terms of my death? That's not so clear to me. I hope you have read Charles Dickens's *A Tale of Two Cities*, because if not, I am about to spoil the plot for you. Here's a central strand of the story. The hero of the novel is in love with a woman who—alas and alack!—does not love him. She loves another man. This other man—alas and alack!—has been condemned to death during the French Revolution. Now as it happens, our hero looks rather like the other man (this is a novel, after all). And so, as the other man is being carted off to be killed on the guillotine, our hero takes his place. Hence the famous speech, "It is a far, far better thing that I do, than I have ever done." Our hero sacrifices himself so that the woman he loves can have the man that she loves. For our purposes, though, the romance isn't crucial. For our purposes, the crucial point is to see that what seems to be going on here is that our hero is taking the place of somebody else who's about to die. Just like somebody else could take my place in the string quartet, it seems that somebody else could take my place at the guillotine.

In the American Civil War there was a military draft, but if you were rich enough you could avoid it by hiring someone to take your place. Suppose, then, that your troop is in some battle, and people are being killed left and right. Imagine that everybody in the troop gets killed, and *you* would have been killed as well had you been there, but instead, the person you hired to take your place gets killed. It doesn't strike me as implausible to say, in such a case, that he took your place and died for you. So if the claim being made is that nobody *can* die for me, nobody can take my place in death, then that still seems to be false.

A fan of the view in question might come back yet again, and note that although it is true that the hero of *A Tale of Two Cities* takes the place of the other man on the guillotine, what ends up happening, of course, is that our hero actually dies his *own* death. He doesn't take over the death of the other man. After all, the death of the *other* man doesn't take place until twenty, thirty, forty years later! Similarly, then, nobody can take my place at *my* death, because, of course, if they take my place what they end up going through is actually *their* death, not *my* death. *My* death is something that only *I* can undergo. So perhaps this is what is meant when people say that everyone dies alone. They mean that no one can die *my* death for me.

If this is in fact what people mean, then once again I want to point out that it seems rather misleading to state the idea in question in terms of the language of "dying alone." That seems a rather confusing way to express the point. But let that pass. Infelicities of expression aside, it does seem to be *true* that each one of us must undergo his own death and nobody else's death. Indeed, it seems to be a *necessary* truth that nobody else can undergo *my* death for me. And, finally, this fact—for it does seem to be a fact—certainly seems to reveal something interesting and deep about death.

But I think this appearance—of having finally captured a deep insight into the nature of death—is misleading. I don't think we are here learning anything particularly special about death at all!

Consider something utterly mundane, getting your hair cut at the barber. Now, of course, somebody else can take your slot at the barber. Someone comes along and says, "I need to get to a date. I'm going to be late. Would you mind my taking your appointment?" And you are a generous sort and reply, "That's okay, I'm willing to wait. Go ahead." So in some loose sense they've gotten your haircut. But of course, as it ended up, they didn't really get *your* haircut. They got *their* haircut. That's how it is with haircuts. Nobody can get *my* haircut for me. *I'm* the only one who can get *my* haircut. If somebody else tries to get my haircut, they just end up getting their *own* haircut.

And of course, that's not anything special about haircuts. Think about getting your kidney stones removed. Nobody else can get *my* kidney stones removed for me. *I'm* the only one who can get my kidney stones removed for me. Or think about eating lunch. Nobody can eat *my* lunch for me. If somebody else tries to eat my lunch for me, it becomes *their* lunch. They've eaten *their* lunch for themselves. Nobody can eat my lunch for me except for *me*.

If you think about it, a similar point is true about just about everything. Maybe, indeed, everything. If you emphasize the word "my" enough, nobody can do much of anything for me and still have it be *my* such and such. In short, even though it's true that nobody can die my death for me, this isn't some deep insight into the special nature of death. It's just a trivial grammatical point about the meaning of the word "my."

So far, then, we have yet to find an interpretation of the claim that everyone dies alone, where that claim—so interpreted—says something about death that is both genuinely interesting (rather than trivial) and true! But maybe I have been tone-deaf in my attempts to understand what's being said. I've been looking for an interpretation of the claim that is literally true, but maybe the claim that we all die alone isn't meant literally at all. Maybe it is intended, rather, as a kind of *metaphor*. It's not that we all really do die alone. It's that when we die, it's *as though* we were alone. It's *like* being alone. Maybe the claim "we all die alone" is a psychological claim—that the psychological state we are in when we die is *similar* to loneliness. It's similar to the *feeling* of being alone that we sometimes have.

Imagine someone dying. We can suppose that she isn't literally alone. On the contrary, perhaps she is surrounded by other people as she lies on her deathbed. And yet, despite this, she feels removed, distant, alienated from the others. She feels lonely, even in the crowd. Perhaps *that* is the kind of "being alone" that people mean to be talking about.

It is certainly easy to believe that there are cases like this, where people die feeling distant and removed from others. Maybe that was true of Tolstoy's Ivan Ilyich. Ivan Ilyich progressively grows more and more distant from his family and friends who, indeed, remove themselves psychologically from him. He faces his death with a feeling of alienation and being alone. He's not literally alone, it's just a metaphor, but still the metaphor does provide an important insight into his psychology.

So the question we have to ask ourselves is whether something similar is true of everybody. Remember, we are looking for a *necessary* truth about death—an insight into its very nature. We aren't looking for something that just happens to be true in a certain percentage of cases. What we need to know is whether *everybody* dies alone in this psychological sense. And all I can say is, it certainly doesn't *seem* to be true.

First of all, notice the obvious point that sometimes people die in their sleep, unexpectedly. They weren't ill. They just die of cardiac arrest while they're sleeping. Such a person presumably is not feeling lonely or alienated while she dies. Of course, it might be suggested that what was meant, rather, was that anyone who is *awake* while they're dying, dies with this feeling of loneliness and alienation. But that's not true either. Suppose you are crossing the street, talking to your friend, engaged in lively discussion. So lively, in fact, that you don't notice the truck that's about to hit you. The truck hits you, and you die, painlessly and immediately. Were you feeling alienated and distant during your final moments? No, of course not. So it certainly doesn't seem true to say that everybody who dies while awake has these particular psychological feelings.

Perhaps we need to revise the claim yet again. Perhaps the claim is simply that everybody who *realizes* that they're dying has the feeling of loneliness and distance from others. Perhaps all of us who *realize* that we are dying, die "alone." That restriction (that is, to people who realize that they are dying) would take care of the sleep case. It would take care of the truck case. And the claim would remain an interesting one, even given the restriction. But is it true? Happily, it doesn't seem to be.

Recall Socrates. Socrates is engaged in philosophical discussion with his friends. He knows he's about to die. He's drunk the hemlock. He's sitting there saying goodbye to everybody. He doesn't *seem* alienated. He doesn't *seem* to be feeling distant and alone. It just doesn't seem true that everybody who knows they're going to die and is facing their death feels lonely.

Another example of this was the philosopher David Hume. Hume was quite sociable while he was dying. During his final illness, Hume used to invite people in, to sit around his deathbed and talk. He was cheerful and pleasant to the end. As far as I can see, there is simply no reason at all to believe that Hume was feeling lonely, distant, or alienated from the people who were keeping him company. In short, the psychological reading of the claim that everyone dies alone doesn't do any better than any of the earlier interpretations.

Of course, there may be yet another interpretation worth considering. But if so, I don't know what it might be. So I invite you to reflect on this question yourself. Is it really true that we all die alone? Is there some way of understanding this claim where it turns out to offer us a genuine insight into the nature of death? If so, I can't find it.[4] Despite the fact that people routinely say that we all die alone, I think the claim is simple nonsense. I rather fear that people are talking without giving half a moment's thought to what they might mean when they say it.

CHAPTER 10

The Badness of Death

Let's take stock. Broadly speaking, up to this point we have been engaged in metaphysics. We tried to get clear about the nature of the person so that we could get clearer about the nature of survival, which in turn allowed us to reach a better understanding of the nature of death.

I have, of course, defended a physicalist view, according to which, essentially, people are just bodies capable of doing some fancy tricks, bodies capable of P functioning. And details aside, death is a matter of the body breaking, so that it's no longer able to engage in the relevant functioning. Of course, as we saw, depending on the particular theory of personal identity that you accept, we might have to say slightly different things about whether the death of my body means that I no longer exist, and we might need to distinguish between the death of the body and the death of the person, and so forth. But details aside, the following is true: when the body breaks, I cease to exist as a person. And even if we can hold out the bare logical possibility of my surviving the death of my body, I see no good reason to believe that any of those logical possibilities actually happen.

As far as I can see, then, when my body dies, that's it. Of course, as a fan of the body view, I believe that I will still exist for a while afterward. I will exist as a corpse. But that's not the kind of existence that gives me what matters, since what I want is not just to exist, nor even just to be alive, but to be a person, and indeed a person with pretty much the same personality. And the truth of the matter is, when my body dies, that's all history.

So that's where we are at in terms of the metaphysics. We could summarize all of this by saying that when I die, I cease to exist. Of course, that's a little bit misleading, given the view I have just endorsed, where even though I'm dead I still exist for a while as a corpse. But those issues won't concern us in what we are about to turn to. Accordingly, in order to simplify the discussion that follows, I propose to leave these complications aside. Let's suppose that my body gets destroyed at the very moment that it dies. Perhaps I will be merrily going my way when a bomb explodes nearby, killing me instantly and blowing my body to bits. If so, then the very same moment will mark the end of my body, the end of my existence, the end of my personhood, and the end of what matters. Death will be the end—full stop. It remains true, of course, that in other less tidy scenarios these various things can come apart; but as I say, these details won't matter for the topics to come.

What we're going to do, then, in the remaining chapters, is to turn to value theory. We spent the first nine chapters of this book trying to get clear about the metaphysical facts. But having done that, I now want to turn to ethical and evaluative questions, investigating them in light of our (slightly simplified) conclusion that death is the end. For example, we all believe that death is bad. But *why* is death bad? How *can* death be bad? And if it is bad, would it indeed be better if we lived *forever*? As we shall quickly discover, there are plenty of puzzling issues to be explored here as well.

The Deprivation Account

The first question we are going to consider is this: *how* and *in what ways* is death bad? I take it, after all, that most of us do believe that death is bad. (Or, at least, *would* be bad, if it really were the end.) So the first thing we need to ask is whether death really is bad, as we typically take it to be, and, if so, what is it about death that *makes* it bad?

Of course, in thinking about this question I am simply going to assume (from here on out) that the metaphysical view that I've been sketching is right, that physicalism is true. The death of my body is the end of my existence as a person. Death is my end. But if that's right, how *can* it be bad for me to die? After all, once I'm dead, I don't exist. If I don't exist, how can it be bad for me that I'm dead?

It is, of course, easy to see how you might worry about the badness of death if you thought you would *survive* your death. If you believed in a soul, for example, then you might reasonably worry about what is going to happen to your soul after you die. Are you going to make it up to heaven? Are you going to go to hell? You might worry about how badly off you're going to be once you're dead. The question makes perfect sense. In contrast, however, it has often seemed to people that if death really is the end—and this is of course precisely what I am assuming—then death can't truly be bad for me. How could *anything* be bad for me once I'm dead? If I don't exist, it seems reasonable to say, it can't be bad for me.

People sometimes respond to this thought by saying that death isn't bad for the person who is dead. Death is bad for the *survivors*. Fred's death isn't bad for Fred. Fred's death is bad for the people who loved Fred and who now have to continue living without Fred. Fred's death is bad for Fred's friends and family. When somebody dies, we lose the chance to continue interacting with the person. We're no longer able to talk with them, spend time with them, watch a movie, look at the sunset, have a laugh. We're no longer able to share our troubles and get their advice. We're no longer able to interact with them. All of that is gone, when somebody dies.

And the claim might be, that's the central bad of death. Not what it does for the person who dies. Death *isn't* bad for the person who dies. It's bad because of what it does to those left behind.

Now I don't in any way want to belittle the importance of the pain and suffering that happen to us when somebody that we care about dies. Death robs us—we, the survivors—of our friends and loved ones. This is certainly one central and very bad thing about death. Here's a poem that emphasizes this thought. It is by the German poet Friedrich Gottlieb Klopstock, and it is called *Separation*:[1]

> You turned so serious when the corpse
> was carried past us;
> are you afraid of death? "Oh, not of that!"
> Of what are you afraid? "Of dying."
>
> I not even of that. "Then you're afraid of nothing?"
> Alas, I am afraid, afraid . . . "Heavens, of what?"
> Of parting from my friends.
> And not mine only, of their parting, too.
>
> That's why I turned more serious even
> than you did, deeper in the soul,
> when the corpse
> was carried past us.

According to Klopstock, it seems, the crucial badness of death is losing your friends. When they die, you lose them. And as I say, I don't in any way want to belittle the central badness of that. But I don't think it can be at the core in terms of what's bad about death. I don't think that can be the central fact about why death is bad. And to see this, I want you to compare two stories.

Story number one. Your friend is about to go on the spaceship which is leaving to explore a distant solar system. She will be gone for years and years. Indeed, by the time the spaceship comes back, one hundred years will have gone by. (Because of "relativistic" effects, your friend will have aged only ten years, but you will be long dead.) Worse still, twenty minutes after the ship takes off, all radio contact between the earth and the ship will be lost, until their return. Thus, all possibility of future communication with your friend is about to be lost forever. Now, this is horrible. You're losing your closest friend. You will no longer be able to talk to her, get her insights and advice. You'll no longer be able to tell her about the things that have been going on in your life or learn about hers. This is the kind of separation that Klopstock was talking about. It's horrible, and it's sad. That was story number one.

Story number two. The spaceship takes off, and then, tragically, twenty-five minutes into the flight, it explodes in a horrible accident and everybody on the spaceship is killed instantly, including your friend.

I take it that story number two is worse. Something worse has taken place. But what is this worse thing? It can't be the separation. Of course, we do have the separation in story number two. You can't communicate in the future with your friend; she can't communicate with you. But we had that already in story number one. If there's something worse about story number two—and I think it's pretty clear that there *is* something worse—it's not the separation. It's something about the fact that your friend has *died*. Admittedly, this is worse for you, too, since you care about your friend. But the explanation of why it upsets you so to have her die presumably lies in the fact that it is bad for *her* to have died. And the badness for her isn't just a matter of separation, because we already had *that* in story number one. You couldn't communicate with her. She couldn't communicate with you.

If we want to get at the central badness of death, it seems to me, we can't focus on the badness of separation, the badness for the survivors. We have to think about how it could be true that death is bad for the person that *dies*. That's the central badness of death and that's the aspect that I'm going to have us focus on. But that only points us in the right direction; it doesn't yet answer our question. How *can* it be true that death is bad for the person that dies? What exactly is it about my death, or the fact that I am going to die, that makes that bad for me?

In thinking about this question it is important to be clear about what we're asking. In particular, we are not asking whether or how the *process* of dying can be bad. For I take it to be quite uncontroversial—and not at all puzzling—that the process of dying can be a painful one. Suppose, for example, that I will someday be ripped to pieces by Bengali tigers. If so, then the actual process of dying would be horrible. It would be incredibly painful. So it obviously makes sense to talk about the process of dying as something that could potentially be bad for me.

But at the same time, it must be admitted that the process *needn't* be particularly painful or otherwise bad for me in itself. I might, after all, die in my sleep, in which case the process of dying would not be bad in itself. At any rate, I take it that for most of us, although we might have some passing concern that our process of dying might be a painful one, that's not the central thing we are concerned about when we face the fact that we are going to die.

Similarly, of course, many of us find the *prospect* of dying to be unpleasant. That is to say, one of the things that's bad about my death for me is that right now I've got some unhappy thoughts as I anticipate the fact that I'm going to die. But again, that can't be the *central* thing that's bad about death, because it would only make sense for the prospect of my death to be a painful or unpleasant one if death *itself* is bad for me. Having fear or anxiety or concern or regret or anguish or whatever it is that I have now at the thought that I'm going to die piggybacks on the logically prior thought that death itself is bad for me. If it didn't piggyback in that way, it wouldn't make any sense to have fear or anxiety or dread or anguish or whatever it is that I may be feeling right now.

Suppose I say to you, "Tomorrow something's going to happen to you and that thing is going to be simply fantastic, absolutely incredible, unqualifiedly wonderful." And you reply, "Well, I believe you and I have to tell you, I'm just filled with dread and foreboding in thinking about it." That wouldn't make any sense at all. It makes sense to be filled with dread or foreboding or what have you only if the thing you're looking forward to, the thing you are anticipating, is itself bad. Maybe, for example, it makes sense to dread going to the dentist, if you believe that being at the dentist is a painful, unpleasant experience. But if being at the dentist isn't itself unpleasant, it doesn't make sense to dread it in anticipation.

So again, if we're thinking about the central badness of death, it seems to me that we've got to focus on my *being* dead. What is it about my *being* dead that's bad for me? And when we pose that question it seems as though the answer should be simple and straightforward. When I'm dead, I won't *exist*. (Remember, we are putting aside the potential complication that I might exist for a while as a corpse; for simplicity, we are supposing that I am killed in an explosion that simultaneously destroys my body.) Doesn't that give us the answer, right there, to what's bad about death? When I'm dead, I won't exist. Isn't that the straightforward explanation about why death is bad?

And what I want to say, in effect, is this. I do think the fact that I won't exist provides the *key* to getting clear about how and why death is bad. But I don't think it's altogether straightforward. As we'll see, it actually takes some work to spell out exactly how nonexistence could be bad for me. And even having done that, some puzzling questions will still remain.

Initially, to be sure, the basic idea seems to be straightforward enough. When I'm dead, I won't exist. Isn't it clear that nonexistence is bad for me? Pretty quickly, however, that answer can come to seem pretty unsatisfactory. How *could* nonexistence be bad for me? After all, the whole idea of nonexistence is that you don't exist! And how could anything be bad for you when you don't exist? Isn't there a kind of logical requirement that for something to be bad for you, you've got to be around to receive that bad thing? A headache, for example, can be bad for you. But of course, you exist during the headache. Headaches couldn't be bad for people who don't exist. They can't experience or have or receive headaches. How could *anything* be bad for you when you don't exist? And in particular, then, how could *nonexistence* be bad for you when you don't exist?

So it's not, as I say, altogether straightforward to see how an appeal to nonexistence genuinely explains the badness of death, as opposed to simply refocusing our attention on the problem. If I say that death is bad for me because when I'm dead I don't exist, we should still find ourselves puzzled as to how it could possibly be that nonexistence *can* be bad for me.

The answer to this objection, I think, is to be found in drawing a distinction between three different ways in which something can be bad for me. First of all, something can be bad for me in an absolute, robust, intrinsic sense. Take a headache, again, or some other kind of pain—stubbing your toe or getting stabbed or being tortured. Pain is *intrinsically* bad. It's bad in its own right. It's something we want to avoid for its own sake. Frequently enough, things that are bad for you are bad intrinsically; they're bad by virtue of their very nature.

Second, many things are *instrumentally* bad: something may not be bad in itself, but bad by virtue of what it causes or *leads* to. In particular, it might lead to something that is, in itself, *intrinsically* bad. Losing your job, for example, is not intrinsically bad—it's not bad in and of itself—but it is instrumentally bad, because it can lead to poverty and debt, which in turn can lead to pain, suffering, and other intrinsic bads.

But there's another way of something being bad for you, a third way that it's easy to overlook. Something can be bad *comparatively*. Something could be bad because of what you're not getting while you get this bad thing. It could be bad by virtue of what economists call the "opportunity costs." It's not that it's intrinsically bad, nor even that it's instrumentally bad; it's bad because while you're doing this, you're not getting something better.

How could that be? Let's have a simple example. Suppose that I stay home and watch some game show on TV. I watch the show and I have a good enough time. How could that be bad for me? In terms of the first way of being bad, being intrinsically bad, it's not bad. It's a pleasant enough way to spend half an hour. And we can certainly imagine that it's not bad in the second way either: it isn't instrumentally bad. (Watching a half hour of TV, let's suppose, won't *lead* to anything bad for me.) But still, for all that, it might be bad in the third way. Suppose, for example, that instead of staying at home, watching a half hour of television, I could be at a really great party. Then we might say that the fact that I'm stuck home watching television is bad for me in this *comparative* sense. It's not that it is, in itself, an unpleasant way to spend some time. It's not that it leads to something unpleasant. It's just that there's a *better* way to spend the time (if only I had remembered). Because I'm forgoing that greater good, there's something bad, comparatively speaking, about the fact that I'm at home watching TV. There's a lack of the better good. A lack is not *intrinsically* bad, and it needn't be an instrumental bad, but it's still a kind of bad in this third, comparative, sense. To be lacking a good is, in this comparative sense, bad for me.

Similarly, suppose I hold out two envelopes and I say, "Pick one." You pick the first one and you open it up and you say, "Hey look, ten bucks! Isn't that good for me?" Well, of course, ten bucks *is* good. Admittedly, it's not intrinsically good (not worth having for its own sake), but it is certainly instrumentally good (it can help you buy ice cream, for example, which can give you pleasure). Suppose, however, that, unbeknownst to you, the other envelope had $1,000 in it! Then we can say, "Look, it's bad for you that you picked the first envelope." Bad in what sense? Bad in the *comparative* sense. You would have been better off had you picked the second envelope. You would have been having more good, or a greater amount of good.

Now I hope it is obvious that nonexistence can't be bad for me in our first sense. It can't be that nonexistence is intrinsically bad, worth avoiding for its own sake. That would make sense only if nonexistence was somehow, for example, painful. But when you don't exist, you have no painful experiences. There's nothing about nonexistence in and of itself that makes us want to avoid it. And similarly, nonexistence isn't bad for me in our second sense. It doesn't cause me to have pains later, for example, nor does it lead to other intrinsic bads. So nonexistence isn't instrumentally bad either. But still, for all that, nonexistence can be bad for me in the *comparative* sense, because of the *lack* that it involves. When I don't exist, I'm lacking stuff.

What am I lacking? What I'm lacking, of course, is *life* and, more particularly still, the *good things* that life can give me. Nonexistence is bad by virtue of the opportunity costs that are involved. Famously, W. C. Fields wanted his tombstone to say "I'd rather be in Philadelphia." What's bad about being dead is that you don't get to experience and enjoy any longer the various good things that life would offer us.

So nonexistence does provide the key to understanding the central badness of death. Why is death bad? Because when I'm dead I don't exist. And if we ask, how can it be the case that nonexistence is bad?—the answer is, because of the lack of the good things in life. When I don't exist, I am not getting the things that I could have otherwise gotten, if only I were still alive. Death is bad because it deprives me of the good things in life.

This is nowadays known as the *deprivation* account of the evil or badness of death, since it holds that what is centrally bad about death is that it *deprives* you of the goods of life you might otherwise be getting. And it seems to me that the deprivation account basically has it right. To be sure, I think that there are additional aspects of death that may also contribute to its badness, aspects above and beyond the one that gets emphasized by the deprivation account. We'll get to these in a later chapter. But still, it seems to me the deprivation account points us correctly to the *central* thing that's bad about death. When I'm dead, I won't be getting the good things in life; I'll be deprived of them. That's the main reason death is bad.

Epicurus

Despite the overall plausibility of the deprivation account, it's not all smooth sailing. There are various objections that still need to be faced. Some people have found these objections so overwhelming that they have concluded that the deprivation account should not be accepted after all. Indeed, some have argued for the rather surprising conclusion that death is not, in fact, bad for me at all!

The first objection starts with what seems to be a quite general metaphysical principle: if something is true, there's got to be a *time* when whatever is being talked about is (or was, or will be) true. Facts can be *dated*. For example, I—Shelly Kagan—am typing some words right now about the badness of death. That's a fact. When was it true? That is, when was I typing? Right now: Tuesday, August 16, 2011, at 10:30 P.M. Here's another fact: Thomas Jefferson used to be president of the United States. When was that true? From March 4, 1801, to March 4, 1809. Things that are facts can be dated.

Okay, that seems right. But if it is right, then immediately we've got a puzzle. Can it really be true that my death is (or was, or will be) bad for me? After all, if my death is bad for me, that would be a fact. So we are entitled to ask, when is that true? *When* is death bad for me? It doesn't seem plausible to answer by saying that it's bad for me now. Death *isn't* bad for me now. I'm not *dead* now! Maybe, then, death is bad for me when I'm dead? But that seems very hard to believe as well. I mean, when I'm dead, I won't even exist. How could anything be bad for me *then*? Surely you've got to exist for something to be bad for you. So, there's a puzzle about dating the badness of death.

Now, it may be that this puzzle about time and the date of the badness of death is what the ancient Greek philosopher Epicurus had in mind in a passage I want to share with you. This passage has troubled people for two thousand years. Epicurus seems to be putting his finger on *something* genuinely puzzling about death, but it's difficult to pin down exactly what it is that's bugging him. Here's the passage from Epicurus that I have in mind:

> So death, the most terrifying of ills, is nothing to us, since so long as we exist, death is not with us; but when death comes, then we do not exist. It does not then concern either the living or the dead, since for the former it is not, and the latter are no more.[2]

As you can see, it's not altogether clear what Epicurus is bothered by here, but one possible interpretation is that he's thinking about our puzzle concerning the timing of the badness of death. Death can't be bad for me now, because I'm alive. And death can't be bad for me when I'm dead, because at that point I will be no more. (How can things be bad for me *then*?) But if death has no time at which it's bad for me, then the purported fact that death is bad for me can't really be a fact after all. Contrary to what we normally believe, death *isn't* bad for me.

Regardless of whether this really is what Epicurus had in mind, we need to ask ourselves, how can we respond to this argument? One way, of course, is to accept it and conclude that death isn't truly bad for me. And some philosophers have indeed embraced that very conclusion (including Epicurus). Most of us, however, want to insist that death really is bad. That requires showing where the argument goes wrong. And as far as I can see, if we are going to reject the argument, there are only two ways to do this. First, we could grab the bull by the horns, agree that facts need to be dated, and then say *when* death is bad for me. Alternatively, second, we could challenge the assumption that all facts are datable.

Let's start with the second. Could there be some facts that we can't date? Maybe. Here's a possible example. Suppose that on Monday I shoot John. I wound him with the bullet that comes out of my gun. But it's not a wound directly into his heart. He simply starts bleeding. And he bleeds slowly. So he doesn't die on Monday. He's wounded and he's dying, but he doesn't die on Monday. Next, imagine that on Tuesday I have a heart attack and I die. John's still around—bleeding, but still around. On Wednesday, though, the loss of blood finally overtakes him and John dies. That's the sequence: I shoot John on Monday, I die on Tuesday, and John dies on Wednesday.

I killed John. I take it we're all in agreement about that. If I hadn't shot him, he wouldn't be dead. I killed him. That's a fact. But *when* did I kill him? Did I kill him on Monday, the day I shot him? That doesn't seem right. He's not *dead* on Monday, so how could I have killed him on Monday? And Tuesday is clearly no better: John is still alive on Tuesday as well. John didn't die until Wednesday. So did I kill him on Wednesday? But how could that be? I don't even exist on Wednesday! I died on Tuesday. How can I kill him after I'm dead? So I didn't kill him on Monday, I didn't kill him on Tuesday, and I didn't kill him on Wednesday. So when did I kill him?

Maybe the answer is that there's no particular time at all when I killed John. But for all that, it's true that I did kill him. What makes it true that

I killed him? What makes it true is that on Monday I shot him, and on Wednesday he died from the wound. That's what makes it true. But *when* did I kill him? Maybe we can't date that. Suppose we can't. If we can't, then there are facts that you can't date, like the fact that I killed John. If there are facts that you can't date, then maybe this is another one: my death is bad for me. *When* is my death bad for me? Maybe that fact simply cannot be dated, but for all that, it really is a fact. So that's one way of trying to resist the argument: we might reject the assumption that all facts can be dated.

Of course, the thought that all facts can be dated is a very powerful one. Perhaps you'll find yourself thinking about this example for a while and come up with an acceptable answer to the question of when I killed John. Indeed, maybe on reflection you will decide that it really is true that *all* facts can be dated. (There are, of course, other puzzling examples besides the one I just gave that you would need to think about as well.) If you do decide that all facts can be dated, and yet you still want to insist that my death is bad for me, then you will need to take the other approach, and come up with the time. Can we do that? Can we say *when* death is bad for me?

I don't think it would be very promising to claim that death is bad for me *now*. I am not *dead* now, so it is very hard for me to see how my death can be bad for me now. But it isn't 100 percent clear to me that the other alternative is similarly unacceptable. Why not say that death is bad for me when I am *dead*? After all, when is a headache bad for me? When the headache is occurring. So why not say, similarly, that death is bad for me when I am dead?

According to the deprivation account, the badness of death consists in the fact that when you're dead, you are deprived of the goods of life. So when is death bad for you? Presumably, during the time when you are being deprived of the goods of life. Okay, when are you deprived of the goods of life? When you're dead. When does the deprivation actually occur? When you're dead. So perhaps we should just say to Epicurus (if this really was Epicurus's argument), "You were right, Epicurus, all facts have to be dated. But we *can* date the badness of death. My death is bad for me during the time I'm dead, since during that time I am deprived of—I'm not getting—the good things in life that I would be getting if only I were still alive."

That does seem to be a possible response to the argument. But of course, it just immediately returns us to an earlier puzzle. How *could* it be that death is bad for me then? How could it be that death is bad for me when I don't even exist? Surely, I have to exist in order for something to be bad for me—or, for that matter, for something to be good for me. Don't you need to exist in order for something to be good or bad for you?

This line of thought points to a different possible interpretation of Epicurus's argument. Perhaps the argument he has in mind is really this:

(A) Something can be bad for you only if you exist.
(B) When you are dead you don't exist.
So (C) death can't be bad for you.

Here's the quote from Epicurus again:

So death, the most terrifying of ills, is nothing to us, since so long as we exist, death is not with us; but when death comes, then we do not exist. It does not then concern either the living or the dead, since for the former it is not, and the latter are no more.

Of course, the passage from Epicurus still isn't altogether clear, but maybe he's got in mind something like this new argument. Maybe Epicurus thinks: (A) something can be bad for you only if you exist; (B) when you're dead you don't exist; so (C) death can't be bad for you.

Regardless of whether this is what Epicurus had in mind, what should we say about this new argument? For our purposes, we are taking (B) as given. When you're dead, you don't exist. And so the conclusion (C), that death can't be bad for you, is going to follow, once we accept (A). Call (A) the *existence requirement*. Something can be bad for you—or, for that matter, good for you—only if you exist. That's the existence requirement for bads and goods.

If we accept the existence requirement, it looks as though we have to accept the conclusion, that death can't be bad for you. So what should we say? Maybe we should just *reject* the existence requirement. Admittedly, in typical cases—cases involving pains, being blind, being crippled, losing your job, and so on—things are bad for you while you exist. Indeed, in the ordinary case, in order to receive bads, you *have* to exist. But perhaps that's only the ordinary case—not all cases. Perhaps for certain kinds of bads you don't even need to *exist* in order for those things to be bad for you.

What kind of bads could be like that? Arguably, the *comparative* bads of deprivation are like that. To lack something, after all, you don't need to exist. Indeed, the very fact that you don't exist might explain why you are deprived, why you are lacking. Of course, not all lacks are like that. Remember the television case, where you are watching TV but could have been at a great party. Obviously enough, you *existed* while you were watching TV and deprived of the party. Similarly, in our envelope example, you existed while you were getting the mere $10 instead of the $1,000. So sometimes deprivations coincide with existence. But the crucial point about deprivations is you don't even need to so much as exist in order to be deprived of something. Nonexistence *guarantees* that you're deprived of something.

So perhaps we should just reject the existence requirement. Perhaps we should say that when we're talking about lacks, when we're talking about deprivations, (A) is wrong. Something can be bad for you even if you *don't* exist. The existence requirement is *false*. That would be a way to respond to this second possible interpretation of Epicurus's argument. By rejecting the existence requirement, we'd be able to retain the thought that death is bad.

Unfortunately, there are some implications of rejecting the existence requirement that may be rather hard to swallow. Think about what we would be saying. In rejecting the existence requirement, we would be saying that something, in particular nonexistence, can be bad for somebody, even though they don't exist. That's why my death can be bad for me. But if nonexistence can be bad for somebody even though they don't exist, then nonexistence could be bad for somebody who *never* exists. It can be bad for somebody who is a merely *possible* person, someone who could have existed but never actually gets born.

It's hard to think about somebody like that. So let's try to get at least a little bit more concrete. I need two volunteers. I need a male volunteer from among my readers. And I need a female volunteer from among my readers. Okay, good. Now what I want the two of you to do is this: go have sex and have a baby.

Let me just suppose that this isn't actually going to happen. Still, we can consider the possible world in which it did happen. We can consider the never-to-be-truly-actualized possibility in which this particular man and that particular woman would have sex and have a baby. His sperm joins with her egg to form a fertilized egg. The fertilized egg develops into a fetus. It's the fetus we created by mixing egg 37, say, with sperm 4,000,309. The fetus is eventually born. The baby grows up. None of this is going to happen, but it could have happened.

Thus, there is a person that *could* have been born but never does, in fact, get born. Let's call that particular person—who could have been born but never does get born—*Larry*. Larry is a *possible* person. He *could* exist (my two readers could have sex), but he *won't* exist (they won't have sex). That's why Larry is *only* a possible person. Now, how many of us feel sorry for Larry? Probably nobody. After all, Larry never even exists. How can we feel sorry for him?

That answer made perfect sense when we accepted the existence requirement—the claim that something can be bad for you only if you exist. Since Larry never exists, nothing can be bad for Larry. But once we give up on the existence requirement, once we say something can be bad for you even if you never exist, then we no longer have any grounds for withholding our sympathy from Larry. We can say, "Oh my gosh! Think of all the goods in life that Larry would have had, if only he'd been born. But he never *is* born, so he's deprived of all those goods." And if death is bad for me, by virtue of being deprived of the goods of life, then nonexistence is bad for Larry too, by virtue of his being deprived of all the goods of life. I've got it bad. I'm going to die. But Larry's got it *worse*. We should really feel much sorrier for Larry. But I bet you *don't* feel sorry for Larry, this never-to-be-born-at-all person.

In thinking about this case, it's important not to slip back into some form of dualism. In particular, don't start imagining Larry as already having a soul, desperately wishing he would be born. There's a scene in Homer, I think, where some sort of sacrifice is being made and all the dead souls hover around, longing to be alive again, wishing they could savor the taste and smell of the food. If you've got a picture of the nonexistent, merely possible but never-to-be-born individuals as somehow really already existing in a kind of ghostlike state, wishing they were born, maybe you *should* feel sorry for them. But that's not at all what is going on in the physicalist picture that I am assuming. Nonexistent people don't have a kind of spooky, I-wish-I-were-alive ghostlike existence. They just don't exist, full stop. So once we keep that in mind about Larry, it's very hard to feel sorry for him.

Of course, while I have been prattling on about how he's deprived of all the good things in life, maybe you *have* started feeling sorry for Larry. So it's worth getting clear about just what it would mean to take seriously the thought that it's bad for merely potential people never to be born. I want you to get a sense of just how many merely potential people there are. It's not just Larry, the unborn person that would exist if we mixed egg 37 and sperm 4,000,309, that would have to be an object of our sympathy. No, we would need to feel sorry for a vastly larger number of merely potential

people. For the fact is, there is an incredibly large number of merely potential, never-to-be-born individuals.

How many? *A lot.* How many? I once tried to do the calculation, and
I recently updated it slightly. As you'll see, the calculation is an utterly
"back of the envelope" sort of thing, extremely rough and completely inadequate in all sorts of ways. But at least it'll give you a sense of just how many
potential people there are.

Let's start modestly and ask: how many possible people could we, the
current generation, produce? Well, how many people *are* there? In round
numbers, as I write in 2011, there are about 7 billion people. Roughly half of
them are men, half of them are women.

What we want to know then is, how many possible people could the
3.5 billion men make altogether with the 3.5 billion women? The crucial
point in thinking about this is to realize that every time you combine a different egg with a different sperm you end up with a different person. If you
combine an egg with a different sperm, you get a different genetic code that
develops into a different person. Or if you combine that sperm with a different egg, you get a different person. Thus, for example, if my parents had had
sex five minutes earlier or five minutes later, presumably some other sperm
would have joined with the egg. The baby that might eventually have been
born would not have been *me*. It would have been some sibling being born
instead of me. Change the egg, change the sperm, you get a different person.
So what we really want to know is, how many sperm-egg combinations are
there with roughly 7 billion people in the world?

Let's see. There are 3.5 billion women. How many eggs can a woman
have? As we will see, the precise number doesn't really matter all that much,
so we can approximate. In round numbers, a woman produces 12 eggs a
year, for roughly 30 years. So that's the number of eggs per woman. Actually,
I discovered some time after having done this calculation that the number
of possible eggs is far greater than this. Although a woman ovulates and
gives off roughly this many eggs during her fertile years, I gather that there
are actually many, many other cells that could have developed into eggs but
never do. So that's a much, much larger number of potential eggs. But this
will do for our purposes: 30 years times 12 eggs a year.

Men next. There are roughly 3.5 billion men. Each man has a much
longer period in which he's able to produce sperm. Let's just use round numbers here, and say he's fertile for 50 years. How many times a day can the
man have sex? Well, certainly more than once, but let's be modest here and

just say once a day. So that's 50 years times 365 times a year. Each time a man ejaculates he gives off a lot of sperm. How much sperm? A *lot*. As it happens, I looked this up once. In round numbers, there are 40 million sperm each time a man ejaculates. So we need to take the number of times the man can ejaculate over his life and multiply this by 40 million sperm.

Okay, so we take all the men that exist now and all the women that exist now, and we ask, how many possible sperm-egg combinations are there? That will give us a sense of the number of possible people the current generation could produce. Of course, most of these people are never going to be born—but what we are looking for is the number of *possible* people.

How many possible people are there? Here's the equation:

3.5 billion women × 30 years/woman × 12 eggs/year × 3.5 billion men × 50 years/man × 365 days/year × 40 million sperm/day = *approximately* 3 million billion billion billion (3×10^{33})

I've done a lot of rounding here, including the final calculation, but in very rough terms that gives us 3 million billion billion billion different possible people. That's 3×10^{33}. That's how many possible people we could have, roughly speaking, in the next generation, of which, obviously, only a minuscule fraction are going to be born. And the crucial point is this: if you're going to feel sorry for Larry, you've got to feel sorry for every merely possible person. Every person who *could* have been born but never *gets* born. And there are 3 million billion billion billion such merely possible people.

And of course, the truth of the matter is, we have barely scratched the surface here. Because now we need to think of all those possible people and think about all the possible children *they* could have. We got this initial number starting with a mere 7 billion people. Imagine the number we would get if we then calculated how many possible grandchildren we could have! (The total is approximately 5×10^{66}.) I don't mean that we could actually have all of those people at the same time, but each one is a possible person that could have existed. And that was after just two generations! If you go to three generations you end up with more possible people than there are particles in the known universe. Four generations, and you'll have even more. If we think about the number of possible people, people who could have existed but will never exist, the number just boggles the mind.

Suppose, then, that we've gotten rid of the existence requirement and so things can be bad for you even if you never actually exist. Then we have to say of each and every single one of those billions upon billions upon billions upon billions upon billions of possible people that it's a tragedy that they never get born, because they're deprived of the goods of life. If we do away with the existence requirement, then the plight of the unborn possible people is a moral tragedy that simply staggers the mind. The worst possible moral horrors of human history don't even begin to be in the same ballpark as the moral horror of the deprivation for all of these unborn possible people.

Now I don't know about you, but when *I* think about it, all I can say is it doesn't strike me as being a moral catastrophe. I don't feel anguish and sorrow and dismay at the deprivation for the untold billion billion billion billions. But if we give up the existence requirement and explain the badness of my death via the deprivation account, we do have to say that the fact that billions upon billions are never born is a moral tragedy of unspeakable proportions.

If we are *not* prepared to say that that's a moral tragedy, we could avoid this conclusion by going back to the existence requirement. But of course, if we do go back to the existence requirement, then we're back with Epicurus's argument. Something can be bad for you only if you exist. When you're dead, you don't exist. So death can't be bad for you.

We've really gotten ourselves in a philosophical pickle now, haven't we? If I accept the existence requirement, we've got an argument that says death isn't bad for me, which is really rather surprising and hard to believe. Alternatively, I can keep the claim that death is bad for me by giving up the existence requirement. But if I give up the existence requirement, I've got to say it's a tragedy that Larry and the untold billion billion billion billions are deprived of life as well. And that seems just as unacceptable. So what should we do? What should we say?

The problem, again, is this. If we don't throw in any existence requirement, we have to feel sorry for the unborn billion billion billions. That doesn't seem acceptable. So it seems that we need *some* kind of existence requirement. But if we throw in the existence requirement, we seem to end up saying that death isn't bad for me, because I don't exist when I'm dead. That doesn't seem acceptable either. But maybe we have been *misinterpreting* the existence requirement. Maybe it demands less than we realize. Or, to put the point in slightly different terms, maybe we can distinguish between two different *versions* of the existence requirement, a bolder and a more modest version, where we have been unwittingly assuming the bold version, while the more modest version would allow us to avoid both unacceptable implications.

I think this is a promising idea, so let me suggest two different ways of understanding what the existence requirement comes to:

Modest: Something can be bad for you only if you exist at *some* time or the other.

Bold: Something can be bad for you only if you exist at the *same* time as that thing.

These are two different ways of understanding what the existence requirement asserts. The modest version is called *modest* because it asks for less. It says that something can be bad for you provided that you exist at some time or the other. The bold existence requirement adds a further requirement. It says that something can be bad for you only if you exist at the very same time as the thing that's supposed to be bad for you. There's got to be a kind of simultaneity. If something's bad for you, you had better exist at the very same time that the bad thing is happening. That's more demanding than the modest requirement. The modest requirement doesn't require that you exist at the *same* time as the bad thing. It only requires that you exist at *some* time or the other.

Suppose we accept the bold claim. For something to be bad for you, you have to exist at the very same time as the bad thing. Then death can't be bad for you, because you don't exist at the time you are dead. Most of us find that an unacceptable conclusion. However, if we accept the modest requirement instead, then things look rather different. Now, for something to be bad for you, you only have to exist at some time or the other; you needn't exist at the very same time as the bad thing. But of course I *do* exist at some time or the other—after all, I exist right now. So death can be bad for me. Admittedly, I won't exist when I'm dead. But that's okay. The modest existence requirement doesn't require that I exist at the very same time as the bad thing. The bold version did, but the modest one doesn't. So the modest version of the existence requirement allows us to say that death is bad for me.

But notice, and this is the crucial point, the modest version does *not* say that nonexistence is bad for Larry, too—because Larry never exists at all! Since Larry never exists at all, he doesn't satisfy even the *modest* existence requirement. So nonexistence is not bad for Larry, or the untold billion billion billions.

In short, with no existence requirement at all, we have to say that the nonexistence of the billions and billions is bad. That seems unacceptable. And with the bold existence requirement, we have to say death isn't even bad for me. That seems unacceptable as well. But if, instead, we accept the *modest* existence requirement, we're able to say that nonexistence is *not* bad for Larry, but death *is* bad for me. We are able to avoid both unacceptable positions. Accordingly, the most plausible position seems to be one that involves accepting the modest existence requirement.

If we accept the modest existence requirement, then we are saying that in order for something to be bad for you, there has to have been a time, some time or the other, when you exist. You've got to exist at least *briefly* in order to get into the "club," as we might put it, of creatures that we care about and are concerned about morally. To get into the club, you have to exist for some period of time (past, present, or future). But once you're *in* the club, things can be bad for you, even if you don't happen to exist at that particular moment.

If we accept the modest existence requirement, then we can say that it's not bad that Larry doesn't exist, because, well, Larry doesn't get into the club. In order to get into the club of things that we feel sorry for, you have to have existed at least for some moment or the other. But Larry and the billions upon billions upon billions of potential people who never actually come into existence don't satisfy the requirement of having existed at some time or the other. So we don't have to feel sorry for them. Nonetheless, we *can* feel sorry for a child who died last week at the age of ten because we can point out that she did exist, even if only very briefly. Such a child is in the club of beings that we can feel sorry for. It can be bad for her that she's not still alive. (Think of all the good things in life she would be getting if she were still alive!) So the modest existence requirement allows us to avoid both extremes. It seems like the position we should accept.

Unfortunately, even the modest existence requirement is not without its counterintuitive implications. Consider somebody's life. Suppose that somebody's got a nice long life. He comes into existence, and lives 10, 20, 30, 40, 50, 60, 70, 80, 90 years. It's a nice life. Now, imagine that we bring it about that instead of living 90 years, he has a somewhat shorter life—10, 20, 30, 40, 50 years. We've caused him to die after 50 years as opposed to the 90 years he might have otherwise had. We will say, of course, that this is worse for him—to live merely 50 years instead of the full 80 or 90 years. And if we accept the modest existence requirement, we can indeed say that, because, after all, whether you live 50 years or 90 years, you did exist at some time or the other. So the fact that you lost the 40 years you otherwise would have gotten is bad for you. Good. That gives us the answer we want. That's not counterintuitive.

Now imagine that instead of living 50 years, the person lives only 10 or 20 years and then dies. That's clearly worse still. Think of all the extra goods he would have gotten if only he hadn't died so young. And if I caused him to die after 20 years instead of 50 or 90 years, I've made things worse. Next, imagine that I caused him to die after one year. That's worse still. All of this is perfectly intuitive. The shorter his life, the worse it is for him, the more he's deprived of the good things in life.

In short: Ninety year life, not bad. Fifty year life, worse. Ten year life, worse still. One year life, worse still. One month life, worse still. One day life, worse still. One minute life, worse still. One second life, worse still.

Finally, imagine that I bring it about that the person never comes into existence at all. Oh, that's fine.

What? How can that be fine? But that's the implication of accepting the modest existence requirement. If I shorten the life he would have had so completely that he never gets born at all (or, more precisely, never comes into existence at all), then he doesn't satisfy the requirement of having existed at some time or the other. So although we were making things worse and worse and worse and worse and worse as we shortened the life, when we finally snip out that last little fraction of a second, it turns out we didn't make things worse at all. Now we haven't done anything objectionable. That, it seems, is what you've got to say if you accept the modest existence requirement.

Of course, if we didn't have an existence requirement at all, we could say that it is indeed worst of all never to have been born at all. But if you do say that, then you've got to feel sorry for Larry. You've got to feel sorry for the untold billion billion billions.

So which view is it that on balance is the most plausible? However you answer, note that being the *most* plausible here doesn't mean that it has to be all that plausible! I think that when we start thinking about these puzzles, *every* alternative seems unattractive in its own way. Maybe the most we should ask is, which is the least *implausible* thing to say here? And the truth is, I'm not altogether certain.

Lucretius

Let me turn to one more puzzle for the deprivation account. This particular puzzle arises whether or not we accept an existence requirement, because we're going to deal with somebody who certainly does exist at some time or the other, namely, you or me. It's a puzzle that we get from Lucretius, a

Roman philosopher.[3] Lucretius was one of those who thought it a mistake to claim that death could be bad for us. He thinks we are confused when we find the prospect of our death upsetting. He recognizes, of course, that most of us *are* upset at the fact that we're going to die. We think death is bad for us. Why? In my own case, of course, it's because after my death I won't exist. As the deprivation account points out, after my death it will be true that if only I were still alive, I could be enjoying the good things in life.

Fair enough, says Lucretius, but wait a minute. The time after I die isn't the *only* period during which I won't exist. It's not the only period in which it is true that if only I were alive, I could be enjoying the good things in life. There's *another* period of nonexistence: the period before my birth. To be sure, there will be an infinite period after my death in which I won't exist—and realizing that fills me with dismay. But be that all as it may, there was of course also an infinite period *before* I came into existence. Well, says Lucretius, if nonexistence is so bad—and by the deprivation account it seems that we want to say that it is—shouldn't I be upset at the fact that there was also this eternity of nonexistence before I was born?

But, Lucretius suggests, that's silly, right? Nobody is upset about the fact that there was an eternity of nonexistence *before* they were born. In which case, he concludes, it doesn't make any sense to be upset about the eternity of nonexistence *after* you die.

Lucretius doesn't offer this as a puzzle. Rather, he offers it as an argument that we should not be concerned about the fact that we're going to die. Unsurprisingly, however, most philosophers aren't willing to go with Lucretius all the way to this conclusion. They insist, instead, that there must be something wrong with this argument someplace. The challenge is to figure out just where the mistake is.

What are the options here? One possibility, of course, is to simply agree with Lucretius. There is nothing bad about the eternity of nonexistence before I was born. So, similarly, there is nothing bad about the eternity of nonexistence after I die. Despite what most of us think, death is not bad for me. That's certainly one possibility—completely agreeing with Lucretius.

A second possibility is to partly agree with Lucretius. Perhaps we really do need to treat these two eternities of nonexistence on a par; but instead of saying with Lucretius that there was nothing bad about the eternity of nonexistence before birth and so nothing bad about the eternity of nonexistence after death, maybe we should say, instead, that just as there is something bad about the eternity of nonexistence after we die, so too there must be something bad about the eternity of nonexistence before we were born!

Maybe we should just stick with the deprivation account and not lose faith in it. The deprivation account tells us that it's bad for us that there's this period after we die, because if only we weren't dead then, we would still be able to enjoy the good things in life. So maybe we should say, similarly, that it *is* bad for us that there's this period before we come into existence. After all, if only we had existed then, we would have been able to enjoy the good things in life. So maybe Lucretius was right when he tells us that we have to treat both periods the same, but for all that he could be wrong in concluding that neither period is bad. Maybe we should think *both* periods are bad. That's a possibility, too.

What other possibilities are there? We might say that although Lucretius is right when he points out that there are two periods of nonexistence, not just one, nonetheless there is a justification for treating them differently. Perhaps there is an important difference between the two periods, a kind of asymmetry that explains why we should care about the one but not the other.

Most philosophers want to take this last way out. They say that there's something that explains why it makes sense, why it's reasonable, to care about the eternity of nonexistence after my death in a way that I don't care about the eternity of nonexistence before my birth. But then the puzzle, of course, is to point to a difference that would *justify* that kind of asymmetrical treatment of the two periods. It's easy to *say* that it's reasonable to treat the two periods differently; the philosophical challenge is to point to something that explains or justifies that asymmetrical treatment.

One very common response is to say something like this. Consider the period after my death. I'm no longer alive. I have *lost* my life. In contrast, during the period before my birth, although I'm not alive, I have not *lost* my life. I have never yet been alive. And, of course, you can't lose something you've never yet had. So what's worse about the period after death is the fact that death involves *loss*, whereas prenatal nonexistence does *not* involve loss. And so (the argument goes), we can see why it's reasonable to care more about the period after death than the period before birth. The one involves loss, while the other does not.

This is, as I say, a very common response. But I am inclined to think that it can't be an adequate answer. It is true, of course, that the period after death involves loss while the period before birth does not. The very definition of "loss," after all, requires that in order to have lost something, it must be true that you don't have something that at an earlier time you did have. Given this definition, it follows trivially that the period after death involves loss, while the period before birth does not. After all, as we just observed, during the period before birth, although I do not *have* life, it is also true that I haven't had life previously. So I haven't *lost* anything.

Of course, there's another thing that's true about this prenatal period, to wit, I don't have life and I'm *going* to get it. So I don't yet have something that's going to come in the future. That's not true about the postlife period. After death I've *lost* life. But it's not true of this postdeath period that I don't have life and I'm going to get it in the future. So this period after death isn't quite like the period before birth: in the period after death, I am not in the state of not yet having something that I am going to get. That's an interesting difference.

As it happens, we don't have a name for this other kind of state— where you don't yet have something that you will get later. It is similar to loss, in one way, but it's not quite like loss. Let's call it "schmoss." When I have *lost* something, then, I don't have it, but I did have it earlier. And when I have *schmost* something, I don't have it yet, but I will get it later.

So here's the deal. During the period after death, there's a loss of life, but no schmoss of life. And during the period before birth, there's no loss of life, but there is a schmoss of life. And now, as philosophers, we need to ask: why do we care more about *loss* of life than *schmoss* of life? What is it about the fact that we don't have something that we used to have, that makes this worse than not having something that we're going to have?

It's easy to overlook the symmetry here, because we've got this nice word "loss," and we don't have the word "schmoss." But that's not really explaining anything, it's just pointing to the thing that needs explaining. Why do we care more about not having what once upon a time we did, than about not having what once upon a time we will? That's really quite puzzling.

Various proposals have been made to explain this difference in attitude toward the two periods of nonexistence. One of them comes from Thomas Nagel, a contemporary philosopher.[4] Nagel starts by pointing out how easy it is to imagine the possibility of living longer. Suppose I die at the age of eighty. Perhaps I will get hit by a car. Imagine, though, that if I didn't die then, I would have continued living until I was ninety or even one hundred. That certainly seems possible, even if in fact I am going to die at eighty. The fact that I am going to die at eighty is a *contingent* fact about me. It is not a necessary fact about me that I die at eighty. So it is an easy enough matter to imagine my living longer, by having my death come later. That's why it makes sense to get upset at the fact of my death coming when it does: I could have lived longer, by having death come later.

In contrast, Nagel notes, if I am going to be upset about my nonexistence before my birth, we have to imagine my being born earlier. We have to imagine my living longer by having my birth come sooner. Is this possible? I was born in 1954. Can I be upset about the fact that I was born in 1954 instead of, say, 1944?

Nagel thinks, however, that I shouldn't be upset about the fact that I wasn't born in 1944, because in fact it isn't *possible* for me to have an earlier birth. The date of my *death* is a contingent fact about me. But the date of my *birth* is not a contingent fact about me. Well, that's not quite right. We could change the time of birth slightly, perhaps by having me delivered prematurely, or through Caesarean section, or what have you. Strictly speaking, of course, the crucial moment is the moment at which I come into *existence*. Let's suppose that this is the time when the egg and the sperm join. Nagel's thought is that this is not a contingent moment in my life story. That's an *essential* moment in my life story.

How could that be? Can't we easily imagine my parents having had sex ten years earlier? Sure we can. But remember, if they had had sex ten years earlier, it would have been a different egg and a different sperm coming together, so it wouldn't be *me*. It would be some sibling of mine that, as it happens, never got born. Obviously, there could have been some sibling of mine that came into existence in 1944, but *I* couldn't have come into existence in 1944. The person we are imagining with the earlier birth date wouldn't be *me*. What this means, Nagel suggests, is that although we can *say* the words "if only I had been born earlier," this isn't really pointing to a genuine metaphysical possibility. So there is no point in being upset at the nonexistence before you started to exist, because you couldn't have had a longer life by coming into existence earlier. (In contrast, as we have seen, you could have a longer life by going out of existence later.)

I must say, that's a pretty intriguing suggestion. But I think it can't be quite right. Or rather, it cannot be the complete story about how to answer Lucretius's puzzle. For in some cases, I think, we *can* easily imagine the possibility of having come into existence earlier. Suppose we've got a fertility clinic that has some sperm on hold and has some eggs on hold. Perhaps they keep them there frozen until they're ready to use them. And they thaw a pair out in, say, 2025. They fertilize the egg and eventually the person is born. That person, it seems to me, can correctly say that he could have come into existence earlier. He could look back and say that if only they had put the relevant sperm and egg together ten years earlier, he would have come into existence ten years earlier. It wouldn't be a sibling; it would have been *him*. After all, it would have been the very same sperm and the very same egg, resulting in the very same person. So if only they had combined the sperm and egg ten years earlier, he would have been born ten years earlier.

If that's right—and it does seem to me to be right—then Nagel is wrong in saying it's not possible to imagine being born earlier. In at least some cases it is. Yet, if we imagine somebody like this, somebody who's an offspring of this kind of fertility clinic, and we ask, "Would they be upset that they weren't born earlier?" it still seems as though most people would say, "No, of course not." So Nagel's solution to our puzzle doesn't seem to me to be an adequate one.

Here's another possible answer. This one comes from Fred Feldman, another contemporary philosopher.[5] If I say, "if only I would die later," what am I imagining? Suppose I will get hit by a car in 2034, when I am eighty. We can certainly imagine what would happen if I *didn't* get killed at that point. What do we imagine? Something like this, I suppose: instead of my living a "mere" eighty years, we imagine that I would live to be eighty-five or ninety, or more. We imagine a longer life. When we imagine my dying later, we imagine my having a longer life.

But what do I imagine when I say, "if only I had been born *earlier*"? According to Feldman, you don't actually imagine a longer life, you just *shift* the entire life and start it earlier. After all, suppose I ask you to imagine being born in 1800 instead of the year you were actually born. Nobody thinks, "Why, if I had been born in 1800, I'd still be alive. I would be more than two hundred years old!" Rather, you think, "If I had been born in 1800 I would have died in 1860, or 1870, or some such."

When we imagine being born earlier, we don't imagine a longer life, just an *earlier* life. And of course there is nothing about having a life that takes place earlier that makes it particularly better, according to the deprivation account. So there is no point in bemoaning the fact that you weren't born earlier. But in contrast, when we imagine dying later, it's not as though we shift the life *forward*. We don't imagine being *born* later, keeping the life the same length. No, we imagine a *longer* life. And so, Feldman says, it's no wonder that you care about nonexistence after death in a way that you don't care about nonexistence before birth. When you imagine death coming later, you imagine a longer life, with more of the goods of life. But when you imagine birth coming earlier, you don't imagine more goods in your life, you just imagine them taking place at a different time.

That too is an interesting suggestion, and I imagine it is probably part of a complete answer to Lucretius. But I don't think it can be the complete story. Because we can in fact imagine cases where the person reasonably thinks that if only she had been born earlier she *would* have had a longer life.

Let's suppose that next week astronomers discover the horrible fact that there's an asteroid that's about to land on the Earth and wipe out all life. Suppose that it is going to crash into the Earth on January 1st of next year. Now imagine someone who is currently only thirty years old. It seems to me to be perfectly reasonable for such a person to think to herself that she has only had thirty years of life, and if only she had been born ten years earlier, she would have had forty years before she died, instead of thirty; if she had been born twenty years earlier, she would have had fifty years, instead of thirty. That all seems perfectly intelligible. So it does seem as though, if we work at it, we can think of cases where an earlier birth does result in a longer life and not merely a shifted life. In cases like this, it seems, we can imagine making life longer in the "pre-birth" direction rather than in the "postdeath" direction.

What does that show us? I am not sure. When I think about the asteroid example, I find myself thinking that maybe symmetry is the right way to go here after all. Maybe in a case like this, the relevant bit of prenatal nonexistence *is* just as bad as a corresponding bit of postmortem nonexistence. Maybe Feldman is right when he says that normally, when thinking about an earlier birth, we just shift the life, instead of lengthening it. But for all that, if we are careful to describe a case where an earlier birth would truly mean a longer life for me, maybe it really *is* bad that I didn't get started sooner. (Feldman would probably agree.)

Here's one more answer to Lucretius that's been proposed. This is by yet another contemporary philosopher, Derek Parfit.[6] Recall the fact that even though nonexistence before birth doesn't involve loss, it does involve schmoss. So it would be helpful if we had an explanation of why loss is worse than schmoss. Why should we care more about the former than the latter? Parfit's idea, in effect, is that this is not an arbitrary preference on our part. Rather, it's part of a quite general pattern we have of caring about the future in a way that we don't care about the past. This is a very deep fact about human caring. We are oriented toward the future and concerned about what will happen in it, in a way that we're not oriented toward and concerned about what happened in the past.

Parfit's got a very nice example to bring the point home. He asks you to imagine that you've got some medical condition that will kill you unless you have an operation. So you're going to have the operation. Unfortunately, in order to perform the operation, they can't have you anesthetized. You have to be awake, perhaps in order to tell the surgeon, "Yes, that's where it hurts." You've got to be awake during the operation, and it's a *very* painful operation. Furthermore, we can't give you painkiller, because then you won't be able to tell the surgeon where it hurts. In short, you need to be awake while you are, in effect, being tortured. Of course, it's still worth it, because this will cure your condition, and you can go on to have a nice long life. But during the operation itself, it is going to hurt like hell.

Since we can't give you painkillers and we can't put you out, all we can do is this: after the operation is over, we'll give you this very powerful medication, which will induce a very localized form of amnesia, destroying your very recent memories. You won't remember anything about the operation itself. And in particular, then, you won't ever have to revisit horrible memories of having been tortured. Any such memory will be completely destroyed. Indeed, *all* memories from the preceding twenty-four hours will be completely wiped out. In sum, you are going to have a horrendously painful operation, and you are going to be awake during it. But after the operation you will be given medication that will make you completely forget the pain of the operation, indeed forget everything about the entire day.

So you're in the hospital and you wake up and you ask yourself, "Have I had the operation yet or not?" And of course, you don't know. You certainly don't remember having had it. But that doesn't tell you anything. On the one hand, if you haven't had it yet, it is no wonder you have no memories of having had it. But on the other hand, even if you *have* had the operation, you would have been given the medication afterwards, so would have no memories of it now. So you ask the nurse, "Have I had the operation yet or not?" She answers, "I don't know. We have several patients like you on the floor today, some of whom have already had the procedure, and some of whom are scheduled to have it later today. I don't remember which group you are in. Let me go look at your file. I'll come back in a moment and I'll tell you." So she wanders off. She's going to come back in a minute or two. And as you are waiting for her to come back, you ask yourself, what do you want the answer to be? Do you care which group you're in? Do you prefer to be someone who has *already* had the operation? Someone who *hasn't* had it yet? Or are you indifferent?

Now, if you're like Parfit, and for that matter like me, then you're going to say that *of course* you care. I certainly want it to be the case that I have *already* had the operation. I don't want to be someone who hasn't had the operation yet.

We might ask, how can that make any sense? You are going to have the operation sooner or later. At some point in your life history, that operation is going to have occurred. And so there's going to be the same amount of pain and torture at some point in your life, regardless of whether you're one of the people that had it yesterday or one of the people that are going to have it later today. But for all that, says Parfit, the fact of the matter is perfectly plain: we *do* care. We want the pain to be in the past. We don't want the pain to be in the future. We care more about what's happening in the future than about what's happened in the past.

That being the case, however, it is no surprise that we care about our nonexistence in the future in a way that we don't care about our nonexistence in the past. So perhaps that is the answer that we should give to Lucretius: the future matters in a way that the past does not.

That too is an intriguing suggestion. And it may well provide us with a convincing explanation of our asymmetrical attitudes. But we might still wonder whether it gives us any kind of *justification* for them. The fact that we've got this deep-seated asymmetrical attitude toward time doesn't in any way, as far as I can see, yet tell us whether or not that's a *justified* attitude. Maybe evolution built us to care about the future in a way that we don't care about the past, and this expresses itself in all sorts of places, including Parfit's hospital case and our attitude toward loss versus schmoss, and so forth and so on. But the fact that we've got this attitude doesn't yet show that it's a *rational* attitude.

How could we show that it's a rational attitude? Perhaps we would have to start doing some heavy-duty metaphysics (if what we have been doing so far isn't yet heavy-duty enough). Maybe we need to talk about the metaphysical difference between the past and the future. Intuitively, after all, the past is fixed, while the future is open, and time seems to have a direction, from past to future. Maybe somehow we could bring all these things in and explain why our attitude toward time is a reasonable one. I'm not going to go there. All I want to say is, it's not altogether obvious what the best answer to Lucretius's puzzle is.

So when I appeal to the deprivation account, and say that the central thing that's bad about death is the fact that you're deprived of the good things in life, I don't mean to suggest that everything is sweetness and light with regard to the deprivation account. I think that there are some residual puzzles—questions that have not yet been completely answered—about how it *can* be that death is bad.

But for all that, it seems to me that the deprivation account is the right way to go. It seems to me that this account does put its finger on the central bad thing about death. Most centrally, what's bad about death is that when you're dead, you're not experiencing the good things in life. Death is bad for you precisely because you don't have what life would bring you if only you hadn't died.

CHAPTER 11

Immortality

If death is bad because it deprives us of the good things in life, does it follow that the best thing of all would be to live forever? Given the deprivation account of the badness of death, does it follow that it would be better to be immortal?

It is natural to think that it does follow. Suppose, for example, that I get hit by a truck next week and die. That's bad, according to the deprivation account, because if only I hadn't gotten hit by a truck I might have lived another twenty or thirty years. I would have gotten the good things in life for another few decades. That would have been better for me. But of course if I die, instead, at eighty—of cancer, let's suppose—that is *still* bad for me. Because if only cancer hadn't killed me at eighty, I might have lived another ten, fifteen, or twenty years and gotten even more of the good things in life. And if, instead, we imagine that I die at one hundred—perhaps of congestive heart failure—that is still bad for me as well. If only I hadn't died at one hundred, I would have gotten even *more* out of life.

Obviously enough, we can keep repeating this kind of remark. If only I hadn't died at 120, if only I hadn't died at 150, if only I hadn't died at 500. *Whenever* it is I die, won't it always be true, if we accept the deprivation account, that if only I hadn't died then, I would have gotten more good things from life? And so whenever it is you die, death is bad for you. From which it follows that the best thing for you would be never to die at all, immortality.

There are actually two questions that we need to ask here. The first question is whether consistency requires that anyone who accepts the deprivation account must also believe that immortality would be a good thing. If I accept the deprivation account, but deny the value of immortality, am I somehow contradicting myself? The second question is this: even if consistency alone doesn't require that we value immortality, is it nonetheless *true* that immortality would be a good thing? I want to start with the first question, because I think that's the easier one to answer.

If I accept the deprivation account, am I thereby committed—on pain of inconsistency—to the claim that immortality would be valuable? Not at all. For the value of immortality simply does not follow as a matter of logic alone from the truth of the deprivation account. After all, what the deprivation account says is that death is bad for you by virtue of the fact that you are deprived of the good things in life. If only you hadn't gotten hit by that truck, say, you would have had an exciting life as a professional dancer or an architect. You would have had a family, or traveled around the world, spent time with your friends, or made important scientific discoveries. Whatever it might be. Life would have given you a lot of great things, and you get *deprived* of those great things when you get hit by that truck. That's why it's bad for you to have died then. That is to say, death is bad, when it's bad, by virtue of the fact that it deprives you of the good things in life.

But suppose that there are no more good things for life to give you. We don't know yet whether this could actually happen, but let's at least consider the logical possibility. Suppose there are no more good things for life to offer. Then when you're deprived of life by death, you're not being deprived of any good things, and so at that point it's *not* bad for you to be dead. Death is only bad, according to the deprivation account, when there are *good* things that would have come your way. Or, more precisely, when the life you would have had next would have been, *on balance,* good for you. (There can be bad mixed in with the good.) When that's true—when your life would have continued to be good *overall*—then to lose that next bit of life is *bad* for you.

But if it should turn out that what life would have offered hereafter, instead of being good, would have been hellish, then it's *not* bad for you to avoid that. It might actually be *good* for you to avoid it. So, even if we accept the deprivation account we're not committed to the claim that death is always bad. We have to look and see: what would life actually hold out for us? Logic alone, plus the deprivation account, doesn't force us to say immortality would be a good thing.

After all—this is really a crucial point to understand—things that are good for you in limited quantities can become bad for you if you get more and more and more and more of them. For example, I love chocolate. Imagine that somebody comes up to me with a box of Godiva chocolate and offers me a few pieces. I say, "Wonderful! I love Godiva chocolate." And then they give me some more, and then some more after that. Ten pieces of chocolate. Fifteen. Twenty pieces. By the time I've had twenty pieces of chocolate, I'm not sure right now if I really want the twenty-first piece. But they keep giving me more. Thirty pieces of chocolate, forty pieces of chocolate, one hundred pieces of chocolate. At some point—I've never actually had his much chocolate, so I don't know what the point is, but at *some* point—I'm going to say that although the first ten, fifteen, or twenty pieces were good, having to eat the twenty-first or the thirtieth or the fiftieth piece of chocolate is no longer good. Logically, at least, it could happen.

Similarly, then, perhaps life is like that across the board. Logically speaking, at least, it might be that although life is good in small quantities—fifty years, eighty years, one hundred years—at some point life would turn bad for us. Just like being force-fed more and more chocolate. And if it *did* turn bad for us, then the deprivation account would allow us to say that at *that* point, dying is not bad for you.

So logic alone doesn't tell us that we *have* to believe that immortality would be a good thing. But for all that, of course, it could still *be* a good thing. So that's question number two. Let's ask, what *should* we think about the prospect of living forever? Would having more and more life in fact be better and better and better? Should we say that if someone dies at age ten in some horrible car accident, then it would be better if they had made it to forty? If somebody dies at age forty, it would have been better if they had made it to eighty? If somebody dies at age eighty, it would have been better if they had made it to one hundred, 120, 170, and beyond? Is it really true that life would get better and better and better, the longer it is?

In asking this question, we have to be careful to be clear about what exactly we're imagining. Here's one way to try to picture immortality. Suppose that aging largely works the same way as it works now, with all the various changes that bodies currently undergo as they get older. But instead of those changes killing you at eighty, ninety, or one hundred, they don't. You get more and more of those changes, but they never actually kill you. This is the sort of thought experiment that Jonathan Swift undertakes in a wonderful passage from *Gulliver's Travels*.[1] Swift imagines Gulliver coming to a country where a certain subset of the people live forever. They are immortals. At first Gulliver says, "Oh, isn't this wonderful?" But he has forgotten to think about the fact that if the kinds of changes that we actually undergo as we age continue to accumulate, then not only are you getting older, you are also getting weaker and more disabled. There is greater and greater discomfort; senility sets in with a vengeance. You've got these creatures that live forever, but eventually their minds are gone, they're in constant pain, and they can't do anything at all because their bodies are utterly infirm, diseased, and sick. That's not a wonderful thing to have. If immortality was like *that*, says Swift, that would be horrible. If immortality was like that, then death would be a blessing. And Montaigne made a very similar point, arguing that death is indeed a blessing, because it puts an end to the pain and suffering and misery that afflict us in our old age.[2]

That certainly seems right, but I suppose we'd be forgiven for objecting that when we wanted to be immortal, we didn't want *this* kind of life going on and on and on, with the same downward trajectory. Rather, we want to live forever, hale and hearty and healthy. So even if the real world wouldn't allow us that, let's just ask whether or not living forever *could* be good. Obviously, in asking this, we are going to have to change some of the facts about what it probably *would* be like to live forever. But let's do that. Let's let our imaginations run wild. Isn't it at least true that in principle, if nothing more, living forever could be good?

We have to be careful here. If you are *not* careful, this is going to end up like one of those horror stories you read now and then, where you've got a couple of wishes but you forget to be careful about how exactly you state the wish. And so you get what you want, but it ends up being a nightmare. If you just tell the fairy who gives you three wishes, "I want to live forever," and you forget to say "and be sure to keep me healthy"—well, that's going to be a nightmare. That's what Swift told us. So let's be careful. Let's throw in health and anything else you want. Be sure to throw in enough money to make sure you're not poor for eternity. (Wouldn't that be horrible, to be healthy but *impoverished* forever?) Throw in *whatever* you want. All we need to ask at this point is, is there any way *at all* to imagine immortality, where being immortal in that way would be a good thing? Is there any way to imagine existing forever where that would be good for you, *forever*?

It is very tempting to think that the answer is that of course there is a way to do this. Nothing could be easier. Just imagine being in *heaven* forever. Eternal heavenly bliss. What could be better? Wouldn't we all love to be in heaven forever? The trouble is, I was a little bit vague just now about what exactly life is like in heaven. It's a striking fact that even those religions that promise us an eternity in heaven are rather shy about the details. Why? Because—one might worry—if you actually try to fill in the details, this wonderful, eternal existence ends up not seeming so wonderful after all.

Imagine that what's going to happen is that we all become angels, and we're going to spend eternity singing psalms. Now as it happens, I actually like psalms. I rather enjoy singing psalms at services. Saturday mornings I sing psalms in Hebrew and I quite enjoy it. But if you ask me about the possibility of spending an *eternity* doing that, then that doesn't really seem so desirable.

This same point was made humorously in the movie *Bedazzled.*[3] In that movie a human meets the devil and asks him, "So why did you rebel against God?" The devil says, "Well, I'll show you. I'll sit here, and you dance around me and say 'Oh, praise the Lord, aren't you wonderful. You're so magnificent. You're so glorious.'" The human does this for a while and then he complains, "This has gotten really boring. Can't we switch?" And the devil says, "That's exactly what I said."

When I try to imagine singing psalms for eternity in heaven, that doesn't seem so attractive. All right, so we won't imagine singing psalms for eternity! We'll just imagine something else. But what? Imagine what? This is the thought experiment that I invite you to perform. What kind of life can you imagine such that having that life forever would be good? Not just for another ten years, not just for another hundred years, not just for another thousand years, or a million years, or a billion years. Remember, eternity is a very, very long time. Forever goes on *forever.* Can you describe an existence that you would want to be stuck with forever?

When the British philosopher Bernard Williams thought about this question, he decided that the answer was no.[4] *No* kind of life would be one that would be desirable and attractive forever. Williams believed that *every* life would eventually become tedious and worse, indeed excruciatingly painful. Every kind of life is a life that you would eventually want to be rid of. In short, far from being a wonderful thing, immortality would be a horrible thing.

Suppose, for the moment, that we were to agree with Williams. What then should we say about death? Strictly speaking, if we are being careful, and we agree that immortality would be bad, then we can't say that death, per se, is bad as well. On the contrary, the fact that we are going to die, the fact of our mortality, is actually a good thing. After all, since the only alternative to dying is living forever, if immortality would actually be a bad thing, then death is not, in fact, a bad thing at all. Death is a *good* thing: it saves us from the undesirable fate of immortality.

Of course, even if we do say this, that doesn't mean that when I get hit by a car tomorrow, that's good for me. We don't have to say that at all. We can still say that it is a bad thing that I got hit by a car—because, after all, if I hadn't gotten hit by a car, it isn't as though I would have been condemned to immortality! I just would have lived another ten or twenty or thirty years. And those years would have been good ones for me. And maybe even when I die—let's suppose I live to the ripe old age of one hundred—when I die at one hundred, we could perhaps still say that it's a bad thing for me that I die at the age of one hundred. Because if I hadn't died then, I might have lived another ten or twenty years and still enjoyed things in life, such as playing with my great grandchildren or great great grandchildren.

To say that immortality is bad is not to say it is a good thing that we die when we do. You can still believe consistently that we die *too soon*. Even if eventually, sooner or later, death would no longer be bad, it could still be true that in point of fact it comes too soon for all of us.

That's what we could say if we agree with Williams that immortality would not, in fact, be desirable. But we haven't yet decided whether we *should* agree with him. So we still need to ask: *is* there a way to imagine an immortal life that would be worth having? Or is Williams right when he tells us that every life, no matter how you imagine it, would eventually grow tedious or worse?

For whatever it's worth, I am inclined to agree with Williams. I think that no matter how we try to fill in the blank, it's a very long blank. The crucial point to keep in mind is that immortality means not just living a very long time or even an extraordinarily long time, but literally living *forever*. And I think it's very difficult, indeed I think it's impossible, to think of anything you would want to do forever.

I have a friend who once claimed to me that he wanted to live forever so that he could have Thai food every day for the rest of eternity. I like Thai food just fine, but the prospect of having Thai food every day, day after day, for thousands, millions, billions, trillions of years does not seem to me an attractive proposal. It seems to me, rather, a kind of a nightmare. Similarly, I have already told you that I love chocolate—but the prospect of having to eat more and more and more chocolate, for all eternity, seems to me a sickening one.

Think of any activity. Perhaps you enjoy doing crossword puzzles. Perhaps you would find the prospect of doing crossword puzzles a couple of hours a day an enjoyable one. But imagine doing crossword puzzles every day for ten years, a thousand years, a million years, a billion years, a trillion years. Eventually, or so it seems to me, you would end up saying, "I'm really *tired* of crossword puzzles." Sure, there would always be some new particular puzzle you hadn't seen before, but you would step up a level and say, "Although I haven't seen this particular one before, I've seen many, many crossword puzzles before. There's really nothing new under the sun here. The fact that I haven't seen this particular combination of words isn't enough to make it interesting."

Admittedly, crossword puzzles aren't a very deep subject, and we might wonder whether we would do better if we were engaged in something more mentally challenging than that. This may indicate something unusual about me, but I rather like math. And the prospect of having a lot of time to pursue math problems of a richer and deeper sort seems fairly attractive. Yet even there, when I imagine an eternity of thinking about math—or for that matter, an eternity of thinking about philosophy, which I obviously like even more than math—the prospect seems an unattractive one. I can't think of any activity I'd want to do *forever.*

Of course, this has all been a bit of a cheat. No one is suggesting that we have to spend all of eternity doing the same single thing over and over. No one is suggesting that we should spend eternity doing math problems and nothing but math problems. Even now, with our 50, 80, or 100 years, we don't fill our days doing only one kind of activity. Rather, we fill our days with a mixture of activities: eating, doing philosophy, spending time with family and friends, traveling. Perhaps, then, we need to mix it up a bit more. Instead of Thai every day for all eternity, perhaps it could be Thai for lunch on Mondays, Wednesdays, and Fridays, with Italian for lunch on Tuesdays and Thursdays, and Ethiopian for dinner on Saturday night, and so forth and so on. Perhaps we could spend three hours in the morning doing philosophy, and then two hours in the afternoon doing math, and then spend the evening watching a movie or going to the theater. I must say, that sounds like a pretty pleasant life. But it doesn't really help. Because, again, when I think of doing this, not just for years, or decades, or even centuries, but for all *eternity*, never getting away from it, never being free from it, it all turns sour. The seemingly positive dream of immortality becomes a nightmare, a nightmare from which we can never escape.

Maybe I am just not being sufficiently imaginative. A former colleague of mine once talked to me about the prospect of having a heavenly vision of the divine. Maybe that would be desirable forever. She asked me to think about what it's like to have a really great conversation with a friend, a conversation that you wish would "never end." She suggested that I should think of

God as being like an *infinitely* fascinating and understanding friend. Communing with God would be like having an incredibly satisfying conversation, one that you would literally want to continue forever.

Well, I can say the words, but when I try to imagine that possibility and take it seriously, I find that I just can't see it. No friend that I've ever talked with is one that I would actually *want* to spend eternity talking to. Of course, it is easy enough for me to *say* that I should just imagine a friend that I would want to talk with through all eternity. But the whole point is, I can't actually imagine what that would be like. When I do my best to imagine some kind of existence that would be desirable or attractive forever, it just doesn't work. It becomes a nightmare.

Maybe what we need to do is not so much imagine cycling through the same mix of activities week after week after week, but moving through whole careers. Maybe you could spend fifty or a hundred years pursuing philosophy as your career. And then, after that, fifty or a hundred years pursuing math as your career. And then fifty or a hundred years traveling around the world, followed by fifty or a hundred years being an artist working on your water colors, and so on. It certainly does seem to me that we could probably get a significantly longer desirable life out of that approach. But the crucial point remains that we have to remember that forever is literally *forever*. And there is *no* life that I am able to imagine for myself that is one that I would want to take on forever.

You might object: surely there could be creatures that *would* want to live forever, that would enjoy an eternal existence. I think that's probably right. Consider the fact that scientists have learned how to do the following. You can take a rat and put an electrode in his brain. If you put the electrode in just the right place, then when the electrode gets turned on, it stimulates the pleasure center in the rat's brain and it gets a little burst of pleasure, a pretty intense burst of pleasure. And in fact, you can take the wire from the electrode and hook it up to a lever and teach the rat how to push the lever and give itself a little burst of pleasure. What happens to rats when you do this? Maybe it won't surprise you to hear that what they do is keep pressing the lever. Indeed, they press the lever and they stop eating. They're no longer interested in sex or anything else. Basically, they just keep giving themselves these little orgasmic bursts of pleasure—until they die.

Of course, it's too bad that the rat dies, but perhaps we can somehow imagine the rat being immortal (maybe you have it on IV fluids, so it gets its nutrients that way). It is easy to imagine the rat simply pressing the lever forever, getting these intense bursts of pleasure and being content to do that for all eternity. If it's so easy to imagine that for the rat, then why not for us too? Why not just put our own orgasmatron hat on with the electrodes directly stimulating our brains so that we constantly get these intense bursts of pleasure? Just imagine that the bursts of pleasure go on forever. What could be more desirable than that?

Except that when I think about it—and I invite you to think about it too—I don't actually find this an especially attractive prospect. Mind you, it's not that I think we couldn't be stimulated to get pleasure forever. It's that there's something that distinguishes humans from rats. No doubt I would enjoy it. And no doubt I would enjoy it for a very long time. But I imagine that after a sufficiently long period, there would be a shift. Humans have this ability to look down on their experiences, or to step back from their experiences, and assess them. Even now, for example, as I'm sitting here typing these words, watching the screen on my computer, listening to the birds outside my window, part of me is thinking about whether I am getting my point across, and whether the light coming in from my window is a bit bright, and so forth and so on. We can all reflect on our first-order or base-level experiences, even while we are having them.

So imagine that you are in the pleasure-making machine. After a while, I think, part of you is going to start thinking, "Hmm, this feels the same as it did yesterday, and the day before that, and the day before that. I imagine that this is how it's going to feel tomorrow, and the day after that, and the day after that." And eventually this question would start nagging at you, "Is this really all there is to life, just simple pleasure like this?"

The thing about being human is that, unlike the rat, you're not just going to stay caught up in the moment. You're going to take this meta-level or higher-level standpoint, look down at the pleasure, and wonder, "Is this all that there is to life?" And I think eventually that question would gnaw at you and sour and override the pleasure. Eventually, you'd become horrified that you were, in effect, stuck in this ratlike existence. Of course, the human part of you is able to say that there is *more* to you than this ratlike existence. But precisely for this reason, the human part of you is going to rebel at the unending parade of simple ratlike pleasures. So I don't think an eternity like that would be such a good thing. Maybe it would be good for a rat, but not for a human.

Of course, we could perhaps deal with that problem by making us more ratlike in terms of our thinking processes. Perhaps the right kind of lobotomy would do the trick. I don't actually know exactly what it would take, but no doubt you could just cut off and snip the relevant nerve endings so that we're no longer able to engage in that higher-order thinking, no longer able to raise the question "Is that all there is?" No longer able to step back from the first-order pleasure. No doubt, you can turn us into creatures like rats in that way. And then, I presume, we would continue to enjoy it forever.

But the question isn't whether there is something you could do to a human being so that he'd be happy, or at least enjoying himself, forever. Rather, it's whether, right here, right now, thinking about that kind of life, you *want* that for yourself. Do you want to be lobotomized so as to ensure that you would enjoy that kind of life forever? I certainly don't. I don't for a moment doubt that there must be ways that you could mess with my brain, screw up my ability to reflect, and then perhaps I could enjoy some form of life forever. But that doesn't mean that I now want that for myself. That doesn't seem to me to be some gift you've given me. Rather, that seems to me to be some sort of horrible *punishment* that you've imposed on me, reducing me from being a human being, able to engage in the full range of reflection, and turning me into something like a rat. So again, when the question is posed, "Is there a kind of life that I or you would want to live forever?" that question is being posed to you here and now. Is there a kind of life that *you* would want to have forever? It's not good enough if we can only get you to want that eternal life by altering you and turning you into something that you—here, now—don't want to be.

Here's a different possibility. Essentially, the problem with immortality seems to be one of inevitable boredom. The problem is tedium. You get tired of doing math after a while. After a hundred years, a thousand years, a million years, whatever it is, eventually you are going to say, "Yes, here's a math problem I haven't solved before, but so what? I've just done *so much* math, it holds no appeal for me anymore." Or, you go through all the great art museums in the world (or the galaxy) and you say, "Yes, I've seen dozens of Picassos. I've seen Rembrandts and Van Goghs, and more. I've seen thousands, millions, billions of incredible works of art. I've gotten what there is to get out of them. Isn't there anything new?" And the problem is that there isn't. There are, of course, things that you haven't seen before—but they are not new in a way that can still engage you afresh.

What's the solution for that? Perhaps a special kind of amnesia—a constantly rolling, progressive loss of memory. So here I am, 100 years old, 1,000 years old, 50,000 years old. I'm getting pretty bored with life. But we now introduce some progressive memory loss, so that I no longer remember what I did ten thousand years earlier. By the time I'm a million, I no longer remember what I was doing when I was a lad of 500,000. By the time

I'm a million and a half, I no longer remember what was happening back when I was a million. I know I was alive, perhaps, but beyond that, it is all rather hazy. I remember the last five or ten thousand years and that's it.

And while we're at it, why not overhaul your interests, desires, and tastes as well? Let's have your tastes and interests change gradually but *radically* over the years. (Minimal alterations presumably won't be enough.) Right now, perhaps, you like math, but eventually—maybe over thousands of years—you lose your interest in math, and you become the kind of person who is, say, interested in Chinese poetry. You lose your taste for jazz and develop a love of Gregorian chants. You lose your love of natural beauty and develop a fascination with the details of molecular biology. You stop wanting to do pottery and instead find yourself wanting to sail the seven seas.

Wouldn't something like that do it? Suppose we had this sort of progressive, ongoing, gradual but radical alteration of memories, beliefs, desires, and tastes. Wouldn't that allow us to have a kind of existence that would be forever enjoyable, without being reduced to a mere ratlike existence? I would be engaged in studying Chinese poetry. I'd be engaged in doing math. I'd be engaged in studying astronomy, practicing the trombone, sailing, what have you. That's far better than the rat's existence. And yet, at no point do I become bored, because, roughly, I'm so different from period to period to period.

I do think you could probably tell a story where something like this was true, especially if we throw in enough doses of memory loss. But this story should remind you of something, because it is similar to one that we have already discussed—the Methuselah case from Chapter 7. In that example, you'll remember, we imagined my living for hundreds and hundreds of years. (That seemed pretty long, at the time—before we started thinking about living *forever*!) In the Methuselah case, by the time I get to be 300, I don't remember all that much about being 100. By the time I get to be 500, I am not all that similar to the way I was when I was 200. By the time I am 800, I have utterly different memories, beliefs, desires, goals, and interests from the ones that I have now.

What I found when I thought about that case was that even though we have stipulated that it is going to still be me at age 800—the very same person as the one who is writing these words today—it didn't really matter. I said, "So what?" When I thought about what I *wanted* in survival, it wasn't good enough that there be somebody in the distant future that is me. It had to be somebody with a *similar* enough personality.

You tell me: "There's going to be somebody alive. He'll be you, but he will be completely *unlike* you. He will have different tastes, no memories of having taught philosophy—no *interest* in philosophy, or politics, or folk music, no concern for your family, and so forth and so on." I say: "That's all rather interesting from a metaphysical point of view, but speaking personally, I don't really care. It's of no interest to me to survive per se; and merely repeating the mantra, 'Oh, but it's me' doesn't make it more desirable to me. What I want isn't merely for somebody to be me. I want them to be sufficiently *like* me." The problem with the Methuselah case was that if you go far enough out, then the person is no longer sufficiently like me. I don't really care that there will still be somebody out there who is *me*, if they are so utterly unlike the way I am now.

But that, I hope you see, is just what we've ended up describing with our little story of eternal life made palatable through progressive memory loss and radical changes in interests, goals, and desires. In that story, there will be somebody around 100,000 years from now, 500,000 years from now, a million years from now, and they will be me. But I don't care. This doesn't give me what I want, when I want to survive. That person may *be* me, but he won't be enough *like* me, to give me what matters.

We can put the point in the form of a dilemma. Could immortality be something worth having forever? On the one hand, if we make that immortal person be *similar* to me, then boredom's going to set in. The only way to avoid that is to lobotomize me, and obviously that's not desirable. On the other hand, if we solve the problem of boredom with progressive memory loss and radical personality changes, then maybe boredom won't set in, but that life isn't anything that I especially want for myself. It just doesn't *matter* to me that it's still going to be me, anymore than it would matter to me if you were to just tell me, "Oh, there'll be somebody *else* around, who happens to like organic chemistry, and atonal music."

So, is there a way of living forever that's attractive? I can't think of what it would look like. I find myself agreeing with Bernard Williams when he says that immortality wouldn't be desirable. It would actually be a nightmare, something you would long to free yourself from.

Of course, having said that doesn't in any way mean that it's a good thing that we die when we *do*—at fifty or eighty or a hundred. Even if it is true (and I do think it is true) that after 1,000 years or 100,000 years or a million years or whatever it is, life would eventually grow tiresome, that hardly shows that life must grow tiresome after fifty years or eighty years or one hundred years. I don't believe I will have come *close* to scratching the surface of what I would enjoy doing by the time I die. And I imagine the same thing is true for you.

So the best form of life would not involve immortality. That, I think, would not be at all desirable. But neither is the best form of life what we have now, where you die after a measly fifty or eighty or one hundred years. Rather, the best thing, I suppose, would be to be able to live as long as you *wanted*.

This is more or less the sort of thing that the author Julian Barnes imagines in his short story "The Dream."[5] Barnes envisions heaven as someplace where you can stick around doing whatever it is that you want to do, for as long as you want to do it. But eventually, Barnes says, you will have had enough. And once you have, you can put an end to it. The suggestion that you will indeed eventually want to put an end to it—that's Barnes's way of expressing the thought that living *forever* would be undesirable. But the new thought here is that what *would* be good is being able to live until we were *satisfied*, until we had gotten *all* of the good that life could offer us.

What all this suggests, then—and this is a point that I have already made—is that the best understanding of the deprivation account doesn't say that it is a bad thing that we are going to die. For if I'm right in thinking that immortality would be undesirable, an unending nightmare, then the fact that we're going to die is actually good, since it guarantees that we don't have to face immortality. But still, for all that, even though it's not a bad thing that we will die, it could still be a bad thing that we die *when* we do. It could still be the case that we die *too soon*.

Finally, before leaving the topic of immortality, I can't resist sharing with you some words of wisdom from a former Miss USA contestant. She was asked the question, would you want to live forever? Here's her response:

> I would not live forever, because we should not live forever. Because if we were supposed to live forever, then we would live forever. But we cannot live forever, which is why I would not live forever.

> Isn't that wonderful?

CHAPTER 12

The Value of Life

I have been arguing that death is bad, when it's bad, because of the fact that it deprives us of the good things in life, insofar as we would have continued to get good things had we not died. But if life would no longer have anything good on balance to offer you—if what you would have had, had you not died, would have been something negative overall instead of something positive—then at that point dying isn't actually a bad thing, but a good thing. Death is bad insofar as it deprives you of a chunk of life that would have been good. But if it deprives you of a future that would have been bad, then death's not actually bad at all, it's good.

Now in saying all of this, I am obviously presupposing that, in principle at least, we can make these kinds of overall judgments with regard to the quality of your life, how well off you are or would be. Is life giving you good things, or is life giving you bad things? Is it worth continuing to live, or is it worth not continuing to live?

But what *is* it for a life to be going well? How do we assess what makes a life (or a portion of a life) a good one rather than a bad one? In asking this question, I don't mean to be asking about what makes a life a *morally* good life. I mean, rather, to be asking what makes a life a good one *for* the person whose life it is. The kind of life where it is reasonable to think, "I am *benefiting* from having this life." What I want to ask is, what are the ingredients or constituents or elements of a good life (versus a bad life) in *that* sense of the term? Of course, it's not just a matter of black or white. It isn't as though a life is either a good one or a bad one, with nothing more to say. There can be better lives and worse lives. So what we want is a yardstick adequate to making these more subtle comparisons as well.

What we want, then, is a theory of well-being, a theory of the value of life. Unfortunately, as with many of the other topics we've talked about in this book, this is a quite complicated subject, one that we could easily spend a great deal of time discussing. I will have to content myself here with merely scratching the surface.

The very first point that needs to be made, I think, is this. If you start listing all of the things worth having in life, it might seem as though you couldn't possibly come to any general organizing principles. Think about it. What's worth having? Well, let's see: Jobs are worth having. Pleasure is worth having. Money is worth having. Sex is worth having. Chocolate is worth having. Ice cream is worth having. Air conditioners are worth having. What are some of the things worth avoiding? Well, being blind is worth avoiding. Being mugged is worth avoiding. Diarrhea is worth avoiding. Pain is worth avoiding. Being unemployed is worth avoiding. War is worth avoiding. Disease is worth avoiding.

What kind of system or order could we possibly bring to all of this? The crucial distinction, I think, is one we have already met. We need to distinguish between instrumental goods and intrinsic goods, between those things that are valuable because of what they lead to—or, more strictly, *only* because of what they lead to—and those things that are valuable in their own right, worth having for their own sake.

Take something like a job. A job is certainly worth having. But why is a job worth having? Because, among other things, it gives you money. And money is certainly worth having, too. But why is money worth having? Because, among other things, you can buy ice cream with it. Okay. But why is ice cream worth having? Because when I eat ice cream it gives me this pleasurable sensation. So far, so good.

Next: why is the pleasurable sensation worth having? At this point, we get a different kind of answer. At this point, we say something like this: pleasure is worth having for its *own* sake. The other things were valuable only as a means—ultimately, a means to pleasure. But pleasure is worth having for its own sake. The things that are valuable as a means are *instrumentally* valuable. The things that are worth having for their own sake philosophers call *intrinsically* valuable.

If we look back at that long, open-ended list of things that were good or bad, we'll find that most of the good things on that list are instrumentally good. They're good because of what they lead to. Similarly, of course, most of the bad things on the list are instrumentally bad. Why, for example, is disease bad? Well, among other things, because disease means that you can't enjoy yourself. So it deprives you of pleasure, and it may cause pain. Or perhaps because if you are sick, you can't hold your job down, and so can't get money, and so forth and so on. If you think about it, you will probably agree that most familiar goods and bads are good or bad precisely because of their instrumental effects.

But if we want to make progress on the question about the nature of the good life, the nature of well-being, what we need to focus on is not the instrumental goods and bads but rather the *intrinsic* goods and bads. You've got to ask yourself, "What things are worth having for their *own* sake? What's worth having in and of itself?"

One natural suggestion—we've already seen it at work—is that pleasure is worth having for its own sake. Similarly, it seems pretty plausible to suggest that pain is worth *avoiding* for its own sake. So pain is intrinsically bad, and pleasure is intrinsically good.

I should mention, if only in passing, that nothing prevents one and the same thing from having both instrumental value (or disvalue) *and* intrinsic value (or disvalue). For example, when I work, I enjoy myself, and the fact that I am enjoying myself makes it easier for me to work harder. So the pleasure here is both intrinsically valuable and instrumentally valuable. Another, more interesting, example is this: when I burn myself on the stove, it hurts, and as a result I am careful not to burn myself even more. Here, then, the pain is *instrumentally* valuable (it prevents more pain down the road) even though it is *intrinsically* bad. Examples like this show that something can have both intrinsic value (or disvalue) and instrumental value (or disvalue); there is no need for us to claim it can have only the one, or the other, but not both.

Nonetheless, in trying to get clear about the nature of well-being, the crucial thing to do is to focus on intrinsic value (or disvalue). The things that are instrumentally helpful or harmful have the kind of instrumental value that they do precisely because of the intrinsic goods or bads that they help bring about. So from a philosophical point of view, the really interesting question is, what things are worth having (or avoiding) for their *own* sake?

I have, of course, already indicated two things that probably belong on any plausible list of intrinsic goods or bads. It seems plausible to think that pleasure is intrinsically good. It may not be the *only* thing that has intrinsic value—the only thing that makes a life intrinsically better—but it certainly seems to be one such thing. And one thing that seems intrinsically bad, one thing that seems to directly reduce the value of a life, is pain. Most of us agree, then, that pleasure is intrinsically good, and pain is intrinsically bad.

Suppose for a moment that we make a bold conjecture. Suppose that we claim that not only is pleasure *one* thing that belongs on our list of intrinsic goods and bads, and pain another thing that belongs on the list—suppose we claim that that's the entire list. Suppose we conjecture that the *only* thing intrinsically valuable is pleasure, and the *only* thing intrinsically bad is pain. That view is called *hedonism*.

Hedonism is a view that many people are attracted to. You may believe it too. It offers us a very simple theory of the nature of well-being. Being well off is a matter of experiencing pleasure and avoiding or minimizing the experience of pain. That's hedonism. A little later we'll turn to the question of what else might belong on the list, if hedonism is not the complete story. But for the time being, let's suppose that hedonism is true. Notice that if hedonism is true, then in principle at least, we should be able to make the kinds of evaluations that I was helping myself to previously when I said, for example, that death isn't bad for you if what life would offer you hereafter is bad overall.

What's going on when we make those judgments? The hedonist offers us a very simple, straightforward answer. In deciding whether what life holds for you is worth having, what you need to do, roughly speaking, is add up all the good times yet to come and subtract all the bad times and see whether the net balance is positive or negative. Add up all the pleasures, subtract all the pains. If the balance is positive, your future life is worth living. And the more positive the balance, the bigger the number, the more your life is worth living. If the balance is negative, though, your future holds more pain overall than pleasure. And in that case, sadly, you would be better off dead. After all, if you were dead, you would have neither pleasure nor pain. Mathematically speaking we should probably represent that with a zero: not a positive number (since there is no pleasure) and not a negative number (since there is no pain)—just a zero. Obviously enough, if the balance of pleasure over pain is positive, that's better than zero, and you are better off living. But if the balance is negative—if there is more pain than pleasure—then that's worse than zero. That's a life not worth having. That's what the hedonist says.

There are, of course, different ways of working out the details of the hedonist view. It's not, after all, as though all pleasures count equally or all pains count equally. The pain of stubbing your toe obviously doesn't count for nearly as much as the pain of a migraine, which in turn doesn't count nearly as much as the pain of being tortured. So we might need to work out a more complicated formula here, where we multiply the intensity of the pain times its duration, and thus arrive at a measure of the sheer *quantity* of pain. And similarly, of course, pleasures can be longer lasting, or more intense. You can imagine how some of those details might go, and I can assure you that some of the questions get rather tricky. But for our purposes, we don't really need to worry about the details. The basic thought should suffice. We need to weigh the pleasures and the pains in some appropriate way. We need to add up the pleasures, and add up the pains, and then see whether the grand total of pleasures is greater than the grand total of pain. The more positive the net balance, the better your life.

Armed with an approach like this, one thing we can do is to evaluate entire lives. There you are at the pearly gates and you look back on your entire life. In principle, at least, you could add up all the pleasures, add up all the pains, subtract the pains from the pleasures and ask yourself, "How good a life did I have? How well off was I, having lived that life?" And perhaps then you could imagine alternative lives. If only you had chosen to become a doctor, instead of having chosen to become a lawyer, how much better off or worse off would you have been? Or if you had decided to become an artist or a scholar or a beach bum or a farmer, how much better off or worse off would you have been? How much greater or smaller would the number be?

Despite my talking about numbers, of course, there's no particular reason to think that we can really give precise numbers to any of this. And we certainly don't think that in fact most of us are in the position to actually crank out any kind of accurate number. I certainly don't know enough to say with a high degree of accuracy how things would have gone had I decided to become a farmer instead of a philosopher. The hedonist isn't saying that we can make these calculations with a high degree of accuracy. But in principle, at least, this is what we're wondering about when we face choices. We can ask ourselves, "What would my life look like? Would it be better or worse?" And the yardstick that we're at least trying to apply is one that involves adding up the pleasure and subtracting the pain.

The hedonist will also hasten to point out that just because we can't do this perfectly or infallibly, that doesn't mean that we can't make educated guesses. Suppose you are trying to decide where to go to college. Should you go to Yale, or should you go to Ohio State, or Harvard, or wherever else you got into? You try to project your future and you ask, "Where do I think I'd be better off? Which of these possible futures is the one that holds out more pleasure and less pain?" That's how the hedonist says we should think about it.

And notice, by the by, that when we make choices about our future, from the hedonist point of view there's no particular need to dwell a whole lot on the past, because what's done is done. You're not going to alter how much pleasure you enjoyed previously, how much suffering you've already undergone. What's open is the future. We're able to evaluate not just lives as a whole, looking back at the pearly gates; we're also able to evaluate lives from here on out. We ask, which of the various alternatives that are open to me are likely to give me the better future, leave me better off in terms of pleasure and pain? And we give it our best shot, however good or bad that may be; we do our best to make such comparative evaluations.

And of course, we can do more than just evaluate the entire rest of my life. We can evaluate the next year or the next six months or, for that matter, just this evening. I can think about how my life might go tonight. Should I stay home tonight and work on my book? Or should I go to the party? Where will I be better off tonight? I might well decide that I will enjoy myself more at the party than I will working on my book. (And the book isn't due at the publisher for a while yet, so I won't feel too bad neglecting it for a bit.) So we make evaluations not just of entire lives but of chunks of lives.

That's what we can do, if we accept hedonism. But we haven't yet asked, *should* we accept hedonism? Now it would not come as news to me if I were to learn that you accept hedonism. It's a very popular view. Not only is it popular among philosophers (it's a view that has been around as long as there has been philosophy), it's popular among people "in the street," too. It's a very tempting view, to think that the only thing worth having for its own sake is pleasure and the only thing worth avoiding for its own sake is pain. But for all that, despite the popularity of that view, I'm inclined to think it must be wrong.

How can that be? It's certainly not as though I think that pleasure isn't good or pain isn't bad. Rather, where hedonism goes wrong is when it says that pleasure and pain are the *only* things that matter intrinsically. I'm inclined to think there's more to the *best* kind of life than just having pleasure and avoiding pain.

I may have already revealed that fact about myself, when I was talking about the rat-lever machine. I said that if you hook me up to the machine

I'll certainly enjoy myself, but for all that, I don't want that kind of life for myself. Why? Because there's *more* to life than just pleasure and the absence of pain. Or so it seems to me.

Of course, a hedonist can point out that rat-lever pleasures are not the only kind of pleasures there are. There is the pleasure of experiencing art or seeing a beautiful sunset, of reading a gripping novel or making an incredible discovery. I don't know about you, but at least when I imagine the rat-lever machine, it's a sort of simple, undifferentiated pleasure. So that really won't do the trick in giving us the *best* quality pleasures, the kinds of pleasures that humans most crave—the pleasures of friendship and discussion, sexual intimacy and love. These are pleasures that the rat-lever machine wasn't giving us.

So couldn't hedonism still be true? Couldn't it still be the case that as long as we take into account the importance of getting the right *kinds* of pleasures, then pleasure really is what it's all about—the *only* thing that it's all about? No, I think that's still not right. But to see this, we'll need to move to something fancier than the rat-lever machine. Here, the relevant thought experiment was suggested by Robert Nozick, a philosopher who died a few years ago, who taught for many years at Harvard.

Nozick invited us to imagine an experience machine.[1] Suppose that scientists have discovered a way not just to stimulate the particular little pleasure center of the brain, but instead a way to give you an utterly complete, totally realistic simulated experience. When you are hooked up to the machine, it seems to you *exactly* the same ("on the inside") as it would seem to you if you were really _____—and now you get to fill in the blank any way you want. You could, for example, have an experience exactly identical to the one you would have if you were climbing Mount Everest. You will, for instance, feel the bracing rush of the wind on your face. Of course, you won't *really* feel any wind. Strictly speaking, you can't feel the wind, because there is no wind to feel, because of course you are not really up on Mount Everest. What's really going on is you're floating in the psychologist's tank in their lab with the electrodes hooked up to your brain. But you don't *know* that you are floating in the tank. Hooked up to the machine, you *believe* you are climbing Mount Everest. You feel the thrill of having made it to the top, you are awed by the stunning vistas, you feel the sense of satisfaction and accomplishment, and you are shaky from the memories of having almost died when the rope broke earlier.

It's not like being at the IMAX (or, for that matter, an ordinary virtual reality machine). When you're at the IMAX, although it's very realistic, part of you is aware that you're just in the theater. But on the experience machine, you *don't* know you're just in the lab. When you're on the experience machine, your brain is being stimulated in such a way that you've got experiences (on the inside) *exactly* identical to the experiences you would be having if you really were *doing* these things.

So imagine a life on the experience machine. Imagine that we have downloaded the data file with all of the best possible experiences, whatever you think those are. Of course, people might disagree about that, but just throw in whatever it is you think the best experiences really would be. If what you want to do is, say, write the great American novel, then imagine that you've got the experience of staying up late at night not knowing how to make the plot work out, crumpling pieces of paper and throwing them away, or deleting rough drafts from your computer, whatever it is you do as you write the great American novel.

Or if you want to be finding the cure for cancer, then imagine that you've got exactly the experience you would have if you were working in your lab, suddenly having the brilliant breakthrough when you finally realize what the combination is that would make the right protein inhibitors, or whatever it is. Or if you want to be observing all the most beautiful sunsets and visiting the most exotic locales, you've got exactly the experiences you would have if you really were doing just that. Or perhaps you want to be doing everything I just said, while at the same time raising a loving family. Then while you are on the experience machine you will have exactly the same experiences as you would have if you really were writing the great American novel, traveling around the world, finding a cure for cancer, and raising a family.

That's life on the experience machine. You're not *doing* any of it. You're floating in the lab. But the experiences are identical. Now ask yourself, would you want to spend your life hooked up to the experience machine? Ask yourself, how would you feel if you discovered that you *have* been living your life hooked up to an experience machine?

I've got to add a footnote here. This perfectly glorious philosophical example has been ruined in recent years by the movie *The Matrix*. Whenever I tell this story now, people start saying, "Oh, well, the evil machines are busy using your body as a battery," or whatever it was that was going on in the movie. Or people worry, "What if aliens are surreptitiously feasting on my liver, while I am having these experiences?" and so forth. So I'm asking you, please don't imagine anything like that! There is no evil scientist deliberately deceiving you so as to conduct his nefarious experiments.

Nothing like that at all. And similarly, while we're at it, please don't worry about what's happening to world poverty or global justice while you are hooked up to the machine. Just imagine that *everyone* is hooked up to an experience machine, everybody is having the very best possible experiences.

Remember, what I am asking you is whether you would want to spend your *life* hooked up to the experience machine. I'm not talking about whether it might be interesting or fun to try it out for a week, or a month, or even a year. Indeed, strictly speaking, the question isn't even whether life on the experience machine might be better for you than life is for you right now. Although it would make me very, very sad to discover this, I suppose it's possible that you have such a bad life that moving on to the experience machine would be a step up. That's not the question.

The question is, does life on the experience machine give you *everything* worth having in life? *Everything*. Is it the *best* possible form of human existence? According to the hedonist, the answer's got to be yes. Life on the experience machine is *perfect*, as long as you've got the right experience file downloaded. By hypothesis, you've got the best possible balance of wonderful pleasures and incredible, fantastic experiences. By hypothesis, the machine is giving us that. And since, according to the hedonist, that's all there is to human well-being, it follows that there couldn't possibly be anything more. There couldn't possibly be anything missing.

But when I think about whether I would want to spend my life hooked up to an experience machine the answer is no. And I find that for most people that I discuss this example with, when I ask them whether they would want to have their entire life spent hooked up to the experience machine, they answer no as well. But if the answer is no, then that means hedonism has to be wrong. If life on the experience machine doesn't give us everything worth having in life, then there is more to the best possible life than getting the insides right. The experience machine gets the pleasures right—it gets the experiences right, it gets the mental states right, it gets the *insides* right—but if life on the experience machine isn't all that's worth wanting out of life, then there's more to the best possible life than getting the insides right. Hedonism is wrong.

Of course, I have been discussing this sort of example for many, many years. So I know that there are always some people who think, yes, life on the experience machine is *perfect*, as long as you've got the right data file playing. But the vast majority of people say no, there's something missing from that life. It's not the ideal of human existence; it's not the best possible life we can imagine ourselves having.

But if you are with me in thinking that something is missing, you have to ask yourself, *what* is missing? What's *wrong* with the experience machine? I think different people will answer that in different ways. If we had the space, I could spell out rival theories of well-being, which differ in interesting ways from one another in terms of how they answer the questions "What's missing from the experience machine?" and "Why are the things that are missing from the experience machine worth having?" Different theories of well-being answer those questions in different ways. But instead of trying to pursue those alternative theories in a systematic fashion, let me just gesture toward some of the things that seem to be missing from that kind of life.

First of all, and perhaps most obviously, if you're just spending your life floating in the scientist's lab, you're not actually accomplishing anything. You're not actually getting the things out of life that you thought you were getting. You wanted to be climbing the mountain, but you're not actually climbing a mountain. You're just floating there. You wanted to be writing the great American novel, but you're not writing the great American novel. You're just floating there. You wanted to be finding the cure for cancer, but you're not actually finding the cure for cancer. You are just floating there. You wanted to be loved, but you're not actually loved. You're just floating there. (Nobody other than the scientist even knows that you exist!) You wanted to know your place in the universe, but you don't even have that kind of knowledge either, because you *think* you are writing novels, finding the cure for cancer, or climbing Mount Everest, and you are completely deceived about all those things. So you don't have that kind of self-knowledge either.

So among the things that seem to be missing from a life on the experience machine are the following: we don't have any accomplishments, we don't have self-knowledge, and we don't stand in loving relationships. It seems plausible to think that an adequate account of well-being will include these things as valuable too—above and beyond the experiences that normally accompany them.

Of course, different theories of well-being will offer different explanations as to why these things are valuable. (For example, are these things valuable because we *want* them? Or do we want them because we recognize that they're independently valuable?) And there will be any number of further details to work out.

Take, for example, accomplishment. Most of us think that accomplishment is important, but it's not as though *any* old accomplishment is important. If somebody sets himself the goal of making the biggest rubber-band ball in the eastern United States, I suppose that in one sense of the word it's an accomplishment if they do it, but it doesn't strike me as the kind of accomplishment that makes for a particularly valuable life. So we'll need a way to distinguish between any old accomplishment and genuinely valuable accomplishments.

Similarly, not every bit of knowledge is equally valuable. It's one thing to know your place in the universe or to know the fundamental laws of physics. It's another thing to know the average rainfall in Bangkok in 1984. I'm not sure that that kind of knowledge gives a whole lot of value to your life. So we need a way to tell the significant, truly valuable sort of knowledge from the mere trivia. And in the same way, we need a way to tell the valuable sorts of relationships—like friendship and love—from the trivial unimportant ones.

All of this would be rather complicated to work out. But let's just suppose that we have done it. The crucial point is that it takes more to have the best kind of life than just getting the insides right. It also requires the right kind of accomplishments and knowledge and relationships. It requires getting the *outsides* right as well. The best life requires not just experience—"internal" goods—but "external" goods as well.

I am not going to try to develop an adequate theory of well-being here. But notice that if we did have such a theory, then in principle at least—whatever the practical difficulties might be—we could still evaluate rival lives. We could still talk about adding up all the goods and all the bads, and looking to see where the balance lies. It's just that now we would have a somewhat broader, more encompassing or inclusive list of goods, as well as a broader and more encompassing list of bads. We would count not just the internal goods and bads of experience, but the various external goods and bads as well, whatever exactly the list comes to.

So we could still evaluate alternative lives, or parts of lives. My life would have gone better had I chosen to become a farmer instead of choosing to become a doctor. Or my life would have gone better for this period of ten years, but then it would have become worse. Similarly, I can ask myself how things will go for me over the next couple of weeks if I go on vacation instead of staying home. To answer questions like these, we add up the goods, as best we can, subtract the bads—whatever our favorite list of the goods and bads might be—and we come to our best educated guesses about the comparative evaluations of not just lives as a whole, but chunks of lives as well.

What do those totals come to? You might well think that this is an empirical question, where the precise answer varies from person to person. But it is worth noting that there are people who think we can generalize across all humans. *Optimists* are people who think that for everybody, in every circumstance, the total is always positive. "Life is always worth living; it's always better than nonexistence." That's what optimists think—not just for themselves individually, but for everybody. The total is always positive.

Against that, you've got *pessimists*, people who think that the overall balance is always negative—for everybody, in every circumstance. Pessimists can admit that life has some good in it (just as optimists can admit that life has some bad); they simply believe that the good is always outweighed. "We would all be better off dead; indeed, it would have been better, for each of us, never to have been born in the first place." That's what the pessimists say.

In between the optimists, on the one hand, and the pessimists, on the other, you've got the *moderates*. These are people who say, "It depends. For some people the balance is positive, for others the balance may be negative. And that can be true for life as a whole, as well as for more particular stretches of their lives." According to the moderate, then, we have to get down to facts about particular cases. Most of us, perhaps, have lives worth living; but some, perhaps, do not. Imagine, for example, someone in the terminal stage of an illness, with a great deal of pain. Perhaps they are bedridden, unable to accomplish anything, and their family has largely abandoned them. Even if this person's life as a whole has been a good one, it might still be the case that the future before them is not. That's what the moderate would say. It varies from case to case.

However we settled this dispute, notice that there is still one further assumption that all of these positions have in common. How good it is to be alive is a matter of adding up all of what we can call the *contents* of life. We add up your pleasures and pains, accomplishments and failures (and so forth and so on), and we look for the total. That's what's relevant in determining the value of your life: what's happening *within* your life. Being alive per se has no value. Rather, life itself is only a container which we fill with various goods or bads. And deciding how valuable it is, how good it is for me to be alive, is a matter of adding up the value of the contents. The container itself is indeed a mere container; it has no value in and of itself.

We could say that what I've been presupposing up to this point is the *neutral container* theory of the value of life. Hedonism is a version of the neutral container theory. How well off you are, how valuable your life is, is a function of the contents—the pleasure and the pain. We've now expanded the list of goods and bads that can occur *within* your life, but for all that, we've still been assuming that the neutral container theory is the right approach.

But there are those who think that in addition to thinking about the value of the contents of life, we also have to remember that life *itself* is worth having. There's a benefit in being alive above and beyond the question of what's going on *within* my life. These people claim that the mere fact that I am indeed *alive* gives my life some additional value. These are *valuable container* theories.

Strictly speaking, of course, it probably isn't accurate to say that on this sort of view what's valuable is being alive *per se*. A blade of grass is alive, after all, and I presume that even fans of valuable container theories don't think there is any value to me in having *that* kind of life. "Life" may have value in and of itself, but it's not *mere* life. What we want, rather, is something like *human* life, life as a *person*. So even though there are people who sometimes say that being alive per se is valuable, presumably what they really mean is being alive as a person. Nonetheless, for simplicity, in discussing these views I too will talk as though the suggestion being made is that life per se is valuable.

Actually, I suppose, there could be a more extreme view still. It seems implausible to me, but I suppose it's worth noticing that there *are* people who think that being alive *per se* is valuable. "Yes, even if my brain has been so thoroughly and irreparably damaged that I am no longer able to know anything, no longer able to experience anything, no longer able to relate to anyone, no longer able to accomplish anything at all—even if I am in this sort of irreparable vegetative state, at least I am *alive*." You can imagine somebody who has that view. I've got to say, though, I find that a pretty implausible view. So I'm going to restrict myself to versions of the valuable container theory that think that it's really the life of a *person* that's valuable per se. But as I just noted, for simplicity I will continue to describe this view as though it holds that what's valuable in and of itself is the very fact that you are *alive*.

Think, then, about what it would mean to accept a valuable container theory. If life per se has some positive value, then to decide how well off someone is you can't just add up the *contents* of their life. It won't suffice to add up all the pleasures and subtract the pains, or add up as well all the accomplishments and knowledge and meaningful relationships, and subtract the failures and ignorance and deception, and so forth. To be sure, doing this—getting the balance of the contents in this way—still gives you a relevant *subtotal*, but that subtotal is no longer the entire story. Rather, if we accept a valuable container theory, we also have to add in something *extra*, to take account of the value in and of itself of being alive. So first we get the content subtotal, and then we add some extra positive points for the very fact that you are alive at all.

Notice that since we are adding extra positive points for the fact that you're alive, then even if the *contents* subtotal is negative, the *grand* total could still be positive. Suppose, for example, that being alive per se is worth +100 (just to make up some number). Then even if your content subtotal was −10, that doesn't mean you're not better off alive, because −10 plus the extra +100 points for the mere fact that you're alive is still going to give you a positive total: +90. Indeed, the main reason for thinking about the possibility of accepting a valuable container theory is precisely to remind us that in deciding whether you are better off dead—whether death would be depriving you of something good, on balance, or not—it may not be sufficient to focus on the *contents* of the life; it may be important to add some positive points above and beyond the content subtotal so as to take into account the value of the sheer fact that you're alive.

Of course, if you are a fan of the *neutral* container theory, you won't have to add anything extra, because life per se is just a zero. The value of a life is strictly a matter of its contents. But if you accept a *valuable* container theory, you have to add something more. So even if my life is going badly overall in terms of its *contents*, it might still be that, on balance, it remains good to be alive. We have to remember to add some extra points.

How *much* extra do we have to add? Here we're going to have to distinguish between different versions of the valuable container theory. Let me just note two broad types. Modest versions of the valuable container theory say that although being alive per se is good, if the contents of your life get bad enough, that can outweigh the value of being alive, so that the grand total is negative. That is to say, *modest* container theories claim that there is *a* value to being alive, but it can in principle be outweighed. Whether it gets outweighed easily, or whether it's very, very difficult and the contents have to be horrible to outweigh it, depends on how much value you think being alive per se has. Still, what modest theories have in common is the thought that although there is positive value in being alive, it can be outweighed.

Against that, you can imagine someone who thinks that being alive per se is so incredibly valuable that no matter *how* horrible the contents are, the grand total will always be positive. It's as though being alive is infinitely valuable in comparison to questions about the contents. We could call this the *fantastic* container theory as opposed to the more modest versions. I suppose that label gives away where I want to come down on this. I find the fantastic container theory fantastic in the sense of being incredible, unbelievable. I simply can't bring myself to believe it.

It's not that I lack sympathy for valuable container theories altogether. Admittedly, I am often drawn to the neutral view; I find myself thinking that life per se has no value at all. But at other times I am indeed drawn to the thought that being alive per se is good for you. Nonetheless, even in those moments when I am drawn to valuable container theories, it is always the modest version I find attractive. I never find myself drawn to the fantastic version at all.

Armed with these distinctions, let's return to the main question we have been asking ourselves: why is death bad? The deprivation account says that death is bad for you when it is true that, by virtue of dying now, what you've been deprived of is another chunk of life that would have been good for you to have. But if, on the other hand, what death deprives you of is a future that would have been bad for you, then death isn't bad for you after all, but good. And what we can now see is that if we are to tell which of these cases we face—or whether, for that matter, both are possible—we need to decide whether we accept the neutral container theory, the modest container theory, or the fantastic container theory.

If we are *neutral* container theorists, we're going to say that the crucial question is, what would the contents of my life have been like for the next week, or year, or ten years? If that would have been worth having—if the next chunk of my life would have been worth having—then it's bad for me that I die *now* instead of living for the next week, or year, or ten years. On the other hand, if the balance from here on out would have been negative, then it's good for me that I die now instead of being kept alive with a life not worth living. That's how neutral theorists think of it.

If we are *modest* container theorists, we agree that we have to look at the contents of the next chunk of life, but we insist, at the same time, that we mustn't forget to add some extra points to the total. Even if, for example, the next five years would have been slightly bad for you in terms of the contents of your life, it might still be the case that the value of being alive per se outweighs that negative subtotal, so that it would still be *better* for you to remain alive. In that case, of course, if death comes now, it is indeed bad for you. On the other hand, if the contents from here on out are bad enough, so that the grand total remains negative even when we add some extra points for being alive, then it is better for you to die now.

Notice, incidentally, that if we accept the modest view, we also need to revisit the question of the value of immortality. For even if you were inclined to agree with Bernard Williams's claim that immortality would be bad for you, we now are in a position to realize that what Williams was talking about only concerned the *contents* of an immortal life. But if we accept the modest container theory, then that no longer settles the issue. Conceivably, we could agree with Williams that inevitably the contents would become negative overall, and yet still insist, for all that, that this is outweighed by the sheer fact that you are alive. Perhaps, then, being immortal would be a good thing, on balance, after all. Of course, whether that's right or not depends on just how bad it would be—in terms of the contents—to be immortal. Because if you accept the modest version of the valuable container theory, then if the contents get bad *enough*, that can still outweigh the positive value of life.

In contrast, fans of the *fantastic* container theory will say that it doesn't really matter if Williams is right about immortality becoming a nightmare. Even if being immortal would become horrendously boring and tedious or worse, it doesn't matter. The value of being alive per se outweighs that, so you are *always* better off being alive. No matter how horrible the contents might be, more life would always be *better*. On a view like this, obviously enough, being immortal really *would* be a good thing for you. Death is *always* a bad thing.

Of course, I have already remarked that I find fantastic container theories implausible. So I don't think we can simply disregard the question of how bad the contents of an immortal life would eventually become. But beyond that, even in those moods where I accept a modest container theory, I still find myself inclined to think that whatever positive value being alive per se may have for us, it would eventually be *outweighed* by the negative contents of an immortal life. That is to say, I am still inclined to think that eventually immortality would become bad, overall, for all of us.

That being the case, I still want to say that it is a good thing that we die—because eventually immortality would be horrible. But let me remind you, this position is still compatible with believing that death comes *too soon*. It could still be the case that we all die before life has *turned* bad. Perhaps we die while it is still the case that living another ten years or twenty years—or for that matter five hundred years—would still have been good for us. It's compatible with thinking that immortality would be bad to think that in fact death always comes too soon.

But of course, at this point, we now need to recall the distinction between optimists, pessimists, and moderates. To be sure, if an immortal life would eventually be a bad one, then the position of an extreme optimist—someone who thinks that every future must be a good one—will have to be rejected. But we can still imagine a *qualified* optimist, someone who thinks that in fact, given the kinds of lives we actually live, a few more years would always be a good thing, on balance. If so, then in life as we actually live it, death always comes too soon. (Admittedly, the label "optimist" may not be an ideal one, given that they think that death always comes too soon; but they are optimists in that they think that the next chunk of life would always be a good one.) In contrast, the pessimist will say that death never comes a moment too soon for any of us. The next chunk of life is always not worth having, always worse than nothing.

For whatever it is worth, though, my sympathies lie with the moderate. I think it clear that death does come too soon for many of us, perhaps even for most of us. But not, I think, for all of us. Some of us, tragically, reach a point in our lives where we are so crippled, so incapacitated, so wracked by pain (with no serious prospect of recovery), that continuing to live is not a benefit at all. In cases like this—however common or rare they may be—death does not, in fact, come too soon. Sometimes, indeed, it is horribly delayed.

CHAPTER 13

Other Aspects of Death

According to the deprivation account, the central way in which death is bad for us—when it is bad for us—is that it deprives us of something good. Initially, of course, I presented this idea by saying that death deprives us of the good things *in* life, but now we have seen that some may want to modify this slightly, so as to take note of the possibility that life itself may be good as well. But regardless of the details, we can capture the basic idea by saying that the central badness of death lies in the fact (when it is a fact) that it deprives me of life worth having.

But although I've been at pains to say this is the central or *fundamental* bad thing about death, I think that one could make the case that this isn't the *only* bad thing about death—not even if we continue to focus on the way in which death is bad for the person who *dies*. There are *other* features of death, as we experience it, that are separable from the deprivation that death involves, so we then have to ask the question, do these further features *add* to the badness of death? Alternatively, conceivably, some of these further features might mitigate it, reduce its badness in one way or another.

Here's an example. It is, of course, true of you that you are going to die. But more than that: it is *inevitable* that you are going to die. There's no avoiding it. Contrast the inevitability of death with the fact, say, that you are reading this book. You are, of course, reading this book, but it wasn't inevitable that you would read it. You had a choice. But death is different. It doesn't matter what you choose, you can't avoid dying. So it's not just merely the case that in fact we are all going to die; it's a *necessary* truth that we're all going to die. Accordingly, we might ask, what about this inevitability of death? Does that make things worse? And here I want to distinguish between two issues: there's the individual issue (it's inevitable that *you* are going to die) and there's the universal issue (it's inevitable that we are *all* going to die).

Let's start by thinking about the fact that it's unavoidable that *you* are going to die. Does the unavoidability of death make it better or worse? The interesting thing is, I think it is easy to feel the pull of *both* possible answers here. On the one hand, you can imagine somebody who says, "Look, it's bad enough that I'm going to die, but the fact that there's nothing I can do about it just makes it worse. It's like adding insult to injury that I'm powerless in the face of death. I cannot escape the Grim Reaper. This sheer impotence with regard to a central fact about my existence makes things even worse."

Against that, however, there are those people who want to say that the inevitability of my death actually *reduces* the badness. To get a feel for this position, just think about the idea behind the expression "Don't cry over spilt milk." What's done is done; you can't change it. The idea, of course, is that when you focus on the fact that you can't change something, that thing loses some of its power to upset you. But if that's right, and if we then realize that there is nothing at all I can do about the fact that I am going to die, then perhaps some of the sting of that realization is eliminated as well.

Here's an especially clear example of this: try getting upset about the fact that two plus two equals four. Try feeling upset at your powerlessness to change that fact. Suppose you wanted two plus two to equal five. Can you work up anger and regret and dismay over that? I assume that you can't. You can't get worked up over something so clearly unalterable.

The philosopher Spinoza thought that if we could only recognize the fact—or, at least, what he took to be a fact—that *everything* that happens in life is necessary, then we would get a kind of emotional distance from it; it would no longer upset us. We would no longer be disappointed by things, because to be disappointed in something presupposes that it could have been some other way. And Spinoza thought that once you see that it *couldn't* go any other way, then you can't be sad about it. Well, then, if we see that our death is *inevitable* and we really internalize that fact, perhaps that would reduce the badness of it.

Maybe that's right. But I am not sure. Perhaps you have read Dostoyevsky's short novel *Notes from Underground*. The Underground Man is upset about the fact that two times two equals four. Or rather, he is upset about the fact that there is nothing at all that he can do about the fact that two times two equals four. He *resents* being so impotent that he can't change the fact that two times two equals four. Similarly, when Descartes thought about God's omnipotence, he suggested that it wouldn't be good enough if God was unable to change the facts of mathematics. Descartes thinks it would be a sign of weakness for God to be stuck with necessities that he couldn't alter. So Descartes claims that God *could* have made it be true that two plus two equals five, but chose not to. In effect, then, Dostoyevsky takes that thought and runs with it. His Underground Man says that it doesn't actually help that something is inevitable. It makes it worse. As I say, I can feel the pull of both sides of this dispute. In different moods, I lean in different directions.

What about the fact that not only is it inevitable that I'm going to die, it's inevitable that we're *all* going to die. Does the *universality* of death make things better or worse? Here too, I find myself pulled both ways. On the one hand, I find myself wanting to say, it's bad that I'm going to die, but I'm not a *monster*. It makes me feel even *worse* that everybody else must die as well. Or perhaps, in light of our discussion of immortality, I should say that what is sad is the fact that we all (or, at least, most of us) die too soon. That makes it even worse.

On the other hand, let's be honest here, we also know the expression "Misery loves company." There's at least some comfort to be had—isn't there?—in the realization that this undesirable thing isn't just true for me. It's not like the universe has singled me out for the injury of dying too soon. That's something that it does to almost everybody. Perhaps there's some comfort in that fact.

Here's a different aspect of death worth thinking about: what about the *variability* of death? After all, it's not just the case that we all die. There's a great deal of *variation* in how much life we get. Some of us make it to the ripe old age of 80, 90, 100, or more. Others of us die at 20, or 15, or 10, or even younger.

Even if death were inevitable, life didn't have to come in different-sized packages. After all, it isn't as though death *has* to involve variability. We could imagine a world in which everybody dies at the same age, perhaps at a hundred. Does it make things worse or better that there's this kind of variability?

From the moral point of view, I suppose, it's fairly straightforward to suggest that it makes things worse. After all, most of us are inclined to think that inequality is morally objectionable. It's bad that, through no fault of their own, some people are poor while other people are rich. But if inequality is morally objectionable, then it's very likely that we're going to think that it is morally horrendous that there is this crucial inequality: some of us die at the age of five while others get to live to ninety. However, in keeping with the general focus of our discussion about the badness of death, I want to put aside the moral question and think about how good or bad it is for *me* that there's variability in death.

We can look at the situation from two basic perspectives: those who get less than the average lifespan, and those who get more than the average lifespan. From the point of view of somebody who gets *less*, this is obviously a bad thing. It's bad enough that I'm going to die too soon. But what's even worse is that I'm going to get even less than the average amount of life. That's clearly an extra bad. But we might then wonder, what about the people who are getting *more* than the average? Suppose we find the median lifespan, the exact length of life such that 50 percent of the people get less than this, and 50 percent get more. Then for every person who gets less than the median amount of life, there's another person who has *more* than the median amount of life. That person gets to say that although it is a pity that he is going to die too soon, at least he is getting more than the average. That seems to count as a plus.

Perhaps these two sides of the equation balance themselves out. There are people who are basically screwed by the fact that they get less than the average amount and there are people who are benefited by getting more than the average amount. Perhaps in terms of the individual badness of death that's a *wash*. Maybe. Except it seems to me there's a further relevant fact about human psychology: we care more about being shortchanged, as we might put it, than we do about being overcompensated. I rather suspect that when people have *less* than the average of something, the amount that this hurts them is *greater* than the amount of benefit that comes to people who have *more* than the average of something. And if that's right—and that seems likely to be the case, especially for something like death—the extra bad arising from the fact that there's variability, and so some people get less than average, outweighs the extra benefit of some people having more than average.

Here's another important feature of death. We considered inevitability; we looked at variability. What about *unpredictability*? Not only is it inevitable that you're going to die, and not only do some people live longer than others—it is also true that you don't know how much more time you've got.

You would be forgiven for thinking that we have already brought in unpredictability, once we start thinking about variability. But in fact, that's not the case. Logically speaking, although variability is a requirement for unpredictability, it doesn't suffice to guarantee unpredictability. You could, in fact, have variability with complete predictability. Imagine, for example, that whenever a baby is born there is a natural birthmark on their wrist that infallibly indicates the precise year, day, and time in which they are going to die. We can certainly imagine a world like this. Death remains inevitable; everybody's got some date marked on their wrist. And more to the point, there could still be variability. Some people live eighty years, some people live fifty-seven years, others only twenty. But there is no unpredictability. Because of the birthmark, everybody knows exactly how much longer they've got.

In our world, of course, we don't have that. In our world, not only do we have variability, we've got unpredictability. Does that make things better? Or does that make things worse? Would it be better to know *when* you were going to die?

One way in which unpredictability has at least the potential of making things worse is this: you don't know how much *more* time you have. So it is hard to make plans. Of course, you can make a guess based on statistics. You can calculate the average lifespan. Suppose that right now, in the United States, it's seventy-nine years. That means that if you are, say, in your late twenties, you have on average another fifty years. But as we have already pointed out, that average covers up a lot of underlying variability. So there you are, you're busy calculating all of this, you're walking across the street, and you get hit by a truck and you die. It could happen, right? Because of unpredictability, you can't really know. And because you can't really know, it's difficult to make the right kinds of plans.

In particular, it's hard to know how to pace yourself. You decide to go off to medical school, to become a doctor. And so not only do you put the time into college, you put the time into medical school, you put the time into your residency, and you put the time into your internship. And that's a very long commitment. It's a long-term plan, which can go wrong if you get sick and die in your early twenties. That's a rather dramatic example, of course, but the same sort of thing can happen in principle to all of us. You make a life plan, figure out what you want to accomplish in your life, and then—boom!—death comes, unexpectedly, screwing up your plans. If only you had known that you were only going to have twenty more years instead of fifty more years, you would have picked a different kind of life for yourself. The unpredictability makes it worse.

Less obviously, it can work the other way as well. You make a life plan, you carry it out, and then, expectedly, you don't die any time close to the time you guessed you would. You continue to stick around, and then your life has this feeling of being anticlimactic. You peaked too soon. You thought you were going to be like the actor James Dean, burn out fast and die young. But you were wrong. If only you had known that you had another seventy years, that you weren't going to die young—if only you had realized that you were going to live to the ripe old age of ninety-four, you would have picked a different life for yourself.

In thinking about these points, I am suggesting, in effect, that the overall value of your life can be affected by some features that we haven't yet talked about. We might put the idea this way: the overall shape of your life matters. Putting the same idea in slightly different language, we could say that "the narrative arc" of your life makes a difference to its overall value.

Let me illustrate the point with some very, very simple graphs. These are not meant to be realistic, but they'll give you the basic idea. The nineteenth-century American author Horatio Alger used to write stories about people who start out poor but who make their way (through hard work, dedication, and effort) to riches and success. Rags to riches—that's a wonderful, inspiring life.

Let's draw a graph of that life. (See Figure 13.1.) Let the Y axis represent well-being, how well off you are at a given moment, and let the X axis represent time. In the first graph in Figure 13.1, you start off with nothing and you end up incredibly well off. That's a great life. That's the Horatio Alger life.

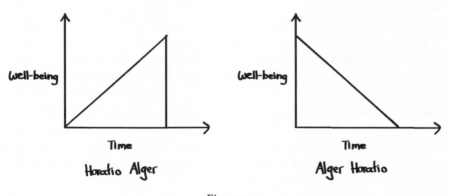

Fig. 13.1

Now consider a different story. This time, instead of going from rags to riches, the person goes from riches to rags. He starts off with everything but ends up with nothing. That's the Alger Horatio life. It is, of course, the reverse of the first story. In Figure 13.1, it's the graph on the right.

Now I doubt if there is anyone who is genuinely indifferent between these alternatives, indifferent with regard to the choice between these two lives. I imagine that pretty much everyone prefers the first life.[1] But notice that in terms of the contents of the life, or at least the *local* contents, it is hard to see why we should care which life we get. Both lives have the same amount of suffering; both lives have the same amount of success. The two graphs are, of course, mirror images of each other, and that means that for every good period in the one, there is an exactly similar good period in the other; for every bad period, there is a corresponding bad period. Roughly but intuitively speaking, the contents of the two lives are the same. (In mathematical terms, the areas under the two lines are the same.) And even if we accept the valuable container theory, and so say that being alive per se is worth something as well, that still doesn't give us reason to prefer one life over the other. Since the two lives last the same number of years, the same number of extra points gets added either way.

If we're not indifferent between these two lives, that seems to show that we think that not only do the various "local" goods make a difference to the value of a life—how happy or unhappy you are at various times—the overall *shape* of the life matters as well. The narrative arc matters. The story "bad to good" is the kind of story we want for ourselves, while the story "good to bad" is the kind of story we don't want for ourselves.

That raises an interesting question: why do we care? And this, of course, should remind us of the puzzle from Lucretius: why do we care more about future nonexistence than past nonexistence? The reason isn't obvious, but the fact remains that when the bad is behind us, that seems less bothersome than when the bad is in front of us. Similarly, it seems, we want the bad to come sooner rather than later. (Recall, as well, the story from Derek Parfit about the painful operation. We're not indifferent between having the bad in the future or in the past.) Whatever the exact explanation may be, the simple fact seems to be that we care about the overall shape and trajectory of our life.

Given that this is the case, however, we have to worry about the possibility that, thanks to the unpredictability of death, our lives may end up lacking the ideal shape. Consider the life shown in Figure 13.2. Here, the problem is that the person peaks too soon. We peak, but then we stick around too long after the climax. A lot of us, I imagine, might be unhappy with a life like that. Think about your life as though it were a novel, where the graph of your life is like the plot of a great story. It isn't as though we think the denouement must occur on the very last page. It's okay to stick around for a while after. But if the high point of the story occurs in chapter 2, and then there are another sixty-seven chapters after that, you're likely to find yourself thinking that this is not a well-constructed novel.

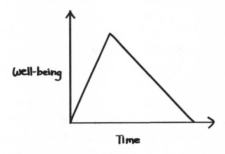

Fig. 13.2

Insofar as we care about the overall shape of our lives, we might worry about life having the *right* shape overall. Where and when do you want your life to peak in terms of your accomplishments? That clearly matters to us, but the trouble is, without predictability you don't know where to put the peak. If you aim for peaking later, you might not make it that long. If you put the peak too soon, you might be around for too long afterwards. All of this suggests, then, that the unpredictability of death adds an extra negative element. It makes it harder to plan what the best way to live my life would be. And from that perspective, it looks as though it would be better to know how much time you've got left.

But then we have to ask, would it really be better to know? Would you really want to know exactly how much time you still have? Suppose we were born with the kinds of birthmarks I was describing earlier, so that you always knew exactly how much longer you had before you were going to die. If you had that kind of birthmark, you would face your entire life with the burden of knowing: I've got 50 years left, I've got 49 years left, 48 years left, 47 . . . Many of us, I think, would indeed find that a burden—something hanging constantly over us, interfering with our ability to enjoy life.

Let's alter the story. Instead of imagining a birthmark, readily visible and interpreted, suppose that there were some sort of genetic marker that could be examined with the right kind of testing. If you wanted to, you could have your DNA examined, and then you would know exactly how much time you had left. Would you want to get that testing done? Of course, that's science fiction, and I presume it is going to stay science fiction. But the fact of the matter is, as we learn more and more about the various genes that carry different diseases, more and more of us face the question of whether we want to get tested for those diseases.

Imagine that there is a horrible genetic disorder that kills its victims at age forty. You are twenty years old, and you already know that you have a 50 percent chance of having the gene (one of your parents had the gene and died young), but you don't yet know whether you yourself have it. If you do, you are going to die in another twenty years. Would you want to be tested? Would you want to know?

Here's a closely related question: if you did know how much time you had left, would you act differently from what you are doing now? Would that knowledge lead you to refocus your attention on doing the things that are most important to you? Thinking about this question can provide a useful way of recognizing what it is in life that you most value. Ask yourself, what would you choose to do if you knew you only had another year, another five years, another ten years?

There's an old *Saturday Night Live* routine where one of the actors is in the doctor's office, and the doctor gives him the very sad news that he's got two minutes left to live. And he says, "I'm going to pack a lifetime of enjoyment into those two minutes." And then, of course, the point of the skit is that he presses the down button on the elevator and a minute and a half goes by while he's waiting for the elevator to come.

If you knew you had a year left or two years left, what would you do with that time? Would you be in school? Would you travel? Would you spend more time hanging out with your friends? An extremely moving instance of someone having to face this question occurred in the class on death that I teach at Yale. There was a student in that class some years ago who was dying. And he knew that he was dying. He'd been diagnosed with cancer as a freshman. His doctor had told him that he pretty much had no chance of recovery, and indeed he had only a couple more years to live. Faced with that knowledge, he had to ask himself, "Well, what should I do with my remaining years?"

He decided that what he wanted to do was finish his Yale degree. He set himself the goal of graduating college before he died. And there he was, second semester of his senior year, taking my class on death. (It was humbling for me to learn that someone in his situation had decided to take a class on death, and then have me get up, week after week, and talk about how there is no soul, there is no afterlife, it's a good thing that we are all going to die . . .) So there he was, in my class—until spring break. By spring vacation he had gotten sufficiently sick that his doctor had told him that he could not continue in school anymore. He had to go home. In effect, his doctor had told him that it was time to go home to die. He went home, and his condition rapidly deteriorated after that.

The faculty members who were teaching his various courses that semester then all faced a question posed to them by the administration. Based on the work that he had done so far that semester, what kind of grades were we prepared to assign for the semester as a whole? Because, of course, depending on which of his classes he passed, and which he failed, he either was, or was not, going to be able to graduate. As it turned out, he had done well enough. And Yale, to its very real credit, sent a member of the administration down to his deathbed to award him his degree before he passed away.

It is a very moving and striking story. I'm not sure how many of us would decide that the thing we most want to do with our few remaining years is to spend them in college. But then, what is it that you *would* want to do? What would you choose? And returning to our original question, would knowing how much time you have left be something that would allow you to embrace those choices, so that you could finish your life in the most meaningful way? Or would it be a burden? That's the kind of question we have to face when we think about the fact that typically we don't *know* how much time we've got left. Is that something that increases the badness of death, or does it reduce it somewhat?

Here's yet another feature of death. In addition to the inevitability, in addition to the variability, in addition to the unpredictability, there's the fact that death is, as I like to think of it, *ubiquitous*. I don't just mean the fact that people are dying all around us. I mean, rather, that you yourself could die at any time. There's never any getting away from the possibility that you'll die *now*. Even if we had unpredictability, it wouldn't necessarily follow that death was pervasive in this way. The point I've got in mind here is this: even when you think you're perfectly safe, you could of course die of a stroke. You could die of a heart attack. Even somebody who's young and strong could die from an aneurysm.

Or—one of my favorite examples—you could be sitting in your living room, when suddenly an airplane crashes into your house, killing you. One reads about this sort of thing in the newspaper occasionally. You thought

you were safe. You were watching reruns on television—and the next minute, you're dead. This takes us beyond unpredictability. The fact that you
don't know when you're going to die doesn't yet entail that you could die at
any moment. But in fact, that's true of all of us as well.

Here is another example, also close to my heart. Once I was driving
down the expressway and a car pulled into my lane without looking, clip-
ping my car and causing it to go spinning out of control, careening across
three lanes of traffic. The whole thing lasted only a few moments, but I remember thinking quite clearly, "I'm going to die." Now as it happens, I didn't
die. I walked away from the accident, and the damage to my car was surprisingly minimal. But it could have happened like *that*.

Death—the possibility of death—is ubiquitous. It's pervasive. So we
have to ask ourselves, does this make things worse? It certainly feels, to my
mind, as though this is an additional bad aspect of death. It would be nice
to get a breather. Imagine, if you will, that there were certain locations, certain vacation spots, where as long as you were there you couldn't die.
Wouldn't it be nice to be able to go someplace and just for a period think to
yourself, "Well, you know, right now I don't have to worry about that. It
doesn't even have to cross my mind."

Of course, if there were death-free zones like this, they'd probably get
rather crowded. So perhaps we should change the example. Instead of having death-free zones, imagine that there were death-free *times*. Just suppose
that, for whatever reason, nobody could die between noon and one. You
could just put it out of your mind. Wouldn't that be nice? To be sure, at one
o'clock you would have to take the burden back on. But wouldn't it be nice
to have a certain period of time every day when death wasn't so much as a
remote possibility? Or suppose there were certain death-free *activities*. Maybe
reading philosophy would be something that as long as you were doing it
you couldn't die; or perhaps, as long as you were engaged in prayer you
couldn't die. Wouldn't that be nice?

Or turn the entire thing the other way around. Suppose that most times
and *most* activities were death free, but certain activities introduced the
possibility of dying. So you couldn't die unless you were engaged in certain
activities. You would be *potentially* immortal, in the sense that you *could* live
forever, but you wouldn't be *forced* to live forever. Some activities—perhaps
putting a gun to your head, for example—would put an end to your life. So
even if immortality would be bad, there would be certain things that you
could do that would end it. But beyond these special death-*ensuring* activities, imagine that there were various other activities that merely carried the

risk of dying (that is, they carried the level of risk that they actually carry in the real world): while doing these things, you would lose the guarantee that you would not die. And then ask yourself, what sorts of activities would you engage in if you knew that those activities carried with them the risk of dying?

What things are so important to you that you would be willing to suddenly risk death for the sake of doing those things? Perhaps you like art. Is art important enough to you that you would be prepared to look at a masterpiece, if you knew that while you were enjoying it you could die, but that you couldn't die otherwise? Is sex great enough that you'd be prepared to run the risk of dying while you were engaged in sex? We can discover what we think is *most* valuable by asking which activities are *so* valuable that you would be prepared to do them even if that would introduce what wouldn't otherwise be there, namely, the risk of death.

In posing the question that way, I've been assuming that these are things you would do *despite* the fact that they run the risk of death. I suppose, however, that there is a further question we have to ask as well: are there things that would be worth doing precisely *because* of the fact that they introduced the risk of death? To be sure, that new idea sounds rather bizarre. At least, it sounds bizarre if we put aside the possibility that we've now lived for a hundred thousand years and have exhausted all that life's got to offer for us. What seems hard to believe is that we might engage in activities now, while life still has so much *more* to offer, precisely *for* the chance of dying. And yet, it seems to me that there are activities—if not many, at least some—that people do exactly for that reason.

For example, let me tell you something that I know is going to shock you. Did you know that there are people who jump out of airplanes? Admittedly, when they jump, they've got this little piece of cloth that gives them a decent chance of not killing themselves. But these things do fail. Every now and then you read in the newspaper about somebody whose parachute failed to open and so they died. And I ask myself, why? What could possibly drive somebody to jump out of an airplane with nothing but a little piece of cloth between them and death? And the answer that strikes me as most plausible is this: it's the very fact that there's a significant chance of death that helps explain why people do this.

Of course, if you talk to some of these people, they'll say, "Oh, no, no, no. The views are so glorious," or something like that. But I think this is rather an implausible suggestion because you could have these glorious views just by going up in the airplane and looking down from the safety of the plane. Part of the thrill—or so it seems to me—has got to be the very fact that they now have an increased risk of death. The chance of dying is part of what drives somebody to jump out of an airplane.

But if that's right, then maybe I was wrong earlier when I suggested that it would be nice to have a death-free time or a death-free location or death-free activities. Maybe I was wrong when I said that the pervasiveness of death, the ubiquity of death, is oppressive. If the chance of death adds a kind of zest, then perhaps the ubiquity of death is actually a *good* thing rather than a bad thing.

However, I'm inclined to think that that's not right, not even for those who are indeed drawn to parachuting because of the risk. I imagine, rather, that for such people the ubiquity of death is a kind of constant, unnoticed hum in the background. It's not really good enough to just have *some* risk of death—it's got to be greater risk than usual. What's attractive about jumping out of an airplane is that it *spikes* the risk of death. If that's right, though, then even for those death thrill seekers, the ubiquity of death won't be a particularly good thing precisely because of its ubiquity. The pervasiveness of the risk of death makes it disappear into the background.

There is one further aspect of death that I want to examine as well— the fact that death *follows* life. Arguably, this is the fundamental fact about the human condition. It isn't merely that we live, or that at some point in time we do not exist. Rather, what's true about humans is that we live and *then* we die. And what I want to ask is, what should we think about that fact? There is, after all, a kind of metaphysical compound here, a particular combination of life and death. We need to ask about the overall value of not just life, and not just death, but the entire combination.

One natural thought here, I suppose, would be that when we want to get clear about the value of a compound, we simply need to determine the value of its various component parts and then sum these values. Accordingly, if we want to understand the overall value of the human condition— life followed by death—we should first get clear about the value of life itself, then get clear about the badness of death, and then add the two up. Find the value of the two parts, and see what the sum comes to.

Of course, even given this strategy, people might disagree about the total. Optimists presumably will think that the sum comes out positive. "Yes," they might say, "death is bad. But life is good—sufficiently good to outweigh the badness arising from the fact that we are going to die. On balance, then, it is a good thing to be born." And pessimists will presumably insist that the sum is negative. "On balance," they will argue, "the bad of death *outweighs* the good (if any!) of life." And moderates might suggest that the answer depends on the facts in the individual case.

But I think there is more to do than merely finding the sum. To evaluate the human condition as a whole, we need to do more than merely add the goodness of life and the badness of death. The issue is actually more complicated than this, because sometimes the value of a compound or combination is different from the total you would get by just thinking about each one of its parts in isolation and then adding up the values of the distinct parts. This simple, "additive" approach to the values of wholes will not always be correct.

Here's an example, to illustrate the point. My two favorite foods in the world are pizza, on the one hand, and chocolate, on the other. I have of course already shared my love of chocolate with you, but I don't think I've mentioned pizza previously. But there they are, my two favorite foods. Pizza—delicious! Chocolate—delicious! Now take these two delicious things and combine them into a chocolate-covered pizza. Yuck! The whole thing just sounds disgusting to me, utterly unappealing.[2] I hope you are with me in finding the idea disgusting. Still, you might not *notice* the disgustingness if you just thought about the value of pizza in isolation and the value of chocolate in isolation. The value of chocolate-covered pizza is not just a matter of summing up the value of the parts taken by themselves. You've got to think about what we might call the "interaction effects."

So let's ask ourselves, are there any interaction effects that need to be taken into account when thinking about the human condition—the fact that life is followed by death? Presumably, there are two main possibilities here. If there are indeed interaction effects, they might be negative—reducing the value of the combination overall—or they might, instead, be positive.

Let me start briefly by mentioning one possible candidate for a *positive* interaction effect. Given that you are going to die, it follows, trivially, that there is a *finite* amount of life that you are going to get. Life is a scarce resource. It's precious. And we might be attracted to the thought that the value of life is increased by its very preciousness. After all, it is a common enough thought that the value of something may be greater if it is fragile or rare. Perhaps, then, the very fact that life is precious, that it won't endure, actually increases its value.

There's a short story by the science fiction writer Orson Scott Card, where the basic idea of the story is that of all the life forms in the universe, we here on Earth are the only ones that are mortal.[3] And because of this we are the envy of the rest of the universe. It's not so much that immortality is unattractive or boring. It's perfectly fine. But still, other beings throughout the universe envy us for our finite lifespans, because what we've got and they don't have is something that for each individual is precious—something that has to be valued during the limited time that we possess it. I'm not sure whether I agree with this idea, but I certainly can see its appeal. If it's right, then the very fact that we're going to die interacts with our life so as to make it more fragile, more ephemeral, and, as a result of that, more valuable.

Whether or not one accepts this first, positive, interaction effect, there remains the possibility of negative interaction effects as well. Here are two further suggestions that I often find plausible. The first idea I think of under the heading "A Taste Is Just a Tease." It starts with the observation that we live life for a while, getting a feel for all the wonderful things that life could offer us, and then a mere moment later, as it were, it's all snatched away from us. In a way, it adds insult to injury that we are offered just a whiff. It is as though somebody put a delicious meal before a hungry man, allowed him to see what it looked like, allowed him to smell the delicious aromas, perhaps gave him just one little tiny forkful to see just how beautifully delicious the food was. And then they snatched the whole thing away.

You can understand someone who says that it would be better never to have had the taste at all than to have the taste and then not be allowed to have the entire meal. Yet this negative feature is something that you might not notice at all, if you just focus on the intrinsic nature of the taste. In itself, after all, the taste of the meal is positive. Similarly, you might not notice this negative feature if you simply focus on the intrinsic character of *not* having the meal. Not having a meal, after all, is just an absence of a certain experience. The deprivation is a comparative bad, but it is not bad in and of itself. If you want to capture what's excruciatingly undesirable about being teased with a taste and then not being allowed to have more, you need to think about the two in combination. It's an interaction effect. And so we might think, similarly, that one of the bad things about the human condition is that we get a taste of life—nothing more—before it's snatched away. That's one possibility.

The second potential negative interaction effect that I want to mention falls under the heading "How the Noble Have Fallen." Right now, there's something amazing about you and me. We are *people*. In the universe as we know it, that is a remarkably rare and extraordinary thing to be. It is of course impossible to say with confidence what other forms of life there may be out there, but here on Earth, at least, we may well be the only people there are. (Who knows? Maybe dolphins or some of the great apes are people as well—in the philosophical sense of the term. But at any rate, it's a rather select club.) Of course, according to the physicalist, a person is just a certain kind of machine. But as I have already explained, we're not just *any* old machine. We are *amazing* machines. We're able to love. We're able to write poetry. We're able to think about the farthest reaches of the universe and ask about our place in that universe. People are amazing. And yet, for all that, we end up rotting. We end up as corpses. For many people, there's something horrifying about the thought that something as amazing as us, as exalted and valuable as we are, could end up something as lowly and unimportant as a piece of rotting flesh.

Whenever I think about this idea, the image that always comes to mind is that of a deposed king who ends up waiting on tables to make a living in New York. You might think, reasonably enough, that the life of a waiter is not the worst thing in the world. But at the same time, there's an extra twist—an insult added to the injury. The waiter has to remember that he used to be something extraordinary, a ruler. Notice, however, that if you just think about life as a ruler—if you just think about that part of the combination in isolation—it is likely to seem pretty good. And even life as a waiter, viewed in isolation, isn't all that bad. So if you want to notice the *problem* with this fate, the potential extra negative feature, you've got to think about the fact that there is an entire package here being evaluated. There is, after all, something especially insulting about having gone from king to waiter. And that fate—or worse—is waiting for all of us. It's a fact about the human condition that the amazing things we are don't stay amazing. We turn into pieces of rotting, decaying flesh.

So there are at least three potential interaction effects worth thinking about when evaluating the human condition. On the one hand, there may be negative effects, arising from the fact that a mere taste can be a special form of torture or that there is something horrifying about going from person to corpse. And yet, at the same time, there may be a positive effect as well, arising from the sheer preciousness of life. In different moods I find myself inclined to accept one or another of these different ideas, sometimes all three. Beyond this, it isn't at all clear to me which of these effects, if real, would be greater.

Presumably, people will have different views on this question. Optimists will say that even when we throw in the negative interaction effects, the overall nature of the human condition remains positive. So it is, indeed, a good thing to be born, even though your life is going to be followed by death. In contrast, of course, pessimists will say that the negative aspects of life are so great—especially when we throw in the negative interaction effects—that it would be better never to have been born at all. In effect, the pessimist's view is that the fact that we are going to die seeps in and poisons the nature of life, or perhaps the nature of the compound as a whole—life followed by death. On balance, they insist, the whole thing is a negative. Better not to have had any of it at all, better not to have been born, than to have this combination package of life followed by death. (Perhaps, then, instead of feeling sorry for Larry, the merely potential and never-to-be born individual from Chapter 10, we should *envy* him.)

Speaking for myself, I'm sufficiently optimistic to think that life can be pretty wonderful. Strictly speaking, though, I am not an optimist, but rather a moderate. There is no single overall value that we should place on the human condition, such that it would be appropriate to say of everyone that it is better to have been born, or better never to have been born. Sadly, it depends on the facts of the given individual's life. But still, it does seem to me that many of us attain lives very much worth living. And even in those moods where I am inclined to agree that we must not forget to take into account one or the other of the negative interaction effects, it still seems to me that for many of us—perhaps most of us—our situation is, on balance, a good one. For those of us fortunate enough to get a reasonable taste of what life can offer, then despite the fact that life must be followed by death, it is, I think, better to have been born than to have never been born at all.

Nonetheless, I want to emphasize the point that even if we were to *accept* the pessimist's conclusion that it would be better never to have been born at all, it wouldn't yet follow that the appropriate response to this realization is to commit suicide. That would take some further arguments.

It is, of course, tempting to think otherwise. That is to say, it is tempting to think that if we decide that it is better never to have been born, it follows without further ado that suicide is the appropriate response to the human condition. But in fact, as a matter of logic at least, that doesn't follow at all. Because if you think about it for a moment, you can readily see that suicide doesn't change the fundamental nature of the human condition— life followed by death. It isn't as though if you kill yourself you somehow bring it about that you've never been born at all! If there is something horrible about having just a taste, for example, then the fact remains that even if you kill yourself, all you have been given is a taste. Indeed, if you commit suicide, you've simply made it an even smaller taste. Similarly, if there is something degrading about being a person who is going to become a corpse, committing suicide doesn't alter that fundamental fact either. It just makes the insult come all the sooner.

So even if we were to agree with the pessimist that it would be better never to have been born at all, we still need to say—in the language of the old joke—show me one person in a thousand who is so lucky! *We* have all been born. And from the fact, even if we were to agree that it is a fact, that it would have been better if we hadn't been born at all—even if that were true, it simply wouldn't follow that suicide was an appropriate response.

Of course, none of this shows that suicide *isn't* ever an appropriate response to one's situation. That's a topic we will turn to in our penultimate chapter. But let's hold off on thinking about that question for a bit longer. First, I think, we need to ask a more general question: how should one *live*, in light of the facts about death that I have been laying out up to this point? Indeed, we also need to ask: *should* death affect the way we live at all?

CHAPTER 14

Living in the Face of Death

Disregarding the Facts

It is natural to think that the fact that we are going to die should have a significant influence on the way we live our lives. But perhaps that's just not true. So the very first question we need to ask may be this: should we really be thinking about all of these issues at all?

I realize of course that for you, my dear reader, it is too late. If you have made it this far in the book, then it is probably too late in the day to be asking whether it is really such a good idea to have spent this much time thinking about death in the first place. Nonetheless, as theorists at least, we can still be interested in the theoretical possibility that the right response to the facts about death might be to not think about death at all!

In principle, after all, there are three different possible reactions to any set of facts. You can deny them. You can respond to them. Or you can *disregard* them. It is that last reaction that I want to examine further.

In the previous chapters I have made any number of claims about the nature of death. In particular, of course, I have argued that we are just physical objects, and when those objects break in the relevant ways, we cease to exist. Obviously enough, then, one possible reaction to everything I have said is to simply disagree with me about the facts. Perhaps you think that there are souls, or that although we are just bodies, those bodies will someday be resurrected, so that death is not the end. If you do disagree with me about these things, then of course I think you are mistaken. I will view you as denying the facts, getting them wrong. But unsurprisingly, I don't have a lot more to say here about why one should hold the views that I think one should hold about the nature of death. So let us put this first reaction aside.

A different possible reaction, one that I will turn to a little bit later, is to admit the facts and then live accordingly—responding to the facts by living appropriately. Of course, we haven't yet asked ourselves, how *should* you live if you recognize and want to take into account the facts about death? That's a question we'll turn to later. But there's a middle possibility worth considering as well. Instead of mistakenly denying the facts, or accepting them and living accordingly, one might simply decide to not think about them. Maybe the best response to the nature of death is to just put it out of your mind. Don't give it any thought at all.

One might understandably complain that this can't possibly be an appropriate response. How can it possibly be appropriate to disregard the facts about *any* subject, to put them out of your mind? But this position, noble and high-minded as it may seem, has got to be mistaken. There is simply nothing unacceptable or inappropriate or misguided about not thinking about all sorts of facts that you might have learned at some point or the other.

Here is my favorite example of some stupid facts that I was forced to learn when I was younger: the state capitals. I've gotten pretty far in my life, and as far as I can tell I've never, ever, ever had to remember the capitals of the fifty states. So I just don't think about it. Indeed, I only think about state capitals about once a year, when I am offering this very example, to make this very point. Then I find myself asking, how many state capitals can I remember? And the answer is, not all that many of them. I knew these facts at one point, but the truth is, not thinking about them is just not all that objectionable.

Suppose, then, that we agree that the facts about life and death are exactly as I have described them. Until we say something more, it's not clear that we shouldn't just note it all, store it away, and then forget about it, just like the facts about the state capitals.

That seems like an odd suggestion; indeed, it seems misguided. But why? What is it about the facts about life and death that seem to make it misguided to think we should just put them aside and pay no attention to them? Presumably, it is because we are attracted to the thought that the facts about death—*whatever* they are—should have an *impact* on how we live. The appropriate way to live gets shaped, at least in part, by the fact that we're going to die, that we won't be around forever. If that's right, then it seems as though there'd be something irrational and inappropriate about simply disregarding those facts.

Of course, a decision to disregard the facts might well be an understandable one. Imagine someone saying the following: "If I thought about the nature of death—the fact that the fifty, eighty, or ninety years I have on Earth are all that I am going to have—it would just be overwhelming. It would be crushing. I would be unable to go on with my life." People do sometimes make claims like that, and they argue that because of this, the right thing to do is to not think about death. Recall Tolstoy's *Death of Ivan Ilyich*. The people in the Tolstoy story seem to have put the fact of mortality out of their mind. Why? Presumably because they think that facing it is just too crushing and overwhelming. So the way they cope with it is by simply *disregarding* the facts, trying not to think about them.

But there does seem to be something amiss about that reaction. That, at any rate, was certainly the point that Tolstoy was trying to get us to see. There's something wrong about lives—something inauthentic about lives— that are lived without facing the fact of our mortality and living accordingly, whatever exactly the appropriate responses might be. There is something odd and inappropriate about disregarding these particular facts. Unlike the facts about the state capitals, the facts about death are *important*.

Here are two stories that should give us a feel for the oddity of deciding to disregard important facts. Neither story has anything to do with death per se. First, then, suppose that you are about to go out on a hot date with Peggy Sue (depending on your sexual preferences, you may prefer to tell the story about Billy Bob). Imagine that your roommate holds up an envelope and says, "Written in this envelope are certain facts about Peggy Sue. I'm not going to tell you what these facts are yet. They're in the envelope. But I'll give you the envelope and you can open it up and read them. But I do want to tell you this one thing. It is indeed the case that if you were to read these facts, if you were to think about these facts, if you were to know the things written down in the envelope, you would not want to go out with Peggy Sue."

Imagine, next, that you believe your roommate. You don't know what's written in the envelope, but you really believe that the things written down in the envelope—whatever they are—are true. It's not that you think, for example, that your roommate has made it all up, that these things are lies or slander. No, what's written in the envelope is true. What's more, you know that if only you were to read these things in the envelope, you would change your mind and no longer want to go out with Peggy Sue. Suppose that all of this is the case, and yet what you tell your roommate is, "Don't show me the envelope." That seems odd. It doesn't seem like it makes sense. If there are facts that would change your mind about how to behave, and you *know* that they would change your mind, how can it be rational to disregard them?

Here's another story. You're about to drink a milkshake. But your roommate comes rushing in and says, "I've got the lab report. I had my suspicions about the milkshake, and so I took a sample and I rushed it down to the lab. I've got the lab report." You're about to drink it. It's a hot day and you love milkshakes, but your roommate says, "Inside the envelope are facts about this milkshake that—I promise you it is indeed the case—if you knew these facts, you would not drink the milkshake anymore." And so you say, "Oh, thank God. Don't open the envelope," and you drink the milkshake, disregarding the facts. That seems inappropriate too.

Suppose, then, that it really is true: if only we faced the facts about our mortality, we would live our lives rather differently than we currently do. How, then, could it be reasonable for us to *disregard* those facts? That seems inappropriate; it seems irrational.

Perhaps then what all of this shows is that the option of disregarding the facts about death isn't really all that intellectually reputable. Perhaps we either have to deny the claims I have been making about the nature of death or else—supposing they really are true—go on to ask how we should live in light of them. Maybe the option of disregarding the facts is one that we simply cannot take on as an intellectually acceptable alternative.

But I suspect that that's probably a little bit too quick, because there are actually two different ways in which facts can influence our behavior. And if we're not careful we'll disregard this distinction, even though I think it's an important one. Here are the two ways. On the one hand, it could be that certain facts, if you knew them, would *cause* you to behave differently without actually giving you any *reason* to behave differently. That's possibility number one. On the other hand, possibility number two, it could be that the facts would change your behavior by giving you a *reason* to behave differently.

Let me show you an example of the first possibility, because that's the one I think we may be overlooking when we assume that disregarding the facts about death can't ever make any sense. So there you are, kissing Peggy Sue, and your roommate bursts in and says, "I have in the envelope certain facts such that if you were to think about them you would no longer want to kiss her." And let me now tell you just what the facts in your roommate's envelope are. They are facts about the nature of Peggy Sue's digestive system. She has already had dinner, and while you are sitting there making out, food is making its way down Peggy Sue's digestive tract, being turned into shit. Eventually it's going to be excreted. And if you started picturing to yourself the feces inside Peggy Sue's digestive tract, and the fact that she's eventually going to be wiping the feces off of her behind, you might find it difficult to continue to engage in making out with her.

Now these are just facts, right? I didn't make any of these things up. But I imagine that even this cursory description might be enough to gross you out. So it is easy to believe that a complete and evocative description—all contained in your roommate's envelope—might indeed be enough to make you lose all desire to kiss Peggy Sue, if only you read it through and thought about the facts being described.

Now, do any of these facts about the digestive system make it inappropriate to kiss another human being? Of course not! But for all that, thinking about those facts can make it rather difficult to continue enjoying kissing the person. So there are certain facts about the digestive tract such that if you think about them you won't do something, kiss Peggy Sue. But it's not because you've got any good *reason* not to kiss her. Thinking about the facts about the human digestive process may *cause* you to change your behavior without giving you any *reason* to change your behavior.

So when your roommate comes running in, holding the envelope, and says, "I have in this envelope certain facts such that if you read these facts, and think about these facts, you will stop kissing Peggy Sue," the question you should put to your roommate is, "Are these facts that would merely *cause* me to change what I'm doing, or are these facts things that would give me some good *reason* to change?" If these are facts about how Peggy Sue likes to kiss and tell—perhaps she talks to her friends about who is a good kisser and who is a bad kisser—maybe that gives you a reason to not continue what you're doing. But if *all* we know is that knowledge of the facts in question would change your behavior, then that doesn't yet tell us whether they are reason-generating facts. If they are mere causes and not reasons, then maybe it's perfectly okay to disregard them. If your roommate comes in and starts trying to tell you facts about the human digestive system, you'll appropriately say, "Not now." Disregarding sometimes *is* the appropriate thing to do.

What about the facts about death? Are these facts ones that it's appropriate to disregard? A bold claim would answer in the affirmative. Perhaps the facts about death, if I thought about them, would change my behavior, but not because they would give me a reason to change my behavior; perhaps they would simply *influence* my behavior. If so, we might conclude, it might be better not to think about them. That would be the bold claim to make at this point.

Suppose, for example, that the right way to live, in light of the facts about death, is to live life to the fullest. But suppose as well that if you think about death you'll just get too depressed and you won't be able to live life to the fullest. It's not that the facts about death give you reason to stay in your room and sulk. It's just that the facts about death *cause* you to stay in your room and sulk. If that was the case, then disregarding the facts—perhaps always disregarding those facts—might well be the appropriate response. That would indeed be a rather bold claim. I am not inclined to believe that the bold claim is right.

So should we conclude instead that you should *always* be thinking about the nature of death? No, I think this alternative position is probably mistaken as well. There you are, one last time, making out with Peggy Sue, and your roommate comes in and starts trying to tell you about how human bodies decay when they turn into corpses. As he begins to tell you this story, you start picturing Peggy Sue as a rotting corpse. Suddenly, you don't really feel like kissing her anymore. It's like the digestive tract story. It's not that, as far as I can see, the fact that she's going to be a corpse gives you any *reason* not to kiss her. It's just that thinking about the fact that she's going to be a corpse *causes* you to not want to kiss her; it leaves you unable to enjoy kissing her.

Accordingly, I'm inclined to think that the right position here is a moderate one. There are times and places for thinking about the facts of death. When you're kissing somebody—that is not the time and that is not the place. So if someone says that you should *always* have the fact of your mortality before your mind's eye, then I think they are mistaken. Similarly, though, if anybody says that you should *never* think about mortality and the nature of death, I think that they're mistaken as well. There is, in fact, a time and a place.

But that still leaves us with a question. Let us suppose that *this* is an appropriate time and place for thinking about death. (After all, if ever there was a time and place for thinking about the facts of death and how it should influence our life, it's right here, right now, while reading a book about death.) So we still have to ask, how *should* you live? What is the *appropriate* response to the facts of life and death?

Fear of Death

It is natural to think that the fact that we are going to die should influence how we live. Indeed, most of us are drawn to the thought that death is so utterly central to our existence that it should have a significant and pervasive influence on how we live. Kafka, for example, said that "the meaning of life is that it ends." That's a nice cryptic saying, as is typical of Kafka, but the suggestion, I suppose, is a fairly common one: the fact that I am going to die, that my life will come to an end, is a deep and fundamental fact about my life, something that should have an important impact on how I live. That's the thought. But what, exactly, is that impact supposed to be? How should recognizing the fact that I am going to die influence the way that I live?

In thinking about this question, it's not enough to notice how recognition of our mortality *does* in fact influence us. It might be, for example—taking a page from Tolstoy—that if you dwelled upon the fact of your mortality you would scream interminably until the moment you died. But that fact, if it were a fact, wouldn't show that that's an appropriate response. That might just be a merely causal fact about how we're built. The question I want to ask, rather, is how is it *appropriate* to react? What reason is there to behave in one way rather than another?

The very first kind of "behavior" that I want us to think about isn't, strictly speaking, a form of behavior at all. I have in mind our emotional response, because one of the most common reactions to death, I suppose, is *fear* of death. Indeed, "fear" may in many cases be too weak a term. An extremely strong form of fear—terror of death—is, I suppose, a very common emotional response to death. So we need to ask: is fear of death a rationally *appropriate* response?

The crucial word here is "appropriate." I don't want to deny at all what I take to be the empirical fact that many people are afraid of death. How common a reaction that is, and how strong the fear is—that, I suppose, would be something for psychologists or sociologists to study. But I am not interested in that question. I take it that fear of death is very common. What I want to know is whether fear of death is an *appropriate* response, a *reasonable* emotion.

In raising that question, I'm obviously presupposing the larger philo-sophical thesis that it makes sense to talk about emotions as being appro-priate or inappropriate. We can ask not only what emotions does somebody have, but also what emotions *should* they have? However, this point may not be an obvious one, so perhaps it's worth dwelling on for a moment or two, before we turn to fear of death per se.

Let's start with an emotion other than fear—pride, for example. Pride is certainly an emotion. But I think we can probably agree that it only makes sense to be proud of something if the relevant conditions are met. What conditions? Two come to mind. First of all, the thing that you are proud of has to be some kind of accomplishment. If you were to say to me right now, "I'm really proud of the fact that I'm breathing," I would look at you in an uncomprehending fashion because breathing isn't difficult in any way that allows it to count as an accomplishment, and as such I can't understand how or why you would be proud of the fact that you're breathing. Of course, if you had had an accident, and had to go through excruciating physical ther-apy in order to learn how to use your lungs again, then we might well be able to see how breathing naturally and normally would be an accomplishment, something to be proud of. But for the rest of us, in any event, it's not an ac-complishment; hence it's not something that it's appropriate to be proud of.

Even if we've got an accomplishment, that may not be enough. For it to make sense for you to be proud of something, it's got to be in some way an accomplishment that reflects *well* on you. In the most straightforward cases, of course, cases where it's *your* accomplishment, the reason that pride makes sense is because you're the one who did this difficult thing. So if you get an A on your philosophy paper and you tell me that you're proud of that, I understand that; getting an A on a philosophy paper is an accom-plishment, and you wrote it, so I understand why you're proud of it. Of course, if what you did was go on the Internet and find one of those sites where you pay money and somebody else writes an A paper for you, well, I understand why maybe *they* should be proud that they've written a great philosophy paper, but I don't see how this reflects especially positively upon *you*. So that's a second condition that must be met if pride is to be appropri-ate: the object or event or activity or feature that you're proud of has to somehow reflect well on *you*.

That's not to say that it has to be *your* accomplishment, at least not in any straightforward, narrow sense. It makes sense, for example, to be proud of your children's accomplishments because there is the right kind of connection between you and your children. In some relevant way, their accomplishments are connected to you. And in still other cases, we might wonder about whether the connection is tight enough, or for that matter what exactly the nature of the connection has to be. Perhaps as an American you take pride when Americans win some event at the Olympics, and you say to yourself, "Well, I didn't run in the race, but for all that, I am an American and an American won, and I feel proud." That makes sense; we can understand how you think the connection there is tight enough. On the other hand, if you say, "The Germans won the race in the Olympics and I'm really proud," I will ask you, are you yourself German? Do you have German roots? Did you give money to support the German Olympic team? If none of that is true, then the appropriateness condition doesn't seem to be satisfied. It doesn't make *sense* to be proud.

We could easily spend more time exploring the precise conditions under which it makes sense to feel pride. But of course that's not really my purpose here. The reason for discussing pride was simply to make plausible the thought that emotions really do have requirements. Notice that these requirements are not necessarily conditions on what must be in place in order to *feel* the emotion. That would be a different question. Rather, these things need to be in place for it to make *sense* for you to have the emotion, for it to be rational or reasonable to feel the emotion—for that emotion to be an appropriate response to your circumstances or situation.

So let's ask, then, what are the appropriateness conditions for fear? Armed with an account of the relevant conditions, we can go on to ask, is it appropriate to feel fear of death? But first we need to know what the relevant requirements come to. When I think about this question, three conditions come to mind. The first is this: in order for it to make sense to feel fear, the thing that you are afraid of has to be *bad*.

I imagine that this first condition is fairly uncontroversial. If somebody were to say to me, "I'm afraid that after work today someone is going to give me an ice cream cone," I would once again look at them uncomprehendingly. I would ask, "Why are you afraid of that? How can it make any sense to be afraid of that?" Of course, it isn't as though an intelligible answer is impossible here. If they tell me, "I'm trying to lose weight, but I'm so weak that if they give me an ice cream cone I will just eat it, and that will ruin my diet for the week," then I would understand. From the point of view of a dieter, an ice cream cone may be a bad thing, and so our first condition on appropriate fear would be satisfied. But if you don't have a story like that, if you're like most of us most of the time, and an ice cream cone's a pretty good thing, a source of some passing but at least genuine pleasure, then I don't see how you can reasonably be afraid of getting an ice cream cone. It doesn't make any sense.

To be appropriately afraid of something, it's got to be bad. That's one of the reasons why we sometimes look askance at people who have various kinds of phobias—fear of spiders or fear of dust or fear of bunnies. We ask, how does this make any sense? Here is a cute little bunny; it's not dangerous. Fear of that bunny is inappropriate. Admittedly, there are poisonous spiders, but the fact of the matter is that the spiders we run across here in the suburbs of Connecticut are not poisonous. So fear of spiders doesn't seem appropriate either. (It might be another matter if you live in Australia, where poisonous spiders are more common.) Again, it's not that people can't have this kind of emotional reaction to spiders or bunnies; it's that it doesn't make *sense*.

So the first condition on appropriate fear is that the object of your fear must be bad. I can reasonably fear getting a migraine, if I'm subject to migraines. I can't reasonably fear the pleasure of looking at a beautiful sunset. The second condition is that there has to be a nonnegligible chance of the bad state of affairs happening, of the bad object coming to you. It's not enough that it's a logical possibility for fear to be a reasonable reaction. There is, for example, nothing logically inconsistent or incoherent about the possibility that you will meet your death by being ripped to pieces by Siberian tigers. It's not as though that's an inconsistent state of affairs. It's just that it is so unlikely—there is such a negligibly small chance of this happening—that if you were to tell me that you are indeed afraid that you will be killed in this way, then I could only say that such a fear doesn't make any sense, it's not appropriate.

Again, we can tell special stories where things might be different. Suppose you tell me that when you are not reading philosophical books on death you work as a wild animal trainer. Or perhaps you are planning to work in the circus where you will be training the tigers. Then of course I will change my tune. There is indeed a nonnegligible chance that you will be mauled and killed by tigers. So I understand the fear, it makes sense. But for the rest of us, I suppose, the chance of being killed by tigers is so close to zero, it's negligible. So fear of being eaten by tigers or being mauled to death by tigers doesn't make any sense.

Once you get the point, it is easy to multiply examples. Suppose I have a fear of being kidnapped by space creatures from Alpha Centauri, who will take me back to their lab and prod and poke me before dissecting me alive.

Yes, I suppose there's some possibility of that; it's not logically impossible. But again, the chance of this happening is so vanishingly small that if I really were afraid of this happening, you would correctly point out to me that such a fear is inappropriate. It's not rational.

So if fear is to be appropriate, there has to be a large enough chance of the bad thing actually happening. No doubt, there would be room for us to argue about how large a chance has to be in order to be large enough, but at least we should be able to agree that when you have a vanishingly small chance, then the fear doesn't make any sense. So that's condition number two.

Condition number three, I think, is somewhat more controversial, but for all that it still seems correct to me. In order for fear to be appropriate, you need to have some uncertainty about whether the bad thing will actually happen. It isn't clear how much uncertainty is required; but there must be at least *some* uncertainty as to whether the bad thing will really happen, or else how bad it will be. To see the point of this third condition, we need to imagine a case where a bad thing will happen, and indeed it is completely certain that this bad thing is going to happen. Indeed, you know precisely how bad this bad thing is going to be. I put it to you that in circumstances like that, fear is not an appropriate emotional response, even though the first two conditions have both been met.

Suppose that what happens is this. Every day you come to the office bringing a bagged lunch, which you put in the office refrigerator. Along with your lunch, you include a dessert; let's say a cookie. And every day at one o'clock, when you go to grab your lunch out of the refrigerator, you look inside the bag and you see that somebody has stolen your cookie! Well, that's a bad thing to happen. Admittedly, it's not the worst thing in the world, but it's a bad thing to have somebody steal your cookie. And furthermore, there is a more than negligible chance that your cookie will be stolen tomorrow as well. So we've got the first two conditions in place. In fact, however, not only is there a more than negligible chance that your cookie will be stolen again tomorrow, it is pretty much guaranteed. It happens day after day after day. So the bad thing is certain to happen, and you know precisely how bad it is (since nothing more than your cookie is ever missing). I put it to you, then, that in a case like this, *fear* doesn't make any sense.

Mind you, there are other negative emotions that probably do make sense, like anger and resentment. Who does this thief, whoever it is, think that he or she is, to be stealing your cookie? They don't have the right to do that! You can be angry, you can be resentful. You can be *sad* that you don't have a dessert, day after day after day. But you shouldn't be *afraid*, because there's nothing here that it makes sense for you to be afraid of. It doesn't make sense to be afraid when you know for a certainty that the bad thing is coming and how bad it is.

In contrast, if the thief strikes at random, taking different people's desserts from different bags at different times of the week, and you never know who he or she is going to steal from next, then you might reasonably be afraid that you'll be the person whose dessert gets stolen tomorrow. Or if cookie theft seems to you too silly an example, imagine that what happens is that somebody has been breaking into apartments in your neighborhood, stealing laptop computers. Here too, fear makes sense; you might reasonably fear that they will steal your computer next. Here, then, all three conditions have been met: there is a bad thing that is feared, there is a nonnegligible chance of that bad thing happening, but the relevant chance nonetheless falls short of certainty.

On the other hand, suppose that we have a situation like you might find in the movies, where the thief is such a master of her craft that she takes pride in her work and announces her heists. She might, for example, take out an ad in the *New York Times* that says "On Wednesday, April 27th, I shall steal the computer from so-and-so's apartment." And it doesn't matter what precautions are taken, something always goes wrong and the given person's computer always gets stolen. If it is *your* apartment that is mentioned for next week's heist, then you could reasonably be angry. You can be pissed, you can be annoyed, you can feel stupid that you can't figure out how to take adequate precautions. But when the ad appears, with your name and the date, and when all year long the thief has always carried through on the announced theft, then I put it to you that *fear* doesn't make any sense, because if you know exactly what the size of the harm is going to be, and you know that the harm is coming, fear is no longer appropriate.

Suppose that I have a little torture machine, a little pain generator. I put your hand down, hook it up to the electrodes, crank the dial and pull the switch, and you feel an electric shock. It makes sense to fear what the next shock is going to feel like, if the shocks vary in their intensity. But if the machine's only got one setting, on and off, and all the shocks feel exactly the same, and I've done it for you several times, so you know exactly what it feels like, and you know there will be exactly three more such shocks—perhaps you are being paid to participate in some weird psychology experiment—then, I suggest, fear doesn't make any sense. When you know exactly what's coming, exactly what it's going to feel like, you may of course dislike what is happening to you, but *fear* is inappropriate.

The experiment is over now. You've been paid your ten dollars for participating, but I refuse to let you go. I say, "I'm going to do it one more time, no worse than before." Obviously, you might not believe me. Perhaps this last shock really will be worse than the others. That would introduce the element of uncertainty, and then perhaps fear would be appropriate. But if you really do *believe* me that there will be exactly one more pain, exactly like the ones you felt before, then anger may make sense (you didn't agree to one more!), resentment may make sense, sadness that you are going to feel this pain may make sense—but *fear* doesn't make sense.

So there are, I think, three conditions that must be met for fear to be appropriate. The object of your fear must be bad, and there must be a nonnegligible chance that the bad thing is going to happen. But you must not be *certain* that the bad thing is going to happen. If you have certainty as to the nature of the bad, and certainty that this bad is coming, then fear doesn't make sense.

One other point, probably worth mentioning in passing, is this. Even when fear does make sense, there's a *proportionality* condition that should be kept in mind as well. Even if there's a nonnegligible chance of a harm coming (that falls short of certainty), and so *some* fear is appropriate, the *amount* of fear might still be inappropriate, if the chance is small but the fear is tremendous. When the risk is slight, mild concern may be all that is appropriate. Similarly, the amount of fear needs to be proportioned to the *size* of the bad. In the case of the cookie thief, for example, even when you are not certain whether you will be the next victim or not and so some fear is not out of place, it should only be slight. Anything more than that is an inappropriate reaction.

Armed with these ideas, it might seem that we are now in a position to ask whether fear of death is appropriate. In fact, however, we first need to clarify something important: when we are afraid of death, what *exactly* are we afraid of? What is the precise object of our fear? As it happens, I think there are importantly different ways to answer this question—and depending on which thing, exactly, we have in mind, fear may, or may not, be appropriate.

One thing you might worry about is the *process* of dying. Some people find that the actual process at the end of their life is a painful and unpleasant one. I've already mentioned the possibility of being mauled to death by tigers, and I certainly imagine that that would be a rather unpleasant way to die. So insofar as there is some nonnegligible chance that you will die a painful death, there does seem to be room for some amount of fear. Of course, we then have to ask, what is the chance that you'll die painfully? As

I've already observed, for most of us the chance of being mauled to death by tigers is vanishingly small. Because of this, I think, no real fear of dying that particular death is appropriate. And for that matter, the fear of dying through a painful operation at the hands of aliens from Alpha Centauri is not appropriate either.

Still, the sad fact of the matter is that there are people in the world who do suffer painful deaths, in particular, of course, because some diseases can be painful in their final stages. It can come as a rather unpleasant bit of news to learn that many hospitals do not yet provide adequate pain medication at the end of life. Why? That's a rather complicated question, but I suppose if somebody were to say to me that in light of this fact they are afraid that this might happen to them, I would certainly understand that reaction. Still, the fear had better be proportionate. If you tell me that you can't sleep at night for fear that this is going to happen to you, then a fear of that magnitude strikes me as being disproportionate.

But at any rate, although it may be true for some people that when they say they are afraid of death what they mean is that they are afraid of the process of dying, I imagine that this is not what most people have in mind when they say that they are afraid of death. What most people mean, I take it, is that they're afraid of death itself—afraid of *being* dead. They are afraid of what it will be *like* to be dead. And with regard to that, I want to suggest, the relevant conditions for appropriate fear are not in fact satisfied.

The main point to bear in mind here is that there is actually *nothing* that it is like to be dead. Being dead involves no kind of experience at all. This is, of course, a point we have already discussed, in Chapter 9. It's not that there is *some* sort of experience when one is dead, but an experience unlike our ordinary ones and so hard to imagine—a troubling mystery. No, there is no mystery here at all: being dead simply involves no experience whatsoever.

But that means that "what it's like" to be dead is not, in fact, intrinsically bad, in and of itself—precisely because there is nothing at all that it is like to be dead. So if what we fear when we fear death is what it is like to be dead, then any such fear is an inappropriate one. The first condition for appropriate fear isn't satisfied, since the object of our fear—what it is like to be dead—is not, in fact, anything bad at all.

Obviously, this argument presupposes the view about the nature of death that I have defended in the first half of this book. Things will look rather different if you believe in an afterlife, or at least the significant possibility of an afterlife. Suppose, for example, that you are worried that you might go to hell. On that sort of view, clearly, fear of what it will be like to be dead makes a lot of sense. (Unless, of course, you are *certain* you are going to hell, and you are certain how much punishment you will receive. In that case, in contrast, the *third* condition for appropriate fear isn't met, so fear remains inappropriate.) But if, as I believe, death is truly the end of experience, then it seems to me that the first condition on appropriate fear isn't satisfied. It makes no sense to be afraid of what it is like to be dead, since there is *nothing* that it is like to be dead at all—and thus nothing *bad* that it is like.

Of course, I am not suggesting that there is nothing bad about death. Although I am insisting that it makes no sense to be afraid of what it is *like* to be dead—precisely because that is not something bad at all—I have not denied that death is bad. On the contrary, I accept the deprivation account, according to which death is bad (when it is bad) by virtue of the fact that one is deprived of the good that one would have if one weren't dead. In short, death isn't bad because of what it feels like to be dead; rather, death is bad because of the deprivation that it involves.

But if that is right, then perhaps we can specify an appropriate object of fear here after all. Instead of fearing what death will be *like*, perhaps we should simply fear the deprivation that it will involve. Admittedly, deprivation isn't an intrinsic bad. But as we have seen, it does seem to be a *comparative* bad. So it seems as though fear of the deprivation involved in death would satisfy the first requirement on appropriate fear—that the thing feared must be bad. Perhaps, then, fear of death is appropriate after all, as long as we are clear that what is to be feared is the deprivation, rather than the experience, of death.

But that's not quite right either. First of all, I have argued that immortality would not, in fact, be good for us; to be condemned to live forever would be a punishment, not a blessing. And if I am right about that, then the fact of our mortality—that we will eventually be deprived of life—is not actually something bad after all, it is something good. So fear of the deprivation involved in death is not appropriate after all. More precisely, if what we are afraid of is the inevitable loss of life, then the object of our fear is not bad, but good, and so fear remains out of place.

Of course, you may not have been persuaded that immortality would be bad. Perhaps you think it *would* be good to live forever, in which case the inevitable loss of life, which is built into the very fact of our mortality, would indeed be something bad, not good. So can we at least agree that on this view—where immortality is good, not bad—the object of our fear is something bad, and so fear is appropriate?

Note, however, that even if I am mistaken to think that immortality would be bad, it won't yet follow that fear of death is appropriate. For I have also argued that appropriate fear requires a lack of certainty with regard to the coming of the object of our fear. And with regard to the fact that eventually I will be deprived of life, there is no uncertainty. I *know* that this comparative bad (supposing, for the sake of argument, that it really is a bad) is coming. I *know* that I am going to die. So *fear* remains out of place.

Suppose I give you an ice cream cone, and you like it. You wish you could have a second ice cream cone. But I don't have a second ice cream cone to share with you. So you know that after the first ice cream cone is over, you won't have a second ice cream cone. That's a pity, that's a lack of something good. And now you tell me, "I'm afraid; I'm afraid of the fact that there will be this period after the first ice cream cone is done in which I'm not getting a second ice cream cone. I'm afraid because of the badness of deprivation of ice cream." I hope it is clear that fear along these lines doesn't make any sense. Since you *know* that there isn't going to be a second ice cream cone, fear of that lack is inappropriate. Similarly, then, even if death per se is bad, because it means that at some point you won't get another "helping" of life, nonetheless, since you *know* that life must come to an end, fear of that eventual lack is inappropriate as well.

But now a different possibility suggests itself. I have just argued that fear of death is inappropriate precisely because death is certain. But what is not at all certain, of course, is *when* you are going to die. Perhaps, then, what one should be afraid of is not the loss of life per se, but rather the possibility that one will die *sooner* rather than later.

Consider an analogy. Suppose that you're at a party. It's a great party, and you wish you could stay and stay and stay, but this is taking place back in high school, and what's going to happen is that your mother is going to call at a certain point and tell you it's time to go home. Now, let's just imagine there's nothing bad about being at home; it's intrinsically neutral. You just wish you could stay at the party. But you know you can't. Finally, suppose that you *know* that the call is going to come at midnight, guaranteed, no chance of her calling earlier or later. Then there really isn't anything to be *afraid* of. You might resent the fact that your mother is going to call you at midnight; you might be annoyed at the fact that she won't let you stay out till one o'clock like your other friends. But there's nothing to be afraid of. If it is 11 o'clock and you're saying, "I'm terrified of the fact that the call's going to come at midnight, since that's when she always calls," then the simple fact is that your fear just doesn't make any sense. You don't have the relevant degree of uncertainty. Since you know exactly what's coming and you know for a certainty that it's coming, fear isn't appropriate.

In contrast, if we imagine that all you know is that your mother is going to call *some* time between 11:00 and 1:00, then some fear makes sense. Perhaps most of the time she calls around 12:00, or 12:30, and sometimes she calls as late as 1:00—but occasionally she calls as early as 11:00. Now, it seems to me, our various conditions for appropriate fear have all been met. There is something bad—the possibility of having to leave the party sooner rather than later—there is a nonnegligible chance that the bad thing will happen (she sometimes does call on the early side), and yet, for all that, there is a lack of certainty that the bad thing will happen (since she sometimes calls later, rather than earlier). Here, then, some degree of fear makes sense. (How much fear? That depends on how *likely* it is that the call will come early.)

Perhaps we have something similar with regard to death. Perhaps what it makes sense to be afraid of is the possibility that death will come sooner rather than later. Notice, incidentally, that a fear of this sort neatly sidesteps the issue of whether immortality would indeed be bad for us. Even if it *would* be bad to live forever, death might still come too soon for most or all of us. If so, we can reasonably worry that death will come sooner rather than later.

Notice as well that the crucial ingredient here, by virtue of which death is something that can be appropriately feared, is death's unpredictability. Indeed, it seems to me that if it weren't for the unpredictability of death, *fear* of death wouldn't make any sense at all. As I have tried to explain, being dead per se is not the sort of thing that it makes sense to be afraid of. As far as I can see, the only reason fear might be appropriate at all here is because of the unpredictability of death.

Even here, further distinctions might be helpful. Am I afraid that I will die *too soon*, in the sense that if only I lived at least a while longer, life would still be, on balance, good? Or is the worry that I will die *soon*, in the sense that, given the range of additional years I might reasonably hope for, death may come sooner rather than later? Or—a third possibility—am I afraid that I will die *young*, with death coming sooner for me than it does for others? These three ways of specifying the precise object of my potential fear differ from one another in important ways, including how *much* fear is appropriate, if any, and when. For your fear needs to be proportioned to the relevant likelihood.

Take, for example, the fear of dying young. Obviously enough, once one has reached middle age, any fear of dying young is utterly irrational, since it is no longer so much as possible. (I am myself approaching sixty; it is far too late for me to die young!) But even among the young themselves, where the possibility of dying young at least remains open, the chance of this actually happening is extremely small. For a healthy twenty-year-old in the United States, for example, the chances of dying in the next five, ten, or even twenty years are virtually negligible, so small that no significant amount of fear seems at all appropriate. Of course, as one grows older, the chance of dying within a given period of time steadily increases, but even here, fear that one will die soon can easily be out of proportion. Even an eighty-year-old woman has a greater than 90 percent chance of living at least another year.

Obviously, fear that death may come soon can make sense among the very sick or the very aged. But for the rest of us, I think, it is typically misplaced. In particular, then, if you are yourself reasonably healthy and yet you say to me, "death is so overwhelming, I am terrified of death," then all I can say in response is that I believe you, but for all that it seems to me that terror of death is not an *appropriate* emotion. It doesn't make sense, given the facts.

Of course, even if I am right about this, and fear of death is for the most part inappropriate, that still leaves open the possibility that there may be some *other* negative emotion that *is* appropriate. I have already suggested that anger, sorrow, and regret can sometimes make sense even though fear does not. So we still need to ask whether one of these other negative emotions is appropriate when thinking about death.

One thing seems clear. Given my views about immortality, the fact that I will eventually die is not, in and of itself, a bad thing. Death per se is not bad but good. Accordingly, I think it doesn't make sense to have a negative attitude of any sort toward death itself—the very fact that I am going to die. But we can focus, instead, on the possibility that I may die *too soon*— that I may die while it is still the case that what life has to offer me remains, on balance, good overall. The possibility of dying too soon is clearly a bad one. So what, if anything, is the appropriate negative emotional response here?

An obvious suggestion is *anger*. It seems natural to suppose that even if *fear* isn't the right response to death, anger may be. Part of me wants to shake my fist at the universe and curse it for giving me only 60 years or 70 years or even 100 years, when the world is such a rich, incredibly fantastic place that it would take hundreds of years, or thousands of years, or longer, to exhaust what it has to offer. Isn't anger an appropriate response to the fact that I am likely to die too soon?

Actually, though, it's not so clear that it is. Like all of the other emotions, anger itself has appropriateness conditions, and it isn't clear that they are met here. Admittedly, the first requirement for appropriate anger—that something bad must happen to you (or be likely to happen)—is, in fact, met, since I am likely to die too soon, and that would be bad for me. But there are additional requirements on appropriate anger, and it is these further conditions that may not be satisfied.

For example, anger is only appropriate if it is directed at a person—at an agent, a being that has some choice over what they are doing to you. So if someone at the office spills coffee on your computer, ruining the hard drive, even though you have told them previously to be more careful, anger makes sense. The anger is directed at your coworker, a person with some control over what they were doing. Similarly, if you get angry at your boss for the poor evaluation you receive at work, at the very least this particular condition is satisfied as well: you are directing your anger at an agent, at an individual person who has some control over how they behave toward you.

Of course, there is no doubt that sometimes we get angry at inanimate objects. Your report is due at work, and you are about to print it out and rush off, when your computer crashes. You get angry at the computer. What's going on here? You have *personified* the computer: you are viewing it as though it were a person who has deliberately chosen to fail right now, letting you down yet again. I certainly understand this sort of behavior; I do this sort of thing as well. But of course you can step back. At the very least, once your anger has subsided you can step back and recognize that getting angry at your computer doesn't really make any sense. Why not? Because your computer is not a person; your computer is not an agent; your computer didn't have any choice or control.

Another condition on appropriate anger, I think, is this: anger makes sense only when the agent has *wronged* you, has treated you in a way that was morally inappropriate. If you deserved that negative evaluation from your boss, then they haven't done anything wrong, and your anger is inappropriate. But if he gave you that poor evaluation to get back at you for beating him at squash, then what he did was wrong, and your anger is no longer out of place. When you are angry at someone, you are revealing the fact that you think they've mistreated you, that they have behaved toward you in a way that they shouldn't.

These two additional conditions may not be the only further requirements on appropriate anger, but they will suffice for our purposes. So let us ask, does it indeed make sense to be angry given the fact that we are likely to die too soon?

The answer may well depend on who it is, or what it is, that you take to be responsible for the fact that we die too soon. Why do we only get our 60, 70, or 80 years? Here are two basic alternative answers. On the one hand, you might accept a classic religious outlook, where God is a person who rules the universe and decides our fate. Perhaps God has condemned us to death and indeed brought it about that almost all of us die too soon. That's what we see in Genesis, for example: God punishes Adam and Eve by making them mortal. On the other hand, you might believe instead in an utterly impersonal universe. On this alternative view, there are just atoms swirling in the void, coming together in various combinations. There is no person behind the scene, controlling all of it. We die because that's the way life happened to evolve.

Let's consider the two possibilities, starting with the theistic picture of the universe. Here, at least, the first of our two further conditions on appropriate anger is met. Since God is a person, it might well be appropriate to be angry at God for condemning us to lives that are so short, relative to the riches that the world offers us. But what about the second of the further conditions? Has God *wronged* us? Has he mistreated us in giving us our 50 or 80 or 100 years? Has God treated us in some morally unjustified way? If not, then anger or resentment at God doesn't make sense.

Suppose that someone at work has a box of candy and she gives you a piece, which you enjoy. Then she gives you a second piece of candy, and you enjoy that as well. And then she gives you a third piece, which you also enjoy. Imagine that you ask her for a *fourth* piece of candy, and she won't give it to you. Has she *wronged* you? Has she treated you immorally? Does she *owe* you more candy? It's not clear that she does. But if not, then being angry is inappropriate. Of course, I might *understand* if you got angry, in that this might be a common enough response. But is anger an *appropriate* response to your officemate for giving you something good and then not giving you more? It's not clear that it *is* an appropriate response. The appropriate response actually seems to me to be, not one of anger, but gratitude. Your officemate didn't owe you any candy at all, and yet she gave you three pieces. You might wish you could have more, you might be sad that you can't have more, but *anger* doesn't seem appropriate. Similarly, then, anger at God might be inappropriate as well. As far as I can see, God doesn't *owe* it to us to give us any more life than what we get.

Suppose, instead, that you accept the second basic picture, with an utterly impersonal universe. In that case, of course, even the first of our two further conditions isn't satisfied. Getting angry at the universe isn't actually a rationally appropriate emotion, precisely because the universe isn't a person, it isn't an agent, it has no choice or control over what it does. Obviously enough, I *can* lift my fist and curse the universe, but what I am doing then is personifying the universe, treating it as though it were a person that deliberately decided to make us die too soon. But however common that response might be, it makes no sense rationally if the universe is not in fact a person, if it's just atoms swirling in the void, forming various kinds of combinations. On this view too, then, anger at the fact that I'm probably going to die too soon just doesn't make sense.

Well, what about sorrow? Maybe I should just be *sad* about the fact that I'm likely to die too soon? In point of fact, it does seem to me that some emotion along this line makes sense. The world is a wonderful place. It would be better to have a larger helping of the amazing things that it can offer us. Accordingly, I am sad—and appropriately sad, I think—that I am not going to get more.

But having had that thought, I immediately find myself with another thought as well. Although it's a pity I don't get more, I'm extremely lucky to have gotten as much as I get. My own view is that the universe is just this swirling mass of atoms, forming clumps of various kinds of things, and then having those clumps dissolve or break apart. Most of those atoms don't get to be alive at all. Most of those atoms don't get to be a person, falling in love, seeing sunsets, eating ice cream. It's extraordinarily lucky of us to be in this select, fortunate few.

Let me share with you one of my favorite expressions of this thought. It comes from Kurt Vonnegut's book *Cat's Cradle*.[1] Vonnegut imagines a kind of prayer that one might recite on one's deathbed:

> God made mud.
> God got lonesome.
> So God said to some of the mud, "Sit up!"
> "See all I've made," said God. "The hills, the sea, the sky, the
>   stars."
> And I was some of the mud that got to sit up and look around.

Lucky me, lucky mud.

I, mud, sat up and saw what a nice job God had done.

Nice going God!

Nobody but you could have done it God! I certainly couldn't
   have.

I feel very unimportant compared to You.

The only way I can feel the least bit important is to think of all
   the mud that didn't even get to sit up and look around.

I got so much, and most mud got so little.

Thank you for the honor!

Now mud lies down again and goes to sleep.

What memories for mud to have!

What interesting other kinds of sitting-up mud I met!

I loved everything I saw.*

It seems to me that the right emotional response isn't fear, it isn't
anger, it's *gratitude* that we're able to be alive at all.

(Might gratitude, like anger, be something that should only be directed to a person? If so, and if one believes in an impersonal universe, then
of course strictly speaking it isn't gratitude that's appropriate, but perhaps
rather a feeling of having been extremely lucky or fortunate.)

Being Careful

So far, we've been considering emotional reactions to death. But what about
behavior? How should we *live* in light of the fact that we're going to die? One
answer that immediately comes to mind seems almost like a joke. I want to
say, well, we should be *careful*.

There used to be a cop show on TV called *Hill Street Blues*. The show
began every day with the sergeant going over the various crimes that had
taken place recently and the various investigations that were under way,
and he'd always end, as he sent off his police, by saying, "Be careful out
there."

---

* I have always made a point of reading this passage from *Cat's Cradle* to the students in my course on death. In April of 2007, just after the class in which I did that, a
visitor brought to my attention the fact that Vonnegut himself had died the night before,
something I had not realized when reading the quote. As I told my students the next day,
I hope that to the very end, Kurt Vonnegut, who lived until he was eighty-four, realized
how lucky he was to be some of the sitting-up mud.

You've got to be careful, of course, because otherwise you are going to end up dying from avoidable causes. If you're not careful, you won't notice the truck coming down the street about to hit you. That much seems obvious. But beyond this trivial observation—that one must look out for dangers that might end one's life prematurely—the fact that we're going to die also seems to require a further, more particular kind of care: you must be careful about what you are *doing* with your life. As people sometimes put it, you only "go around" once; you don't get to do it again. And so, it seems, the fact that we're mortal, the fact that we've got a finite lifespan, requires us to recognize that we can blow it. We could do it wrong.

Now, the nitpicky part of me wants to point out that it can't be mortality per se that has this implication. Even if we lived forever, we could still do it wrong. After all, even with an infinitely long life there is still going to be some particular pattern of actions and activities that you engage in. And that particular pattern could still be one that wasn't the best pattern available to you. So the possibility of having blown it, of having lived the wrong kind of life, is a possibility that's going to be true of us whether or not we're mortal. To see this, consider the following simplistic example. Suppose that we live forever, and then imagine someone who spends eternity simply counting the integers: 1, 2, 3, 4, 5, 6 . . . That might be a considerably less valuable way to spend eternity than, say, doing more complicated math. So even immortals can squander their lives.

And yet, for all that, it seems as though if we are mortal, rather than immortal, this adds an extra risk, an extra danger of blowing it. After all, if you really will live forever, then even if you have already spent a million years or a billion years counting the integers and only then realize that this is a pointless thing to do, you can always start over. You have plenty of time to start doing deeper, more valuable math. Immortality gives you a chance of *starting over*. It gives you the possibility of do-overs.

Should we conclude, therefore, that what's especially troubling about mortality is the fact that it robs us of the chance to start over? But of course, that's not quite right either. Even if you don't live forever, indeed, even if you live for only 60, 70, or 80 years, you have the chance to reappraise your life at the age of 20 or 30 or 50 and decide you need to change course. So it's not exactly as though the possibility of do-overs disappears as a result of our mortality per se. Nonetheless, the fact that death comes as *quickly* as it does, does seem to mean that we have to be especially careful, since we have such a short period of time in which to try again. There is precious little time to correct our mistakes.

There are two kinds of mistakes, really, that we might catch ourselves in. We might discover, on the one hand, that we made some bad choices in terms of what we were aiming for. And on the other hand, we might find that, even if we made the right choices in terms of our goals, we flubbed it in terms of actually accomplishing what we were trying to accomplish. And so we literally have to start over and try again. So there are two kinds of care that we have to take. We have to be careful in our choice of aims and we have to be careful in the execution of our aims, because we have, as it were, a rather limited amount of time to get things right.

Here too, the nitpicky part of me wants to say that, strictly speaking, the need to be careful doesn't follow from the mere fact that we live relatively brief lives—typically less than, say, a hundred years. A short life in absolute terms does not all by itself entail that we have to be especially careful. After all, suppose there just weren't all that many things worth doing. And suppose that they weren't all that difficult to do well. Suppose, for example, that there were only *five* things worth doing. And even if you couldn't necessarily do every single one of them right the first time out, at most it would take two or three tries, with each try taking at most an hour or two. Obviously, that would be a pretty impoverished world, if it could only offer us that much. Still, if that really was the way the world worked and we had *one hundred years* to live our lives, we wouldn't really have to worry all that much about being careful. We would have plenty of time to aim for each of the five things worth having and plenty of time to get each one of the five things right. A hundred years of life would be more than enough. *Twenty* years would be more than enough! We wouldn't have to be careful at all.

So it's not just the fact that we're mortal that requires us to be careful, nor the fact that we live for only a short period of time, measured in some absolute way. Rather, it's the fact that we have a short span of life relative to how *much* there is worth aiming for, and how complicated and *difficult* it can be to achieve those things. It's because of the fact that there's so much to do and it's so hard to do it properly that we have to be careful. We just don't have the time to flail around and try a little of this, a little of that.

As I say, there are really two dangers here. First of all, we may eventually discover that the things that we have aimed for weren't really the best choices. Notice, by the way, that the most serious risk here isn't that we will discover that the things we have tried to accomplish weren't really worth doing *at all*. Rather, the danger is that we will discover that we wasted our time on things that were simply significantly *less* valuable than *other* goals we might have set ourselves. Given the relatively short period of time that we've got—far too little time to try to achieve everything at all that might be worth achieving—we have the extra burden of needing to decide what are the things *most* worth going after. We all face the possibility that we may eventually look back and realize that when setting our goals we simply didn't choose wisely. So that is one way in which death forces us to be careful. But beyond this, of course—second—whatever our goals may be, we also have to be attentive to how we try to accomplish them. Life may well give you enough time for an occasional chance at a do-over, but the simple fact of the matter is that you don't have time for a whole lot of them. So here too, death forces us to be careful.

As an analogy, imagine that you are a musician who goes into a recording studio, planning to record an album. If you've got a long enough period of time, let's say a month in the studio, then you don't have to be particularly careful. You can pick a few songs from your repertoire and see how they go. Maybe these wouldn't be the best things to record? Not a problem, let's just give it a try and we'll see. Didn't get the song right the first time? Not a problem, we can record it again. We can try it a third time, or a fourth. Or maybe try a different song altogether. If you've got enough time, it isn't especially important to be clear which songs are the ones to record; and it isn't especially important to get those songs down in one take, or at most two.

But if instead of having a month in the recording studio, you've got only a week in the studio, or a day in the studio, suddenly everything's much more pressing. Time is much more precious. You've got to decide early on: which are the songs that it makes sense to record? Sure, there are other songs you could record instead, but these seem to be the better choices. And when you record them, you can't be as careless and inattentive as you try to get them down. You've got to try to get it right the first time or, at worst, the second time.

That, it seems to me, is the situation we find ourselves in, given how incredibly rich the world is, how many things it offers us, how many choices we have in terms of what's worth going after—and given how very difficult it can be to achieve many of these things. Admittedly, life is long enough that we do have *some* chance at trying again, both in terms of changing our mind about what we should be aiming at, and trying a second or third time to achieve our various goals, whatever they might be. But the fact of the matter is, we don't have that many chances; we don't have all that much time. So we've got to pay attention. We've got to be careful.

Of course, having said that, we immediately need to ask, what *should* I do with my life? Here I am. I'm paying attention. I'm trying to be careful. But what should I *do*? How should I fill my life? What should I aim for?

I have to tell you, I am not going to try to answer that question here. To ask what things are really worth going after in life is to come up to the edge of asking, what is the *meaning* of life? What goals, what purposes, what aims are the most valuable, the most rewarding, the most significant? That is clearly an important question, indeed perhaps *the* important question. But it is, I think, a question for a different book. And so, having come close enough to the question to touch it, I am now going to slowly back away from it.

Strategies

How should I live, given that I am going to die? One natural thought is this: we haven't got much time, so we should pack as much as we can into life. Pack as much in as you can, *while* you can.

That's a common enough thought, but there are, I think, at least two different broad strategies for putting that idea into practice. The first strategy emphasizes the dangers of failure if your aims are too ambitious. It counsels us to aim, instead, for the kinds of goals that you are virtually guaranteed to achieve. It tells us to aim for the pleasures of food, company, and sex. "Eat, drink, and be merry, for tomorrow we die." That's the first strategy. We're going to be dead tomorrow, so while we are here we should try to pack in as much as we can by going for the things that we've got a very high chance of actually attaining.

The second strategy remarks that that's all well and good: you've certainly got a pretty high chance of succeeding, if that's what you aim at. The trouble with strategy number one, however, is that the goods that you can achieve, if you aspire only to sure things, are small ones. They're rather small potatoes, as things go. The second strategy reminds us that some of the most valuable goods in life don't come with a guarantee of success. You might want to write a novel, compose a symphony, or for that matter marry and raise a family. Things like this—more ambitious goods—are among the most valuable things that life can offer us. A life filled with these larger but less certain goods is a more valuable life than one filled only with the easily acquired and quickly passing pleasures of food, drink, and entertainment.

Suppose God were to say to you, "Which life do you want? A life filled with food and drink and passing pleasures, or a life filled with lasting accomplishments? I promise you, whatever your choice, you will be completely successful." I imagine that most of us would readily agree that the life filled with genuine accomplishment is the more valuable life. The trouble, of course, is that in the *real* world, this sort of life—a life in which one *aims* at significant accomplishments—is also a life with a greater chance of failure. You aim for writing the great American novel and ten years later you still haven't finished it. Twenty years later, you decide you don't have it in you to write the great American novel. Now what do you have to show for your time? Or perhaps you try to start a thriving business, and after years and years of hard work and struggle it goes under.

So, what's the right strategy to take? I suppose many of us would be inclined to say that there is actually a *third* strategy here as well, and it is this third strategy that should be adopted: we should aim for the right *mixture* of large and small goods. On the one hand, we should aim for a certain number of more significant accomplishments, precisely because if you do manage to get them your life will have more value. But at the same time, on the other hand, you should also throw in a certain sprinkling of the smaller things, so you are at least assured of having gotten *something* out of life.

Of course, even if we were to agree that this sort of mixed strategy is the most reasonable one, that would still leave us wondering, what is the *right* mixture? But I am not going to try to answer that question either. Instead, I want to ask whether we are right to accept the common idea that underlies each of these three different strategies—the idea of trying to pack in as much as possible. Regardless of whether we are talking about large goods or small, or some mixture of the two, is it really true that the more we add, the greater the value of the life? Are we right to assume that the more, the better?

I have, of course, already argued that immortality would not actually be a good thing. Rich and incredible as the world is, eventually the goods of life would run out for each of us; immortality would be dreadful. But most of us never come anywhere *close* to running out. Most of us die way too soon. If you die at thirty, for example, it would have been better to live to forty. And if you die at forty, it would have been better to live to fifty—or sixty, or seventy, or eighty. So, one thing that most of us are inclined to agree upon is this: other things being equal, the longer your life, the better.

Compare the two lives shown in Figure 14.1. The width of a given box represents how long the life lasts, and the height represents how well the life is going at a given time. The two lives shown are going equally well. For the sake of concreteness, we can suppose that each has a value of 100 points at each moment, and let's suppose that that's a rather high level of well-being. I imagine, then, that most of us would prefer the life on the right. We would agree that it is better to have a life at that value that lasts one hundred years, rather than one that lasts only fifty years. Other things being equal (and here, I've stipulated, they are), the greater the length or duration of life, the better.

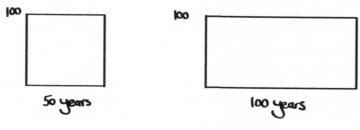

Fig. 14.1

But at the same time, I assume we will all agree that the length of a life isn't the *only* thing that matters. The *quality* of the life matters as well. Suppose, for example, that you had to choose between a life of fifty years at 100 "quality points" and a life of fifty years at 130 quality points. (See Figure 14.2.) Presumably you would rather have the second life. So length of life isn't the only thing we care about; we want to pay attention to quality as well.

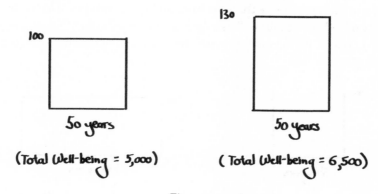

Fig. 14.2

Thinking about it mathematically, we might say that *quantity* of well-being is a function of both duration and quality. Somewhat more precisely, we can say that the quantity of well-being within a life is equal to the area of the given box, a quantity that we find, of course, by multiplying duration times quality. So in the first life shown in Figure 14.2 we have 50 × 100, for a total of 5,000 units of well-being. And in the second life we have 50 × 130, for a total of 6,500. Of course, we don't have to believe that the numbers could ever be this precise; what's important here is simply the underlying idea, that the area of the box represents the overall quantity of well-being that you managed to fit into your life in your fifty years.

(If we accept a valuable container theory, rather than a neutral container theory, we would need a more complicated formula. Multiplying duration times quality merely captures the value of the *contents* of the life. But if being alive per se has value as well, then we will need to add a further amount—one reflecting the value of life in and of itself—to get the grand total. Presumably this further amount will be a function of duration alone. For simplicity, however, I won't pursue this complication here. I am also putting aside—again, for reasons of simplicity—the sort of view considered in Chapter 13, according to which the value of a life can be affected by its overall *shape*.)

If well-being is a function of both duration and quality, then we have to face the fact that we might have to *choose* between the two. Consider Figure 14.3. Here, the second life lasts considerably longer than the first (one hundred years rather than only fifty), but it does so at a somewhat lower level in terms of quality (90 quality points rather than 100). We need to ask, is this drop in quality sufficiently offset by the gain in duration, so as to make the second life a better one than the first? So long as we appeal to the overall *quantity* of well-being, we will answer the question in the affirmative, since the total area of the second box is greater than that of the first (9,000 units versus 5,000).

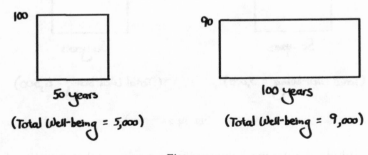

Fig. 14.3

Obviously enough, thinking in terms of the quantity of well-being—where quantity is defined as the product of quality and duration—is one way to take into account the importance of quality. But is it the right way? Does this approach give an *adequate* place to the quality of one's life?

It isn't clear that it does. Consider yet another choice between lives. In the first life shown in Figure 14.4, you live a nice long time, one hundred years. And you do so at an extremely high level, 150 quality points. Let's suppose that the best life lived on earth so far had a quality level of 125—so this really is an incredible life. And you get to live it for a hundred years! Now compare this with the second life shown. Here the quality of life is extremely unimpressive, a mere +1. Mind you, this is still a life worth having, since +1 is still a positive number. But a life like this is just barely worth having at any given moment. (Zero would be a life not worth having, though no worse than nonexistence; negative numbers would be lives worse than nothing.) Still, although the quality of life is extremely low, the life itself lasts a very, *very* long time—so long, in fact, that I can't draw it to scale. (That's why I've drawn the "..." in the middle of the lines.) Imagine that this life goes on for *30,000 years*.

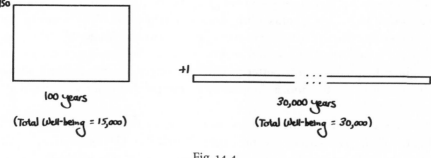

Fig. 14.4

Now ask yourself: which of these two lives would you prefer, the first or the second? Most of us, I think, would prefer the first life to the second. Admittedly, the second life is vastly longer than the first, but for all that, it's barely worth having at any given moment. In contrast, of course, the first life, though much shorter, is lived at a considerably higher level. Faced with this choice, I think, most of us would conclude that the extra duration of the second life is not sufficient to offset the tremendous drop in quality.

Notice, however, that if we are forced to choose between the two lives simply in terms of the quantity of well-being that each contains, we would actually have to say that it is the second life that is preferable to the first. After all, the area of the second box is twice that of the first one (30,000 versus 15,000); the second life contains twice as large a total amount of the good things in life. So what this shows, I suppose, is this. If you agree that it is actually the first life that is superior, despite having a smaller total *quantity* of well-being, then it turns out that quantity isn't really what it's all about. Put in slightly different terms, although quantity takes quality into account, it may not do this in the right way; it may not give quality *enough* weight.[2]

Here's a natural thought to have when comparing the two lives. Although the first life is shorter, it attains a kind of peak level of quality that simply isn't approached at any point in the second life. Perhaps, then, when evaluating lives and choosing between them, we can't just look for the quantity of good, we have to particularly look at the peaks, the heights. In thinking about a life, it's important to ask not just how much you packed in, in total, but what the *greatest* goods were that you gained or accomplished in that life. In short, perhaps quality can trump quantity.

There are various ways to work out a view like this. It might be, at a minimum, that quality needs to be given extra weight, so that it can sometimes—but not always—outweigh quantity. Alternatively, on a bolder version of this view, quality *always* outweighs quantity. That's not to say that quantity doesn't matter. Given a choice between a longer life where we achieve great things and a shorter life where we achieve great things, we might still agree that it is better to have the longer life. We can still admit that quantity matters too, as long as we recognize that quality is what matters the most.

An even more radical version of the theory would say that, actually, quality is *all* that matters. The peaks are all that should concern us. That, at any rate, is the position that gets expressed by Friedrich Holderlin in his poem "To the Parcae" (to the Fates):[3]

> A single summer grant me, great powers, and
> a single autumn for fully ripened song
> that, sated with the sweetness of my
> playing, my heart may more willingly die.
>
> The soul that, living, did not attain its divine
> right cannot repose in the nether world.
> But once what I am bent on, what is
> holy, my poetry, is accomplished:

Be welcome then, stillness of the shadows' world!
I shall be satisfied though my lyre will not
accompany me down there. Once I
lived like the gods, and more is not needed.

Holderlin is saying that he doesn't care about quantity at all. If he can accomplish something really significant, if he can ascend to the heights and do something great with his poetry, that's enough. Having once lived like the gods, more is not needed.

So, in thinking about what we want to do with our lives, it's not enough to ask *which* things are worth having in life. We also have to address this question of quality versus quantity. Is quality important only insofar as it gets folded into quantity—so that what really matters is actually quantity alone? Or does quality matter in its own right as something that's worth going for, even when it means a smaller *quantity* of what's worth having? And if quality does matter, does quantity matter as well? Or is quality, indeed, all that matters? Is Holderlin right when he says that having once lived like the gods, more is not needed?

I imagine that at least part of the reason that Holderlin is confident that "more is not needed" is because he is thinking about the lasting contribution that his poetry will make. Often enough, when we think we have accomplished something significant, we feel as though we have attained a certain kind of immortality. We will live on through our works. And so the next thing I want to turn to in thinking about strategies for living in the face of death is to ask whether this *kind* of immortality is worth going after. I emphasize the word "kind," of course, because strictly speaking, if you live on through your works—or through your children, and so forth—it's not as though you are literally living on. It's semi-immortality or quasi-immortality, at best. I suppose that people who don't believe in the value of this sort of thing would prefer to call it *pseudo*-immortality. (As Woody Allen says, "I don't want to be immortal through my work; I want to be immortal through not dying.")

It seems to me that these sorts of appeals to the value of "semi-immortality" take two broad forms. Sometimes people say that even though you are not literally living on, there is something very much like that going on, insofar as a *part* of you continues. If I have children, for example, then there is literally a part of myself that goes into my child. One of my cells continues in someone else. And if my children have children, then their cells continue in their children, and their children's cells continue in their children's children, and so on. If you think of an amoeba splitting and splitting, and splitting and splitting again, part of the original amoeba could be there for many, many, many generations. Some people take comfort in the thought that, literally speaking, a part of them will continue. Even if I never have children, at the very least my atoms will get recycled and used again. Ultimately, I get absorbed back into the universe; but I never completely disappear. Some people take comfort in that thought.

The German philosopher Schopenhauer thought that this should reduce somewhat the sting of death. He said, "But it will be asked, 'How is the permanence of mere dust, of crude matter, to be regarded as a continuance of our true inner nature?'" And he answers,

> Oh! Do you know this dust then? Do you know what it is and what it can do? Learn to know it before you despise it. This matter, now lying there as dust and ashes, will soon form into crystals when dissolved in water; it will shine as metal; it will then emit electric sparks. . . . It will, indeed, of its own accord, form itself into plant and animal; and from its mysterious womb it will develop that life, about the loss of which you in your narrowness of mind are so nervous and anxious.[4]

Well, that's a very stirring passage, but I have to say, I don't buy it. I don't find any comfort at all in the thought that my atoms will still be around getting reused in something else. So this first type of semi-immortality, where you take comfort in the thought that there are literally parts of you that will continue, this strikes me as a kind of desperate reaching for straws. "Oh, it's not so bad that I'm going to die soon. At least my atoms will still be around." If Schopenhauer thinks that, I think he's just deluding himself. At any rate, it doesn't work for me.

There's a second approach to semi-immortality, though, where it's not so much that you are supposed to be comforted by the thought that your *parts* will continue to last after you, but that your *accomplishments* will continue to last after you. Holderlin wrote poetry which we're still reading some two hundred years later. You can write a novel which can be read for twenty or fifty or one hundred or more years. You might make some contribution to math or philosophy or science, and fifty or one hundred years later, people could still be talking about that philosophical argument or that mathematical result.

And there are, of course, many other kinds of lasting accomplishments. You might, for example, help construct a building that will continue on after you. I've read interviews with stonecutters who take pride and comfort in the thought that long after they're gone, the buildings that they helped build will still be there. Or you might try to build a company that will continue after you die. Or, for that matter, you might take pleasure and comfort in the accomplishment of having raised a family. Here, the idea is not so much that some of your cells are in your offspring, but rather that to have raised another decent human being is a nontrivial accomplishment, something worth having done with your life. And that accomplishment continues after you're gone.

What should we think about this second type of semi-immortality? I have to confess, I am of two minds. Unlike the stuff about dust and atoms— where I think you just must be deluding yourself if you find it comforting to realize that your parts go on after you—I do find myself drawn to the thought that this second kind of semi-immortality does have genuine value. I find myself tempted by the thought that there's something valuable about producing something significant that continues for a while. Even if my life here on earth is a short one, if something that I've accomplished continues, my life is the better for it. That's Holderlin's thought, I suppose. And it's a view that appeals to me. I suppose it explains, in part, why I write philosophy—there's the hope that the things I write might still be read twenty years after I die, or fifty years, or, if I'm so lucky, one hundred years after I die.

So in certain moods, perhaps in most moods, I'm attracted to that thought. But in other moods, I've got to admit, I'm skeptical of it. I remind myself of Schopenhauer writing his little passage, his *Ode to Dust*, and I find myself saying that I am deluding myself, just like Schopenhauer did. Schopenhauer was so desperate that he deluded himself into thinking, "Oh, it doesn't matter that I'm about to turn into dust. Dust is really, really important." Similarly, then, I worry, perhaps I'm just deluding myself as well when I think that there's something grander, something significant, something valuable about having achieved something that will continue beyond me. In certain dark moods, at least, I find myself thinking that I am just deluding myself.

But that's only in certain moods. And at least most of the time I find myself in agreement with Holderlin. To be sure, I don't find myself agreeing with him that quantity doesn't matter at all. When Holderlin suggests that to have written one great work is all you need, so that writing further great works wouldn't add anything at all—that strikes me as going too far. Quantity

matters too. But he's right about this much: to have done something significant that abides, that really does seem to me to add to the value and significance of my life.

Let me quickly mention one final approach to facing death. I'm going
to give very, very short shrift to this last strategy, but it is certainly worth
mentioning as well. All of the strategies that we have considered so far
share an underlying belief: that life is or can be good, so that it makes sense
to try to have your life be as valuable as it possibly can be. Although the different strategies differ about the details, they all agree that since we can't do
anything about the loss of life, the right response is to make the life that we've
got as valuable as it can be—indeed, to recognize (and enhance) its value
while we've got it.

But there's a rather different approach one might adopt. That alternative approach says, yes, we're going to lose life and that seems horrible. But
it's only truly horrible if life is something that it is indeed bad to lose. After
all, if we were to decide that life wasn't really a valuable gift, something
worth embracing, something potentially full of value, then its loss wouldn't
actually be a *loss* at all. The idea here is actually closely related to a point
that we have seen before. According to the deprivation account, the central
badness of death lies in the fact that you are deprived of an additional period of life that would have been worth living. But this means, of course,
that if the pessimist is right and life *isn't* worth having, then its loss is not
a bad thing after all, but a good thing. The trick, then, isn't to make life as
valuable as it could be, but rather to come to recognize that on balance, life
isn't positive, but negative.

I know that what I'm about to say has a kind of *Classics Illustrated*
simplicity to it, and I am overgeneralizing horribly, but perhaps we could
say that the first basic outlook—according to which life is good, and so the
loss of life is bad and the answer is to make as much of life as we possibly
can while we've got it—this is, in broad strokes, the Western outlook. Similarly, if we are painting in very broad strokes, we can say that the second
basic outlook—according to which life isn't really as good as we normally
take it to be, and so the loss of life needn't be viewed as bad after all—this is
perhaps the Eastern outlook. No doubt it is an oversimplification to call
this *the* Eastern outlook, but at least it is a perspective that gets expressed
more frequently in Eastern thought than in Western thought.

A prominent example of this second outlook can be found in certain
strands of Buddhism. Buddhism teaches four "noble truths," and the first
noble truth is that life is suffering. Buddhists believe (or, at least, certain

Buddhists believe) that if you think hard about the underlying nature of life, you'll see that loss and suffering are *everywhere*.[5] There is suffering. There is disease. There is death. There is pain. To be sure, there are also things that we want, and if we're lucky we get them. But then we lose them—and that just adds to the suffering and the pain and the misery. On balance, then, life isn't good. Armed with this judgment, what Buddhists try to do is to free you from attachment to these goods, so that when you lose them, the loss is minimized. And indeed, Buddhists try to free you from what they take to be the illusion of there being a self at all. There is no *me* to lose anything.

Death is terrifying insofar as I worry about it being the dissolution of myself. But if there is no self, there's nothing to dissolve.

I want to say, I have tremendous respect for Buddhism. It all makes sense, given the assumption that life is suffering. But for better or for worse, I'm a child of the West. I'm a child of the book of Genesis—where God looks at the world and judges that it is good. For me, at least, a strategy of minimizing your loss by recognizing that life is negative is not one that I can accept. For me, then, and perhaps for most of us, the relevant choice is among the various more optimistic strategies that we have already discussed. We need to ask, how is it that we can make our lives most valuable? What is it that we can do that will allow us to say, with Holderlin, "Once we lived like the gods"?

CHAPTER 15

Suicide

The Rationality of Suicide

In the last chapter I asked how the fact of our mortality should affect the way we live. I considered various possible suggestions, but there is one possible reaction that we have not yet considered: suicide. Mortality opens the door to *ending* one's life.

Strictly speaking, I suppose, being mortal, per se, does not guarantee that suicide is an option. If we all lived exactly eighty years, for example, and could do nothing about it, we would still be mortal, but suicide would be impossible. Indeed, even if there was variability in how long we lived, as long as we could do nothing to *alter* the length of our life, suicide would remain impossible. So the possibility of suicide opens up only given the fact that we can *control* how long we live. But this is, in fact, one of the few things about death that we can indeed control: if I choose to, I can end my life earlier than it would otherwise end.

So the last question I want to explore about death is this: under what circumstances, if any, does suicide make sense? Under what circumstances, if any, is it an appropriate thing to do?

It is, of course, a fairly widespread feature of our culture that suicide is looked upon with such a mixture of disdain, fear, and disapproval that it's very hard to discuss the topic calmly and clearly. Most people think that you've got to be crazy to kill yourself. Indeed, the very fact that you are contemplating suicide is *evidence* that you're crazy. And if you're not crazy, then it shows that you're immoral. Suicide, they say, is never the morally right thing to do.

So it's easy to let our emotions get the better of us when thinking about this subject. Still, what I propose to do is to examine the issue systematically, carefully considering both sides of the question. And the very first thing to do, I think, in thinking about the topic of suicide, is to distinguish questions of rationality from questions of morality. I'm going to begin the discussion by focusing exclusively on the former, asking under what circumstances, if any, suicide would be the *rational* thing to do. Only later will we turn to questions about morality, asking when, if ever, suicide would be a morally legitimate or morally permissible thing to do.

In posing this distinction, I'm obviously presupposing that these questions can come apart, or at least that they need to be examined separately. There are questions about rationality, on the one hand, and questions of morality, on the other. To be sure, these are all questions about *oughts*, as we might put it. They're evaluative questions. But at least most people are inclined to think that we are drawing on different evaluative standards when we raise the one set of questions, as opposed to when we raise the other.

In many cases, no doubt, rationality and morality go hand in hand. And there are philosophical views about the nature of rationality and the nature of morality according to which they *always* go hand in hand. But many of us are inclined to think that in principle, at least, they can indeed come apart. Take, for example, the possibility of cheating on your income taxes. The rate at which income tax returns get audited is very, very low, and the fines tend to be fairly modest, even if you do get caught. So from the point of view of rational self-interest, at least, the decision to cheat might well be a reasonable one. (You're not likely to get caught, and even if you do, how bad is the fine anyway?) But even if we were to agree that it is rational to cheat, most of us would then immediately want to follow that remark up by pointing out that this doesn't at all mean that it's *morally* acceptable to cheat on your income tax. So perhaps that's a case where you are morally required to do something (pay your full taxes) that you are not rationally required to do.

Of course, it might be a mistake to construe rationality quite that narrowly—as though rationality were simply a matter of doing what is in one's rational self-interest and nothing more. Arguably, there can be reasons to perform a given act (or to refrain from performing a given act) that do not reduce to questions of what best benefits the agent. But that's a complicated philosophical question that we need not try to settle here.

Instead, let's simply stipulate, as we turn to the evaluation of suicide from the rational point of view, that we are going to restrict our attention to questions of rational self-interest, questions of what benefits or harms the person who is contemplating suicide. Even if there is more to rationality than simply doing what is best for oneself, it is plausible to think that normally, at least, considerations of self-interest are the most significant ones for determining the rationality of suicide. Accordingly, we can simplify our discussion by focusing on these considerations exclusively.

This means, however, that certain types of cases are simply going to be put aside. For example, we are not going to consider cases where your life is a valuable and satisfying one, but you kill yourself nonetheless so as to help promote a cause that you deeply support or to protect your friends or loved ones. Strictly, it seems to me, cases like this should also be counted as instances of suicide, albeit atypical ones; and a complete discussion of suicide would certainly need to consider such cases as well. But for simplicity I am going to put them aside, so as to focus on the more standard case where you kill yourself out of a concern for *yourself*—that is to say, because you feel that you would be better off dead. Restricting the discussion of the rationality of suicide to questions of rational self-interest may be simplifying somewhat, but doing this will allow us to focus on what I take to be the central and paradigmatic case.

So when, if ever, is suicide a rational decision to make? Here, too, the first thing I want to do is to distinguish between two different questions. The first question is going to be this: when, if ever, would it be true that you would be better off dead? Could it be the case that your life is going so badly that it would be better for you not to be alive at all? Suppose that the answer to the first question is that under such and such circumstances you would indeed be better off dead. That still leaves the second question: could it ever be rational for you to *trust* your judgment that this is one of those cases? Could it ever be rational for you to *act* on that judgment? Conceivably, the answer to this second question might be no. Indeed, even if it were *true* that you would be better off dead, perhaps it would never be rational to believe this and then act accordingly.

After all, it is conceivable that precisely in those circumstances in which life has gotten so horrible that you'd be better off dead, you can't think clearly. And the very fact that you can't think clearly would entail that you shouldn't trust your judgment that you are, in fact, in one of those cases. Whether that's a good argument or not is something we'll have to turn to later. But it's because of the possibility of an argument like that, that

I want to distinguish the first question (could it ever be true that you would be better off dead?) from the second (could it ever be reasonable for you to act on your judgment that you are actually in one of those situations?). We need to examine them separately. Unless both questions can be answered affirmatively, it doesn't seem likely that it is ever going to be rational to commit suicide.

The very first question we have to ask, then, is whether it could ever be true that you would be better off dead. And immediately, there's a kind of logical worry that may occur to you. It isn't obvious that judgments along the lines of "Jones would be better off dead" even make sense!

After all, it seems that in order to make comparisons of this sort ("he would be better off—or worse off—if such and such were to happen"), you've got to be able to talk about what condition or state the person is *already* in (or is going to be in) and what condition or state the person *would* be in (if the change occurred). You've got to be able to describe the two alternative conditions or states and compare them—otherwise the comparison doesn't even make sense. Call this the *two-state requirement*.

(Sometimes, of course, when we make comparisons, *neither* alternative is going to happen unless we first do something. But even here, it seems, we need to be able to compare the condition you would be in under the first alternative, with the condition you would be in under the second alternative. So the two-state requirement is relevant there, too.)

Normally, at any rate, when we make judgments about whether something would leave you better off or worse off, we satisfy the two-state requirement. Perhaps, for example, you're trying to decide whether or not to lose some weight. You think to yourself, "Here's how well off I am right now, being overweight, and that's how well off I would be later, if I were to lose the weight." You compare the two states and recognize that the second state is better than the first. That's what makes it *true* that you would be better off losing the weight. And something similar happens when you decide whether to marry your girlfriend, quit your job, divorce your spouse, or move to the country. You compare the two relevant states and see which is better. That's what allows us to say, "Yes, I'd be better off," or "No, I would be worse off." Indeed, it seems to be the very fact that there are two possible states to compare that makes it *true* that you would be better off or worse off, as the case may be.

But if I am contemplating suicide, and start talking about whether or not I would be better off dead, the two-state requirement doesn't seem to be met. So how can the judgment that I would be better off dead possibly make sense? Here I am now, in whatever particular condition I happen to be in (or will eventually be in), so we certainly can talk about *that* state. But if I try to describe the condition I would be in if I kill myself, something seems to go wrong. There is no such condition to describe at all. Nonexistence isn't a state I will be in after I am dead; it's not a condition. If death really is the end, if I really won't exist after I am dead, then there is no state or condition that I will be in afterwards to describe! So there simply doesn't seem to be a second state or condition of Shelly Kagan to *compare* to the first. And this means, of course, that the two-state requirement for making comparisons isn't met.

The thought, in effect, is this. States and conditions presuppose existence. We can ask: Are you happy? Are you sad? Are you bored? Are you excited? All of those things presuppose your existence. Even *sleeping* is a state or condition you can be in, because you exist while you are asleep. But if I kill myself, I won't exist. There is no second state to compare. So, how could we possibly say that I would be *better off* dead? For something like that to be true, there has to be a second state that we can compare to my actual state. And since there isn't one—or so the argument goes—the judgment that I would be better off dead can't even get off the ground. A comparison like that doesn't make any sense.

Various philosophers have been attracted to this line of argument. But it seems to me that it must be mistaken.

Consider the sort of thing we wanted to say when we were discussing the deprivation account: dying would be bad for most of us because it would deprive us of the good things in life that we would get, if only we didn't die then. That seemed like a natural thing to say. It seemed like an appropriate thing to say. But if we believe in the two-state requirement, then we need to object: how *could* we have said that? After all, to say that dying right now would be bad for me seems to come to the same thing as saying that I would be better off staying alive. And if we believe in the two-state requirement, then we need to say that this sort of judgment (that I am better off staying alive) only makes sense if there is some state I would be in were I to die that we can compare with the state that I would be in if I didn't die. But of course, nonexistence *isn't* a state, so the two-state requirement isn't met. So I *can't* say that I am better off staying alive. I can't say that death would be *bad* for me.

That should give one pause. It would, I suppose, be one thing if the only implication of accepting the two-state requirement were that we couldn't ever say that someone would be better off dead. Maybe we could accept that implication. But it turns out that the two-state requirement also has the implication that we can't even say that you are better off staying *alive*! And that's very, very hard to believe.

Imagine some incredibly happy person with a wonderful life filled with whatever goods you think are worth having in life—love and accomplishment and knowledge and whatever it is. She's walking across the street, and she's about to get hit by a truck. And so, at some risk to yourself, you leap into the street, pushing her out of the way and saving her life. Happily, you don't get hurt either. She looks up, realizes that she was this close to death, and she says, "Thank you. Thank you for saving my life."

And now what you have to say is, "I'm afraid you're rather confused. Because to thank me for saying your life is to presuppose I've benefited you in some way. To presuppose I've benefited you is to assume that it's a good thing that your life has continued, that you are better off staying alive! But, you see, given the two-state requirement, we can't say it's a good thing that your life continued, because the two-state requirement says we can make that kind of remark only when there is a state that you would have been in had I let you die. But had you died, you wouldn't have existed at all, and nonexistence is not a *condition* you would have been in. So you see, you are really rather philosophically confused in thinking that I've done you some sort of favor by saving your life."

I can't take that argument seriously. I hope you don't either. *Of course* you are doing someone a favor when you save their life, given the assumption that their life has been and would continue to be wonderful. So what does that show? Certainly not that nonexistence really is a kind of spooky, super thin state or condition after all. No, nonexistence is nonexistence. It's no kind of condition or state that I am in at all. What it shows, rather, is that the two-state requirement isn't a genuine requirement on these sorts of evaluations. When we point to the person whose life you have saved, and say that you did her a favor, that she's better off alive, we don't have to be claiming that had she died she would have been in some inferior state. We simply have to be claiming that the life she will have (thanks to your having saved her) is a great life. Since it is (and will continue to be) good, to have lost it would have been bad. Since losing it would have been bad, saving her life is benefiting her. It is doing her a favor. If the two-state requirement says otherwise, then it is the two-state requirement that has to go.

But having gotten rid of it, we can, in principle, say something similar in the opposite case. Imagine someone whose life is *horrible*, full of pain and suffering and misery. Whether there really could be such a person is a question that we'll turn to in a moment. But if there were such a person, then we can say that for their life to continue isn't good for them; it's bad for them. Their life is full of misery and suffering and frustration and disappointment. And the longer the life goes on like that, the worse it is. To live a life of one hundred years, where every moment is torture and pain, is worse than to live a life of thirty years where every moment is torture and pain. So if you had such a person, for their life to go on longer would be bad for them. In which case, of course, having a shorter life would be *better* for them.

And that's all we mean when we say they'd be better off dead. We're not claiming that there is some spooky super thin and hard-to-describe condition that they'd be in if they were dead. We are simply comparing the two different *lives* that they could have. Think again about the person with the wonderful life who you save. We compare the life with ninety wonderful years to the life she would have if it ended after a mere thirty years, and we immediately see that the first life is better. So saving her life is a good thing for her. Similarly, when thinking about someone with a miserable life, we compare the long life of misery with a shorter life of misery, and we see that the long life of misery is a worse life to have than the shorter life. That being the case, we simply say that he would be better off dead. It is not that, were he dead, he would be in some condition that is a good one, or a better one than being alive. It is simply that were he dead he would *avoid* this miserable condition, which is clearly a bad one. That's all it takes for it to be true that he would be better off dead. If the two-state requirement says otherwise, so much the worse for the two-state requirement.

Of course, this doesn't yet tell us whether it could, in fact, be the case that somebody's life is so bad that they'd be better off dead, whether a life could indeed be worse than not existing at all. All we've done so far is open the door to the possibility of saying that coherently. But that doesn't mean it's ever true. Whether there could be such lives depends on your view about the correct account of well-being, what makes someone's life worthwhile. And as we have seen, this is a controversial topic. People disagree about the ingredients of the best kind of life. Given these differences, we're going to get philosophical differences of opinion with regard to whether or not a life could be so bad that it would be better for it to come to an end.

Suppose, for example, that you accept hedonism, according to which the quality of life is a matter of adding up all the pleasure and subtracting all the pain. Since the question we are asking is whether it would be better for me to have my life end now, what we want to know is whether the life I would have from *here on out* (that is, if I don't die now) would be good on the whole, or bad. So we add up the total amount of pleasure I would have, and we add up the total amount of pain—taking intensity and duration into account for both calculations—subtract the pain from the pleasure, and look to see what the grand total is. If it's positive, your life is worth continuing. And the greater the positive number, the more your life is worth continuing.

If it's negative, though, if the life you would have from here on out would be filled with sufficient pain and suffering to outweigh whatever pleasures you would have, then your life is not worth continuing. If it has a negative balance, then that's a life that it is *bad* for you to have, and you would be better off not having it. You would be better off dead. That, at any rate, is the verdict of hedonism.

Of course, if we are not hedonists we'll accept a more complicated theory of well-being. So when doing the calculations we will need to take into account other things besides pleasure and pain. In evaluating what your life would be like from here on out, we will need to take into account not just what your mental states would be like, but also what your life would be like in terms of the various relevant *external* goods and bads. For example, will you continue to accomplish things with your life, or will you be frustrated and crippled, unable to achieve your significant aims? Will you continue to have friendships and other loving relationships, or will others neglect you, abuse you, or abandon you? Will you continue to learn and know about your place in the universe, or will your future life be one of ignorance and illusion? I won't try here to settle the exact list of external goods and bads. Whatever the list might be, we're going to want to somehow add up *all* the various goods and bads—internal *and* external—and see where the balance lies. If it is positive, if the goods will outweigh the bads from here on out, then your life is worth continuing—you are better off alive. But if the balance is negative, if the bad will outweigh the good, then your life is not worth continuing. You are better off dead.

It is important to notice, however, that all of our calculations so far have been concerned solely with determining the value of the *contents* of a life (from here on out). On some views, of course, that's enough. If you accept a neutral container theory—where life has no value in and of itself, and the only thing that matters is the contents of the life—then our calculations are complete once we have determined whether your life would contain more good than bad. But the requisite calculations will be more complicated still if you accept a valuable container theory, according to which the very fact that you are alive is a good thing, in and of itself. On a view like this, after we have calculated the value of the contents of the future life that you would have, we also have to add an appropriate additional (positive) amount, so as to reflect the additional value arising from the sheer fact that you would be alive. How much will we need to add? That will depend on the particular version of the valuable container theory. But the point, of course, is that even if the contents of your life would be negative overall from here on out, it might still be the case that you are better off alive, since the *grand* balance (once we have added the additional value of life per se) might still be positive. It is only if the overall balance—the value of the contents *plus* the value of life per se—is negative, that we can correctly say that you would be better off dead.

Can this happen? Can someone's grand balance be negative? According to those who accept modest container theories, it might. In principle, at least, the positive value of being alive could be outweighed if the contents would be bad enough. But according to those who accept fantastic container theories, it cannot. On views of this sort, the value of being alive is so tremendous that it doesn't matter *how* bad the contents get (from here on out)—the grand total will *always* be a positive one. Thus it will *never* be true that somebody could be better off dead. Pretty clearly, then, from the perspective of fantastic container theories, suicide will never be rational, because it is never true that it would be better for you to have a shorter life rather than a longer one.

Most of us, I imagine, find the fantastic container theory implausible; we believe in either the neutral container theory or a modest container theory. Either way, then, if the contents of a life are bad enough, this can result in the life having a negative value overall. And if the contents of the life you would have from here on out are sufficiently negative, then it might well be true that you would be better off dead.

Of course, at this point optimists will insist that in point of fact *no one's* life ever is so bad that they would indeed be better off dead. And pessimists will insist that *everyone's* life is bad enough that they would be better off dead. But I imagine that the commonsense view is that *neither* of these extremes is correct. *Some* lives are so full of suffering, inability, misery, and failure—or, at least, they will be—that these people would indeed be better off dead. But not all lives are like this. It depends on the facts of the individual case.

I share this moderate perspective. As far as I can see, it's just not true that everyone has a life that is and will continue to be worse than nothing.

But neither is it true that everyone has a life that is and will continue to be *better* than nothing. Horribly enough, there are cases where things are going to be so bad from here on out that this simply outweighs whatever value there might be in being alive per se.

We might, for example, imagine someone in the late stages of a debilitating (and eventually fatal) illness. Perhaps his cancer is causing him a great deal of pain—so much pain, in fact, that he really can't do much of anything other than suffer. It isn't as though he can work on his novel, or tend his garden, enjoy poetry, or even, for that matter, enjoy the company of other members of his family. He is just distracted by the pain, overcome by the pain, wishing the pain would come to an end. Or perhaps he has a degenerative disease which is progressively leaving him less and less capable of doing the things that give life value, less and less capable of taking care of himself in even the most basic of ways. (Indeed, the very realization that he is in that situation and no longer able to do much of anything may itself be a source of significant pain, misery, and frustration.)

Obviously, I wouldn't want to claim that lives like these become not worth living at the very onset of the disease, or as soon as the illness begins to take any kind of toll at all. And for that matter, I also don't want to claim that for every disease that will eventually prove fatal there must come a point at which you would be better off dead. But in at least some such cases, it seems to me, the patient does reach such a moment. Horribly enough, in some cases the future holds an ever worsening balance of pain, suffering, incapacity, and misery. So as your condition becomes worse and worse, you may well reach a point at which it is truly the case that you would be better off dead.

Taking this point as given—that in at least some cases, at some point, one would be better off dead—let me now try to say something a bit more precise about when suicide would make sense. Once again, I think it may be helpful to illustrate the main ideas with graphs that show how well-being varies over time. In Figure 15.1, as well as in the other graphs in this chapter, the X axis represents time, with later times shown further to the right. The Y axis represents how good or bad it is to be alive at a given time. (The higher up the Y axis, the better the life; the lower down the Y axis, the worse the life.) Points below the X axis are sufficiently bad that one would (if it continued like that) be better off dead. Note, incidentally, that the Y coordinate is intended to represent the *overall* value of the life; it represents not merely the value of the *contents* of the life, but rather the value of the contents plus the extra value, if any, that one gets from being alive per se. Thus, regardless of whether you accept a neutral container theory or a valuable container theory, the Y coordinate represents the overall bottom line: how good (or bad) it is to be alive at that time.[1]

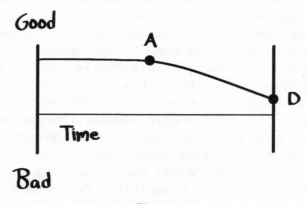

Fig. 15.1

Figure 15.1 is an example of what a life might look like. It's going along pretty well and then, starting at point A, things get worse. (Perhaps you get ill at point A, or your disease begins to show symptoms.) The quality of life begins to deteriorate. Point D, at the far right end of the line, represents the moment when you will die of natural causes. Thus, the line represents how your life will go. Or rather, somewhat more precisely, it represents how your life will go if you do not *kill yourself* somewhere along the way.

Our question, of course, is whether it would be *rational* to kill yourself, whether suicide would make sense in a case like this. And it is pretty clear that the answer is no. Admittedly, toward the end of the life, things are not as good as they were when you were young and healthy and vigorous, and had all sorts of opportunities and accomplishments. But still, up till the very end, the value of your life remains positive (it is always above the X axis). Things never become so bad that you would be better off dead. So suicide doesn't make any sense.

In particular, then, it would be a mistake to point to A and say that this is the moment when suicide first becomes reasonable since that marks the moment when things start to get worse. Yes, after point A the value of your life is lower, and eventually it is *significantly* lower, but it is never so bad that you would be better off dead. With a life like this, it always remains the case that more is better. So suicide wouldn't make any sense at all.

For suicide to make sense, it's got to be the case that your life takes *such* a dramatic turn for the worse that for some stretch of your life the line goes *below* the X axis. There has to be some period of your life where we can truly say that your life is *worse* than nonexistence. In short, for suicide to make sense there has to come a time when you would be better off dead! And we simply don't have that in Figure 15.1.

But we do in Figure 15.2. In Figure 15.2 you start out, again, healthy, vigorous, and successful. But you've got some degenerative disease (let's suppose) that is going to make things worse and worse for you. Once again, point A marks the moment when the overall value of your life begins to decline. But this time around, things get sufficiently bad so that, starting at point C, your existence is going to be worse than nothing. D again marks the point at which you will die from natural causes—your disease—unless you kill yourself first. And what we are struck by, in looking at Figure 15.2, is the realization that here there *is* a period in which it is true that you would be better off dead. From C to D you are *not* better off staying alive. Rather, you would be better off dying sooner rather than later.

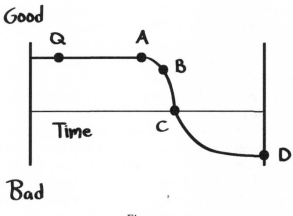

Fig. 15.2

In this case, then, it seems that we can reasonably broach the question of suicide. Here, it seems, it might well be rational to think about ending your life.

There is, however, a crucial qualification that must be made explicit. Suppose that there is some cure for your disease that is available, or at the very least there is a treatment that would significantly improve the quality of your life. Imagine that if only you were willing to be treated, the line would never dip below the X axis at all! And yet, foolishly, and without any good reason, you simply refuse to get the relevant treatment. In such a case, obviously enough, suicide is not a reasonable course of action. Even though it would be true, after point C, that you would be better off dead, nonetheless in a case like this what you have reason to do is to *improve* the quality of your life—not end it!

Accordingly, in discussing this case (and, for that matter, our other cases as well), we need to assume that there is *no* further suitable treatment available. We need to assume that you will indeed readily avail yourself of appropriate ways of improving the quality of your life. Thus the line shown cannot be improved upon. If it dips down, there is no reasonable course of action available to you that would make things better. The only way to avoid a life worse than nothing is to end it.

If this is the way we understand the example shown in Figure 15.2, then it does seem that suicide may well be a rational choice. From point C on, you would be better off dead. Suicide allows you to avoid that.

But at what point does suicide become a rational choice? Not at point A. Admittedly, from A on there is a downturn, and things begin to get worse. But life doesn't become worse than nonexistence until point C. And what this means, of course, is that there is a period of time *between* A and C—whether it is six months, a year, or five years—where even though it is true that life isn't as good as it had been earlier (before A), it remains better than nothing. So killing yourself at point A (let alone at any earlier moment) would be premature. It is throwing away a "chunk" of life that would still be worth having.

Instead, the relevant time for ending your life seems to be point C. That marks the precise moment when life becomes worse than nothing. Up until that moment, after all, your life was worth living; after that moment, it isn't. To be sure, for some initial stretch after C life won't be *very* much worse than nothing. Nonetheless, from C onward the overall value of your life is and remains negative: you are better off dead. So if you have complete control over when to kill yourself, it is clear that C would be the time to do it.

Suppose, however, that you *don't* have complete control. Imagine that your degenerative disease is going to progressively strip you of the ability to control your body, but your mind will be in perfect working order for a much longer time. So there may come a period of time in which you will be confined to your hospital bed, unable to take care of yourself, unable to even feed yourself. But even though you can't use your arms, you will still be able to listen to your family as they tell you the news; you will still be able to enjoy reading, or listening to music, or conversing with friends. During this time your life certainly might still be worth living—though we can imagine that the time is eventually going to come when your life *won't* be worth living. Suppose, however, that at that *later* point you will no longer have the ability to kill yourself, because you won't have the relevant ability to control your body.

As I am sure you can see, the question of suicide here turns into the question of euthanasia, mercy killing. Under what circumstances, we might ask, is it ever rational to ask someone to kill you? Under what circumstances, if ever, is it morally legitimate to kill somebody *else*?

But let's continue to focus on the case of suicide itself. Suppose you live in a society that is so unenlightened as to have ruled out euthanasia. In fact, you live in *our* society. And so you cannot plan on having someone end your life when the appropriate time comes. Your situation, rather, is this. You know that at a certain point in the future—C—it will be true of you that you would be better off dead. But once you are at that point, sadly, it will be too late: you won't have the ability to kill yourself, and nobody else will be able to do it for you. In a case like this, I think, killing yourself earlier than C might well make sense.

Consider point B. Suppose that B is the last moment at which you are still able to kill yourself. Should you do it? Admittedly, if you do, you will be throwing away some life that is worth living: the period between B and C. But if, as we are assuming, you will be unable to kill yourself *after* B, then it still might make sense, rationally, to do it *at* B. After all, you don't really have the choice of ending your life at C. Instead, your choice comes down to this: you can end your life at B, and thus throw away the *entire* last bit (B to D), or you can *not* end it then, and continue on until you die from the disease at D.

So the question you need to ask yourself is, what is the overall value of that last bit—from B to D? Obviously enough, it's got a good part (B to C) and a bad part (C to D). Is it better to have both the good part *and* the bad part, or is it better to have neither? And the answer, roughly, is that if the bad part is going to continue on *long* enough (and be bad enough), then it is better to have neither than to have both. The bad will outweigh the good. That is, in fact, what we have in the case as I have drawn it. So in this case, at least, the rational thing to do would be to decide to end your life at a point like B, while you still can, rather than to condemn yourself to the long final stretch of life not worth living.

But what if the last time that you are able to kill yourself is well *before* B? Indeed, what if it is way before A—all the way back at Q? Imagine that, for whatever reason, you have access to the means to kill yourself back at Q, but you won't have access later. Would suicide still make sense? Notice that your life is going to have tremendous value for a very long time after Q. Of course, as we also know, it will eventually have a bad period (C to D) as well. So here too you face a choice between having a good part and a bad part, or having neither. But this time the good part is significantly *greater* than the bad part. So even though it is true that unless you kill yourself at Q you are condemning yourself to the entire future that I've drawn, including the bad finish, nonetheless, killing yourself at Q simply doesn't make sense.

Here's a rather different way things might go. Suppose your life is going along really well, but then it is going to take a drastic turn for the worse. Eventually, however, it is going to get better. Would suicide make sense here? In Figure 15.3, life becomes worse than nothing for a while, but you *recover*; unless you kill yourself, you're going to return to a life that's worth having. Indeed, the final stage of your life is *well* worth having. Here, then, the crucial point to notice is that even though for a while your life will be worse than nothing, that doesn't actually suffice to establish that it ever makes sense to kill yourself. For if you do kill yourself—for example, at point A—although you avoid the bit below the X axis (A to B), doing this also throws away the large final part (B to D) where your life returns to being *better* than nothing. This has to be taken into account when deciding whether suicide makes sense.

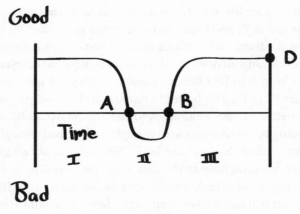

Fig. 15.3

Think of this life as potentially having three stages or three acts. In the first act (up to point A) life is clearly worth living, in the second act (A to B) it is worse than nothing, and in the third act (B to D) it is worth living once again. Ideally, you would like to have act one and act three without having to live through act two. But of course you don't have this choice. You must either take both act three *and* act two (along with act one) or do without either (and have act one alone). And given that the value of the positive third act is as great as it is, it makes sense to suffer through the negative second act in order to get it. So even though your life will be worse than nothing for some stretch, suicide wouldn't be a rational decision.

Note, however, that this argument makes essential use of the fact that the positive value of the third act is sufficiently great (it lasts long enough, and at a high enough level) that it outweighs the negative value of the second act. That is certainly true in Figure 15.3, but it is easy to imagine a variant of this graph where that isn't in fact the case.

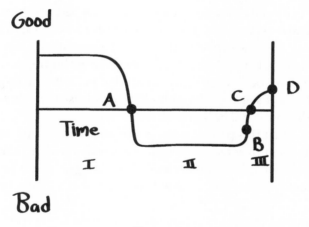

Fig. 15.4

In Figure 15.4, although you can still recover from the second act (where life is not worth living), and go on to have a third act (where life is once again worth having), nonetheless the positive value of act three *isn't* great enough to outweigh act two. There is indeed a recovery, but it is too short and at too low a level to outweigh the bad of the second act. Thus, if you are contemplating killing yourself at point A, this might well be a rational decision.

Of course, here too the rationality of suicide depends on *when* it can be done. Suicide at point A may well be rational—given that it allows you to completely avoid act two. But it is a different matter altogether if what is under consideration is suicide at point C. At C, obviously enough, the fact that you've gone through act two is now history. There's nothing you can do about it. To be sure, you've had an utterly horrible period of your life. But now it's *over.* Your question is not, should you avoid act two? It's too late for that. You are simply asking yourself what you should do about act *three.* Yet act three is worth living; throwing it away makes no sense. So suicide at point C wouldn't be rational, even though it *would* have been rational earlier, at point A. More complicatedly, suicide may well be rational even after A—*during* act two—provided that what *remains* of the second act is bad enough to outweigh the good of act three. Nonetheless, at a *late* enough stage of the second act—such as, for example, point B—suicide will *no longer* be rational, since what remains of act two won't be great enough to outweigh act three.

Consider an accident victim who suffers horrible burns over large parts of his body and has to go through a very long period of treatment, immobilized and in a great deal of pain, while his nerves and skin regenerate. Such a person might well believe that he will eventually recover and go on to have a life worth living. And yet, for all that, during his treatment he might also believe—and believe correctly—that what he will have to go through to reach that final stage will be so horrible that it isn't worth it. He might well insist that he would be better off dead.

Imagine that this patient is physically unable to kill himself. He asks others to do it, but they refuse. So he undergoes years of incredibly painful medical treatment and eventually reaches the stage at which he has recovered sufficiently so that he can now have a life worth living. Finally, he is released.

This person might well acknowledge that his life is now once again worth living. And since it is worth living, suicide—now that he is physically able to do it—*no longer* makes sense. And yet, for all that, he might still insist—and insist correctly—that it would have been better for him to have died *earlier,* before being forced to undergo the years of pain and suffering. Had he been able to kill himself earlier, it would have been rational for him to do that.[2]

So there are cases, I think, where suicide may well make sense, rationally speaking. At least, it makes sense given our assumption that you are thinking clearly, and able to objectively assess your situation, so that you can correctly appraise the future that continued life holds out for you. I do, however, want to emphasize a point I made earlier—that suicide *only* makes sense from the standpoint of rational self-interest if at some point your life will be sufficiently bad that you *would* in fact be better off dead. For I have no doubt at all that in many actual cases of suicide, this crucial condition is not, in fact, met.

The point to remember is this: even if your situation deteriorates—and, indeed, even if your situation will never improve—that still doesn't make suicide rational. The question is not are you worse off than you were before, nor is it are you worse off than you might have been. The question is, rather, will you be *so* badly off that you are better off dead? And the truth of the matter is, if the earlier part of your life is sufficiently good then there is a great deal of room for things to get worse, while still ending up at a level that is better than nothing. In such a case, suicide is not rational at all.

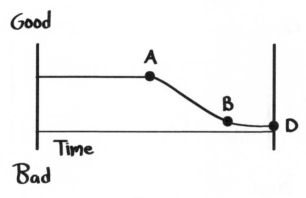

Fig. 15.5

In Figure 15.5, for example, suicide simply does not make sense. Even though the life you will have after point A is worse than the life you had before—and even though the life you will have after point B is *significantly* worse than the life you had before—at no point does the line ever dip below the X axis. By hypothesis, this is still a life worth living. Suicide is unjustified.

It is easy to lose sight of this point. After all, from A on you are sliding further and further down. Sometimes all that you can *see* is the fact that your life is getting worse and worse. So it is natural to find yourself thinking, "I am better off dead." But in Figure 15.5, at least, that's a mistake. You *aren't* better off dead.

Many cases of suicide, I am sure, find their origin in a mistake of this sort. Your girlfriend has left you. You've lost your job. You didn't get into law school. You've been in an accident and will have to spend the rest of your life in a wheelchair. You've been through an ugly divorce. So you compare your life to the way it was, or to the way you dreamed it would be, or to the way that others around you are living, and you conclude that your life is not worth having. But frequently enough, that's just not the case. Even though your life is *less* worth living than you had hoped it would be, it is still better than nothing.

Indeed, I imagine that for many people contemplating suicide, a more accurate graph might look like Figure 15.6. Things take a temporary turn for the worse—and from down in the middle of the dip you just don't see that if you can just hold on, things will eventually get better. In cases like this, obviously enough, suicide would be a horrible mistake.

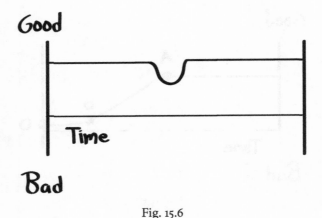

Fig. 15.6

Nonetheless, it does seem to me that there are cases in which the line really does cut below the X axis and remains there for a sufficiently long time (perhaps staying there until the very end), so that it really is true that the person would be better off dead. It is terrible that such cases ever arise, but given that they do, it seems to me plausible to say that if only the person could recognize the facts and know for a certainty that this is what their life would be like, suicide would, at certain times, be rational.

Of course, I have been deliberately bracketing the question of whether you could ever reasonably judge that you *are* in this situation. Someone who believes that suicide is never rationally justified might well agree that suicide *would* be reasonable if you *could* know you would be better off dying now, but in fact you never *can* know this. Perhaps suicide would be rational in certain cases if you had a crystal ball. But you don't, and you never will.

It is, after all, easy enough for me to draw my various lines and confidently assert that given what the future holds in this case or that case, suicide makes sense. But in real life we never have the guarantee that this is, in fact, the way things are going to go. So the question we need to turn to next is whether it could ever be rational for you to judge that your own situation is one in which you would be better off dead, and whether it could ever be rational for you to *act* on that judgment.

It will probably be helpful to think about this question in two stages. First, let's ask what we should say if you were thinking clearly. After that we can take into account the possibility that your thinking may be clouded. After all, it is reasonable to worry that in the type of cases where suicide might otherwise be rationally warranted, it is going to be so stressful that nobody in those circumstances can think clearly. And so, even if it were true that you might reasonably decide to commit suicide if only you were thinking clearly, perhaps nobody ever does think clearly in those situations, and so no one should trust their own judgment that they would be better off dead.

We can come back to that worry about cloudy thinking in a moment. First, though, let's suppose that you can think clearly about your situation. Perhaps you've got some sort of painful disease, but the disease is not painful constantly. There are periods in which the pain comes to an end, brief periods in which you're able to assess your situation and weigh up the facts. Could it ever be rational in a situation like that to decide to kill yourself? Perhaps we would agree that if you had a crystal ball, and knew for a certainty that you would never recover, it would be rational to commit suicide. But as I have already noted, you *don't* have a crystal ball. What should we say in light of that fact?

Those who deny the rationality of suicide might insist that since you never know for sure that you won't recover, suicide never makes sense. After all, we all know that medicine is constantly making advances. Researchers are always making breakthroughs. What seems like an incurable disease one day may have some sort of cure the next. But if you kill yourself, you throw away any chance of getting that cure. What's more, diseases sometimes simply have miraculous remissions. You might just get better spontaneously. That's always a possibility, too. It doesn't happen very often, but it does happen now and then. And so, here too, if you've killed yourself, you've thrown away any chance of recovery.

Some will argue that given that there's a *chance*, however small, of recovery—whether through medical progress or just some sort of medical miracle—suicide simply doesn't make any sense. It's not a rational choice. But I think that this position has got to be mistaken.

It is, of course, true that we don't have a crystal ball, and so in deciding whether to kill yourself, what you are doing is playing the odds. You are gambling. But gambling in this sense is something we do all the time. Indeed, there is no getting away from the need to take chances. The necessity of making decisions in the face of uncertainty is simply one of the facts of life. And if somebody suggests that given this uncertainty it never makes sense to throw away the small chance of recovery, then I can only answer that this position doesn't seem to accord with the principles that we would *normally* use in deciding how to make a decision.

Imagine you are in a kind of twisted game show. You are in a room with two doors. And you have to decide which one to go through. Suppose that if you go through door number one it is virtually guaranteed that what will happen is that you will be kidnapped, and your kidnappers will then torture you for a week, after which you will be released. As I say, it is virtually certain that this is what will happen: it is 90% certain, 99% certain, perhaps 99.9% certain.

There is, however, a *small* chance that you won't be kidnapped and tortured. Instead, you might be whisked away to a wonderful tropical vacation, where you will have a fantastic time for a week and then be sent home. Admittedly, it's not very likely, but it isn't *impossible*. Perhaps the chances are 1 in 1,000. Or 1 in 10,000. Maybe less.

So if you go through door number one, you have a 99.9% chance or a 99.99% chance of being tortured for a week, and a 0.1% or a 0.01% chance of having a wonderful vacation.

On the other hand, if you go through door number two, it is 100% guaranteed that the following is going to happen: you will immediately fall asleep, and you will remain in a deep, dreamless state for the entire week, at which point you'll wake up.

What should you do? Which door should you pick? Notice that this choice isn't quite the same as simply choosing between being tortured and sleeping. For if you choose the first door, you can't quite be *certain* that you will be tortured. I suppose we would all agree that if we had to choose between the certainty of being tortured and the certainty of sleeping, the rational thing to do would be to choose the second door, and fall asleep. Dreamless sleep has no intrinsic value in and of itself, but on the other hand there is nothing particularly negative about it either. I suppose that if we were going to slap a number on it, we would give it a zero. But torture is clearly a negative. And a week of torture is obviously a *very* large negative. So if it was a choice between the certainty of torture and the certainty of sleep, we would all agree that you should pick dreamless sleep for a week. Given certainty, the rational choice is the second door.

But of course, it isn't *certain* that you will be tortured if you go through the first door. It is just very, very likely. So imagine someone saying that in light of this uncertainty the rational choice is actually to choose the first door. "Go for the gold!" they insist. "Sure, it is overwhelmingly likely that you will end up being tortured if you pick the first door. But there is, after all, a very small chance that you will get a wonderful vacation! In contrast, if you pick door number two, you are throwing that chance away. Because of this, the only rational decision is to pick the first door—holding out for the chance, no matter how small, of getting that fantastic vacation. No other decision would be rational."

If anybody were to say that, I'd laugh at them. Admittedly, if you tweak the case, the rational choice might depend on the details. (What if the "torture" is actually no more severe than a bad paper cut? What if the odds of winning the vacation are actually somewhat higher than 1 in 1,000?) But in the case as I have described it, there is an overwhelming likelihood of genuine torture and only a desperately small chance of winning the vacation. And if anyone were to say of *that* choice that the *only* rational decision is to hold out for the chance of the vacation, I would have to say that they are simply mistaken. You are not rationally *required* to disregard the odds and pick the first door.

Am I cheating in spelling out the example this way? I am hoping that you will agree with me that suicide may be a rational choice if the chance of recovery is small enough (and what you face otherwise is bad enough). Just as it may be rational to choose sleep so as to avoid torture—even though this throws away any chance of a vacation—it may be rational to choose death so as to avoid a life of pain and suffering, even though this throws away your only chance of recovering a life worth living. But perhaps the analogy is a flawed one. After all, I deliberately framed the example in terms of a choice between being tortured for a week and being asleep for a week. But death doesn't merely last a week; death is forever. If you kill yourself, you throw away the *only* chance you will ever have of having a life worth living. In contrast, if you refuse to go through the first door, you only throw away the chance of going on vacation *this week*! There will be other chances in the future.

So let's change the example. Suppose that instead of everything lasting only a week, each outcome—sleep, torture, or vacation—will last the
rest of your life! Thus if you go through the first door there is a 99% or a
99.9% chance that you will be tortured for years, perhaps decades, until
you die. And there is a 1% or 0.1% chance that you will be whisked away
to a wonderful vacation that will also last for years or decades, until you
die. But if you go through the second door, you will immediately fall into
a deep, dreamless sleep, from which you will never awaken. You will stay
in that dreamless sleep until you die of natural causes, years or decades
later.

Now imagine that someone comes along and insists that the only
rational decision to make in this case is to go through the first door. After
all, they point out, if you choose the second door, you are throwing away
the *only* chance you will ever have of gaining the wonderful experiences
you would have if you win the vacation. In light of this, they insist, the only
rational decision is to choose the first door, despite the fact that you will
probably end up being tortured for the rest of your life.

That still seems to me to be wrong. Even when I think about the
modified example, where you are throwing away your only chance of ever
getting the vacation, it still seems to me that choosing the second door is a
perfectly rational choice. It is, after all, *overwhelmingly* likely that if you
choose the first door you will end up being tortured for the rest of your life.
And we are assuming that this is genuine torture we are talking about: the
pain and suffering will be great enough that it will indeed be the case that
you would be better off dead, rather than having it continue. But continue
it will, for months, years, or decades. Given all of this, it seems to me clear
that it might well be rational to prefer the dreamless sleep—even though
this throws away the only chance you will ever have for the vacation. If the
torture is great enough, and the chance of winning the vacation slight
enough, choosing the second door may well be a rational choice. It just isn't
right to say that the *only* rational choice is door number one.

Mind you, I am not claiming that one *must* choose the second door.
While I have some sympathy for this position, that's a bolder view than the
one I am trying to defend here. All I am saying is that choosing the second
door is a perfectly reasonable decision. It is rationally *acceptable*. If anyone
says otherwise, it seems to me that they are wrong.

Similarly, then, when it comes to choosing suicide, if the life you
would otherwise have is overwhelmingly likely to be one that is not worth
living, suicide may well be a rationally acceptable choice as well. To be sure,

if you do kill yourself, you throw away forever any chance of recovery. That's an important point, one worth thinking about. But it is also important to think realistically about the *likelihood* of recovery, and just how *badly off* you will be if your life continues in the way that it most likely will. In short, it seems to me that there are cases in which suicide would be a rational choice—or at least, it would be rational *given* the assumption that you are able to think clearly about your situation.

But that still leaves us with the question, *can* one really think clearly about these issues if one is in the middle of the sort of situation that we have been talking about? Even if we grant, for the sake of argument, that there could be cases in which a person's life is so bad that unless they recover dramatically and unexpectedly they would be better off dead, and even if we grant that if only they could think clearly about their situation, suicide would be a rational or reasonable choice—still, isn't it plausible to think that in real life, people just *can't* think objectively and reliably about their situation, precisely when they are *in* situations like that?

Look, it is one thing for me to be writing calmly about these issues as I sit in my office, healthy and comfortable, with a life very much worth living. Similarly, I certainly hope that you too have a life worth living, so that you too are able to consider these questions in a calm, clear-headed, and objective fashion. But things are going to be quite different for anyone who actually must face these questions as something more than philosophically interesting possibilities! Think about it. What would have to be true of you for your life to be so bad that suicide might be a rational choice, so bad that you would be better off dead? The odds are that you would have to be in a tremendous amount of physical pain, a great deal of physical pain. Beyond that, it would probably also have to be the case that you were incapacitated in a large number of ways. You would probably have to be bedridden, unable to accomplish anything, unable to read novels, unable to enjoy discussions with your friends, unable even to enjoy television. (A life watching television may not be as fantastic as the life that *you* are able to have, but it still might be better than nothing.)

To imagine a life this bad, we have to imagine a life with so much pain and physical disability that the amount of emotional distress is simply going to be overwhelming. But precisely because it would be overwhelming, we have to ask: how could anybody think *clearly* in a situation like that? Yet if you can't think clearly, how can you rationally *trust* any judgment you might make that you are in fact in a situation where suicide is indeed a reasonable choice?

To be sure, you might *believe* that you would be better off dead. But should you trust your own opinion on the matter? Probably not! The odds are, after all, that your own thinking on the subject is clouded by your pain, suffering, and emotional distress! Indeed—the argument goes—anyone for whom it is *true* that they would be better off dead would have to be in so much pain and distress that they simply wouldn't be able to think clearly about their own situation. But if they aren't able to think clearly, their judgment on the matter isn't trustworthy. And if their judgment isn't trustworthy, they shouldn't trust it! And so, it seems, suicide could never turn out to be a rational decision after all.

That's certainly an interesting argument; it's an argument worth taking seriously. For it does seem as though we should be more skeptical about decisions made when we are in a lot of pain or under a great deal of stress. But even here, I'm not convinced. To evaluate this line of thought properly we need to ask, is it *always* unreasonable to trust the decisions you make when your thinking is potentially clouded by pain and stress?

Suppose you've got some medical condition that causes you a great deal of pain and has severely limited your physical abilities. But as it happens, there is a surgical procedure that can be done, and the surgical procedure is almost always successful—leaving the patient pain free and able to return to their previous life. It is almost always successful, but not always.

What are your choices? One option is to have the surgery. Surgery almost always works. In 99% of the cases, 99.9%, 99.99% of the cases, it works. Of course, like all surgery, there are risks. Sometimes, after one puts this sort of patient under general anesthesia, the patient doesn't wake up. It doesn't happen very often, maybe once every 1,000 operations, or once every 10,000 or 100,000 operations. Still, there is some chance the surgery won't work, some chance that you will die on the operating table. But it is a very, very small chance. It is overwhelmingly likely that the surgery will succeed. And if it does succeed, your recovery will be complete. That's option number one.

Your second option, of course, is to refuse the surgery and continue in your current state, suffering and incapacitated, unable to lead a rewarding life. That, at any rate, is the most likely outcome of refusing surgery. But sometimes—not often, but sometimes—the condition clears up spontaneously, even without surgery. This is, of course, extremely rare. Perhaps one patient in 1,000 has the condition clear up on its own, or one in 10,000. But in 999 out of 1,000 cases or 9,999 out of 10,000 cases, if surgery is refused the condition just continues without improvement until the patient dies some years down the road.

So there's your choice: should you have surgery or not? And I imagine that what we all think is that *of course* you should have the surgery. You'd be a fool not to have the surgery. It is, after all, overwhelmingly likely that it will cure you! So let us suppose that this is, indeed, the decision that you reach.

But now we worry. Wait a minute. Can you *trust* that judgment? The condition you are in is so stressful, and so painful, that you are obviously very emotionally worked up. Any judgment that you make—that it's reasonable to have this surgery—is a judgment that you're making while under a cloud of pain and emotional distress. How could you possibly trust that judgment? And so, someone might argue, you *shouldn't* trust the judgment. It would never be rational to agree to the surgery in this situation.

But that can't be right. Surely we agree that it *could* be reasonable to trust your judgment in this situation. Now, to be sure, the fact that you are in all of this pain should make you pause, it should make you hesitate, it should make you think twice, and then think again, before deciding what to do. But still, if somebody says that since you are so worked up, it could *never* be rational to decide to have the surgery—that just seems to be going too far. After all, you've got to make *some* kind of decision. You can decide to have the surgery or you can decide not to have the surgery, but either way you are making a decision. And *either* decision is one that you will have to make while worked up, stressed, and under the cloud of pain and suffering. There's no getting around *that*. So think twice. Think a third time. Seek out the opinions of others. All of that seems appropriate. But if somebody says it could *never* be rational to decide to have the surgery and then to act on that decision, they're just wrong.

Return, then, to the case of suicide. It seems to me that in the relevant respects this is (or can be) similar to the example we were just discussing. On the one hand, if you decide *not* to commit suicide, it might be overwhelmingly likely that you will continue to suffer. And while there may be some slight chance that if you don't kill yourself you will eventually recover a life worth living, it can be far, far more likely your suffering will simply continue or even grow worse. On the other hand, if you do kill yourself your suffering will come to an end. Obviously, that's not nearly as good as actually having a *cure* for your condition—and in this regard, perhaps, the analogy to surgery isn't perfect—but still: if your condition is so bad that you are better off dead, and the chance of recovery is vanishingly small, then it might well be rational to decide to kill yourself. And if someone insists that since you are suffering so greatly your judgment must be cloudy, and so you should not trust your own judgment about the matter, I can only reply that this can't be a good argument. If it wasn't a good argument in the surgery case—and it wasn't—then I can't see how it could suddenly become a good argument in the suicide case.

What does seem right, rather, is that *precisely* because you're working and deciding under the cloud of emotional stress and pain, you should think twice, and think a third time, and perhaps think yet again. The decision to kill yourself should not be made in haste. You should discuss it with your doctors. You should discuss it with your loved ones. But if somebody insists that you could *never* reasonably trust the judgment that you make while in these circumstances, I can only say that this doesn't seem like a sound piece of advice. That claim doesn't seem right to me.

I conclude, accordingly, that as long as we're focused on the question of the *rationality* of suicide, suicide is sometimes justified. More precisely, suicide can be rationally justified under certain circumstances if we are evaluating suicide from the perspective of rational self-interest. You could have a life that is worse than nothing. You could have good reason to believe you are in that situation. And you might be able to assess your situation calmly and objectively. Alternatively, even if pain and stress inevitably cloud your thinking and leave you worried and uncertain, you might nonetheless still find the odds in favor of suicide sufficiently strong so as to eventually make it reasonable to trust your judgment on the matter. In principle, then, suicide can be a rational choice.

The Morality of Suicide

But for all that, of course, suicide could still be *immoral*. There could be actions that are rationally permissible but, for all that, morally forbidden. Perhaps suicide is one of them.

Of course, as I mentioned earlier, there is a huge debate in philosophy as to whether or not these two notions—morality and rationality—can really come apart. Arguably, reason actually *requires* you to obey morality—so that even if something is in your self-interest, if it is genuinely immoral perhaps it's not really rational to do it after all. That is, obviously, a fascinating and important question. But it is a question for a different book, so I simply want to put it aside. Let's bracket the philosophical debate con-

cerning the precise connection between rationality and morality, and simply focus directly on the moral issue itself: what should we say about the
morality of suicide?

To do justice to this question, of course, we would really need to work
out an entire theory of morality, and unsurprisingly I am not going to try
to do that here. But I do think I can say enough to put in place some basic
elements of a plausible moral theory. We won't have time to explore these
ideas in detail, but at least we'll get the outlines of a basic moral theory and
see what it might say about suicide.

First, however, I want to consider two quick arguments against suicide that have a somewhat moral tinge to them. Actually, the first argument
isn't so much a moral argument as a theological argument. For the most
part, of course, I have tried to avoid directly discussing theological matters
(although many of the topics I have discussed are of more than passing interest from a religious point of view), but in thinking about suicide it is almost impossible to avoid bringing in God at some point, given the prevalence
of the thought that it is God's will that we stay alive and so it would be going against God's will to kill oneself. At any rate, that's the first quick argument that I want to examine: that suicide is wrong because it goes against
God's will.

I think that the best response to this line of thought was given by
David Hume more than two centuries ago.[3] Hume points out that if all we
have to go on is simply the idea of a Creator who has built us and given us
life, then we can't infer that suicide is against God's will. At the very least, if
you have found the thought that killing yourself goes against God's will a
compelling one, then why wouldn't you also find it compelling to say that it
goes against God's will when you *save* somebody's life? Perhaps God intended for them to die!

There you are, walking along Main Street, and you see that the woman
you are talking to is about to be hit by a truck. So you push her out of the
way. Previously, when we considered an example like this, the question
was whether she should be grateful to you. This time, though, the question
is whether she should *object.* "How dare you do that!" she exclaims, "You
have thwarted God's will. It was God's will that I be hit by that truck."

When we're about to save somebody's life, should we decide not to do
that on the grounds that it must be God's will that they die? If you are a
doctor and somebody is in cardiac arrest and you could now perform CPR
in order to get their heart going again, should you say, "Oh no, I must not
do that. It is God's will that they die. If I try to save their life, I'm thwarting

God's will." Nobody says that. But then, why is the argument any better in the case of suicide?

When you save your friend from being killed by the truck, and she says, "Oh, you thwarted God's will," perhaps you should come back and reply, "Oh, no, no. You see, it was God's will that I *save* your life. Yes, it was God's will that you be in the situation where the truck was going to hit you unless I saved you. But it was also God's will that I save your life." Maybe the doctor should say something similar: "It was God's will that I *respond* to this situation by acting as I did and *altering* it." That's not an obviously implausible thing to say. But if it's *not* an implausible thing to say, why not say the same sort of thing about suicide? Perhaps it is God's will that I respond to my situation by killing myself. Absent any special instruction manual from God, the appeal to God's will doesn't give us any real guidance. We don't know whether it is God's will that we act or God's will that we don't act. So you can't just insist that suicide is obviously wrong, because it violates God's will.

Unless, of course, you've got a divine instruction manual. You might think, for example, that the Bible tells us not to commit suicide, and that since the Bible is God's word we must do whatever the Bible tells us. That would be a much longer argument, one that in principle I'm perfectly prepared to consider, though I don't have the space to do that properly here. For present purposes I will simply have to content myself with pointing out that there are a lot of assumptions made by that argument that we would need to examine with care. Beyond some assumptions that it shares with the initial attempt to appeal to God's will (for example, that there is a God, and that we have moral reason to obey God's will), there is the crucial assumption that God has revealed his will in a book, and that the relevant book is the Bible.

A lot of people do claim, of course, that the Bible is indeed God's instruction manual, and they say that we should be guided by it. But often enough the only real commitment here is to pick and choose among the instructions that they like anyway, throwing away the rest. Even if there is a sentence in this instruction manual that says not to commit suicide (a controversial question in its own right), there are a lot of other things the instruction manual also says that most of us are *not* inclined to listen to. The instruction manual says not to eat pork. But most people are perfectly happy to eat pork. The instruction manual tells you not to mix various kinds of material together in a single item of clothing. But few people find that unacceptable. The instruction manual tells you that a teenager who is rude to his parents should be stoned to death. But few of us think that that's a genuine moral requirement.[4] If you are going to pick and choose which bits of the instruction manual you actually think are morally relevant, then you can't come to me and say that suicide is wrong because the instruction manual says so. You're not really using the instruction manual to give you moral guidance. Instead, you are just starting with the moral beliefs you already accept and then picking and choosing among the various bits of the instruction manual to see which ones you're prepared to endorse. And that means that you aren't really using the appeal to God's will to help you decide whether suicide is morally legitimate or not.

Obviously, there is a great deal more to say about this topic, but for present purposes that will have to do. Instead of considering the appeal to God's will further, there is a second quick argument against suicide that I want to consider as well. Like the first, this new argument can also be run in theological garb, although it need not be presented in that way. This second argument turns on an appeal to the idea of gratitude. It begins by pointing out that we have been given life, and life is a pretty wonderful thing. But that means (it continues) that we owe a debt of gratitude, a debt we discharge by keeping the gift that we have been given. Thus, we have an obligation to stay alive: suicide is immoral.

Now gratitude is not a moral virtue that gets a lot of discussion nowadays. It's fallen on rather hard times. But I see no reason to dismiss it. It does seem to me there is such a thing as a debt of gratitude. If someone does you a favor, you owe them something; you owe them a debt of gratitude.

We might disagree about who or what it is that we should be grateful to. Perhaps it is God who gave us life, or our parents, or maybe we should just say that it is nature. Whatever or whoever it was, isn't it true that we owe a debt of gratitude for this wonderful gift? And as such, how do you repay the debt? You repay the debt by *keeping* the gift. If you kill yourself, you're rejecting the gift. That's being ungrateful, and ingratitude is immoral, it's wrong. So that's why suicide is wrong: it is failing to show proper gratitude for the gift of life.

That's the second quick argument against suicide, and perhaps it won't surprise you to learn that I don't find this second argument persuasive either. Not because I'm skeptical about debts of gratitude, but rather because we need to pay attention to what exactly obligations of gratitude come to.

The first point to consider, I suppose, is that it isn't clear whether one can owe a debt of gratitude to anyone other than a person. If we say that it is *nature* to whom we should be grateful, then it isn't obvious whether we can indeed owe a debt of gratitude in this case, since nature is not in fact a person. But we can let this point pass and assume that either debts of gratitude can be owed to nonpersons, or else that it is God or our parents to whom we owe the debt. The more important point to bear in mind, I think, is this: you owe a person (say) a debt of gratitude for giving you something only when what they give you is, indeed, a *gift*.

Imagine that somebody gives you a pie and says, "Eat it!" But it's not an apple pie. It's not a cherry pie. It's some gross, disgusting, rotting *slime* pie—and he cuts out a big piece and he says, "Eat it!" Do you owe this person a debt of gratitude? Do you have an obligation to this person—by virtue of that very bestowal of pie—to eat it, or continue eating it? That would seem like a rather odd thing to claim. After all, if he is giving you a slice of rotting slime pie and commanding you to eat it, he is nothing more than a bully!

Now of course, typical bullies, at least the ones in the movies, are big and strong. The bully might say the following to you, "You eat this pie or I will beat you up. I'll beat the crap out of you." And maybe you aren't particularly strong yourself. He might well be able to do it. You might well *know* that he'll do it. So it might be *prudent* for you to eat the slime pie, disgusting and appalling as it may be. It might be better to eat a couple of slices of slime pie than to be beaten to a pulp. But there's no moral *obligation* here. There's no *moral* requirement to eat the pie.

Suppose that God takes on the role of bully and says, "Eat the pie or I'll send you to hell." It would probably be prudent of you to do what he says. Similarly, of course, if God takes on the role of bully and says, "Even though your life has become so horrible that you'd be better off dead, I insist that you keep living; I'll send you to hell forever if you kill yourself," maybe it's prudent of you not to kill yourself. But there's no *moral* requirement here. God's just a bully in this story.

That's not to say that I think God *is* a bully. If you believe, plausibly enough, that God is good, then God is not going to want you to continue eating the pie once it has spoiled. He gives you an apple pie. He says, "Eat it. It's good for you. You'll like it." Out of gratitude, you eat it. But then God, not being a bully, also says, "If the pie ever spoils, you can stop eating." If God's not a bully, why in the world would he insist that we continue to eat a spoiled pie? So I can't see how any argument against suicide based on an appeal to gratitude is going to get off the ground.

The bottom line is this. If there is indeed something immoral about suicide, we're not going to establish that fact by means of the two quick arguments we have just been examining. We're going to have to turn to a more systematic appeal to moral theory. So, holding off on the particular topic of suicide for the moment, let's ask ourselves more generally, what is it exactly that makes an action morally acceptable or morally forbidden?

This is, unsurprisingly, something that different moral theories disagree about. But there is at least one idea that all, or almost all, moral theories share, and that is the idea that the consequences of your action matter. Of course, we might or might not think that the consequences are the *only* thing that matters for determining the morality of a given action, but surely it is *one* thing that matters. It is always morally relevant to ask what the consequences of your action are going to be. So let's think about the morality of suicide with an eye toward the consequences, bearing in mind the fact that since we're looking at things from a moral point of view, we need to take into account the consequences as they affect everybody.

Now I suppose it is obvious that the person who is typically *most* affected by suicide is the person who is killing himself. And at first glance, at least, it seems pretty clear that the consequences of suicide are bad with regard to that person. After all, the person was alive, and now they're dead— and we normally take death to be a bad result.

Suppose, for example, that I point to a switch on the wall and tell you that if you flip the switch, a thousand people who would otherwise remain alive will end up dead. You would normally take that to be a pretty compelling argument against flipping the switch! Why? Because the result would be bad: a thousand people would end up dead. Of course, *one* person ending up dead isn't as bad as a *thousand* people ending up dead, but for all that, shouldn't we still say it's a bad consequence? But if so, then don't we have to say that to whatever extent consequences matter in morality, to that extent, at least, suicide is morally objectionable?

But not so quick! Even though it's true that death is normally a bad thing, it's not *always* a bad thing. This is a point we learned long ago, when thinking about the nature of the badness of death. In typical cases, no doubt, the person's dying robs them of a chunk of life that would have been good for them overall, and because of that fact dying now is bad for the person. But in the kinds of cases that we're thinking about here, cases where suicide would be rationally acceptable from a self-interested perspective, the person is *better off* dead. What life now holds out for them is on balance negative; they are better off dying sooner rather than later. And what that means, of course, is that death is not *bad* for them but, rather, *good* for them. So death, in this case, is not a bad consequence, it's a good consequence.

Thus, provided that you are prepared to accept the possibility of cases in which somebody would be better off if his life ended sooner rather than later, we're led to the conclusion that the consequences of suicide might actually be good rather than bad. The person will free himself, let's suppose, of the suffering he would otherwise have to undergo. Thus, even though at first glance it seems as though an appeal to consequences will oppose suicide, a second glance suggests that at least in the right circumstances an appeal to consequences may actually *support* the decision to kill oneself.

But a third glance reminds us that we can't just focus on the consequences for the person who is contemplating suicide. As we have already noted, from the point of view of morality we have to consider the consequences for everyone. So we need to ask, who else might be affected by the death or suicide of the person? And presumably, the most important people for us to think about in this connection are the family and loved ones—the people who most directly know about and care about the person who is contemplating suicide. Yet with regard to this wider circle of individuals, at least, it does seem plausible to suggest that the consequences of suicide are normally bad. Typically, after all, when a person kills himself, this causes a great deal of distress and suffering for the person's family and friends.

Of course, even if that's true, we still have to ask, how do the various consequences compare to one another? After all, we live in a world in which few, if any, acts have only good consequences or only bad consequences. More typically the consequences of our actions are mixed—some good, some bad—and we have to ask whether the good that we would bring about with a given act is greater than the bad we would bring about, or vice versa. (And then we have to compare this mixed set of results with the mixed results that would come about if we performed some different act instead.) So even if there are negative consequences from suicide in terms of distress and pain for the family, friends, and loved ones of the person who kills himself, all of that might still be outweighed by the benefit to the person himself, if it really was the case that he would be better off dying.

Furthermore, it is also worth bearing in mind that insofar as we are thinking about people who love and care about the person who is considering death, then they may actually be *relieved*, on balance, if the suffering of their loved one comes to an end. They will, of course, all be horribly distressed that nature—or God, or the Fates, or what have you—has brought it about that this person's choices are now reduced to killing himself or continuing through the terminal stages of some illness where he's incapacitated and in pain. They will, of course, wish there was a serious prospect of a cure, some chance of recovery. They will wish he had never gotten ill in the first place. But given the limited choices—continued suffering and pain, on the one hand, or having an end to that suffering and pain, on the other—if the person can rationally assess his prospects and reasonably come to believe that he is better off dead, then that's a judgment his loved ones can come to share as well. They may well regret the fact—more than regret, *curse* the fact—that these are the only choices he has, but still, given these limited choices they may come to agree that it is better to put an end to the suffering. And so, if the person kills himself, they may second that choice. They may say, "At least he's not in pain and agony anymore."

As far as consequences are concerned, then, it might well be the case that suicide is sometimes justified. Imagine, then, a moral view according to which consequences aren't just *one* thing that matters morally when thinking about what makes an action right or wrong, they are the *only* thing. Imagine that we take the bold position that the consequences are the only things that are morally relevant. There are, in fact, moral theories that take this position. I suppose that the best known example of this kind of consequences-only approach to morality is *utilitarianism*. Utilitarianism is the moral doctrine that says right and wrong is a matter of producing as much happiness for everybody as possible, counting everybody's happiness equally. And when you can't produce happiness, then at least you should try to minimize the misery and suffering, counting everybody's misery and suffering equally.

Suppose we accept this utilitarian position. What conclusions would we come to with regard to the morality of suicide? I believe the conclusion would be a moderate one. On the one hand, we would reject the extreme view that says that suicide is *never* morally acceptable, because to say that, you would have to be claiming that suicide always has bad consequences overall (as compared to the alternatives). And that strikes me as a rather implausible empirical claim. Sadly enough, it is not too difficult to describe cases in which the results may actually be better if the person kills himself rather than having his suffering continue. It may be better for him and better for his family.

On the other hand, if we are utilitarians we also won't want to go to the other extreme and say that suicide is *always* morally acceptable, because, of course, to say that it's always morally acceptable is to say that the consequences are never bad overall when you kill yourself. And that's also pretty obviously an implausible thing to claim. Many people, for example, are young and healthy, with great futures in front of them. If someone like that kills herself, the results aren't good overall, they're bad. In such cases, suicide cannot be justified morally.

So the utilitarian position is in the middle. It doesn't say that suicide is never acceptable, and it doesn't say that suicide is always acceptable. It says, perhaps unsurprisingly, that suicide is *sometimes* acceptable; it depends on the facts of the case. It depends on the results. We have to compare the results of killing yourself with the results of the various alternatives open to you. For example, even if your life right now is horrifically bad and it would be better for you to be dead than to have it continue like that, if there is some medical procedure available to you that would cure you or significantly improve your condition, then suicide is not in fact the act with the best consequences. Getting medical help is preferable.

We can even think of cases where you would be better off being dead than having your life continue like this, and there is *no* medical treatment available, and yet, for all that, it *still* isn't morally legitimate to kill yourself as far as utilitarianism is concerned. This is because, as always, we have to think about the consequences for others. There may be others who would be *so* adversely affected by your death that the harm to them outweighs the cost to you of keeping yourself alive. Suppose, for example, that you are the single parent of young children. You've got a moral obligation to look after them. If you were to die, it would be simply horrible for them. It's conceivable, in a case like that, that the suffering of your children, were you to kill yourself, would outweigh the suffering that you yourself would have to undergo were you to keep yourself alive for the sake of your children. So it all depends on the facts.

Still, if we accept the utilitarian position we do end up with a moderate conclusion. In certain circumstances suicide will be morally justified. Roughly speaking, it will be justified in those cases where you would be better off dead and the effects on others aren't so great as to outweigh that fact. Those will be the paradigm cases in which suicide would be morally legitimate, according to utilitarianism.

But of course, that doesn't necessarily mean that suicide is indeed ever morally legitimate; for we may not want to embrace a utilitarian theory of morality. Utilitarianism is (very roughly) what you get when you say that consequences matter and they're *all* that matters. But most of us are inclined to think that there's more to morality than consequences. Most of us are inclined to think that there are cases in which actions can have good results and yet still be, for all that, morally forbidden. That's not to say that consequences don't matter morally; it's to claim, rather, that consequences aren't the *only* things that matter morally. Consequences can be outweighed by other morally relevant factors. At any rate, that's the position that's held by those who accept the approach in ethics known as *deontology*.

Deontologists say that other things matter morally besides consequences. In deciding whether your action is right or wrong, you do have to pay attention to the consequences, but you have to pay attention to other things as well. What other things? Unsurprisingly, deontologists differ with one another over the details, but a common enough thought here is that in addition to paying attention to the results, we also have to pay attention to how you *bring about* those results. We can't just ask what the results will be; we also have to ask about your *means* of achieving those results. And in particular, most deontologists say that it is highly relevant whether you have to *harm* anybody to produce the results.

Most of us are inclined to think it's wrong to harm people, or at least innocent people. Indeed, it's wrong to harm innocent people even if the results of doing that might be good. To be sure, I do have to throw in that qualification about harming *innocent* people because it's also true that most of us are inclined to think that *self-defense* can be justified; it may well be legitimate to harm someone who is unjustifiably attacking you or your friends or your fellow countrymen. So it's not as though we want to say that it is *never* legitimate to harm someone. But those people are guilty; they're aggressors. What most of us are inclined to think, in our deontological moods, is that it is never legitimate to harm an *innocent* person. But the crucial point, at any rate, is this: deontologists think it's wrong to harm an innocent person even if the overall results would be better if you did!

Of course, in practice even utilitarians will almost always condemn killing innocent people, since the results of harming an innocent person are almost always bad (compared to the results of the alternative acts one could perform). If I walk into a crowded room, for example, and start shooting people with my Uzi submachine gun, the results would obviously be horrible; so it isn't just the deontologist who is going to condemn that action, the utilitarian will do so as well. Precisely because killing an innocent person almost always has very bad results, it normally doesn't make much of a practical difference whether it is utilitarianism or deontology that we accept.

Accordingly, if we want to think about the differences between utilitarians and deontologists, we shouldn't focus on a typical case. We need, instead, to think about an *atypical* case—a case where killing an innocent person has *good* results. In real life, of course, it's hard to think of cases like that; but we can go science-fictiony and imagine an appropriate example. Doing this will allow us to zero in on the crucial difference between utilitarianism and deontology.

Suppose that we have five patients in a hospital who are going to die because of organ failures of one sort or another. One of them needs a heart transplant, one of them needs a kidney transplant, one of them needs a liver transplant, and so forth and so on. Unfortunately, because of tissue incompatibilities we can't use the organs from any of the five (after they die) to save the others. Meanwhile, here in the hospital for a routine check-up is Fred. Fred is perfectly healthy. And as you examine him—you're the doctor—you discover that he's exactly suitable to be an organ donor for all five of the patients. It occurs to you that if you were to find some way to kill him, but cover up the cause of death so it looked like he died of a seizure, you could then use his organs to save the five. This one gets the kidney, that one gets the heart, that one gets the liver, and so forth and so on. So your choice, roughly, is this: just give Fred his routine medical exam, in which case the five other patients die, or kill Fred and chop him up, using his organs to save the five patients.[5]

What should we say is the right thing to do in the organ transplant case? In terms of consequences it looks as though—if we tell the story right—the results would be better if you chop Fred up. After all, it's one versus five. And although the death of Fred is a horrible result, the death of the five is an even worse result. And so the results would be better if you were to kill innocent Fred.

Obviously, there is a lot to dispute about the way I have just told this story. Will the results *really* be better if you kill Fred? What if the organ transplants fail and you end up with *six* people dead? What will the long-term effects on health care be if you get caught and it comes out that sometimes doctors murder their healthy patients? But rather than trying to tweak the example here, let's just suppose that we could eventually get the details right: the results really would be better if you chop up Fred. Is that the right thing to do?

It seems as though utilitarianism should say that it *is* the right thing to do. But exactly for that reason most of us would then want to say that there is more to morality than what utilitarianism says! Now whether that objection is a good one is a very, very complicated question, and if you want to pursue it then I invite you look at some introductory books on moral philosophy. But for present purposes, let's just suppose that most of us are on board with the deontologists when they say that there is more to morality than bringing about the best results. Intuitively, at least, it's wrong to kill somebody who is innocent, even though by hypothesis the results would be better (in our example, five alive versus only one). As we might put it, people have a *right to life*, a right not to be killed. More generally, most of us accept a deontological moral prohibition against *harming* an innocent person— even when the results really would be better.

In a book on moral philosophy we would immediately want to ask a lot of important questions about this prohibition, including, for example, what its basis is, and what exactly it rules out. But for present purposes we can just ask, suppose we do accept a deontological prohibition like that, what are its implications for the morality of suicide? And it seems that the answer to that question is this: we have to say that suicide is wrong; it is morally unacceptable. Because when I kill myself, I'm *killing* somebody. And didn't we just say, as deontologists, that killing an innocent person is morally wrong? Well, I'm a person. In fact, I am an *innocent* person. So, killing *me* is morally wrong. So my killing *myself* is morally wrong.

And if we do say that, then it won't really change anything to point out that in the sort of case that concerns us I am better off dead. Even if we suppose that the results will be better overall if I kill myself, that fact is neither here nor there, because as deontologists we said that the right to life is so powerful that it outweighs consequences. Just as it was wrong to chop up Fred, even though the results would be better (five alive versus one), it's wrong to kill *yourself*, even if the results would be better. In short, even if suicide is the only way to put an end to your pain, and so has good results overall, that just doesn't matter since the right to life outweighs the appeal to consequences. As deontologists, it seems, we have to say that suicide is forbidden—full stop.

As usual in philosophy, however, it's not quite as simple as that. Some people argue that morality is only about how I treat *others*, not how I treat *myself*: how one treats *oneself* falls outside of the scope of morality altogether. Obviously, if we were to accept a claim like that then it would immediately follow that although the right to life rules out killing *other* people (even when the results would be good), it simply does not apply to cases where a person kills *himself*. And of course, if the right to life doesn't exclude self-killing, then suicide may be morally acceptable after all.

It should be noted, however, that it is not at all obvious why we should *accept* the claim that morality only concerns the treatment of others. Suppose we took it upon ourselves to try to explain why it would be wrong for me to kill *you*. Doubtless, we would point to things like the fact that you are a person, and as such you can't be treated as a mere object, as a mere means of bringing about some goal, no matter how worthy. As a person, there are certain things that shouldn't be done to you, even if the results would be better overall if we did. But of course, *I'm* a person too. Even when I contemplate killing myself, I'm contemplating destroying a person. And it is difficult to see why the mere fact that I am contemplating killing *myself* should suddenly render the fact that I am contemplating killing a person altogether morally irrelevant.

Admittedly, the issue is a complicated one, and to do justice to it we would need to consider rival theories concerning the ultimate basis of morality, a complex subject that I won't try to examine here. So let's simply suppose, for the sake of argument, that morality *isn't* limited to the treatment of others. Can't we at least agree that *if* that's right then suicide is immoral? If morality is indeed concerned (at least in part) with how I treat myself, and if, among the moral rules, there is a deontological prohibition against harming innocent people, doesn't it follow that suicide is wrong?

But at this point it seems important to point out a significant difference between the organ transplant case—where I chop up Fred to save five others—and the case of suicide. When I kill Fred, I am harming one person so as to benefit others. But if I kill myself, I am doing it for my *own* sake. That fact seems highly relevant when thinking about the morality of suicide.

It certainly does seem relevant. But it's not 100 percent clear what to do with that thought. Here are two possible suggestions. First of all, you might think that the relevance of saying that I'm harming myself for my own sake is this. In the kinds of cases we are focusing on, suicide is rational from a self-interested perspective. The person would be better off dead. This means that if I do kill myself, although I am certainly harming myself in one way, I am not harming myself *overall*. On the contrary, I'm actually *benefiting* myself overall. That's obviously an important difference from what happens in the organ transplant case, where I clearly do harm Fred overall.

This fact is relevant because it's possible that the deontological prohibition against harming is really only a prohibition against harming people *overall*. Suppose, for example, that you have an infection in your leg that will kill you unless your leg is amputated. So you go to the surgeon and she removes the leg. Has she done something immoral? It doesn't seem as though she has. But wait a minute: she chopped off your leg! She harmed you! You used to have a leg and now you don't have one. That's clearly a form of harm.

So isn't what she did immoral? Presumably, however, what we want to say is that although she harmed you, she didn't harm you *overall*. She left you better off overall, not worse (compared to the alternatives available to her). And since she didn't harm you overall, she didn't really violate the deontological rule against doing harm.

If that's the right thing to say, then maybe suicide needn't be considered immoral after all. Even if there is a deontological prohibition against harming innocent people, maybe what this prohibition really comes to is a prohibition against harming people in such a way as to leave them worse off overall. But if I would really be better off dead, then when I kill myself I am *not* harming myself overall, I am benefiting myself. So the prohibition against overall harm hasn't been violated. If that's right, then even from the deontological perspective suicide may be morally legitimate in certain cases.

That is one way of developing the thought that when I kill myself, I act for my own sake. Here's another. When I kill myself, given that I'm doing it for my own benefit, I am obviously in favor of what I am doing. I approve of my action; I've agreed to it. Notice how different this is from the organ transplant case. When I kill Fred, presumably, I *don't* have his approval. I act against his will. But since suicide is something that I do to myself, I can't do it against my own will. I always act with my own consent. And that seems to be a morally relevant fact as well.

To accept this idea is to say that we need to add yet another factor into our deontological theory. We already know that consequences are morally relevant, and so is the question of whether innocent people are being harmed to bring about those consequences, but now we also have to take into account the relevance of *consent*. And on reflection, I suspect, most of us would be inclined to agree that consent can make it acceptable to treat people in ways that would otherwise be wrong. In particular, although it is normally wrong to harm people, it is quite a different matter when you have the consent of the person being harmed. For example, in the amputation case it certainly seems relevant that the surgeon has your permission to operate. (We'd feel quite differently about some random stranger who started to amputate your leg without your permission!)

Here's another example that shows the relevance of consent. It would not be morally permissible for me to go up and hit you on the nose. Similarly, it wouldn't be okay for you to come up and hit me in the gut. And yet boxing matches are, I suppose, morally acceptable. Why is that? An important part of the answer, I imagine, is that when people are boxing, they have *agreed* to it. I give you permission to hit me, or at least to try to hit me, in exchange for your giving me permission to hit you, or at least to try to hit you. And it's the presence of that consent that makes it permissible for me to harm you, or for you to harm me.

So consent makes it morally legitimate to harm people, even though in the absence of consent it wouldn't be legitimate. And if that's right, this has a bearing on the morality of suicide. Admittedly, when I kill myself, I am harming an innocent person. But since I am killing *myself*, I obviously have given myself permission to do this. I act with the consent of my "victim." So if consent makes it permissible to do what would normally be forbidden, then consent makes it permissible for me to kill myself. Thus, from the perspective of this more fully developed deontological theory—one that takes into account the relevance of consent—it seems that we have to say that suicide is morally permissible after all.

Indeed, this line of thought may quickly lead us to a rather extreme position concerning the morality of suicide. If the consent of the victim always makes it permissible to do what would otherwise be morally forbidden, then it will turn out that suicide is *always* morally permissible. For in every case of suicide, I take it, the person killing himself has consented to what he is doing to himself.

But we probably shouldn't agree that the power of consent is unlimited in this way. Suppose that you and I meet one day and you say to me, "Shelly, you've got my permission to kill me." So I get out my gun and I shoot you to death. That certainly doesn't seem morally acceptable, even though you gave me your permission. Or suppose that you are feeling guilty because you believe you killed John Smith. As it happens, you are just crazy. You didn't kill John Smith. John Smith isn't even dead. But in your insanity you think you did do it, and so you say, "Shelly, please kill me." Imagine that I know that you are insane, but I kill you anyway. Well, that clearly isn't acceptable either. Or suppose you are playing with your three-year-old nephew, and he says, "I don't like being alive. Kill me." Clearly that doesn't make it permissible to kill him either.

If we accept the *unlimited* power of consent, we are led to some pretty implausible conclusions. So I take it that on reflection we won't want to embrace an unlimited consent principle. Perhaps, then, we should rethink our position and deny the relevance of consent altogether? Maybe consent doesn't really have the kind of moral significance that it initially seemed to have. Maybe it doesn't actually have any genuine moral relevance at all.

I suspect, however, that saying this would be to go too far in the other direction. We need *some* kind of consent principle—even if only a qualified one—because otherwise we won't be able to say some things that most of us very much want to say. Imagine, for example, a soldier in a war, where a hand grenade has been thrown into the dugout. Unless something happens very quickly, the grenade is going to blow up and kill the soldier's five buddies. Unfortunately, they don't see the grenade, and there isn't enough time to warn them. So the soldier's choices are these: He can do nothing, in which case his friends will get killed, but he won't be badly harmed (he is farther away from the grenade). Or he can throw himself on the grenade, in which case his body will absorb the blow from the explosion and he will be killed, but his buddies will be saved. Imagine that he throws himself on the grenade. He has sacrificed himself for his friends.

Few of us, I fear, would have it within ourselves to do this, but amazingly enough, some people do. And we admire and praise these people for their incredible acts of heroic self-sacrifice. We say that such actions are morally praiseworthy, above and beyond the call of duty. But wait a minute: how can they be praiseworthy? The soldier threw himself on a hand grenade, knowing the result of this was that he was going to die. And so he killed a person—an innocent person—apparently violating the deontological prohibition against killing innocent people.

It won't help to point out that the results are better if the soldier sacrifices his life. To be sure, the results are better—five alive rather than just one—but in our deontological moods that shouldn't sway us. After all, suppose that when the soldier sees the hand grenade what he does is push *another* soldier onto the grenade! That's obviously not permissible, even though the results are the same (five alive rather than one). That's deliberately killing an innocent person! And deontologists think that that's wrong, even though the results are good.

So what explains the difference? Why is it morally legitimate for the soldier to throw *himself* on the grenade, but not to push someone else? The most plausible answer, I think, is that it is permissible for him to throw himself because he *agrees* to it. When the soldier throws himself, he has *consented* to being harmed. That makes an act that would otherwise be impermissible into something permissible. Yet if we reject the consent principle altogether, we're forced to say that the soldier's act of self-sacrifice *isn't* morally admirable. It's morally appalling, morally forbidden. I can't believe that.

So deontologists need *some* kind of consent principle. But on the other hand, we don't want to go with such a bold consent principle that we claim that it is okay to kill people just because they say, "Oh, kill me." What we need, then, is a more *moderate* form of the consent principle. We need to say that consent can make the impermissible permissible—but only under certain conditions.

What exactly are the relevant conditions? This is, of course, one more topic open to debate. But among the more plausible suggestions are these: We might insist that the consent has to be given freely. And it has to be given by someone who understands what the results of the relevant action are going to be (or what they might be). It has to be given by someone who is sane, rational, and competent to make this kind of decision. Finally, we might want to require that the person have good *reasons* for giving his consent. (That might be necessary to deal with the case where you just come up to me and tell me to kill you. In that case, after all, you needn't be *insane*; it's just that you don't have any good reason to say what you say. Maybe that's enough to undermine the force of consent.)

Suppose, then, that we have a suitably modified version of the consent principle. What will we end up saying about suicide? It seems to me likely that what we will be led to, once again, is a *moderate* view about suicide. The mere fact that some person wants to kill herself won't suffice to show that it is morally permissible for her to do so because, of course, even though she has given herself permission to do this, she may be insane, or not competent at that moment to make that kind of decision, or she may simply lack good reason for killing herself. But for all that, if we can have cases—and I take it that we *can* have such cases—where someone rationally assesses their situation, sees that they would be better off dead, thinks the case through, doesn't rush into it, makes an informed and voluntary decision, with good reason behind it, then the modified consent principle might well come into play, in which case consent will trump or nullify the force of the deontological prohibition against harming innocent people. So suicide will again be acceptable in some cases, though not in all.

And that's the conclusion that seems to me to be the correct one, whether we accept the utilitarian position or a deontological alternative. Suicide isn't always legitimate, but it is *sometimes* legitimate.

This still leaves an important question: what should we do when we come across somebody trying to kill himself? Here, I think, there is good reason to ask yourself, are you confident that the person has satisfied the relevant conditions on the consent principle? Perhaps we should err on the side of caution, and assume that the person is acting under distress, not thinking clearly, not informed, not altogether competent, not acting for good reasons. But to accept this sort of initial negative presumption is not the same as accepting the stronger conclusion that we must *never* permit anyone to kill himself. Suppose we become convinced that they have thought it through, that they do have good reason, that they are informed, and that they are acting voluntarily. In some such cases, it seems to me, it may well be legitimate for the person to kill himself, and for us to let him.

CHAPTER 16
Conclusion
An Invitation

At the start of this book, I invited you to think about the nature of death. Most of us try very hard not to do that. Death is an unpleasant topic, and we try to put it out of our mind. We don't think about it, even when it is staring us in the face. How often, for example, have you walked past a cemetery without even noticing it? How often do you stop to think about the fact that we are on this Earth for a little while, and then we're not? Most of us just don't like to think about it.

Of course, you are an exception. You've just finished reading an entire book about death, and to a considerable extent I will be content if you have taken the time, while reading it, to take a hard look at the things you believe. Whether or not you end up agreeing with me about the various claims that I have put forward is less important than that you've taken the opportunity to critically examine your beliefs—asking yourself not just what you hope or wish or assume is true, but what you can actually defend.

Still, having said that, it would be disingenuous of me to pretend that I don't care whether you end up believing what I believe about death. I do care, because of course I want you to believe the truth.

As I explained in our opening pages, most people accept all or much of a package of beliefs about the nature of life and death. They believe that we have a soul, that there's something more to us than our bodies. And they believe that, given the existence of the soul, we have the possibility of living forever. Of course, death remains the ultimate mystery, but immortality is nonetheless a genuine possibility, one that we hope for and crave, because the thought that death is the end is simply unbearable. It's so horrible that we try not to think about it. It's so horrible that when we do think about death we're filled with dread, terror, and fear. And it seems perfectly obvious that this is the only sensible reaction one could have to the facts of life and death. Life is so incredible that under no circumstances could it ever make sense to want it to come to an end. Immortality would be wonderful, and suicide can never be a reasonable decision.

In contrast to all of this, I have argued that this package of beliefs, common as it may be, is mistaken—virtually from start to finish. There is no soul; we are just machines. Of course, we are not just any old machine; we are *amazing* machines. We are machines capable of loving, dreaming, being creative; machines able to make plans and to share them with others. We are *people*. But we're just machines anyway. And when the machine breaks, that's the end. Death is not some big mystery that we can't get our heads around. Ultimately, death is no more mysterious than the fact that your lamp or your computer can break, or that any machine will eventually fail.

I hope it has been clear that I haven't tried to suggest that it's not regrettable that we die the way we do. As I argued when discussing immortality, it would certainly be better if we had the power to live until life no longer had something valuable left to offer us. For as long as living a while longer would be good for me overall, death is bad; and for most of us, at least, death comes too soon. But having said that, it certainly doesn't follow that immortality would be a good thing. In truth, immortality would actually be a curse, not a blessing.

When we think about death, then, it isn't appropriate to view it as a great mystery, too dreadful to face, something overwhelming and frightening. On the contrary, far from being the uniquely rational response to death, I think that fear of death is an *inappropriate* response. And while we can certainly be sad that we will likely die too soon, perhaps that emotion should be balanced by the recognition of just how incredibly lucky we are to ever have been alive at all.

At the same time, recognizing our good fortune in having lived doesn't mean that we are always better off *staying* alive. For some of us, tragically, the time will come in which that's no longer true. And when that happens, life is not something to be held onto, come what may, under any and all circumstances. The time may come when it is time to let go.

Over the course of this book, then, I have invited you to think for yourself about the facts of life and death. But more than that, I have invited you to face death without fear and without illusion.

Notes

CHAPTER 2
Dualism versus Physicalism

1. One version of this objection is helpfully discussed by Jay Rosenberg in *Thinking Clearly About Death* (Prentice-Hall, 1983), pp. 18–22.

CHAPTER 4
Descartes' Argument

1. René Descartes, *Meditations on First Philosophy*, the Sixth Meditation.
2. In point of fact, I think Descartes' argument goes wrong at the very first premise. I am not actually imagining a world in which my mind exists but my body doesn't. Rather, I am imagining a world where someone without a body mistakenly *thinks* he is me! It is *his* mind that exists without a body in the imagined scenario, not mine. This may suffice to show that *his* mind would be distinct from his body, and thus that there *could* be souls (that immaterial minds are logically possible); but it won't help to establish that *my* mind is distinct from my body. It won't help show that there *are* souls.

CHAPTER 5
Plato on the Immortality of the Soul

1. Quotations from the *Phaedo* are from the translation by G. M. A. Grube (Hackett, 1977).
2. I discuss some of the other arguments in the *Phaedo* in (parts of) lectures 7, 8, and 9 of the online course on which this book is based. See oyc.yale.edu/philosophy/death.

CHAPTER 6
Personal Identity

1. I learned these analogies (should the relation between objects and stages be seen as more like a sandwich or more like a salami?) from David Kaplan, a philosopher at the University of California at Los Angeles.
2. John Locke, *An Essay Concerning Human Understanding*, book II, chapter 27.
3. Peter van Inwagen, "The Possibility of Resurrection," in *The Possibility of Resurrection and Other Essays in Christian Apologetics* (Westview, 1997).
4. That's the view put forward by Gertrude, the heroine of John Perry's *A Dialogue on Personal Identity and Immortality* (Hackett, 1978). There are, of course, still other versions of the body view, which I won't try to discuss here.

CHAPTER 7
Choosing between the Theories

1. I'm actually going to give a *pair* of cases. Both of them come from Bernard Williams, a British philosopher who died a few years ago. He described these cases in his essay "The Self and the Future," in *Problems of the Self* (Cambridge, 1973).
2. It comes from Derek Parfit, *Reasons and Persons* (Oxford, 1984), part III.

CHAPTER 8
The Nature of Death

1. Fred Feldman notes this implication of the body view, and likens the situation to a bad joke, in his *Confrontations with the Reaper* (Oxford, 1992), chapter 6.

CHAPTER 9
Two Surprising Claims about Death

1. Sigmund Freud is quoted in Walter Kaufmann's essay "Death," in *The Faith of a Heretic* (Doubleday, 1961), pp. 356–357.
2. Loudon Wainwright III, "Last Man on Earth," from his album *Last Man on Earth* (Red House Records, 2001).
3. Christopher Paolini, *Eldest* (Knopf, 2005), p. 441.
4. What about a religious interpretation? Is the claim that we all die alone a way of saying that we enter heaven alone? Or that we stand in judgment before God without anyone to plead our case? Perhaps some religions have taught something like this, and if so that may be the origin of the idea. But in any event, it is difficult to find any plausible (and true) interpretation of the claim that we all die alone if one denies the relevant religious outlook.

CHAPTER 10
The Badness of Death

1. "Separation" by Friedrich Klopstock, translated by Walter Kaufmann in his essay "Death Without Dread," in *Existentialism, Religion, and Death* (New American Library, 1976), p. 227.
2. Epicurus, *Letter to Menoeceus*, quoted in *The Oxford Book of Death*, edited by D. J. Enright (Oxford, 1983), p. 8.
3. Lucretius, *On the Nature of Things*.
4. Thomas Nagel, "Death," in *Mortal Questions* (Cambridge, 1979).
5. Fred Feldman, *Confrontations with the Reaper* (Oxford, 1992), pp. 154–156.
6. This example comes from Derek Parfit, *Reasons and Persons* (Oxford, 1984), pp. 165–166. I should note, however, that Parfit isn't here explicitly discussing Lucretius. I am simply applying some of his ideas to that puzzle. (Parfit's own discussion of the puzzle can be found in *Reasons and Persons*, pp. 174–177.)

CHAPTER 11
Immortality

1. Jonathan Swift, *Gulliver's Travels*, part III, chapter 10.
2. Michel de Montaigne, "That to Philosophize Is to Learn to Die," in *The Complete Essays*.
3. I'm thinking of the wonderful 1967 original, with Peter Cooke and Dudley Moore. I don't know if this scene is still in the more recent remake.
4. Bernard Williams, "The Makropulos Case: Reflections on the Tedium of Immortality," in *Problems of the Self* (Cambridge, 1973). Williams, incidentally, was also the author of the two thought experiments discussed at the start of Chapter 7.
5. Julian Barnes, "The Dream," in *A History of the World in 10 ½ Chapters* (1989).

CHAPTER 12
The Value of Life

1. Robert Nozick, *Anarchy, State, and Utopia* (Basic Books, 1974), pp. 42–45.

CHAPTER 13
Other Aspects of Death

1. In chapter 6 of *Pleasure and the Good Life* (Oxford, 2004), Fred Feldman argues that we should be indifferent between these two lives. But I imagine that Feldman too has an immediate intuitive preference for the former, even if ultimately he disavows that intuition.
2. Actually, I've been told that in some countries chocolate-covered pizza is considered a delicacy! But as far as I can tell, this treat lacks the cheese, tomato sauce, and standard toppings that I had in mind.
3. Orson Scott Card, "Mortal Gods," in *Maps in a Mirror* (Tor Books, 1990), pp. 440–445.

CHAPTER 14
Living in the Face of Death

1. Kurt Vonnegut, *Cat's Cradle* (1963).
2. My discussion here is indebted to Derek Parfit, *Reasons and Persons* (Oxford, 1984), part IV, where Parfit discusses analogous questions with regard to entire populations.
3. "To the Parcae" by Friedrich Holderlin, translated by Walter Kaufmann in his essay "Death Without Dread," in *Existentialism, Religion, and Death* (New American Library, 1976), p. 231.
4. Arthur Schopenhauer, *The World as Will and Representation*, quoted in Jeff McMahan, *The Ethics of Killing* (Oxford, 2002), p. 96.
5. As with all great religious traditions, there are many strands in Buddhism and many divergent interpretations; the pessimistic strand in Buddhist thought is certainly not the only one. But I am not aiming at a complete and nuanced overview of Buddhism here, only a quick sketch of one possible approach to facing death.

CHAPTER 15
Suicide

1. If you accept the possibility (mentioned in Chapter 13) that the value of a life can also be affected by its overall *shape*, then you would need somewhat different graphs to illustrate and discuss the points I am about to make. (Briefly, on these alternative graphs, the Y axis should represent how good or bad the overall value of one's life would be if it *ended* at a given moment, rather than how *well off* one is at any given moment; and being better off dead would then be represented by a line that dips *down*, rather than by one that crosses below the X axis.) However, since the essential philosophical points I am making here wouldn't be affected, I won't pursue this alternative approach further.
2. Although I have modified it for my own purposes, this example is loosely based on the true story of Donald "Dax" Cowart.
3. David Hume, "On Suicide," in *Essays: Moral, Political, and Literary*.
4. On pork, see Leviticus 11:4–7. On mixed material, see Leviticus 19:19 and Deuteronomy 22:11. On stoning, see Deuteronomy 21:18–21.
5. This example (one of my favorites) was introduced by Philippa Foot in her essay "The Problem of Abortion and the Doctrine of the Double Effect," in *Virtues and Vices* (University of California, 1978).

Suggestions for Further Reading

The philosophical literature on death (and related topics) is vast, and much of it makes for difficult reading for those without a background in philosophy. But here are a few suggestions for those who would like to read more.

General: Two excellent books that cover many of the same topics as this one are Fred Feldman, *Confrontations with the Reaper* (Oxford, 1992), and Stephen Luper, *The Philosophy of Death* (Cambridge, 2009). The book by Feldman is particularly accessible. *The Metaphysics of Death* (Stanford, 1993), edited by John Fischer, is a valuable collection of important papers.

Dualism versus physicalism: Peter Lipton's book *Inference to the Best Explanation* (Routledge, 2nd ed., 2004) provides a helpful discussion of this general form of argument. Jaegwon Kim's *Philosophy of Mind* (Westview, 3rd ed., 2010) is a very good introduction to contemporary philosophical theories about the mind. A brief introduction to free will can be found in Peter van Inwagen, *Metaphysics* (Westview, 1993), chapter 11. A skeptical discussion of near-death experiences can be found in Theodore Schick and Lewis Vaughn, "Near-Death Experiences," in *How to Think About Weird Things* (McGraw-Hill, 2005), pp. 307–323.

Descartes and Plato: René Descartes' argument is given in the Sixth Meditation. (The *Meditations on First Philosophy* provide a wonderful introduction to Descartes' entire philosophical system.) Plato's dialogues were written for a general, educated audience, so by all means have a crack at the *Phaedo*; although some passages are difficult to follow, the simple fact of the matter is that Plato is one of the greatest writers in the history of philosophy. If you have never read a Platonic dialogue before, you are in for a treat.

Surprising claims about death: A lively attempt to cut through some common mistakes about death can be found in Paul Edwards's essay "Existentialism and Death: A Survey of Some Confusions and Absurdities," in *Philosophy, Science, and Method,* edited by Sidney Morgenbesser, Patrick Suppes, and Morton White (St. Martin's Press, 1969).

Personal identity: A very short, accessible introduction is John Perry's *A Dialogue on Personal Identity and Immortality* (Hackett, 1978). One of the most influential contemporary discussions of personal identity is Derek

Parfit, *Reasons and Persons* (Oxford, 1984), part III. (Parfit also discusses the distinction between survival and what *matters* in survival.) John Locke's arguments against the soul view (and a defense of the personality view) can be found in *An Essay Concerning Human Understanding*, book II, chapter 27.

The badness of death: Important contemporary discussions of the deprivation account can be found in Thomas Nagel, "Death," in *Mortal Questions* (Cambridge, 1979), and Fred Feldman, "Some Puzzles About the Evil of Death"—both of which are reprinted in the Fischer anthology. Ben Bradley, *Well-Being and Death* (Oxford, 2009), is a detailed discussion of the topic. Part II of Parfit's *Reasons and Persons* discusses the rationality of different possible attitudes to time.

Immortality: The most important paper here is Bernard Williams, "The Makropulos Case: Reflections on the Tedium of Immortality," in his *Problems of the Self* (Cambridge, 1973).

The value of life: A short introduction to some of the basic theories of well-being can be found in my *Normative Ethics* (Westview, 1998), pp. 29–41. Appendix I of Parfit's *Reasons and Persons* is an influential discussion.

Living in the face of death: Two interesting essays, both by Walter Kaufmann, are "Death Without Dread," in *Existentialism, Religion, and Death* (New American Library, 1976), and "Death," in *The Faith of a Heretic* (Doubleday, 1961).

Suicide: A very readable discussion can be found in Richard Brandt, "The Morality and Rationality of Suicide," in *Moral Problems*, edited by James Rachels (Harper & Row, 1979). Finally, for those who would like to learn more about utilitarianism and deontology (and the differences between them), I offer a more systematic introduction in *Normative Ethics*, part I.

Index

ability: to function, 178–185; to think
clearly, 341–344
abstract objects, 73
accomplishments, 256–257, 289–290,
307–308, 313–316
actions, consequences of, 349–355
afterlife: badness of death and, 206–207,
295–296; existence of, 7–8
alienation, 202–204
alive, being, 173–178
Allen, Woody, 313
aloneness, at death, 196–204
amnesia, 136, 164, 243–245
amoebas, 151
anger, 299–302
animate body, 29–31
appropriateness conditions, 288–303
argument from simplicity, 80–92
argument from the nature of the Forms,
76–80
astronomy argument, 61–68

badness of death, 2, 205–233; afterlife
and, 206–207; deprivation account of,
210–212, 215, 221, 224–235, 247, 261,
264, 316, 322; Epicurus and, 213–224;
existence requirement and, 215–224;
Lucretius and, 224–233; nonexistence
and, 210–212; process of dying and,
209; for survivors, 207–208; timing
of, 213–224
Barnes, Julian, 246
behavioral aspect of mental life, 36–37
beliefs, 32–33; about death, 3–4, 362–363
best explanation, inference to the, 25–28
B functioning body, 170–176, 178–185

Bible, 346–347
birth: existence of soul before, 94; time
before, 225–233
bodily resurrection, 119–122, 179–181
body: animation of, 29–31; death of,
9–10, 15, 17–18, 28–29, 171–178; as
distinct from the soul, 11–12; dualist
view of, 13–18; essential parts of,
122–126; functioning, 20–21, 29–30,
170–185; harmony of, 92–97; interaction between soul and, 13–14,
17–18, 95–97; as material, 11; mental
abilities of, 19–21; physicalist view of,
18–23; separation from desires of, 72,
75–77
body functions, 170–185
body theory of personal identity,
118–127, 161–162, 164, 168; compared
with personality view, 132–139; fission
case and, 150–162; moment of death
and, 174–176, 178, 182–184; what
matters and, 164, 169, 174–175
boredom, 238–245
brain, vs. mind, 21
brain theory of personal identity, 124–126,
138–139; fission case and, 152–155
Buddhism, 316–317
burden of proof, 99–102

Card, Orson Scott, 277
careful, being, 303–307
Cebes, 83–84
changelessness, 81–82, 91
changes: bodily, 122–126; in personality,
129–131
chess-playing computer, 32–34, 42

371